Modular Deficits in Alzheimer-Type Dementia

Issues in the Biology of Language and Cognition
John C. Marshall, editor

What the Hands Reveal about the Brain
Howard Poizner, Edward S. Klima, and Ursula Bellugi, 1987

Disorders of Syntactic Comprehension
David N. Caplan and Nancy Hildebrandt, 1987

Missing the Meaning? A Cognitive Neuropsychological Study of the Processing of Words by an Aphasic Patient
David Howard and Sue Franklin, 1988

The Psychobiology of Down Syndrome
edited by Lynn Nadel, 1988

From Reading to Neurons
edited by Albert M. Galaburda, 1989

Modular Deficits in Alzheimer-Type Dementia
edited by Myrna F. Schwartz, 1990

Modular Deficits in Alzheimer-Type Dementia

edited by Myrna F. Schwartz

A Bradford Book
The MIT Press
Cambridge, Massachusetts
London, England

© 1990 Massachusetts Institute of Technology

All rights reserved. No part of this book may be reproduced in any form by any electronic or mechanical means (including photocopying, recording, or information storage and retrieval) without permission in writing from the publisher.

This book was typeset by Asco Trade Typesetting Ltd, Hong Kong, and printed and bound in the United States of America.

Library of Congress Cataloging-in-Publication Data

Modular deficits in Alzheimer-type dementia / edited by Myrna F. Schwartz.
    p.   cm.—(Issues in the biology of language and cognition)
    "A Bradford book."
    Includes bibliographical references.
    ISBN 0-262-19298-5
    1. Alzheimer's disease—Physiological aspects. 2. Dementia—
Physiological aspects. 3. Neuropsychology. I. Schwartz, Myrna F.
II. Series.
    [DNLM: 1. Alzheimer's Disease. 2. Dementia, Senile. 3. Models,
Biological. 4. Neuropsychology. WM 220 M691]
    RC523.M63 1990
    616.89'83—dc20
    DNLM/DLC
    for Library of Congress   90-5843
                                              CIP

To my beloved parents Helen and Murray Feigelson

Contents

Contributors

Abass Alavi, M.D.
Division of Nuclear Medicine
University of Pennsylvania
Philadelphia, Pennsylvania

Jonathan Baron, Ph.D.
Department of Psychology
University of Pennsylvania
Philadelphia, Pennsylvania

Daniel Bub, Ph.D.
Department of Neurolinguistics
Montreal Neurological Institute
Montreal, Quebec, Canada

Julio A. Calcano-Perez, M.D.
Cerebrovascular Research Center
University of Pennsylvania
Philadelphia, Pennsylvania

John B. Chawluk, M.D.
Cerebrovascular Research Center
University of Pennsylvania
Philadelphia, Pennsylvania

Howard Chertkow, M.D.
Lady Davis Research Institute
Jewish General Hospital
Montreal, Quebec, Canada

H. Branch Coslett, M.D.
Department of Neurology
Temple University School of
   Medicine
Philadelphia, Pennsylvania

Antonio R. Damasio, M.D.,
   Ph.D.
Department of Neurology
University of Iowa College of
   Medicine
Iowa City, Iowa

Eileen J. Fitzpatrick-DeSalme,
   M.S.
Department of Neurology
Temple University School of
   Medicine
Philadelphia, Pennsylvania

Murray Grossman, M.D.
Cerebrovascular Research Center
University of Pennsylvania
Philadelphia, Pennsylvania

Howard I. Hurtig, M.D.
Cerebrovascular Research Center
University of Pennsylvania
Philadelphia, Pennsylvania

Alex Martin, Ph.D.
Cognitive Studies Unit
Laboratory of Clinical Science
National Institute of Mental
   Health
Bethesda, Maryland

Bradley T. Hyman, M.D., Ph.D.
Department of Neurology
University of Iowa College of
   Medicine
Iowa City, Iowa

Morris Moscovitch, Ph.D.
Department of Psychology
Erindale College
University of Toronto
Mississauga, Ontario, Canada
and
Rotman Research Institute
Baycrest Centre for Geriatric
    Care
North York, Ontario, Canada

Martin Reivich, M.D.
Cerebrovascular Research Center
University of Pennsylvania
Philadelphia, Pennsylvania

Eleanor M. Saffran, Ph.D.
Department of Neurology
Temple University School of
    Medicine
Philadelphia, Pennsylvania

Myrna F. Schwartz, Ph.D.
Neuropsychology Research Lab
Moss Rehabilitation Hospital
Philadelphia, Pennsylvania

Jacqueline Ann Stark, Ph.D.
Department of Linguistics and
    Communication Research
Austrian Academy of Sciences
Vienna, Austria

Carlo Umilta, Ph.D.
Instituto di Fisiologia Umana
Universita di Parma
Parma, Italy

Gary W. Van Hoesen, Ph.D.
Department of Neurology
University of Iowa College of
    Medicine
Iowa City, Iowa

Series Foreword

Neurology, Cognition, and Dementia

Let us begin not with dementia but with apoplexy. Apoplexy (or stroke) is "a sudden impairment of brain function due to hemorrhage from or obstruction of one or more cerebral blood vessels" (Walton, Beeson, and Bodley Scott 1986). With respect to the art and science of neurology, stroke is a "natural kind." There may be different types of stroke and differing loci of involvement, but stroke per se must nonetheless be firmly distinguished from other proximate causes of brain malfunction, such as tumor, encephalitis, or neuritic plaques. It is upon accurate differential diagnosis that rational management and treatment is predicated (Wade et al. 1985). And the rationality of that care is in turn dependent on knowing the place of stroke within an overall theory of the vascular system and its pathologies.

The cognitive consequences of stroke can include aphasia, apraxia, agnosia, amnesia . . . and hence stroke is emphatically *not* a natural kind with respect to cognitive neuroscience. To a first approximation, at least, the human brain is partially characterized by punctate localization of functions (Marshall 1984). Whatever the ultimate status of connectionist models (Nadel et al. 1989) turns out to be, it remains a fact that the behavioral consequences of parietal lobe lesions, for example, are typically distinct from those of temporal lobe lesions. There are, in other words, limits on the distribution of parallel distributed processing. And from this it follows (again to a first approximation) that the locus of brain damage is a more pertinent associate of cognitive deficit than is the nature of brain damage. Data relevant to the theory of, say, language or spatial perception and their pathologies may therefore draw (relatively) indiscriminately upon studies of behavioral impairment after stroke, space-occupying lesion, penetrating missile injury, degenerative disease of the central nervous system, and so on.

In addition one might expect considerable biological variation in the precise neuronal representation of higher psychological functions from individual to individual (Basso et al. 1985, De Bleser 1988); it is not plausible to assume an absolutely constant neurological substrate for any "mental organ" in a system as complex as a human brain (Caplan and Hildebrandt 1988).

These considerations complement the now well-known arguments against grouping patients on the basis of "polytypic" symptom-complexes (Schwartz 1984). Groups formed on the basis of syndromes that allow the behavioral characterization of the individuals therein to differ substantially merely introduce noise into the data base (Caramazza and McCloskey 1988), and likewise groups defined solely by lesion type or locus will perforce span a vast variety of different functional impairments (Newcombe and Marshall 1988). Within what Shallice (1988) calls *ultra-cognitive neuropsychology*, the methodological resolution of the chaos explicit in traditional neuropsychology has involved two steps: First, the replacement of group studies by single-case studies (and case-series) and, second, concentration on the functional architecture of cognition with a (temporary) disavowal of interest in the neuroanatomical structures that realize mental life.

There is, to my mind, no doubt but that this cleaning of the Aegean stables has been entirely beneficial. The "special sciences" (Fodor 1974) do indeed cross-classify the phenomena that fall within their respective domains. And consequently the natural kinds of one science will not reduce one-to-one to the natural kinds of another science. An exceptionally clear account is provided by Marr (1976):

> The CNS needs to be understood at four nearly independent levels of description: (1) that at which the nature of a computation is expressed; (2) that at which the algorithms that implement a computation are characterized; (3) that at which an algorithm is committed to particular mechanisms; and (4) that at which the mechanisms are realized in hardware.

But even without moving to a schema as constrained as Marr's, it is apparent that conceptual confusion has been endemic in neuropsychology. It is apparent also that a failure to heed Hughlings Jackson's early warning against mixing levels of explanation (structural and functional) has been responsible for much of this havoc (Marshall 1989).

Nowhere perhaps has the confusion been more rife than in the study of *dementia*—a specific disease entity? a pathological symptom-complex? or a "normal" behavioral manifestation of old age? In ordinary speech *dementia* carries the connotation of severe impairment affecting *all* domains of cognitive, affective, and conative life. Yet clinicians are of course well aware that "few if any dementias are truly global" (Cummings and Benson 1983). It is thus customary to propose polytypic definitions:

> Operationally, dementia can be defined as an acquired persistent impairment of intellectual function with compromise in at least three of the following spheres of mental activity: language, memory, visuospatial skills, emotion or personality, and cognition (abstraction, calculation, judgment, etc.). (Cummings and Benson 1983)

But such definitions immediately raise questions (Marshall 1987): Why this *particular* list of spheres (including the etc.)? and Why "at least three" (what's wrong with two or four)? And it won't wash to shrug one's shoulders and say that the definition is *merely* operational—definitions may be good, bad, or indifferent, but they are never merely mere. And it certainly won't do to argue that the definition is merely clinical. Definitions of clinical entities should be better than those of most other theoretical constructs. Management, treatment, and rehabilitation depend (to a large extent) on the physician (or other clinician) getting the diagnosis correct. The patient's well-being (in some instances, life or death) is at stake.

At the moment, little can be done to halt (or even slow) the degenerative changes that take place in Alzheimer-type dementia; likewise little (but something) can be done to enable patients (and their caregivers) to achieve a reasonable quality of life despite dementing illness. But there is reasonable hope that specific drug therapies will become available in the not-too-distant future and that more effective coping strategies can be devised. In both instances the role of neuropsychological inquiry will be crucial.

In a short, sharp editorial, Poeck (1988) writes: "Why should a Mini-Mental Scale suffice to identify a patient who is then examined with a machine that costs a million?" It is not likely that there is only one degenerative disease that attacks the central nervous system; nor is it likely that the course of each such disease is identical in all patients. Assessment of the efficacy (or otherwise) of any psychopharmacological intervention will thus have to be based on longitudinal neuropsychological assessments that are considerably more sophisticated than those currently obtained in some centers.

Similarly it is unlikely that all patients are alike in how they respond to and cope with their particular set of impaired cognitive functions. Study of what functions remain intact in progressive dementing illnesses is therefore vital if we (and, more important, the patients) are to learn how relatively preserved abilities can be used to compensate for loss. In brief then, as Poeck (1988) forceably argues: "If a group cannot afford a trained neuropsychologist or establish cooperation with a group of experienced neuropsychologists, it should not embark on research on SDAT."

Fortunately the notion of global deterioration is rapidly disappearing from the literature as the role of modern clinical and experimental neuropsychology in the examination of patients with progressive symptomatology comes to be appreciated (Spinnler and Della Sala 1988). The frequency with which "a single neuropsychological disturbance" (not necessarily memory impairment) is experienced early in the history of (putative) Alzheimer's disease is now recognized (Spinnler and Della Sala 1988). Memory loss itself is no longer seen as a unitary function (Spinnler et al. 1988). Slowly progressive aphasias (Scheltens et al. 1990), agnosias, and apraxias (De Renzi 1986) are revealing yet further specificity in the fractionation of cognition by degenerative disease processes of unknown (or only partially known) causes.

It is in this context that *Modular Deficits in Alzheimer-Type Dementia* takes its place. The book is informed by the firm (and empirically well-supported) conviction that "the primary degenerative dementias are selective in their sites of action and that this selectivity has important functional consequences." Myrna Schwartz has brought together a small group of outstanding scientists with expertise in both the neuropathology and the neuropsychology of the dementias and has organized within these pages an interaction that is at the cutting edge of current research.

As the title states, the notion of modularity (Marshall 1984) plays a large role in state-of-the-art interpretations of the dementias. But the book expands upon early accounts of modular functions to include serious discussion of how even central systems can be fractionated; the components thereof have specific responsibilities for integrating and modulating the outputs of dedicated representational mechanisms. Due consideration is given to anatomy, physiology, and biochemistry without falling into the old trap of equating (relatively) diffuse pathology with generalized behavioral impairment (or focal lesion with single-symptom presentation). The relation between structure and function cannot be as simple as that in a system with the complexity and interconnectedness of a human brain (Basso, Capitani, and Laiacona 1988, Warrington 1975).

Modular Deficits in Alzheimer-Type Dementia—the first book to approach the topic from the standpoint of information-processing neuropsychology—points a clear way forward. It will, I hope and expect, have an entirely salutary effect on research and (eventual) remediation for one of the most distressing conditions encountered in current medical practice.

John C. Marshall

References

Basso, A., Capitani, E., and Laiacona, M. 1988. Progressive language impairment without dementia: A case with isolated category-specific semantic defect. *Journal of Neurology, Neurosurgery, and Psychiatry* 51: 1201–1207.

Basso, A., Roch Lecours, A., Moraschini, S., and Vanier, M. 1985. Anatomoclinical correlations of the aphasias as defined through computerized tomography: Exceptions. *Brain and Language* 26: 201–229.

Caplan, D., and Hildebrandt, N. 1988. *Disorders of Syntactic Comprehension.* Cambridge, Mass.: MIT Press.

Caramazza, A., and McCloskey, M. 1988. The case for single-patient studies. *Cognitive Neuropsychology* 5: 517–528.

Cummings, J. L., and Benson, D. F. 1983. *Dementia: A Clinical Approach.* London: Butterworth.

De Bleser, R. 1988. Localization of aphasia: Science or fiction. In G. Denes, C. Semenza, and P. Bisiacchi (eds.), *Perspectives on Cognitive Neuropsychology.* London: Erlbaum.

De Renzi, E. 1986. Slowly progressive visual agnosia or apraxia without dementia. *Cortex* 22: 171–180.

Fodor, J. A. 1974. Special sciences. *Synthese* 28: 77–115.

Marr. D. 1976. Early processing of visual information. *Philosophical Transactions of the Royal Society of London B* 275: 483–524.

Marshall, J. C. 1984. Multiple perspectives on modularity. *Cognition* 17: 209–242.

Marshall, J. C. 1987. Behavioural fractionation in the dementias. In R. A. Griffiths and S. T. McCarthy (eds.), *Degenerative Neurological Disease in the Elderly.* Bristol: Wright.

Marshall, J. C. 1989. Carving the cognitive chicken. *Aphasiology* 3: 735–740.

Nadel, L., Culicover, P., Cooper, L. A., and Harnish, R. M. (eds.). 1989. *Neural Connections, Mental Computation.* Cambridge, Mass.: MIT Press.

Newcombe, F., and Marshall, J. C. 1988. Idealization meets psychometrics: The case for the right groups and the right individuals. *Cognitive Neuropsychology* 5: 549–564.

Poeck, K. 1988. A case for neuropsychology in dementia research. *Journal of Neurology* 235: 257.

Scheltens, Ph., Hazenberg, G. J., Lindeboom, J., Valk, J., and Wolters, E.Ch. 1990. A case of progressive aphasia without dementia: "Temporal" Pick's disease? *Journal of Neurology, Neurosurgery, and Psychiatry* 53: 79–80.

Schwartz, M. F. 1984. What the classical aphasia categories can't do for us, and why. *Brain and Language* 21: 3–8.

Shallice, T. 1988. *From Neuropsychology to Mental Structure.* Cambridge: Cambridge University Press.

Spinnler, H., and Della Sala, S. 1988. The role of clinical neuropsychology in the neurological diagnosis of Alzheimer's disease. *Journal of Neurology* 235: 258–271.

Spinnler, H., Della Sala, S., Bandera, R., and Baddeley, A. 1988. Dementia, ageing, and the structure of human memory. *Cognitive Neuropsychology* 5: 193–211.

Wade, D. T., Langton Hewer, R., Skilbeck, C. E., and David, R. N. 1985. *Stroke: A critical approach to diagnosis, treatment and management.* London: Chapman and Hall.

Walton, J., Beeson, P. B., Bodley Scott, R. (eds.). 1986. *The Oxford Companion to Medicine*. Oxford: Oxford University Press.

Warrington, E. K. 1975. The selective impairment of semantic memory. *Quarterly Journal of Experimental Psychology* 27: 635–657.

Preface

The idea that primary degenerative dementias are selective in their sites and mechanisms of action and that this selectivity has important functional consequences is fast becoming the conventional wisdom. But it was a fairly heretical view back in 1974, when I first heard it espoused by my teacher, Dr. Oscar Marin. I am grateful for having had the benefit of his foresight and direction. It has also been my good fortune to work in a long-term collaboration with Dr. Eleanor Saffran, who is my friend as well as colleague. Our endeavors to bring to the study of dementing disorders the models and methods of cognitive neuropsychology, including its emphasis on single-case studies, have met with many rewards—and not a few frustrations. Through it all I have relied heavily on her wisdom and stability.

Like most researchers who work in this area, I am continually amazed at the generosity of the many individuals—patients and caregivers—who make themselves available to our projects with little hope of practical return. Future generations will benefit from their selflessness. I want to acknowledge my special indebtedness to those who participated over the years in our long-term case studies, and to their families, for admitting us into their homes and lives and allowing us to learn from their experiences. The learning goes well beyond what is represented in this book; it has to do with courage and enduring love in the face of agonizing loss.

I would like to acknowledge also former colleagues and staff whose efforts are represented in one way or another in this book: Susan Williamson, Karen Nolan, Kim Moore, Sara Black, Barry Katz, Mildred Hughes, and the late Benita Hale. Also my coworkers at Moss Rehab: Nathaniel Mayer, Edward Reed, Michael Montgomery, Carolyn Palmer, Jessica Myers, Ruth Fink, Gary Goldberg, and Stephen Braverman. If their patience was strained on those occasions when my efforts here pushed other projects to the back burner, they never allowed it to show.

John Marshall made valuable editorial suggestions and, along with Harry and Betty Stanton, provided support and encouragement during the lengthy process of bringing the book to print. Grants from the National Institutes of Health (#AG02231 and #NS18429) and from the MacArthur Foundation helped support the research and the preparation of chapters. Jessica Myers, Nancy Rosenbauer, and Tania Giovannetti helped out with the final stages of preparation.

My final thanks are reserved for those on whom I depend for all the important intangibles: my sister Annette Berson, my daughters Allie and Becca, and above all Barry, who keeps the home fires burning.

Introduction

These days everyone has heard of Alzheimer's disease; its tragic symptoms have become all too recognizable. But one doesn't have to look more than 15 years into the past for a time when Alzheimer's was unknown to all but a handful of medical specialists, who looked upon it as rare, and etiologically distinct from the dementia of old age (Schwartz and Stark, chapter 2). The dramatic change in perspective came about in the late 1970s and early 1980s, through a series of studies that documented the essential overlap between Alzheimer's disease and senile dementia with respect to both clinical presentation and neuropathological findings at autopsy. These studies established senile dementia as a medical condition resulting from a disease state, rather than the normal manifestation of the brain's aging. Furthermore, with Alzheimer's disease and senile dementia viewed as a single disease entity, estimates of prevalence and malignancy were high enough to justify a call for an all-out effort aimed at prevention or cure (Katzman 1976).[1] In the 1980s the infusion of millions of dollars into research on Alzheimer's disease fueled the formation of interdisciplinary research teams in academic hospitals across the country, and workshops and conferences promoted the sharing and dissemination of information on an international scale. As a result of this effort, there is today an accepted wisdom about what Alzheimer's disease is and what it is not, and this wisdom guides the conduct of research and continuing efforts to refine clinical diagnoses (for example, McKhann et al. 1984).

Alzheimer's disease is identified clinically on the basis of progressive decline in two or more major areas of cognition (for example, memory, language, visual-spatial orientation, praxis) where this decline cannot be attributed to other known systemic diseases or brain disorders. The diagnosis is confirmed by histopathologic evidence obtained from a biopsy or autopsy—evidence of neurofibrillary tangles and neuritic plaques in concentrations that exceed age-graded thresholds (see Damasio, Van Hoesen, and Hyman, chapter 3). When the diagnosis is made on the basis of clinical criteria alone (that is, without histopathologic confirmation), the patient is said to be suffering from *probable* or *possible* Alzheimer's disease, or from dementia of the Alzheimer type (DAT) or Alzheimer-type dementia. The various qualifications acknowledge that a sizable proportion of patients who are seen with the clinical picture of Alzheimer's will not meet the pathological criteria at autopsy. In some of these individuals the postmortem examination of the brain reveals only nonspecific manifestations of cerebral atrophy, for example, spongiform degeneration, nerve cell depletion, and reactive gliosis. In others the examination turns up one or more of the pathological markers that indicate Pick's disease—focal atrophy restricted tò the frontal and/or anterior temporal lobes, distinctive "ballooned" nerve cells, argyrophillic cytoplasmic inclusion bodies—occasionally in combination with Alzheimer plaques and/or tangles (see Morris et al. 1984). The various clinical entities subsumed under Alzheimer-type dementia (Alzheimer's disease, simple or nonspecific dementia, Pick's disease) are all thought to arise as a consequence of primary, idiopathic neuronal degeneration. These conditions are to be contrasted with multi-infarct dementia, which arises from multiple vascular occlusions (strokes), and with the various toxic, metabolic, and viral encephalopathies that are known to cause dementia.

An early discovery in the scientific war on Alzheimer's disease was that acetylcholine (ACh) is depleted in the cortex and hippocampus of affected individuals (as indexed by levels of choline acetyltransferase, the enzyme that synthesizes ACh). This neurochemical deficiency, involving a neurotransmitter known to play a role in memory consolidation, was subsequently found to correlate with plaque concentration and mental status in life (Perry et al. 1978). Moreover it appeared that the deficiency could be traced to the degeneration of cells in nuclei of the basal forebrain, which provide the major cholinergic innervation to cortex and hippocampus (Whitehouse et al. 1981). According to the *cholinergic hypothesis*, the deterioration of cholinergic-bearing cells in forebrain nuclei is the primary pathologic event in Alzheimer's disease, from which other diverse manifestations follow. Based on this hypothesis and the supporting evidence, a succession of clinical trials was conducted with pharmacological agents thought to have the potential to enhance levels of cortical ACh and thus abort or retard the decline in mental status. These studies are continuing, but to date they have not succeeded in yielding the miracle drug that will do for Alzheimer's what L-dopa has done for Parkinson's disease. (For more on the cholinergic hypothesis, see Bartus et al. 1982, Collerton 1986, Coyle, Price, and Delong 1983, and

Drachman and Leavitt 1974. A summary of attempted pharmacological interventions is available in Corkin et al. 1982.)

Overall the cholinergic hypothesis has not been well supported. For one thing the neurochemical disorder in Alzheimer's disease is not specific to the acetylcholine system. The subcortical afferent projections supplying cortical noradrenaline and serotonin are also affected, and there is also a marked reduction in cortical somatostatin traceable to deterioration of intrinsic somatostatin-containing neurons. This is not to say that the neurochemical disorder is all-encompassing. To date the evidence suggests minor involvement, if any, of the dopaminergic system, of several neuropeptide transmitter systems, and of the putative amino acid neurotransmitter systems of the cortex: glutamate, aspartate, GABA (γ-aminobutyric acid).

The several neurotransmitter systems that are severely affected in Alzheimer's disease have in common that their nerve cell bodies are located within the cerebral cortex or lying outside and projecting to it (Mann and Yates 1986). This fact has suggested to some that the primary damage in Alzheimer's disease is to cortical nerve terminals, with neurotransmitter alterations and perikaryal loss following as secondary changes (Mann and Yates 1986, Morrison et al. 1986, Damasio, Van Hoesen, and Hyman, chapter 3).

What lies behind the destruction of cortical neurons and neurites? It now seems clear that the search for ultimate causes will trace back to the aberrant synthesis of one or more proteins and beyond that to defects in the genome. Thus recent evidence has established that families with a clearly inherited form of Alzheimer's disease share one or more abnormal genes on chromosome 21 (St. George-Hyslop et al. 1987). The hypothesis, unproved as of the time of this writing, is that the abnormal gene is that which codes for amyloid β-protein, the protein that forms the core of neuritic plaques (see Goldgaber et al. 1987, Tanzi et al. 1987).

One possible causal account of Alzheimer's disease then is that aberrant synthesis of the amyloid β-protein leads to the deposit of amyloid in the cortical nerve terminals. The accumulation of amyloid has a toxic effect, bringing about the destruction and death of the parent cell, through the mechanism of neurofibrillary tangle formation (see Mann and Yates 1986). Of course because these same plaques and tangles occur in lesser numbers in the brains of non-demented aged individuals, a complete account along these lines will have to explain the quantitative variation that occurs. It will also have to explain the regional and laminar distribution of the changes in both the normal aged and demented brains (Damasio et al., chapter 3). A potentially more significant problem perhaps is the fact that plaques and tangles are quite clearly dissociable events. The brains of patients with Alzheimer-type dementia occasionally show abundant plaques with no neurofibrillary tangles, and in other dementing conditions (for example, dementia pugilistica) it is common for neurofibrillary tangles to occur without plaques.

There are other pathological events too that are frequently, but not invariably, seen alongside the plaque and tangle pathology. Many of these also occur alone as major indicators of other degenerative dementing conditions. As examples we can point to the white matter disorder described by Brun and Englund (1986) and to the variety of vacular alterations in the neuropil, recently studied by Smith and colleagues (1987). The latter alterations are especially interesting because they, like the morphological indicators of Alzheimer's disease, can sometimes show remarkable selectivity in their distribution and their functional consequences. Thus in their recent report of postmortem findings in two patients with isolated, progressive aphasia, Kirshner and colleagues (1987) reported vacuolation, gliosis, and neuronal loss limited to the superficial cortical layers, especially layer 2, in circumscribed regions of left frontal and left temporal lobe.

Finally, with respect to the neurochemical disorder, the possibility must be allowed that in addition to the secondary changes initiated by cortical cell breakdown, there is another pathological process that specifically targets the transmitter-rich cells of the basal forebrain. Based on the evidence available, a disorder of this type, affecting the *isodentritic core* (Rossor 1981), may play an especially important role in early-onset Alzheimer's disease (Bondareff 1983, Rossor et al. 1984).

The general point to be made here is that the search for a primary pathological event in Alzheimer's disease is confounded by the plethora of pathological markers of the disease and the uncertain relation among them. Increasingly researchers are coming to suspect that there is not one but several etiological factors at work here and hence that Alzheimer's disease is not one but a complex of disease states. This possibility is suggested not only by the complexity of the neuropathological picture but also, and even more insistently, by the heterogeneous clinical presentation of the disease.

Among the theses promoted in this book are (1) that this clinical diversity is an essential feature of Alzheimer's disease and Alzheimer-type dementia (Martin, chapter 5; Schwartz, Baron, and Moscovitch, chapter 6); (2) that this clinical diversity reflects to a large degree the differential involvement of particular neural systems that support cognition (Damasio, Van Hoesen, and Hyman, chapter 3; Chawluk et al., chapter 4); and (3) that when suitable methods and models are applied, studies of Alzheimer-type dementia have the potential to greatly expand our understanding of basic brain-behavior relations.

I refer in this last point to the methods and models that constitute the cognitive neuroscience approach to the study of clinical populations. In terms of design it entails an emphasis on detailed case studies, including the study of atypical cases; longitudinal follow-up of patients, and a systematic attempt to correlate symptom profiles with outcomes and with neurophysiologic and neuropathologic findings. It means that behavioral observations should be guided by cognitive and cognitive neuropsychologic theory, including the theory of the modular organization of cognitive systems (Moscovitch and Umilta, chapter 1). Examples of this approach are found in chapter 7 by Chertkow and Bub, chapter 8 by Schwartz and Chawluk, and chapter 9 by Saffran, Fitzpatrick-DeSalme, and Coslett. On the neuropathologic side this approach entails a shift in emphasis away from regional analysis and toward analyses aimed at the cellular distribution of degenerative changes and their consequences for local and distributed neural networks serving behavior and cognition. Damasio and his colleagues at the University of Iowa have been at the forefront of this exciting effort. They summarize their approach and findings in chapter 3. Together these contributing chapters make the case for the relevance of Alzheimer's disease to the elucidation of the neurocognitive modules of mind. As Van Hoesen and Damasio (1987, p. 56) have written elsewhere, "Few opportunities exist to study human behavior in cellular terms, especially in relation to the cerebral cortex. Alzheimer's disease offers one of the exceptions."

Note

1. At the time that Katzman wrote this article, there was no information available concerning prevalence rates in the United States, so Katzman based his figures on studies carried out in northern Europe. Since then a number of studies have been conducted, the most recent one involving the Massachusetts community of East Boston (Evans, Funkenstein, Albert, et al. 1989). In that study an estimated 10.3 percent of noninstitutionalized community residents over 65 had probable Alzheimer's disease. And there was a strong age effect: For persons between 65 and 74, the prevalence rate was 3 percent, compared with 10.7 percent for persons 75 to 84 years old, and 47.2 percent for those 85 and over.

References

Bartus, R. T., Dean, R. L., III, Beer, B., and Lippa, A. S. (1982). The cholinergic hypothesis of geriatric memory dysfunction. *Science* 217: 408–417.

Bondareff, W. (1983). Age and Alzheimer disease. *Lancet* 1: 1447.

Brun, A., and Englund, E. (1986). A white matter disorder in dementia of the Alzheimer type: A pathoanatomical study. *Annals of Neurology* 19: 253–262.

Collerton, D. (1986). Cholinergic function and intellectual decline in Alzheimer's disease. *Neuroscience* 19: 1–28.

Corkin, S., Davis, K. L., Growdon, J. H., Usdin, E., and Wurtman, R. J. (Eds.) (1982). *Alzheimer's Disease: A Report of Progress in Research.* New York: Raven.

Coyle, J. T., Price, D. L., and DeLong, M. R. (1983). Alzheimer's disease: A disorder of cortical cholinergic innervation. *Science* 219: 1184–1189.

Drachman, D. A., and Leavitt, J. (1974). Human memory and the cholinergic system: A relationship to aging? *Archives of Neurology* 30: 113–121.

Evans, D. A., Funkenstein, H. H., Albert, M. S., et al. (1989). Prevalence of Alzheimer's disease in a community population of older persons. *JAMA* 262: 2551–2556.

Goldgaber, D., Lerman, M. I., McBride, O. W., Saffiotti, U., and Gajdusek, D. C. (1987). Characterization and chromosomal localization of a cDNA encoding brain amyloid of Alzheimer's disease. *Science* 235: 877–880.

Katzman, R. (1976). The prevalence and malignancy of Alzheimer disease: A major killer. *Archives of Neurology* 33: 217–218.

Kirshner, H. S., Tanridag, O., Thurman, L., and Whetsell, W. O., Jr. (1987). Progressive aphasia without dementia: Two cases with focal spongiform degeneration. *Annals of Neurology* 22: 527–532.

Mann, D. M. A., and Yates, P. O. (1986). Neurotransmitter deficits in Alzheimer's disease and in other dementing disorders. *Human Neurobiology* 5: 147–158.

McKhann, G., Drachman, D., Folstein, M., et al. (1984). Clinical diagnosis of Alzheimer's disease: Report of the NINCDS-ADRDA Work Group. *Neurology* 34: 939–944.

Morris, J. C., Cole, M., Banker, B. Q., and Wright, D. (1984). Hereditary dysphasic dementia and the Pick-Alzheimer spectrum. *Annals of Neurology* 16: 455–466.

Morrison, J. H., Scherr, S., Lewis, D. A., Campbell, M. J., and Bloom, F. E. (1986). The laminar and regional distribution of neocortical somatostatin and neuritic plaques: Implications for Alzheimer's disease as a global neocortical disconnection syndrome. In A. B. Scheibel, A. F. Wechsler, and M. A. B. Brazier (Eds.) *The Biological Substrates of Alzheimer's Disease,* Orlando: Academic Press.

Perry, E. K., Tomlinson, B. E., Blessed, G., Bergmann, K., Gibson, P. H., and Perry, R. H. (1978). Correlations of cholinergic abnormalities with senile plaques and mental test scores in senile dementia. *British Medical Journal* 2: 1457–1459.

Rossor, M. (1981). Parkinson's disease and Alzheimer's disease as disorders of the isodendritic core. *British Medical Journal* 283: 1588–1590.

Rossor, M. N., Iversen, L. L., Reynolds, G. P., Mountjoy, C. Q., and Roth, M. (1984). Neurochemical characteristics of early and late onset types of Alzheimer's disease. *British Medical Journal* 288: 961–964.

St. George-Hyslop, P., Tanzi, R., Polinsky, R., et al. (1987). The genetic defect causing familial Alzheimer's disease maps on chromosome 21. *Science* 235: 885–890.

Smith, T. W., Anwer, U., DeGirolami, U., and Drachman, D. A. (1987). Vacuolar change in Alzheimer's disease. *Archives of Neurology* 44: 1225–1228.

Tanzi, R. E., Gusella, J. F., Watkins, P. C., et al. (1987). Amyloid β protein gene: cDNA, mRNA distribution, and genetic linkage near the Alzheimer locus. *Science* 235: 880–884.

Van Hoesen, G. W., and Damasio, A. R. (1987). Neural correlates of cognitive impairment in Alzheimer's disease. In V. Mountcastle and F. Plum (Eds.) *Higher Functions of the Nervous System.* Bethesda, MD: American Physiological Society.

Whitehouse, P. J., Price, D. L., Clark, A. W., et al. (1981). Alzheimer disease: Evidence for selective loss of cholinergic neurons in the nucleus basalis. *Annals of Neurology* 10: 122–126.

Modular Deficits in Alzheimer-Type Dementia

Chapter 1

Modularity and Neuropsychology: Modules and Central Processes in Attention and Memory

Morris Moscovitch and Carlo Umilta

Fodor's 1983 monograph, The Modularity of Mind, *rekindled the centuries-old debate on the nature of mental faculties and how they are represented in the brain. Cognitivists and neuroscientists continue to argue the merits of Fodor's twofold distinction between modules and central systems. Here Moscovitch and Umilta examine the distinction from the perspective of cognitive neuropsychology and find it wanting. Their reformulation expands the possibilities for modular organization and suggests that if we want to carve up central systems at the joints, so to speak, we should begin by looking at the functions they serve as integrators and modulators of modular systems.*

Central systems are clearly important in the functional characterization of dementing disorders. Indeed the term dementia is reserved for conditions that heavily affect memory, generic knowledge, and attention, prototypically non-modular systems in Fodor's typology or anyone else's. Moscovitch and Umilta provide detailed models of the neuropsychology of attention and memory to show how the functions we attribute to each, and the deficits associated with them, are based on the delicate interplay of modular and central processes, involving neural networks that are widely distributed in the brain. Degenerative diseases, which have a tendency to disturb cortico-cortical and cortico-limbic connectivity (see Damasio, Van Hoesen, and Hyman, chapter 3), naturally have a disruptive effect on integrative systems of this type.

But the impact of degenerative dementia is not limited to these central systems. The disorders detailed in subsequent chapters of this book implicate more specialized mental faculties, such as those that locate visual arrays in space or interpret words and pictures as semantic tokens. How are these faculties to be understood within the taxonomy of modular systems? Moscovitch and Umilta's answer draws on the notion of assembled modules, whose domain is broad but circumscribed and in whose operation central systems play a definite, albeit constrained, role.

These and other aspects of Moscovitch and Umilta's thesis come up again in following chapters and chapter notes. One point worth emphasizing here is their contention that negative evidence from dementia in some cases constitutes the most compelling evidence for encapsulation of modular systems.

Thus in patients who have serious limitations in retrieving and manipulating information in memory, particularly semantic- or generic-type memory, the continued preservation of functioning within a domain like object identification limits the role that can reasonably be attributed to top-down influences. Considerations of this type figure prominently in other chapters in this book (especially chapters 7 and 8).

M.F.S.

In computer science there are two ways of solving computational problems: One is to design a general purpose processor that can deal with a wide range of data. The second way is to design a stupid, but highly efficient, specific processor that can operate only in a very restricted domain. For example, to read postal codes or bank account numbers, you can build a machine that can read anything or a device that can decode only digits and letters written in a certain format in a particular location.

Nature is faced with similar problems in designing nervous systems. In lower organisms there are many examples of the second type of solution. In humans it has generally been accepted that such rigid "stupid" systems have given way to general purpose processors that can handle any stimulus that is within its sensory capacities and that can use that information to guide a virtually unlimited range of behaviors (Rozin 1976, Sherry and Schacter 1987). A few people, however, have claimed that domain-specific processors continue to exist for higher processes, even in humans. The most obvious examples are those for speech (Liberman and Mattingly 1985) and possibly for face perception (de Schonen, Gil de Diaz, and Mathivet 1986, de Schonen and Mathivet 1989, Yin 1970). Except for Rozin (1976) no one had proposed that these mechanisms may be fundamentally similar to the stupid and "devoted" processors found in lower organisms. It remained for Fodor (1983), however, to make the strongest case that much of what passes for higher-order cognitive processing in humans is of this stupid sort (in Fodor's words it is *modular*) and that it coexists with more central processes on which intelligent behavior depends.

In the first section of this chapter, we briefly sketch what we believe is the current neuropsychological approach to modularity and evaluate Fodor's criteria for modularity from a neuropsychological perspective. To do so, we first make some specific proposals as to what would constitute neuropsychological evidence for Fodor's criteria for modularity. Based on this critique, we offer an alternative view of modularity and apply it to some neuropsychological data. The third section presents a view of central processes and their functions that is consistent with the neuropsychological literature. In the fourth section we apply the framework we have developed of a coordinated system of modular and central processes to problems of memory and attention.

Current Neuropsychological Approach to Modularity

Double Dissociation
In neuropsychology the typical approach used to relate structure to function is *double dissociation* (Teuber 1955). In this paradigm lesions to area A are associated with deficits to function A, but not function B (or C or D . . .), whereas lesions to area B are associated with damage to function B but not A. (Often it is implicitly assumed that double dissociation exists even in a single case study because one knows that other single cases with different lesions will spare the function in question, but affect another function.) This type of evidence has been used to argue that function A or B is modular (for example, Shallice 1981, 1988). However, double dissociation, or lesion evidence in general, is neutral with regard to modularity as defined by Fodor. It could just as easily be two central processes that are doubly dissociated as two modular ones.

Showing a double dissociation is just the first in a series of steps that the investigator would have to follow to use neuropsychological evidence in favor (or against) modularity. What is necessary is to examine the evidence to see if it conforms to accepted criteria of modularity. As we argue, it is not always possible to determine from the data whether these criteria apply, and sometimes it is impossible in principle to do so.

Characteristics of Modules and Central Processes
Modules are computational devices that receive input, transform it as a result of the computations performed on it, and emit an output. These are common features of all computational devices that are accepted by information processing theories and models and are not unique to modules. What distinguishes one type of computational device from another is the type of input that each accepts, the type of computations it performs, and the nature of the output it emits. Because the criteria for distinguishing modules from other computational devices were set down most explicitly by Fodor, we refer to his criteria in our discussion. According to Fodor, "modular cognitive

systems are domain specific, innately specified, hard-wired, auto-nomous, and not assembled" (1983, p. 37). They are informationally encapsulated, their processes are mandatory and rapid, and their out-put is shallow. They follow a characteristic pattern of development and deterioration. These modules are not mere computational de-vices, but have informational or propositional content. Many of these properties are necessary if perceptual modules are to fulfill their func-tion, which is "to represent the world and make it accessible to thought" (p. 40).

Central processes are the antithesis of modular systems. They are "slow, deep, global rather than local, largely under voluntary (or, as one says, "executive") control, typically distributed with diffuse neurological structures, [and] characterized by computations in which information flows in every which way. Above all they are para-digmatically unencapsulated; the higher the cognitive process, the more it turns on the integration of information across superficially dissimilar domains" (Fodor 1985, p. 4). Central cognitive systems are thus concerned with knowledge that can be, and often is, inferential. It is knowledge concerned with, and influenced by, the fixation of belief.

Nonessential Characteristics of Modules
Even a superficial examination of the criteria used to distinguish be-tween modular and central cognitive systems, however, indicates that many of the criteria that distinguish them do not apply. Thus deployment of attention, which can be mediated by a central process, can be both mandatory and rapid (Jonides 1981, Umilta 1988b). To take an obvious example, it is probably impossible not to attend im-mediately to one's name if it is spoken loudly or to a sudden flash of light or movement in the periphery.

Three other features that also seem not to be unique to modules are (1) association with a fixed neural architecture, (2) manifestation of characteristic and specific breakdown patterns, and (3) a characteristic pace and sequencing during development. The neuropsychological literature is replete with cases in which functions mediated by central processes, such as memory, attention, and problem solving, are im-paired after focal brain damage, which suggests that these functions are closely linked to the operation of circumscribed neural structures (Shallice 1988, Walsh 1988). Moreover, the idea of a fixed neural architecture does not necessarily imply a focal location, but can also be realized by a distributed neural network whose components are nonetheless fixed. Memory and attention also have a characteristic breakdown pattern (Butters and Miliotis 1985, Heilman, Watson, and

Valenstein 1985) and a regular developmental sequence (Cohen and Salapatek 1975). Both short- and long-term memory are known to alter their capacity and mode of operation respectively during development and to undergo predictable modification after brain damage, fatigue, or intoxication (Case, Kurland, and Goldberg 1982, Frank and Rabinovitch 1974 a, b).

The distinction between central and cognitive systems does not depend on these criteria; other criteria are much more critical. It is to these essential criteria that we now turn. As we shall see, these too have their problems.

We are not the first to note the deficiencies with Fodor's conceptions of modularity. The interested reader is referred to excellent critiques by Schwartz and Schwartz (1984), Marshall (1984), Shallice (1984), and the respondents to Fodor's 1985 article. Instead, we wish to indicate how these criteria can be translated (operationalized) in neuropsychological terms. What, if anything, would constitute neuropsychological evidence in favor of or against each of the criteria and, by implication, in favor of or against a particular view of the modular organization of mind? Because this book is concerned with both modularity and dementia, we wish to emphasize the special place that evidence from dementing patients holds in evaluating these criteria, identifying modules, and distinguishing them from central cognitive systems.

Essential Characteristics of Modules

Domain Specificity   Each module operates only in a restricted domain. The information a module receives and processes and the hypotheses it projects are highly circumscribed. It cannot accept or deliver information about anything outside its domain. At the neuropsychological level domain specificity is linked to localization of function. Indeed, one interpretation of the results of a double dissociation experiment might be that damage to each region is associated with deficits in a domain that is specific to that region.

There is a problem at both a conceptual and neuropsychological level in defining the domain and determining exactly how restricted it is. A domain can be specified only after one has a theory about the function a module serves and the kind of input it accepts. In the absence of such a theory, it is often difficult to evaluate the neuropsychological evidence. This point can be illustrated with reference to speech perception, where the domain is clearly specified by theory. According to Liberman and Mattingly (1985, 1989), the domain of a speech module is a speech gesture—not a particular set of acoustic features, but the intended gesture that the waveform conveys. This means that the same information can be conveyed not only through sound but also through vision, as in lip-reading (McGurk and MacDonald 1976). At the psychological level this is clearly shown by the McGurk effect, in which the phoneme subjects perceive is a combination of the phoneme they hear and the different phoneme that they simultaneously see being mouthed. Neuropsychologically, this theory suggests that the same structure mediates both speech perception and lip-reading of speech, but no other information. Campbell, Landis, and Regard's (1986) recent experiments on lip-reading in aphasics confirms this prediction. Had the theory specified the domain as one restricted to the acoustic waveform of speech, the experiment by Campbell and colleagues would have been interpreted as evidence against either domain specificity or a particular theoretical instantiation of it to speech.

In this context it may be argued that the neuropsychological deficits of patients with brain damage may provide the best estimate of what the domain of particular modules might be. Unfortunately, few of the deficits ever appear in isolation, as a strict criterion of domain specificity would require. Aphasias, for example, are typically accompanied by deficits in domains that ostensibly have little to do with language (Benson 1985, Kimura 1982). One can always argue that the constellation of deficits one observes results from a lesion that is too diffuse and encompasses more than one functional area (that is, more than one module). Patients in whom, by chance, the lesion seems to be extremely specific and produces the highly circumscribed deficit that the module predicts are rare; yet they sustain our belief in domain specificity even where, as in aphasia, there are no published reports, to our knowledge, of patients without other accompanying cognitive deficits.

Even when some well-documented neuropsychological deficits do appear in relative isolation, it is often difficult to specify the domain involved or even if the structure that was damaged was modular. Consider, for example, visual object agnosia on the one hand and amnesia and hemi-inattention on the other. Whereas object recognition is considered by Fodor to be a modular process, memory and attention are prototypical horizontal faculties that are mediated by central processes. Yet from a neuropsychological perspective there is little to distinguish between, say, amnesia, neglect, and agnosia with regard to the issue of domain specificity. All are caused by focal lesions and can occur in relative isolation from other cognitive deficits. Whereas agnosias are typically modality specific, memory disorders can be material specific (verbal or nonverbal, motor or cognitive—

Milner 1974, Squire 1987) in much the same way that deficits in identifying speech gestures are material, rather than modality, specific. Admittedly, the domain of a memory module may be difficult to specify, but, then, without an adequate theory, so is the domain of any complex, cognitive module. What is the domain of a visual object recognition module? All possible objects, even those not yet invented? Some integral feature input? What makes Fodor and others willing to accept that object recognition is modular, yet reluctant to concede that memory is modular, is probably less a concern about domain specificity than about other essential criteria, such as information encapsulation.

Before we discuss information encapsulation, let us anticipate the argument we will make with regard to both memory and attention. The reason that memory and attention appear to behave as vertical faculties under some circumstances and as horizontal ones under others is that they are mediated by both modular and central cognitive systems. Damage to the modular parts produces a deficit that is as domain specific as damage to a speech gesture or object-recognition module. In fact it is precisely because it is a modular process that is damaged, rather than a central one, that the deficit can be so circumscribed. Where memory and attentional impairments are caused by damage to a central processor, they are accompanied by a more general cognitive impairment that affects other functions (or faculties) in the same way.

Information Encapsulation: Evidence from Dementia   Information encapsulation refers to the resistance of modular processes to top-down cognitive influences. In other words general knowledge of the world cannot affect the operations and outputs of modules—"They go off largely without regard to the beliefs and utilities of the functioning organism" (Fodor 1985, p. 3). Visual illusions and impossible figures persist despite all attempts to have the image conform with the way we know the world must be organized (Kanizsa 1979).

Whereas the idea of domain specificity has figured in neuropsychological investigation, the concern with informational encapsulation is new. The traditional approach of studying patients with focal lesions is not applicable in this instance. If function A is absent, then it makes no sense to try to determine whether the absent function is informationally encapsulated. To test adequately for informational encapsulation, the function under question would have to be intact.

How could questions related to informational encapsulation be framed in neuropsychologically relevant terms? We propose that this issue resembles one that has been taken into account by neuropsychologists and in fact gave rise to the method of double dissociation. The question is related to whether neural damage causes general intellectual impairment or a specific loss of function. By and large, until recently, neuropsychologists interested in localization of function have not been concerned with conditions that lead to a general intellectual deficit. Yet it is precisely this kind of evidence that is critical to the issue of informational encapsulation. If a particular function remains intact despite evidence of gross intellectual loss, one can assume that it is informationally encapsulated because the malfunctioning of a central cognitive system, which is the repository of general knowledge, has no effect on that function. A particularly striking example is the patient reported by Geschwind, Quadfasel, and Segarra (1966) who had her hearing and speech areas isolated from the rest of the cortex. This patient could repeat speech and even correct grammatical errors without any ostensible degree of understanding (though the report of the case is not precise regarding just how much intellectual ability remained). Other examples come from patients with Alzheimer's disease who, despite gross intellectual deficits, can continue to read, to repeat and correct grammatically incorrect sentences (for example, Schwartz, Marin, and Saffran 1979) and, in one rare case, to match different views of particular objects without any idea of what the objects were (Moscovitch, personal observation).

A problem with using residual capacities (sparing of function) in the face of generalized intellectual loss as an index for informational encapsulation is that the conditions that gave rise to the general intellectual deficit are likely also to affect each particular module. Even if some modules are not affected, the patient's inability to follow instructions may make it impossible to evaluate the state of the modules. For these reasons, failure to find that a particular modular function is spared, in the face of general intellectual loss, does not constitute evidence against informational encapsulation. Only positive evidence counts.

Bearing this proviso in mind, we suggest the following: *If domain specificity and information encapsulation are the primary characteristics of modules, then neuropsychological evidence both of double dissociation in patients with focal brain damage and of sparing of function in dementia are necessary for establishing that a cognitive system (or process) is modular.* Taking recognition of noncanonical views of objects as an example, evidence from patients with focal brain damage establishes a domain-specific deficit related to perception of those objects (Warrington and Taylor 1973, 1978), whereas evidence from patients with dementia establishes that the operation of that object-recognition module can be normal despite marked changes in cognition.

Shallow Output   The output of a module is shallow if it is not already semantically interpreted, but is instead confined to domain-specific features. That is, the output cannot convey any information about either how that output was derived or the relation of that output to our general knowledge of the world. Massaro's (1986; p. 440) explanation of shallow output of a language module captures its essence: We can all agree on what was said, but we can argue forever about what was meant.

What constitutes neuropsychological evidence of shallow output? We propose that it is evidence from patients whose lesion prevents them from interpreting and commenting semantically on the information that they had processed successfully in a specific domain. Ideally the evidence should be obtained from demented patients about whom there is little doubt that their ability to interpret and comment on their perceptions is severely impaired. In short, the ideal patient is one whose central processes are so impoverished that it is reasonably safe to assume that performance is determined primarily by modular output. If demented patients are not available, evidence can be obtained from patients with circumscribed deficits that satisfy the criteria we have proposed.

The relevant neuropsychological evidence can be found in two classes of studies: those using explicit tests of knowledge and those using implicit tests (Graf and Schacter 1985, Schacter 1987b). An explicit test is one in which relevant information regarding an aspect of the subject's knowledge is gathered directly and with the subject's awareness. On implicit tests the relevant information is inferred indirectly from the subject's performance and often without the subject's awareness that a particular aspect of knowledge is being tested. For evidence from explicit tests, let us return to the demented patient who matched objects for identity even when they were presented from noncanonical viewpoints. This ability was almost perfectly intact despite the patient's having no conscious awareness, irrespective of the methods we used for testing, of what the object was, to which taxonomic category it belonged, or what function it served. Thus although she matched noncanonical views of objects almost perfectly, the patient performed at chance on the much simpler task of matching different examplars of dogs, cats, and fish to prototypes of each. On the basis of her performance, we conclude that the patient retained an intact module for representing objects in 3D (Marr 1982, Ratcliffe and Newcombe 1982) and that the shallow output of the module was "pictorial" nonsemantic and highly specific to that object—toaster A or toaster B, but not a generic toaster (as Fodor (1983) proposed).

Other examples of performance determined only by such shallow output are not difficult to find. Demented (and nondemented) patients are reported who can read with no understanding (Schwartz, Saffran, and Marin 1980); there are patients who can judge the grammaticality or well-formedness of sentences, and even correct faulty grammar when repeating the sentence, but not assign meaning to the syntactic structure (Linebarger, Schwartz, and Saffran 1983, Linebarger, in press).

The evidence from implicit tests of knowledge may speak to the issue of shallow output more directly. Because on such tests the aspect of the subject's knowledge that is of interest is tested without the subject's awareness, there is little reason to suspect that central processes, as defined by Fodor, can influence performance. Many of the studies relevant to this issue are discussed at length by Schacter, McAndrews, and Moscovitch (1988). Here we restrict ourselves to only a few brief examples.

Many patients with Wernicke's aphasia or Alzheimer's disease display semantic deficits when asked to define words or match them with each other or with corresponding objects. These patients, however, show normal semantic priming effects on a lexical decision task where explicit knowledge of the word's meaning is not a prerequisite for successful performance (Millberg and Blumstein 1981, Milberg, Blumstein, and Dworetzky 1987, Chertkow and Bub, chapter 7). An interpretation of these results consistent with the notion of shallow output is that the module contains all the semantic associations necessary for normal priming performance on this task so that the output can be shallow, yet appear to be deceptively "deep."

A related effect has been observed in patients with prosopagnosia, (Damasio, Damasio, and Van Hoesen 1982) who often cannot even identify the faces of close relatives or their own face in a mirror when tested explicity. These same patients respond with a higher Skin-conductance response (SCR) to familiar than to unfamiliar faces (Bauer 1984, Tranel and Damasio 1985) and showed interference and facilitation effects, respectively, in reading names that are accompanied by a picture of a noncorresponding or corresponding face (De-Haan, Young, and Newcombe 1987). Indeed on the very same trial the patient may deny recognizing the face even as the SCR indicates that the subject is familiar with it.

Evidence of shallow output, however, is not restricted to perceptual or input modules. The output of memory processes, which are prototypically central, according to Fodor, can also be shallow. Patients who are amnesic on explicit tests of memory may perform normally on implicit tests. They provide the correct answer from memory even as they claim that they were guessing and had no recollection of the study episode, let alone of the particular item that they produced correctly on the implicit test. (For review, see Moscovitch 1982a, 1984, Schacter 1987a, Schacter et al. 1988, and Shimamura 1986).

Inaccessibility of Intermediate-Level Representations (Nonassembly)   There may be several intermediate steps in computing the final output of a module, resulting in different representations at each step. Because modules are informationally encapsulated, only the final output can gain free and full access to consciousness. Intermediate-level representations should not be available to consciousness at all. At a neuropsychological level this means that brain damage should not reveal intermediate-level representations for processes that have been identified as (or are strongly suspected to be) modular. And if they do, the behavior of those processes themselves should not be modular.

Before proceeding further, we distinguish between two senses of the term *inaccessible*. One sense refers only to the subject's being unaware of the representations. The second sense, however, leaves open the possibility that though the subject is not aware of the interlevel representations, they can nonetheless be shown to influence behavior. Our discussion first deals with the latter sense of the term.

Fodor (1983, 1985) noted, for example, that normal subjects are not aware of subphonetic differences, yet their reaction times (RTs) in a phoneme-matching task are influenced by them (Pisoni and Tash 1974, Hanson 1977). Similarly experiments on size constancy have shown that judgments that two objects are identical in size are faster when their retinal images are also identical than when they are not (Blount 1979). In both examples subjects utilize information at interlevel representations of which they are not aware.[2]

As we have noted, both normal and clinical neuropsychological literatures are replete with evidence that higher-order processes of which the subject is unaware can influence behavior (Bisiach et al. 1983, Behrmann, Moscovitch, Black, and Mozer (in press), Schacter et al. 1988, Marcel 1983, Fowler, Wolford, Slade, and Tassinary 1981, Forster and Davis 1984, Cheesman and Merikle 1985; see Dixon 1971, 1981 for review and criticisms of this area).

When the brain is functioning normally, it is probably true that people are not aware of intermediate-level representations. Neurological damage, however, can make available to consciousness those representations that were previously completely inaccessible. One striking example concerns motion perception. Ordinarily we see objects moving smoothly from one location to another. Even when the motion may not be smooth, as in the phi-phenomenon, the operation of the module gives as its shallow output a smoothly moving object. After lesions to the visual system, however, some patients report seeing the smoothly moving object as a set of static pictures located at various points in the trajectory, much like superimposed stop-action, stroboscopic pictures of a moving object (Teuber, Battersby, and Bender 1960).

A related phenomenon has been reported in face perception by prosopagnosics. Rather than having the shallow output of a face available to consciousness, the patient instead reports seeing visual patches of dark and light (Hécaen, Angelergues, Bernhard, and Chiarelli 1957). The micropsias and macropsias may also be a case in point (Hécaen and Albert 1978). Objects seem unusually large or small because information is accessed before the computations necessary for size constancy are implemented. In the case of agnosias associated with object perception, some theorists believe that what is available to consciousness after brain damage is a $2\frac{1}{2}$D representation or even a primal sketch of the object (Marr 1982, Marr and Nishihara 1978, Ratcliff and Newcombe 1982), rather than the 3D representation, which is typically the only one available to a normal person. In all these cases it seems that the subject's perception is determined more by direct access to projections of the retinal image than would be the case otherwise, that is, when those projections represent intermediate steps of modular processes.[3]

The latter examples strongly suggest that interlevel representations can be accessible to consciousness and imply that modules can be assembled. If more proof that modules can be assembled were needed, one would only have to examine the neuropsychological literature on reading. Unlike language, with which it is obviously intimately related, learning to read typically requires specific training. Learning is often slow and effortful. Much of the child's knowledge outside the specific domain of reading as well as general strategies are recruited (Miller 1988). Nevertheless a significant proportion of children never acquire adequate reading skills. In short, learning to read seems to involve central processes as much as, if not more than, modular processes. Yet once the skill is mastered, reading appears to be modular. If we accept the evidence, the conclusion is that reading modules must be assembled. In fact we are willing to go further and say that the processes involved in many other learned, automated skills are modular by Fodor's criteria and, by extension, must also have been assembled.

Although there are problems associated with many of the criteria for modularity, it is the proposal that modules cannot be assembled that we consider unacceptable. We use our rejection of this criterion as a point of departure for our own speculation about the functional organization of the mind and brain.

To summarize at this point: *At a neuropsychological level a function is considered to be modular if it can be selectively impaired after focal brain damage (domain specificity) and selectively spared in cases of dementia caused by degenerative brain damage (informationally encapsulated).* The neuropsychological evidence that bears on the four[4] essential characteristics of modules was examined and was found inconsistent with a strict interpretation of modularity. Domain specificity was found wanting for a number of reasons: Except for damage to sensory, cortical areas, the domain effected by focal brain damage was difficult to specify in the absence of a proper theory of the affected function. Often the effect of brain damage was not as circumscribed as one would expect if damage affected a single module. Finally, the selective deficits seen after focal lesions were not only restricted to functions that are identified as modular but also obtained for functions that, according to Fodor, are prototypically nonmodular, such as memory and attention. The same seems to be the case for shallow output. With regard to informational encapsulation, the neuropsychological evidence from patients with dementia and sparing of some (modular?) functions is too sparse to be conclusive. The evidence from patients with brain damage also strongly suggests that functions that are believed to be modular can be assembled.

Can Modules Be Assembled? A Proposal for a Different Modular Organization

Why Modules?
In the previous section we noted that among the various features that are characteristic of modules, some seem to be common to almost any biologically relevant computational device, and others have a variety of problems associated with them. Why then subscribe to the notion of modularity at all? The reason is that we believe, with Fodor, that to present to the central processes veridical information about the world quickly, efficiently, and without distortion from the beliefs, motivations, and expectations of the organism, something like modules that are immune to higher-order influences must exist.

Three Types of Modular Organization
We believe, however, that there are three types of modules, differing in complexity and composition. One type consists of a basic module similar to the one proposed by Fodor. The other two types are modules that are assembled from basic modules to form a collection that usually behaves as an indissoluble unit.

Type I: Basic Modules   The basic modules are those that alone carry out a single function. These modules probably evolved to deal only with highly relevant and predictable environmental stimuli. Among these would be modules for the perception of basic sensory features in each modality. In addition there may be basic modules that pick up complex sensory information such as faces and emotional expressions, where the relevant information is configurational rather than restricted to a single feature. Alternatively this type of complex information may be handled by type II modules.

The neuropsychological evidence suggests that perception of colors, acoustic frequency, sound location, visual location, motion, depth, faces, and perhaps emotions can each be impaired in isolation (Benton 1985, De Renzi 1982, 1986, Hécaen and Albert 1978, Bowers, Bauer, Coslett, and Heilman 1985) and may continue to function normally when the patient is severely demented. Because in each of these cases all the criteria that define a module seem to be met, the evidence in favor of considering each of these to be modular functions is quite good. The slight discrepancies that might arise concerning the domain over which damage to a module produces some impairment can typically be accounted for by the size of the lesion.

It is less clear that other functions can be subserved by type I or basic modules. A case in point is language: The neuropsychological evidence that modules exist for even theoretically separable aspects of language, such as phonology and syntax, is inconclusive (Saffran 1982). On the positive side are reports of word-deafness and agrammatism, suggesting that phonological and syntactic operations, respectively, can be impaired in relative isolation. The main negative evidence is the failure of many of the patients, certainly the ones with syntactic impairment, to meet the criterion of domain specificity—we are not aware of reports of even a single patient in which speech output or syntactic processing is impaired and all other functions appear normal. Unlike the case for perceptual modules, it is difficult to argue that the size of the lesion can account for the violation of domain specificity in agrammatic aphasia. The reason is that there have been too many studies, from Jackson's (1878/1932) in the last century to Kimura's (1977) and others' in the past decade, linking speech output and syntactic deficits to more general cognitive and motor impairments. The main conclusion of these studies is that speech output and syntactic deficits are only one set of symptoms that arise from the impairment of more basic functions such as sequencing and resolution of rapid temporal patterns (Keele, Pokorny, Corcos, and Ivry 1985, Luria 1966). The alternative is either to consider both speech and syntactic processing as dependent on central processes, or, if they are modular, to consider their domain to be neither speech nor syntax but some other basic property whose features have yet to be specified.

Type II: Innately Assembled Modules   consist of a collection of modules whose organization is innately given and whose output is integrated or synthesized by a devoted, nonmodular processor. We use the term *devoted* to indicate that this processor can deal with information coming only from a particular group of modules and no other. This organization is similar to one proposed by Turvey for vision (1973, Michaels and Turvey 1979) in which a devoted central processor integrates input from modular feature analyzers. Like basic modules, type II modules are domain specific, though their domain is much broader. They correspond to the units or mechanisms in Luria's secondary zone (1966). The reason for proposing type II modules is that it is inconceivable to us that there can exist a module for every class of objects that one encounters in the same way that a module exists for faces. If recognizable objects and modules stand in 1:1 correspondence, there would have to be too many modules, conceivably an infinite variety of them. If object recognition is served by a single module or even a small numbers of them, the domain over which each module would have to operate would be so large as to make it indistinguishable from a central cognitive system. Proposals for modules whose single, dedicated function is to provide structural descriptions of objects (Riddoch and Humphreys 1987) would seem to us to be more consistent with type II modules than with the basic modules of Fodor.

Additionally, as we noted, evidence that even primitive modular functions may be fragmented into simpler, modular processes leads us to postulate the existence of type II modules. Deficits in object perception can be due to lesions that affect component modules, damage to the devoted central processor that integrates the output from those modules, or disconnection of that output from a higher-order central processor that makes general knowledge available and that is associated with consciousness (Johnson-Laird 1988, Umilta 1988a). The disconnection from the higher order central processor is common to all types of modular organization and is not relevant to a discussion dealing only with type II modules (Schacter et al. 1988).

It follows from our account that type II modules are capable of modification or learning. Information about specific exemplars of objects, faces, or words are picked up and stored by these modules. Performance on implicit tests of recognition, identification, and memory supports this view (see especially the following section on implicit memory).

The neuropsychological evidence for the existence of type II modules comes from the more complex types of agnosia, such as visual object agnosia, topographic agnosia, agnosia for body parts, and astereoagnosia (object agnosia in the tactile modality) (Bauer and Rubens 1985, Benton 1985, De Renzi 1982). What is characteristic of these agnosias is that they are domain and modality specific, though in each case the domain is quite large; another of their characteristics is that knowledge about the object does not improve its perceptibility in the impaired domain. In some cases the deficits arise, in part, because the output from basic modules seem to be impaired. Here deficits in perceiving basic features accompany the agnosia. In other instances, basic sensory deficits are minimal, but the agnosia arises instead because the devoted central processor seems incapable of integrating the output from the basic modules. In some cases subjects can even copy a line drawing of the object perfectly, but cannot identify it. In addition subjects often cannot imagine what the object would look like in response to a verbal cue, though they can state its function and use the word denoting it properly. Together the evidence supports the idea that it is a devoted central processor rather than a basic input module or a higher-order central processor that is damaged.

From our point of view language is also, in part, mediated by a collection of modules, each with its own function, which are organized to form an intricately related system. The organization is either innately given or innately specified in the sense that early experience modifies it only along prespecified lines and "fixes" the organization so that later experience has little influence on it.

The evidence that language is mediated by a type II module comes from the various aphasias. We have already noted that there are rare cases of language isolation in which phonological, syntactic, and speech output processes can be intact despite the subject's inability to assign meaning to them. In agrammatic aphasia the subject is unable to make conscious use of grammatical knowledge to assign the proper grammatical roles for the lexical items in a sentence (though the ability to do so implicitly may be preserved) (Linebarger et al. 1983,

Saffran 1982, Schwartz et al. 1979). Lexical access, however, and assignment of meaning outside of syntax may be relatively spared. In some forms of receptive aphasia, the converse is the case. The subject may speak grammatically, but has difficulty in assigning meaning consciously to the lexical items. At a simple level one can interpret these results by saying that agrammatic aphasia results from damage to a syntactic module and receptive aphasia from damage to a semantic module. Some might argue that this is hardly an adequate explanation because one merely substitutes one type of nomenclature with another. We simply wish to call attention, however, to the fact the language cannot be conceived as a unitary module, but may be an assembly of modules, each with its own function (Linebarger, in press).

As we noted previously, it is quite possible that language may not fit a modular organization very well. Both agrammatic and receptive aphasias are accompanied by phonological deficits in perception and often in production as well as in other sequential and analytic tasks that have little ostensible relation to language. Is this the result of a lesion overlapping more than one module, or is each module's domain larger than its theoretically assigned function would require? Judging from neurosurgical, stimulation, and CT (computed tomographic) scan studies, the former interpretation would seem preferable because the affected areas are typically quite large. Nonetheless finding a consistent association between two unrelated deficits undermines the case for modular organization.

This type of modular interpretation of language can accommodate recent evidence that agrammatic aphasics are capable of making grammatical judgments (Linebarger et al. 1983) and that receptive aphasics show semantic priming effects for words they do not understand (Millberg and Blumstein 1981, Millberg et al. 1987). This suggests that aphasias, like some agnosias, can arise from a disconnection from a higher-order central processor. According to this view, the syntactic module is intact in the agrammatic aphasic. What is impaired is either the shallow output of the module to a higher-order central processor that assigns syntactic status or role to the different items or the central processor itself. For similar reasons the receptive aphasic patient may not be able to assign the appropriate meaning to the automatic output of an intact lexical module.

Type III: Experientially Assembled Modules   are similar to type II modules except that central processes are involved in assembling the component basic and type II modules which, once integrated, carry out functions that become modular with practice. The difference between type II and type III modules is illustrated by considering the difference between walking and riding a bicycle, or speaking and reading. In the first two instances the organization of the modules is innate in the sense that it is prespecified, though experience is necessary to allow that organization to unfold. In the latter two instances the organization is guided and formed by experience. In the cognitive literature acquired automatized processes would qualify as examples of type III modules. A number of studies have suggested that attention is necessary for assembling subroutines which are then run off automatically (Logan 1978, 1985, Norman and Shallice 1986, Duncan 1986).

Neuropsychological evidence for type III modules are the acquired dyslexias (Coltheart, Patterson, and Marshall 1980, Patterson, Coltheart, and Marshall 1985, Saffran 1984, Shallice 1988) and ideational apraxias (De Renzi and Lucchelli 1988, Heilman and Gonzales Rothi 1985). Automatized processes in reading and learned motor sequences are clearly acquired.

The dissolution of function in ideational apraxia is particularly informative in this regard. Ideational apraxia is the inability to carry out a learned complex action, such as making spaghetti or brewing coffee or shaving, in the proper sequence despite no loss of understanding and no motor disorder. What is particularly striking, and critical from our point of view, is that each element in the sequence can appear normal. It is merely the order in which the sequence is run off that is impaired. Ideational apraxia may be the motor analog of object agnosia and dyslexia in the sense that the output of basic modules are intact, but their integration by a central processor is impaired (Roy 1983).

One prediction is that recovery of function should be better and different after damage to type III than to type II modules because in the former instance new modules could be assembled that together can perform the lost function, albeit in a different way. For type II modules the central processor is devoted, and another one cannot be substituted to take its place. To take reading as an example, damage to type III modules (or to their components) can lead to different forms of reading disorders. Phonological dyslexia results from damage to a type III module that automatically converts graphemes to phonemes. When this module is damaged, the individual must rely on alternate routes to reading (Patterson and Coltheart 1987). An even more dramatic instance occurs in alexia without agraphia, where difficulty of access to the whole word forces the individual to read letter by letter. (Landis, Regard, and Serrant 1980, Shallice 1988, Shallice and Saffran 1986, Patterson and Kay 1982, Coltheart 1985.)

Summary   Three different types of modules are proposed: Type I is a *basic module* that meets all the characteristics ascribed to modules by Fodor. Modules that process and deliver information about sensory features, and perhaps about speech and faces, are of this type. The other two types of modules, though assembled, retain many of the features of basic modules. Type II is *innately assembled* from a collection of basic modules by a devoted central processor. Object recognition modules are of this sort. Type III is an *experientially assembled* module in which a central processor effortfully assembles the component basic and type II modules. With repeated use, these component processes become fully integrated and automated and as a result assume the characteristics of module. Examples of type III modules are those concerned with reading and learned, skilled motor sequences.

Central Processes

Fodor (1983, p. 4) conceived higher cognitive faculties as "slow, deep, global rather than local, largely under voluntary (or, as one now says, "executive") control, typically associated with diffuse neurological structures, neither bottom-to-top nor top-to-bottom in their modes of processing, but characterized by computations which flow every which way. Above all, they are paradigmatically unencapsulated; the higher the cognitive process, the more it turns on the integration of information across superifically dissimilar domains." In short, central processes that mediate higher cognitive functions are everything that modular processes are not.

At the beginning of the chapter, we noted that some of the characteristics mentioned here, such as processing speed, direction of information flow, and localization of function, do not always distinguish central from modular processes. The critical differentiating factor, as Fodor emphasizes, is informational encapsulation (and perhaps also domain specificity). Modules are defined by their informational content, which is used in their computations and which determines and restricts the type of hypotheses or propositions they project to central processes. Never mind that often it is difficult to specify the kind of information that modules receive, contain, and project. The crucial points are that the information is limited to a certain type in modules, whereas the information received by central processes and used in their computations can be infinitely diverse. In contrast to modules there is, in principle, no restriction on the information central systems can bring to bear in projecting hypotheses *and* in the types of hypotheses they can project.[5]

Faced with the prospect of accounting for this potentially infinite diversity of information and the hyptheses that central systems can receive, compute, and project, Fodor, from his perspective, sensibly concluded that one cannot have a scientific psychology of central processes. This conclusion is valid only if psychology's goal is to capture the content of thought. Fodor's concern with informational encapsulation, and the theory of knowledge that it implies, led him to dismiss, or at least belittle, the possibility that in some areas of inquiry it is the processes themselves that should be the focus of scientific psychology (or neuropsychology) rather than the information that the processes compute.

In truth, it is probably impossible to separate the information that is represented from the processes involved in representing it (Anderson 1978). When the information content is obvious and the process that computes that information is not evident, then the proper research strategy is to focus on content; when content is unspecifiable, then a clue can be gained by studying the process. Thus by virtue of their properties, especially of domain specificity and informational encapsulation, modules are typically defined by the kind of information they receive, compute, and project. In contrast, we suggest, central processes are defined by the function they serve.

At the neurological level the distinction between modules and central systems is not necessarily that one is more focal in its structural organization and that the other is more diffuse or distributed, as Fodor suggests. The specificity of the deficit following damage, however, should be equivalent in each case, except that in one case the deficit is typically described in terms of loss of knowledge and in the other in terms of loss of function. The defining characteristics of modules, however, suggest that the major difference between modules and central systems lies in their connections; input pathways to modules should be fewer than those to central systems. Sometimes the input pathways to the central systems are known precisely, so that it is possible to specify with some confidence the type of information that each of the pathways deliver. In those cases a kind of paradoxical effect is found that blurs the distinction between modules and central processes. Small local lesions that damage that part of the central system that receives input from only one pathway can lead to deficits of a particular function that are as domain specific as any observed after damage to modules. When the neuronal architecture is known, the distinction between modules and central systems becomes very fuzzy.

An example will help us illustrate our points. More than any other structure in the brain, the prefrontal cortex is associated with the higher-order functions that are prototypical of central systems. Damage to sizable portions of the prefrontal cortex in humans produces deficits in attention, problem solving, memory, spatial orientation, as well as changes in social interaction and personality (Damasio 1985, Duncan 1986, Milner 1982, Walsh 1988). The prefrontal cortex, which comprises about 30 percent of the cortex in humans, is not a homogeneous structure. A number of cytoarchitectonically distinct zones have been identified, some of which are believed to comprise functionally distinct subsystems on the basis of double dissociation experiments in humans and in monkeys.

One such region that has been extensively studied in monkeys is area 46, a region on the dorsolateral convexity surrounding the sulcus principalis. Lesions in this region produce deficits on delayed response tests only in the visuospatial domain. Performance on a variety of visual tests that do not require memory for a specific location in space is normal. Recent experiments by Goldman-Rakic (1987) and her colleagues have demonstrated that by making ever smaller lesions, the deficit can be restricted to only that portion of space that projects its input, via the parietal lobes, to the damaged zone of area 46. Thus a lesion restricted to a portion receiving projections from only one quadrant of the visual field produces deficits on delayed response tests only if the stimuli appear in the affected quadrant. Performance is normal in response to stimuli in other quadrants. Moreover, with the exception of delayed response, the monkeys' visual responsiveness to stimuli in the affected quadrant is normal. Despite the extreme domain specificity of the deficit, one should not lose sight of the fact that it is caused by a lesion to a part of the prefrontal system that has been characterized as central rather than modular. Indeed, according to Goldman-Rakic (1987), the general function of sulcus principalis may not be different from that of the prefrontal cortex in general—"it is to use short-term representational memory (i.e., internalized knowledge) to guide behavior in the absence of informative external cues." What distinguishes the sulcus principalis from other regions is the specific domain over which this function is performed. Though damage to large portions of the prefrontal cortex produces the kind of global deficits in cognition (and emotion and personality) that one predicts would occur after damage to a central system, the deficits observed following small circumscribed lesions are reminiscent of those that occur after damage to perceptual and motor modules.[6] *Thus, at the global level the prefrontal cortex behaves as a central system, but at the local level the prefrontal cortex (and other cortical areas) may resemble modules.* As Goldman-Rakic put it, "The principal sulcus is therefore as specialized for performance based on visuospatial memory as is the dorsal motor cortex for voluntary limb movement and the lateral striate cortex for central vision" (p. 381).

We do not have a solution to the potential difficulties that this illustration causes for neuropsychologists wishing to maintain hard distinctions between central and modular systems. The criterion of domain specificity seems to be met by the preceding example. Whether informational encapsulation and shallow output are also satisfied has not been determined.

Until a solution is found, we will continue to adhere to some of the basic distinctions between central and modular systems because we believe, for the moment at least, that the interplay of central and modular systems provides the most useful explanation of normal and impaired cognition. Having committed ourselves to this enterprise, let us proceed with the discussion of central processes.

The criteria used for identifying central processes are criteria of exclusion. If they do not satisfy the criteria for modular processes, then they are central. Because central processes are not domain specific or informationally encapsulated, the focus in studying them will be on the operations they perform, rather than on their informational content. As we noted previously, the technique of double dissociation can be applied as easily to central processes as to modular ones. Consistent with this point of view, we should be able to find evidence of brain damage that impairs one of these processes yet leaves the others intact. In the following paragraphs we briefly review the neuropsychological evidence to support this prediction. Four different types of central systems, defined according to their function, are identified. They illustrate, but do not exhaust, all the different types of central systems that may exist.

Function 1: Forming Type II Modules
As we have already discussed, this function is performed by a devoted central processor in conjunction with type I modules to form type II modules. In many ways the operation of the devoted processor is similar to that proposed by Treisman and her colleagues (Treisman and Gelade 1980, Treisman and Souther 1986) to account for the conjunction of separable features into an object. The features are provided by the basic modules and their conjunction by the devoted processor (see also Turvey 1973). Though Treisman and her colleagues assume that the operation of this processor always requires attention, it is possible that noticeable amounts of attention are necessary only under the conditions of tachistoscopic presentation, when the combination of features is artificial, and a demanding search is required.

In more naturalistic settings, the processor may execute its functions relatively effortlessly. Phoneme identification and syntactic parsing may also require the services of a devoted central processor.

We believe that devoted central processors are associated with each modality and that each is located in different cortical regions, usually in close proximity to the sensory region that delivers modular input to them. Thus, though the domain may be large, its boundaries are typically confined to a single modality. They are essentially linked to the modules whose input they receive and in combination with which they form a type II module. In other words they are a kind of bridge between basic modules on the one hand and higher-order central systems on the other. Evidence for this type of devoted central processor was noted previously.

Function 2: Formation and Maintenance of Type III Modules

Damage to the central systems having this function leaves the components of type III modules intact, but impairs their organization into an operational unit. In the case of type III motor modules, the order in which the various components are activated will be disrupted, but each component act will be performed normally. Such disorders can be manifested in two different ways, each of which is associated with damage to different regions of the brain: The best known and the one with the longest history in neuropsychology is *ideational apraxia* (De Renzi and Lucchelli 1988, Heilman and Gonzales Rothi 1985, Roy 1983). This condition is associated with damage to the posterior portion of the left hemisphere and results in the disruption of well-learned motor acts in which each of the elements is intact, but which cannot be ordered properly. For example, when asked to shave, the patient knows how to pick up the razor, lather his face, scrape his face, and so on, but the sequence in which these separate acts are conducted is incorrect. As we already noted, the deficit involved in this type of apraxia and the lesion associated with it bear a strong similarity to object agnosia. In ideational apraxia the central systems are required to maintain and run a particular and limited set of highly organized subroutines, whereas in object agnosia they are devoted to integrating input from a restricted set of modules (see also similar proposals by Goldberg 1989, Goldberg and Costa 1986, Goldberg and Bilder 1987).

The central processes involved in maintaining and running off old action sequences are not the same as those involved in organizing new ones. The processes presumed to be impaired in ideational apraxia normally operate only when the sequence has been well learned or is routinized. Before being routinized, the components forming the sequence must be learned and then effortfully strung together. The function of establishing, rather than maintaining, the appropriate organization of the components is relegated to other central processes. It follows that damage to different brain regions should disrupt these two related functions. This is indeed the case. Damage to anterior frontal cortex impairs the establishment of new routines, which can range from simple motor sequences to solving problems that have many steps. Patients have difficulty in learning to sequence a set of hand movements, face movements, arm movements (Kimura 1977, Kolb and Milner 1981), and a series of actions performed on a latch box (Kimura 1977), though each of the components can be executed flawlessly (see summary in Kolb and Whishaw 1984).

When it comes to problem solving or memory for temporal order, it is not clear that the deficit can be characterized as an impairment in collating new action sequences, even though it is caused by frontal damage. The deficit may arise from impairments in planning or in relating the outcome of each step to the general goal or in subordinating one act to another or in changing sets (Duncan 1986, Milner 1982, Norman and Shallice 1986, Shallice 1982). These last possibilities are to a large extent subsumed under function 4, and they depend on closely related, and maybe even overlapping, but different cortical regions.

The central processes associated with the frontal lobes operate over a larger domain than those in the posterior region, but there are still some constraints. The systems on each side of the brain seem to confine their operations primarily to input received from the same hemisphere or to output governed by that hemisphere. For example, memory for temporal order is impaired by left frontal lesions if the material is verbal, but by right frontal lesions if the material is non-verbal. As more becomes known about the neuroanatomical connections of different regions of the frontal lobes, and about the effects of small focal lesions to these regions, the more likely it is that their operation will satisfy the criterion of domain specificity.

Function 3: Relating Information to General Knowledge
It is this function that perhaps is most problematic to followers of Fodor. How much knowledge is stored in a module? How much information about an object or a word is contained in the shallow output of an object, face, or lexical module? We have already argued that for objects the information seems to be modality and item specific, but does the output provide information about, say, the object's weight, texture, and function (Chertkow and Bub, chapter 7)? If the item is a word, is information made available about its meaning in

different contexts? or if it is a face, is there information about the person's name, occupation, personality trait (Bruce and Young 1986)? These questions were raised in discussing information encapsulation and shallow output, and suggestions were put forward about the type of evidence that might be used to derive answers. What concerns us here, however, is the role that central systems play in supplying the information that is not made available by modules. Two aspects of the central systems' role can be distinguished: one is receiving informational content from modules and the other is the process that relates semantic knowledge to modular output. By combining both aspects, central processes assign meaning to modular output.[7]

For example, systems having this function will interpret the meaning of a 3D representation of an object delivered to it by a type II module. That is, a name could be assigned to the object, its function and relation to other objects made known, and so on. To do this, contact has to be made with general knowledge.

Deficits in this function can arise either because the knowledge base, the semantic core, is "depleted" or because the process that delivers (some of) the necessary semantic information is impaired. In principle it might be possible to distinguish between these two aspects, but in practice it has proved very difficult. What constitutes evidence that the semantic core is deficient? Presumably evidence from patients with global or restricted semantic memory loss in all domains who nonetheless show evidence of adequate processing at the modular level. Such patients should be able, say, to read, repeat words, and recognize items as identical within a modality, yet not know the meaning of the item regardless of the modality in which it is presented. This type of global semantic loss, reported in some demented patients, is in contrast to the modality specific semantic loss associated with the various agnosias (for further discussion, see Chertkow and Bub, chapter 7, and Schwartz and Chawluk, chapter 8).

Though central, the process used to derive the prototypical semantic knowledge of an item—its accepted, common meaning and function—is an *associative process* that is automatically activated by the item. Confronted with the item *chair*, its prototypical meaning and function is immediately apprehended by associative process in anyone who is not demented. This associative process is in contrast to a *strategic process* that allows one to gain access to all the other things one knows, or can infer, about chairs, their potential functions, and even their symbolic value. It is also this kind of process that seems to be involved in identifying by inference stimuli that are either physically degraded or are perceptually distorted because the modules that ordinarily code these stimuli are damaged.

This distinction between associative and strategic processes related to item knowledge is borrowed from research in episodic memory. Whether the distinction will prove useful in studies of semantic memory remains to be seen. At the neurological level the evidence suggests that damage to the posterior temporal-parietal cortex, either on the left or bilaterally, leads to *associative* semantic memory deficits, whereas damage to the prefrontal cortex leads to *strategic* semantic memory deficits (Luria 1966, Goldberg, 1989).

We should note that strategic aspects of function 3 are also necessary in planning. Indeed it stands at the junction between those central systems that assign meaning to sensation and those that use central, internal representations of the perceptual world to organize action. To execute or choose the appropriate plan, one must bring to bear one's general knowledge on the problem at hand, and one must evaluate the plan in relation to what one knows about the world. The planning function itself, we think, is separate from the function that is necessary for relating information to general knowledge. Patients with function 3 impairment may have ineffective plans because they are based on poor knowledge, but a patient with function 4 impairment may have all the necessary knowledge without being able to formulate an appropriate course of action.

Function 4: Planning
In planning, a goal has to be set, a strategy adopted, the action sequences selected, the process monitored, and the outcome verified against an internal representation of the goal that is to be achieved. Selecting the goal and strategy also requires function 3, and collating subroutines requires function 2. All these functions need conscious intervention of a central processing device that has been termed the supervisory attentional system by Norman and Shallice (1986), a central monitor by Weiskrantz (1988), a central processor by Umiltà (1988a), the central executive by Baddeley (1986), and the operating system by Johnson-Laird (1983, 1988). The operations of this device are assumed to be effortful, slow, and serial. Among its functions is the inhibition of irrelevant or interfering subroutines. Though we agree that some central device is necessary for coordinating all the functions involved in planning, we would like to reserve judgment on whether all the functions are carried out by a single processor or whether they are relegated to a number of processors that are interrelated, but than can be selectively impaired. From the foregoing discussion it should be clear that we exclude from function 4 the

mere collating of action sequences, whether automatic or otherwise, which is achieved through function 2.

Anecdotal evidence has existed since the last century that patients with frontal damage have difficulty in setting goals, organizing purposeful behavior, and adhering to the plan of action in mundane daily activities (Harlow 1868, Bianchi 1922). These patients are easily distracted from their goals and tend to omit relevant activities and insert inappropriate ones. These deficits are highlighted in control laboratory tests. Shallice (1982, 1988) suggests that frontal patients fail in their attempt to solve puzzles such as the Tower of London (or Hanoi) because they follow the solution of least resistance rather than correcting false starts by evaluating their moves with respect to prescribed goals. In finding their way through visual and tactile mazes, frontal patients cannot adhere to the structure of the task, but break rules even in those parts of the task that are easy for them to solve. Frontal patients may even have difficulty in learning because they cannot monitor or keep track of their own current responses in relation to previous events and future goals (Petrides and Milner 1982, Milner 1982).

Apart from rule breaking, these are all what Jackson (1932) would term negative symptoms associated with frontal lobe damage. The most prevalent of the positive symptoms is perseveration (Milner 1966, Luria 1966). It is important to distinguish between perseveration restricted to a specific domain (Goldberg and Costa 1986, Goldberg and Bilder 1989, Duncan 1986), which can occur following lesions to a variety of structures, from a general perseverative loss, which is typically associated with frontal impairment (and perhaps associated subcortical structures; Freedman and Oscar-Berman 1986, Kimura, Hahn, and Barnett 1989). General perseveration can occur either because the subject does not monitor performance, so that an action is repeated after it has already been executed, or because the subject has difficulty in abandoning an unsuccessful strategy or inhibiting a prepotent response and choosing a new one.

Sometimes subjects' inability to plan may cause them to adopt routinized strategies automatically even though they are unsuccessful. Another type of deficit occurs because subjects are too easily deflected from the plan or strategy they have devised by irrelevant salient stimuli that trigger automatized subroutines. Whether this results from a failure in monitoring performance, from an inability to focus attention, or from a tendency for abandoning long-term strategies for a seemingly more immediate, but inappropriate, goal is currently open to debate. Shallice (1982, 1988) attributes these positive symptoms to the release of *contention scheduling*, which is an automatic process of activating subroutines, from the control of the supervisory attentional system. To use our terminology, the subjects rely on associative rather than strategic processes to guide their behavior.

Summary
Where central systems are concerned, it is generally neither feasible nor interesting to characterize the system in terms of its input domain or the information that it can potentially encode or transmit. The particular function of a central system, however, may be known or open to discovery. Four such functions, each associated with different central processes, were proposed: (1) forming type II modules, (2) forming type III modules, (3) relating information to general knowledge, and (4) planning. At the neurological level, structures mediating central processes can be as localized as those associated with modules, though the former should have more varied and extensive connections to other structures. The deficits resulting from damage to central systems are often as specific as those following damage to modules. Indeed, small, highly circumscribed lesions in a single pathway (or in the central system structure itself) can produce deficits that satisfy all the neuropsychological criteria of modularity. That some systems behave as modules at a local level, but as central processes at a global level, is a paradox that makes it difficult to maintain hard distinctions between modules and central processes, but that may point to a fundamental organizing principle of the brain.

The following section applies the conceptual framework we have developed to memory and attention.

Attention and Memory

Memory and attention figure in almost every cognitive act. Fodor (1983), following Gall, confers special status on memory and attention by making them, and not other horizontal faculties, part of every module. Fodor treats memory as merely stored information, an engram, specific to the module to which it belongs. Attention for him is simply a resource that activates the module of which it is a part and modulates the efficiency of its operation. We believe that Fodor takes too narrow a view of memory and attention. For us, as for others, memory is a complex function, akin to problem solving. Attention is no less complex primarily because its selectional aspect makes use of general knowledge and links it to the executive or supervisory functions of central systems. For these reasons, both memory and attention are best understood as reflections of the operations of modular *and* central systems. The following discussion elaborates these points.

Attention and Working Memory

Because attention and working memory (WM) are interrelated, to understand one, one must also understand the other. There are two major aspects to attention: selection and resource allocation or expenditure. Resources refer to the mental energy needed to execute cognitive operations (Wickens 1984). We will assume that resources are limited.[8] Selective attention is the process by which cognitive operations and internal representations enter WM, where resources are allocated to them under the supervisory guidance of information already in WM. Information may also enter WM automatically (Navon 1984, Schneider, Dumais, and Shiffrin 1984, Umilta 1988a, b; Underwood 1982).

According to Baddeley (1986, p. 34), WM refers to "the temporary storage of information that is being processed in any range of cognitive tasks." The processing components of the tasks being executed, as well as their informational content, also occupy WM. The cognitive operations and representations in working memory are under conscious control. The capacity of WM is limited. Although not universally accepted, we will assume that the limits of WM are not defined by a fixed number of items or bits of information but rather are set by the cognitive resources necessary for maintaining information and operating on it. The greater the demands of the operations on cognitive resources, the fewer items can be held and attentively processed in WM (Daneman and Green 1986, Baddeley 1986).

One can conceive of selective attention as a process whereby information is conveyed into WM and maintained there or as a spotlight that illuminates whatever cognitive process-representation it focuses on (Baddeley 1986, Klatzky 1984, Posner 1980). Consciousness is the quality we ascribe to experiencing the contents and processes of WM. Put another way, it is only when cognitive information and processes are in WM that we can be conscious of them. Conversely only information that is in WM is consciously apprehended.

For modules, only the output can be available to WM, whereas for most central processes the intermediate steps or outcomes, as well as some aspects of the computations involved, may also be available. This statement needs to be qualified in considering type II and III modules. In the case of type II modules, because a central process is needed to integrate modular output, we may become aware of the output of both modules and the devoted central processor, though not of the way either operates. Such awareness may be evident when type II modular processes break down after brain damage. It is not known, however, whether conscious awareness of the separate components is also possible when type II modules are functioning normally. With respect to type III modules, such as reading or executing a complex motor skill, like a stroke in golf or tennis, there is conscious awareness of all the intermediate steps during compilation of the modules, but typically only of the final output once the process has been assembled and automatized. For example, in learning to read a nonalphabetic script like Hebrew after one has mastered an alpabetic script, one is acutely aware of the separate graphemes, their sound correspondence, the blending of these, the dawning recognition that it sounds like a familiar word, and the search for what the word might mean. With practice the entire process seems to become as automatic as reading the alphabetic script. However, even once it has become automatized, it may still be possible to make available to WM some of the intermediate steps at the expense of slowing the activity down or breaking it up into its separate components. Consider what happens when one tries to bring under conscious control the intermediate steps of such activities as hitting a ball, driving, or reading.

For central processes, as for modular ones, we are never conscious of the internal working of the algorithms that act on the representations. As we have noted, in this way central processes resemble modular ones: The working of the devices themselves are cognitively impenetrable and computationally autonomous.

Within this framework, neuropsychological evidence of attentional deficits can be listed under the following headings: (1) the capacity of WM is reduced or appears to be reduced, (2) the mechanism for allocating attention is damaged, and (3) entry of information into WM is impaired or blocked.

Attentional Deficits

Reduction in WM Capacity: General Versus Specific Deficits in Demented and Nondemented Patients If WM is assumed to be a single system and its capacity is reduced, there should be a comparable reduction in capacity across all processes in which WM is involved. That appears to happen in conditions, such as dementia or intoxication, that affect the general operation of the nervous system (Baddeley 1986, Morris and Kopelman 1986). However, the idea of a single WM with a fixed capacity runs afoul of data from both the normal and clinical literature that show that WM capacity can vary depending on the task the subject is asked to perform. WM memory capacity as measured by reading span is different from that measured by listening span or digit span, which in turn differs from that measured by spatial span (Daneman and Tardif 1987, Baddeley 1986). Similarly, verbal auditory WM can be selectively impaired in patients with conduction aphasia, with visual and spatial WM left relatively intact (Shallice and Warrington 1970, Warrington and Shallice 1969, 1972, Vallar and Baddeley 1984a, b). The converse syndrome can also occur (De Renzi 1982). One solution for interpreting these data is to posit multiple WM systems, each of which is allocated to different functions. Put in Fodor's terms, WM is an integral part of each module.

An alternate more parsimonious, and psychologically and neurologically more plausible solution is that there is neither a single WM in Baddeley's sense nor are there multiple WM systems. Instead WM is that entity that reflects or represents whatever processes are currently active and whose outcomes or operations are consciously apprehended. If a processor has a reduced capacity or is damaged, it will appear as if WM capacity is also reduced whenever that processor is operating. In other words, specific deficits in WM are related to specific deficits in the processes to which attention is allocated. To repeat, the capacity of WM will vary depending on which central (and sometimes modular) process is currently active, not because there are multiple WM systems but because multiple processes and their output are capable of capturing and occupying our attention (and conscious awareness).

This proposal makes it possible to distinguish between the effects on WM produced by a general reduction in resources that is caused by neuronal loss or by diffuse neuronal inactivation and those produced by a specific impairment to a particular process, whether modular or central, that is caused by focal damage. If the loss is general, WM capcity will appear to be reduced in many domains and across many cognitive functions, whereas if it is specific, WM capacity will be impaired only within a specific domain or for a particular cognitive function. Moreover, in the general case, the type of cognitive opertions performed by a central system or by a module will not change if resource loss does not exceed a certain threshold, though the efficiency with which those operations are performed may suffer. If a particular central system or module is damaged, however, its operation will be abnormal or, in the extreme case, lost entirely.

The latter points are illustrated clearly in contrasting WM deficits in patients with Alzheimer's dementia and in those with conduction aphasia. Certain patients with conduction aphasia appear to have an impairment restricted to the phonological store (Vallar and Baddeley 1984a, b). These patients have a highly circumscribed deficit in verbal memory span that expresses itself as a difficulty in verbatim repetition. The case for a phonological storage deficit rests primarily on demonstrations that factors normally thought to interfere with phonological storage capacity, such as word length, or articulatory suppression and phonemic similarity when the words are presented visually, have little or no effect on patients' performance (Vallar and Baddeley 1984a,b, Baddeley, Lewis, and Vallar 1984). For the most part language comprehension and production, as well as nonverbal abilities, are normal. In contrast patients with Alzheimer's disease and a reduced verbal memory span have a phonological store that operates normally, but inefficiently, as evidenced by their sensitivity to factors whose influences depend on a functioning phonological store (Morris 1984). As a consequence of the generalized loss of cognitive resources, the verbal memory deficits of Alzheimer's patients, as measured by their performance on the Brown-Peterson test, were exacerbated when they had to perform even simple concurrent tasks that drew on their already-reduced resources (Morris 1986).

If we assume that as a rule central processes demand more cognitive resources than modular processes, then deficits in Alzheimer patients should be greatest for central as opposed to modular processes. One set of findings seems ideal to illustrate our point: Item search—a slow, serial, effortful, attention-demanding process (Treisman and Gelade 1980) that is almost prototypically central—is impaired in some patients with Alzheimer's disease (Saffran et al., chapter 9). On the other hand feature search—a parallel, automatic process in which target detection appears to be mandatory and modular—is relatively spared in the same patients.

Not merely searching for a particular item but the very process of integration that we believe is accomplished by devoted central processors (type II modules) is also impaired in Alzheimer's patients. Schlotterer, Moscovitch, and Crapper-McLachlan (1983) asked patients to attempt to identify a single target letter that was followed by a visual mask. They measued the interstimulus interval between the target and mask at which the mask no longer affected perception of the target. A homogeneous mask, such as a bright flash of light, impairs target identification by interfering with the pickup of basic features (the operation of a type I module), whereas a pattern mask interrupts a central processor that integrates these basic features (type II module, Kolers 1968, Turvey 1973). Consistent with our prediction Alzheimer patients were impaired only on the pattern-masking task.

A critical component of WM is a central executive (Baddeley 1986), whose function is to summon, coordinate, and maintain processes and information that are active in WM, to allocate resources to them, and to delete them when they are no longer needed. The central executive itself requires resources to perform its function. This central executive is probably part of the set of central systems that we mentioned in connection with function 4.

A malfunctioning central executive is typically an early symptom of dementia. As we noted, central processes are distinguished from modules by the number of pathways and by the cognitive resources they require. The widespread neural degeneration that causes dementia is very likely to disrupt the broad associative and integrative communication pathways that the central executive requires to perform its function, but not necessarily the more limited and restricted modular pathways. A reduction in cognitive resources is also expected to accompany neuronal loss. Last, neural degeneration is often accentuated in the prefrontal cortex and its related structures, which are considered among the critical areas mediating central executive functions. As a result of one or a combination of these causes, performance on tests of WM that depend critically on the central executive are expected to be impaired in dementia.

Baddeley (1986) and Morris (1986) cite the drop in retention on the Brown-Peterson test as evidence of a WM deficit in patients with Alzheimer's disease. That deficit may be caused as much by the central executive's reduced ability to coordinate rehearsal of the items in the face of even limited interference as by the lower level of functioning of the other mechanisms that Baddeley (1986) postulates comprise WM. Similar deficits are observed in patients with closed head injuries (Levin 1990). It is important to note, however, that patients with unilateral left or right frontal lobe lesions perform normally on the Brown-Peterson test (Corsi 1971, cited in Milner 1974) and on Daneman and Carpenter's (1980) reading span test (Frisk 1988), which is also considered a prototypical test of WM. Although it is still possible that the prefrontal cortex mediates some other functions of the central executive, it is unlikely that the WM deficits in dementia that are inferred from these two tests are caused by frontal degeneration alone.

Deficits in Allocation of Attention: Hemineglect and Related Syndromes   Although it is not always possible, it is important to distinguish between deficits in attention caused by a malfunctioning central executive and those caused by an impaired processor that is summoned by the central executive. As a rule of thumb the former type of deficit should be broader, encompassing all domains, whereas the latter should be more restricted. The former entails a deficiency in the voluntary allocation of attention that is influenced by current and past knowledge and by motivation; the latter seems to be best described as the loss of automatic attentional processes that can be overcome, or compensated for, by the recruitment of a more central, voluntary deployment of attention. The former is prototypically central; the latter, we suggest, shares characteristics with modules. Finally, the former is associated, as we noted, with prefrontal lesions, whereas the latter may be affected more by parietal lesions.

Some studies on allocation of attention in space help highlight the differences between these two types of deficits in attention. Damage to the frontal eye fields might initially produce a deficit in allocating attention automatically. However, damage to wider areas of the frontal lobe produces deficits in the voluntary deployment of attention. Guitton, Buchtel, and Douglas (1985) found that patients with frontal lesions cannot reorient attention voluntarily to a side of space contralateral to the lesion when attention is captured automatically on the opposite side. Also Alivisatos and Milner (1989) found that frontal patients do not benefit from a foveally presented stimulus that provides information about the probable location of targets in space. In short they seem unable to make use of expectancies to direct their attention voluntarily in space.

Patients with hemineglect that arises from parietal damage (Heilman, Watson, and Valenstein 1985), however, seem to suffer from a deficit in the automatic deployment of attention. In contrast to the patients with frontal lesions, those with parietal lesions can often benefit from information about the probable location of a target, even if it appears in the neglected field, and can direct their attention toward the target voluntarily in response to a cue (Posner, Cohen, and Rafal 1982, Posner, Walker, Friedrich, and Rafal 1984). They fail, however, to pick up targets that occur unexpectedly in the neglected field when their attention is engaged elsewhere. According to Posner, Inhoff, Friedrich, and Cohen (1987), orienting of attention in space, even when it is unaccompanied by eye, head, or other body movements, can be subdivided into three phases: disengagement of attention from the attended location, movement toward a new position, and engagement of attention there. Parietal lobe lesions impair the disengagement of attention, a process we propose is initiated automatically by the appearance of the stimulus. As will be seen in the next section, we conceive of parietal neglect as a failure of access to WM (and consciousness).

Failure of Access to WM: Deficits in the Automatic Deployment of Attention
Detecting a salient stimulus change, we propose, is a modular process that delivers its output to WM. The domain is not a particular physical feature—it is a change in background stimulation (Jonides

and Yantis 1988). The output is shallow; it provides information that a change occurred, not about what that change was. Once noticed, voluntary attentional mechanisms are deployed to examine the change and interpret it. Whether detection of change is informationally encapsulated is a matter of controversy. Our belief is that expectancies operate postmodularly, after detection has occurred. Indeed one would not want expectancies to play a large role in this process, otherwise one would detect only the expected. In patients with parietal neglect the output of this process does not gain access to WM if the change occurs on the neglected side of space.

If such a detection mechanism exists, one would have to posit that there also exist modules in each sensory modality that are allocated to a particular region of space as it is internally represented and also a higher-order module (type II) in which these sensory-specific spatial maps are integrated into a common one. Salient changes in the information picked up by these modules are automatically delivered into WM. Deficits in deployment of attention arise when the output of these modules fail to gain access to WM. The phenomenon of neglect is not restricted only to the left or right side of space, but can occur even within various regions in front of the subject, as has been shown in monkeys (Rizzolatti and Camarda 1987, Rizzolatti and Gallese 1988). Such specific attentional deficits are exactly what is predicted if separate modular processes are involved. As with other modular processes, deficits in the automatic deployment of attention is rarely seen in the early stages of dementia, though focal lesions can produce a specific impairment (Heilman et al. 1985, Mesulam 1981).

Neglect of the left side of space is not restricted to situations involving stimulus change, but in extreme cases involves the left side of any stimulus or internal representation of it, whether or not it is changing (Bisiach and Vallar 1988). To be consistent, we propose that the subject has information available about the complete extent of the external world and of the stored imagined representation of a scene or object or word from a particular point of view. As with detection the output of the spatial modules of the left side of those representations cannot gain access automatically into WM. Because attentional mechanisms are thus allocated only to the right half of space, what is available to WM and consciousness is the right half representation of the object that is the focus of attention. This interpretation is similar to one offered by Bisiach and colleagues (1983, 1985). If attentional mechanisms are then deployed voluntarily to the neglected space, information there is picked up and consciously apprehended.

One aspect of this proposal that was provocative when we wrote the first draft in 1986, but has become more acceptable since then, is that the information on the left, though neglected, is available to the subject at a preconscious level. As we discussed in relation to some cases of aphasia, prosopagnosia, and dyslexia, the output of modules, though not in WM and therefore unavailable to consciousness, are nonetheless available to other action or procedural systems. Their influence is detectable on implicit or tacit tests of knowledge. Evidence in favor of this view with regard to neglect is slowly accumulating. The neglect patient's midpoint of a line is influenced by the length of the line in the neglected field (Bisiach, Bulgarelli, Sterzi, and Vallar 1983). This suggests that neglect patients are using information in the neglected field, of which they are not consciously aware, to guide their behavior in bisecting lines. Similarly reading in patients who often ignore the left half of words is determined by the information on the neglected left side. Failure to read the left side correctly is greatest in nonwords (for example, *gencil*), less in compound words (*snowman*), and least in noncompound words (*pencil*) (Behrmann, Moscovitch, Black, and Mozer in press). Judging whether tachistoscopically presented stimuli on the neglected side are identical or different from other stimuli can also be done accurately, although subjects are unaware of the stimulus and believe they are guessing (Volpe, LeDoux, and Gazzaniga 1979). In a recent clever demonstration Marshall and Halligan (1988) showed two pictures of identical houses to a woman with severe left-neglect. One picture showed the house in flames on the left side and the other did not. Although on repeated tests the woman did not detect the flames, and believed the houses were identical, she reliably chose the nonburning house as the one in which she would prefer to live.

The similarity of these neglect phenomena with those in other domains reinforces our belief that both modular as well as central processes are involved in the deployment of attention. The same seems to be true of episodic memory, a topic to which we now turn.

Episodic Memory: Explicit and Implicit Tests

Episodic memory is memory for autobiographic episodes or events that retain a spatiotemporal context. Semantic memory on the other hand is concerned with general knowledge and is usually independent of the spatiotemporal context in which that knowledge was acquired (Tulving 1972). As with attention the key elements of episodic memory are input modules, WM (conscious awareness), and the central executive that regulates memory. To these another key element is added that is unique to episodic memory, namely, a process involved in encoding and consolidating information into long-term memory and retrieving it from there. Mediated by the hippocampus and its related limbic structures, this process, we argue, is modular. Because our neuropsychological model of episodic memory has been presented in some detail elsewhere (Moscovitch 1989), we only sketch it briefly here.

First, though, we distinguish between two types of memory tests: Explicit tests of memory depend on the subject's conscious recollection of the experienced event. Implicit tests do not rely on the subject's conscious awareness of the remembered event, but merely investigate whether the subject's behavior was modified by it (Graf and Schacter 1985, Moscovitch 1984, Schacter 1987b). Because the mnemonic processes involved in these two types of tests are different, we examine each separately.

Explicit Tests of Memory   Because conscious awareness of a previous episode is a necessary property of explicit tests, if follows that WM must be involved. In the sense that strategies and general knowledge are involved in encoding and retrieving what is to be remembered, remembering a previous event is no different in principle from attending to a stimulus or solving a problem. As in attention the entire process may be automatized and appear to be modular so that only the outputs are delivered to WM, in which case the memory simply pops into mind, much as some stimuli seem to pop out perceptually and grab our attention. We refer to this memory process as *associative*. Alternatively WM may be extensively involved at all stages so that the subject is aware not only of the remembered event but also of the strategies and knowledge used to bring that event to mind. We refer to this process as *strategic*.

We agree with Fodor that there is no limit to the type of knowledge that a person can use to try to remember a past event or the type of strategies he recruits to aid in the process. But these concerns apply primarily to memory processes we called strategic. Associative memory processes, as we shall see, are different. Besides, there are regularities in the processes that are used in remembering and in the specific breakdown patterns associated with brain damage. These suggest that there are subcomponents of memory processes that can be identified functionally and that are associated with particular neural structures.

According to our model (figure 1.1), the hippocampus facilitates the formation and retrieval of a cross-modular associative structure. An event, that is, the stimulus information that comprises it, is picked up by perceptual modules. They are modified by the process of decoding the information, thereby creating an engram of it. The output

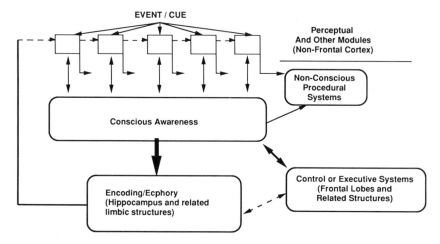

Figure 1.1
A neuropsychological model of memory. The dashed lines indicate that the interaction is optional. The cortical modules that interact with the hippocampal system will vary depending on the information about the event that is available to consciousness when the event is initially experienced and when it is being remembered. (See text for details. From Moscovitch 1989.)

of the perceptual modules are delivered to WM and to central systems that are involved in interpreting them. This consciously experienced, semantically interpreted event, or signals related to it, are then relayed automatically to the hippocampus and its related limbic structures. The hippocampus in turn mandatorily binds the information it receives with the engrams in the various modules and central processes that recorded the experience. Simultaneously the hippocampus encodes all the bound information as a file entry. We propose that consolidation is the process of establishing a long-lasting record or file entry of the encoded event information.

At retrieval an externally presented or internally generated cue enters WM and automatically interacts via the file entry in the hippocampal system with the stored engram in the modules and central systems. The product of that interaction yields an output that enters WM and forms the basis of our conscious experience of remembering. This automatic, mandatory "process by which retrieval information is brought into interaction with stored information" is called *ecphory* by Tulving (1983, p. 169), a term along with *engram* that was first coined by Semon (1921, cited in Schacter, Eich, and Tulving 1978). The information thus retrieved is a product of the cue-engram interaction and may or may not be veridical. Because our colleagues found the term *ecphory* abstruse, the term *automatic retrieval* can be substituted for it. The processes of consolidation and automatic retrieval are all subsumed under associative memory processes.

This associative system, with the hippocampus at its core, we suggest is modular. The specific domain of this module is the information available in WM. Because that information is usually semantically interpreted, semantic information is typically more useful in remembering a past experience explicitly than is information about the sensory attributes of the stimulus. The shallow output of the associative system is ecphoric, or automatically retrieved, information usually about semantic attributes of the stimulus, but also about sensory attributes if they received attention at encoding. Once initiated, the hippocampally based process is rapid, obligatory, informationally encapsulated, and cognitively impenetrable, that is, once the cue is presented, memory retrieval is automatic and "stupid."

The hippocampal-associative memory system also meets the neuropsychological criteria of modularity. Bilateral damage to the hippocampus produces highly circumscribed deficits restricted to the specific domain of the system—explicit memory for consciously apprehended information. Other cognitive functions, and even performance on other types of memory tests, are relatively unaffected. Conversely episodic memory can be relatively preserved in individuals with semantic memory loss, if the disorder spares the hippocampal formation (Warrington 1982, De Renzi, Liotti, and Nichelli 1987).

Yet, as we noted at the outset, memory often is more akin to intelligent behavior such as problem solving than to the stupid, reflexive behaviors one associates with modules. What confers "intelligence" on memory are the *strategic processes* associated with the prefrontal executive system and other central systems. These strategic processes coordinate, interpret, and elaborate the information in WM to provide the hippocampal-associative-memory system with the appropriate encoding information and retrieval cues that it takes as its input. Comparable processes are involved in evaluating the hippocampal system's shallow output and placing those retrieved memories in a proper spatiotemporal context. What makes us conscious of the various processes involved in memory search are not the workings of the hippocampal-associative system but the operations of the strategic system that occupy WM. We are aware of the questions we deliver to the hippocampus, the answers we get from it, and the evaluation of the answers, but we are not aware of the ecphoric operations of the hippocampus itself (Moscovitch 1989).

As might be predicted, memory impairments associated with prefrontal damage do not occur in isolation but invariably are accompanied by related cognitive deficits in other domains. In patients with recovery of frontal functions, the memory impairments resolved along with the other frontal deficits (Kapur and Coughlan 1980, Stuss et al. 1978).

The type of memory deficits seen after damage to the frontal areas of the brain do not involve item information but rather information about temporal or spatial context related to a particular item (Schacter 1987a, Moscovitch 1982a, Milner 1974, 1982). Memory for temporal order (Milner 1974), list differentiation (Cermak, Butters, and Moreines 1974, Moscovitch 1982a, Huppert and Piercy 1976), monitoring productions (Petrides and Milner 1982), and frequency of occurrence (Smith and Milner 1984) are all impaired following frontal lobe damage. It is not surprising that this is the case because we have already noted that central processes associated with the frontal lobes are important in learning sequences of movements and in keeping plans in proper sequence. Presumably similar or identical processes are involved in remembering contextual information about experienced events.

Perhaps the most striking illustration of an associative memory system operating without the control of the strategic system can be seen in patients who confabulate. These patients typically have large frontal lesions attested by radiological evidence and frontal dysfunction as demonstrated by their performance on psychometric tests. These patients "haphazardly combine information from disparate events, jumble their sequence, and essentially accept as veridical whatever the ecphoric process delivers to consciousness. The minimal organization that their memories show is dependent on loose rules of plausibility and association rather than on systematic strategies aimed at recovering additional ecphoric information. In cases of fantastic confabulation (for example, Berlyne 1972, Stuss et al. 1978), retrieval information interacts with whatever information is currently active in the perceptual and semantic modules to deliver ecphoric information that reflects recent thoughts, perceptions, of fantasies rather than relevant past experiences" (Moscovitch 1989, p. 155).

Significantly recall is much more severely affected in many confabulating patients than recognition, suggesting that recall depends more on central strategic process than does recognition. Recognition may provide a more veridical measure of the operation of the hippocampal-associative-system. In patients with bilateral hippocampal damage, both recall and recognition are severely impaired.

The effects of loss of cognitive resources are consistent with the interpretation of the involvement of associative and strategic processes in memory. Aging, intoxication, fatigue, depression, and some forms of dementia that spare the hippocampal formation have their initial and greatest effects on those tasks in which encoding and retrieval are highly dependent on strategic processes. Thus list differentiation and source attribution, two tests that require resolution of temporal context, are affected early in aging (Craik 1977, McIntyre and Craik 1987). The high susceptibility to interference seen in the elderly may have a similar source (Winocur 1982a,b). Similarly, free recall is almost always more impaired than recognition. Providing subjects with appropriate encoding and retrieval strategies and cues to compensate for their lack of resources improves their performance (Craik 1977, Craik and Byrd 1982). Similar effects are observed in patients with Huntington's disease, whose memory impairment is associated with caudate-frontal dysfunction (Butters, Salmon, Heindel, and Granholm, in press). Again, as expected, manipulations such as those that involve strategic processes have little lasting effect on amnesics with bilateral hippocampal damage (Cermak and Reale 1978, Cermak 1982).

The distinction between the effects of damage to frontal strategic systems and hippocampal-associative systems is also observed in performance on tests of recent and remote memory. Temporal ordering of both recent and remote memories is impaired in patients with frontal damage or dysfunction (Milner 1974, Moscovitch 1989, Rubin 1986, Sagar et al. 1988a,b, Shimamura, Janowsky, and Squire 1988). This is consistent with the idea that equivalent strategic processes are operating in all domains. In contrast damage to hippocampal-associative memory typically affects recent memories much more than remote ones (Milner and Scoville 1957, Milner 1966, Rubin 1986, Squire and Cohen 1982, Squire, Cohen, and Nadel 1984, Marslen-Wilson and Teuber 1975), although there is not universal agreement on this point (Warrington and Sanders 1971).

Let us assume that the differential effect on retrograde and anterograde memories is real. How can we account for it? The only solution we envisage is that there is a nonhippocampal route to memory traces that also uses WM. This suggestion implies that the hippocampus is necessary for encoding and automatic retrieval only for a short time after the experience. Subsequently alternate routes to those traces can be established that use central processes or the traces can be revived and their content delivered to WM by newly-established automatic associations for those pieces of information that have been retrieved often (Schacter 1989, Squire, Nadel, and Cohen, 1983, Moscovitch 1989).

It follows from this account that old memory traces are retrieved differently from new ones. For infrequently remembered events their retrieval may be more laborious because they depend on central processes. (Yet if those events had been retrieved only once or twice, they might still require a hippocampal route guided by WM.) For events that have been experienced or remembered frequently, the process would be relatively rapid and automatic, requiring simply their reactivation through firmly established connections outside the hippocampal system. Those memories, moreover, may be quite stereotyped because they are essentially automated subroutines. It would not be unthinkable to say that semantic memories and automatized episodic memories are equivalent in this way (see Cermak 1984 for a similar suggestion).

This type of analysis allows us to rethink the distinction between semantic and episodic memory. After hippocampal lesions it may be as difficult to recall new semantic memories as it is to recollect new episodic memories. What distinguishes semantic from episodic memory is the autobiographical context in which the latter is embedded and that can be used for retrieval. Newly acquired semantic information is learned and retrieved in probably the same manner as episodic memories. With practice semantic memories may be retrieved via a nonhippocampal route. Old semantic memories may be immune from hippocampal damage for that reason. Old, nonroutinized semantic memories may be as laboriously retrieved after hippocampal lesions as nonroutinized episodic memories (Butters and Cermak 1986, Goldberg, in press, Goldberg and Bilder 1986b, Moscovitch 1989, Tulving, Schacter, McLachlan, and Moscovitch 1988).

Implicit Tests of Memory   Unlike explicit tests of memory, like recognition and recall, which require conscious recollection of the past, implicit tests assess memory by measuring the effects of past experience on performance. Even a single presentation of a stimulus item is sufficient to improve one's ability to classify, identify, or generate that item if it is presented again in a complete or degraded form or if it is elicited by perceptual or conceptual information. This improvement can occur though the subject may not explicitly remember having been exposed to that item (Schacter 1987, Shimamura 1986).

If the role of the hippocampus is to make information about recent experiences available to WM, then one possible implication is that without the hippocampus information about these experiences is stored, but unavailable to consciousness. Neither the hippocampus nor the frontal systems are the repository of memory traces, nor are they necessary for storing these memory traces, though hippocampal input might strengthen them once they are laid down. As we indicated in the previous section, we believe that these traces reside in, or are represented by, the modules and central systems involved in encoding the event when it first occurred. As we noted earlier, type II and type III modules are modifiable by experience. The modules store new information relevant to their own function, but they have no access to other memories; their memories are domain specific. On the other hand the information stored in central systems or accessible to them is generic. Thus there is no unique location where memories are stored. Instead we believe, along with others (Squire 1987, Schacter 1985, Mishkin 1982), that memories are distributed in the brain and associated with structures, be they modular or central, involved in processing different kinds of information.

On implicit tests of memory the information and procedures in those modules and central systems can be reactivated directly by priming, rather than through the hippocampal-associative system. With experience or practice the output of the module and associated central systems are delivered more quickly and efficiently. It is this change that serves as an index of memory on implicit tests. We can become aware of the output of either the modules or the central systems, but have no conscious recollection of the previous experience that makes this altered (or speeded) output possible. It is only when the modules and central systems are activated through the hippocampal-associative system that we experience the retrieved information as a memory, as having a sense of familiárity and pastness. As expected, performance on implicit tests of memory is spared in amnesia caused by damage to the hippocampal-associative memory system (for reviews, see Moscovitch, 1982a, 1984, Schacter 1987a, Squire 1987).

A similar proposal has recently been advanced by Schacter (1990). His analysis suggests that research on the effects of structural/sensory features versus semantic attributes on implicit tests of memory may provide a way of distinguishing between the contribution of modular and central processes. The sensitivity of many implicit tests primarily to sensory or structural features of the stimulus, but not to semantic features, suggests that performance on those tests is driven primarily by the output of modular processes that lack semantic content. This is not unexpected because many implicit tests have a strong perceptual component and are believed to be perceptually, or data, driven. In some cases, however, semantic elaboration during the study phase does influence performance on implicit tests. It is significant that in such cases either new associations are formed during the study phase or the implicit tests are conceptually driven rather than data-driven. Instead of it being an implicit test, say, in which the degraded material must be identified, it is a test in which responses must be generated to semantic cues (Roediger, Srinivas, and Weldon 1989). Our model would suggest that performance on implicit tests that are sensitive to semantic manipulations is mediated by the reactivation of old or newly formed associations in central systems or perhaps type III modules. A prediction that follows from this suggestion is that performance on conceptual, but not perceptual, tests of implicit memory would be impaired in dementia. Recent findings that Alzheimer patients are more impaired on conceptual- than data-driven tests is consistent with our prediction (Butters 1990, Gabrielli 1989). Similarly, in conditions that produce a more modest loss of cognitive resources, such as aging, performance on implicit tests of memory is spared only insofar as it depends on reactivation of perceptual modules (Moscovitch 1982b, Moscovitch et al. 1986, Light and Singh 1987). If central or strategic processes need to be recruited to perform the test at hand, as in learning to solve the Tower of Hanoi in its various versions, then performance will be impaired and possibly associated with frontal dysfunction (Shallice 1982, Saint-Cyr, Taylor, and Lang 1988).

Though the outcome of central and modular processes are delivered to WM on implicit tests, and we use WM to gauge changes in performance, there is no reason why working memory cannot be bypassed entirely. One can imagine that other testing procedures, such as measuring SCR or event-related potentials (ERPs) or heart rate, might also reflect the acquisition of new information, though the subject might not be aware at all of the input that was used to trigger these responses. Some progress has already been made in that direction (for SCR, see Rees-Nishio 1984, cited in Moscovitch 1985; for ERP, see Bentin and Moscovitch 1990).

The traces that are laid down and accessed by implicit tests of memory are the same traces that are accessed by explicit tests of memory. It is the process by which they are accessed that leads to different phenomenological experiences. Also because on explicit tests one is conscious of having experienced an event and of retrieving information about it, conscious recollection is amenable to strategic influences and other operations associated with central processes, whereas memories that are retrieved implicitly cannot be influenced by mnemonic strategies at retrieval.

Because the hippocampal-associative memory system receives as its input the contents of WM, bilateral damage to the hippocampus produces an amnesia that affects explicit tests of memory in all domains. If our hypotheses concerning the processes that mediate performance on implicit tests are correct, such global deficits should not be observed on implicit tests after damage to any single system.

Deficits on implicit tests of memory should be restricted only to performance on tests that directly implicate the affected module or central processor.

The evidence on this matter is sparse, but consistent with this prediction. Patients with Parkinson's disease are impaired on implicit tests involving motor learning and frontally mediated problem-solving (St.-Cyr et al. 1988), but perform normally on word-stem completion and reading of geometrically transformed script (Butters et al. in press, Heindel et al. 1988, Huberman, Freedman, and Moscovitch 1988). Patients with Alzheimer's disease, who have a semantic memory impairment, perform poorly on word-stem completion of infrequent words (Shimamura, Salmon, Squire, and Butters 1987), but not of frequent words (Huberman et al. 1988), and have no difficulty acquiring motor skills or learning to read transformed script early in their disease (Moscovitch, Winocur, and McLachlan 1986).

An interesting prediction that follows from our analysis concerns patients with agnosia, aphasia, or dyslexia whose deficit can be interpreted as a failure of modular output to gain access to consciousness. In those patients in whom modular processes can be shown to be intact, but dissociated from consciousness on tests that do not involve episodic memory, it should be possible to demonstrate normal performance on implicit tests of memory for information coded by those intact modules. Because the outputs do not gain access to consciousness, performance on explicit tests for that information should be severely impaired. For material not processed by those modules, performance on implicit and explicit tests should be normal. To our knowledge, there are no published studies with evidence that can be used to determine whether these predictions are correct.

Conclusion

The conceptual framework of modules and central systems that we developed in the first part of this chapter was used to construct neuropsychological models of attention and memory in the second part. In these models it is assumed that more processing goes on in our minds than enters our awareness. Consciousness can be identified with the phenomenal experience of the contents and operation of a limited-capacity central system. This system can also control cognitive processes to some extent by selectively allocating attention to some mental representations and cognitive processes at the expense of others. As a result those receiving attention become conscious, whereas the others remain nonconscious. In other words the notion that emerges is that of consciousness as the experiential equivalent of a central processor that selectively receives and operates on the input of the multitude of nonconscious, modular processes (Umilta 1988a).

In recent years this notion has been supported by neuropsychological studies that have provided evidence of a dissociation between implicit and explicit forms of knowledge. The dissociation takes the following form: A brain-damaged patient is asked to perform a task that requires the explicit use of his or her impaired function. Not surprisingly a severe deficit is observed. When, however, the same patient is asked to perform another task that also taps the impaired function, but in an implicit manner, performance may be quite good, sometimes even normal. Apparently the patient does not have conscious access to the necessary knowledge, even though that knowledge can be accessed unconsciously. Variants of this striking dissociation between normal or near-normal performance on tests requiring implicit knowledge and severely impaired performance on tests requiring explicit knowledge have been observed in many neuropsychological syndromes, some of which have been mentioned in the preceding sections of this chapter. In our view, and in accordance with a proposal by Schacter and coworkers (1988), the implicit/ explicit dissociation shows that (1) conscious or explicit experiences depend on the activity of a common mechanism, the central processor, (2) this mechanism accepts domain-specific input from modules, and (3) neuropsychological impairments can originate because the output from the modules are disconnected from the central processor. Of course the central processor itself is not completely damaged, and thus a global disruption of consciousness does not occur.

There are alternative explanations of explicit/implicit dissociations that are compatible with the type of neuropsychological models we have proposed. Multiple conscious mechanisms may exist, in which case the dissociation results from a disconnection between the module and its specific central processor (Schacter 1990). It is also conceivable that modules project degraded outputs that are sufficient for performance on implicit, but not explicit, tests of knowledge. This possibility is not likely, given that performance of patients resembles that of normal people on the same implicit tests (see Schacter et al. 1988). Alternatively, if damage occurs to a module needed for demonstrating explicit knowledge, performance may then depend on another module that does not have access to the central processor.

Dissociations between performance on implicit and explicit tests constitute only one source of evidence on which our models are based. Neuropsychological deficits can arise from damage to the modules themselves and from damage to central systems that mediate the control processes or functions of the central processor. In this chapter we also tried to indicate how the specific disorders that can arise from these causes can be distinguished from those involving disconnections between modules and the central processor.

According to the models we developed, attention and memory are composed of both central systems and modules. By specifying the functions of central systems and modules and how they interact, as well as by indicating the critical role played by consciousness (and nonconscious processes), the models were able to explain a variety of phenomena in attention and memory of both normal and brain-damaged people. The models also predicted the existence, or presaged the importance, of other phenomena that had been previously overlooked, but that had attracted attention since we first began work on these models in 1986. Among the latter phenomena are the dissociations between implicit and explicit knowledge in neuropsychological syndromes, such as neglect, that had not figured prominently in the literature (Behrmann et al., in press, Marshall and Halligan 1988, Schacter et al. 1989); the distinction between memory disorders that are primarily associative and those that are strategic (Moscovitch 1989, Shallice 1988); and the separation of implicit memory tests, at both the psychological and neurological level, into those that are conceptually driven and those that are perceptually or data driven (Schacter 1990, Roediger, Srinivas, and Weldon 1989). It must be admitted that both the discovery of the phenomena and their coming into prominence owed far less to our models than to the research of other investigators who were working independently of us. Nonetheless it is good to know that we are on the right track. This knowledge encourages us and, we hope, others to develop such models more fully and to use them to guide future research.

Acknowledgments

The first, much longer draft of this chapter was written in the summer of 1986, at the end of a wonderful year in which we were Fellows at the Institute for Advanced Studies of the Hebrew University in Jerusalem. We are grateful to the staff of the Institute for providing us with an ideal environment in which to pursue our studies and to our colleagues at the Institute for the many stimulating discussions on modularity and brain function. Those colleagues who formed the study group at the Institute were led by Israel Nachshon and included Shlomo Bentin, Harvey Babkoff, Elkhonon Goldberg, Gita Ben-Dov, Asher Koriat, Eran Zaidel, Dahlia W. Zaidel, Sonny Kugelmass, and Sally Springer, who visited for a number of weeks. Subsequent drafts of this paper benefited greatly from discussions we had with Myrna Schwartz and Dan Schacter and from their editorial comments. Thanks are also due to Marlene Behrmann, Meredyth Daneman, Mary Pat McAndrews, Eli Saffran, and Endel Tulving for their suggestions and comments.

Notes

1. The patient's performance can be interpreted as disconfirming Fodor's proposal that the output of visual perceptual modules are basic perceptual categories, that is, that if the input is the visual image of a poodle, the output is "dog" and not poodle or animal.

2. One cannot invariably conclude that interlevel representations are being tapped whenever performance is influenced by information of which the subject is unaware. It is equally possible that the output of a module or the outcome of computations performed by the central processes can also affect behavior without gaining access to consciousness.

3. Sometimes dissolution of function only makes it *seem* as if interlevel representations are available to consciousness, but in fact what occurs is a reorganization of function or change in information processing consequent to brain damage. For example, one type of acquired dyslexia, letter-by-letter reading, may be interpreted as making available to consciousness an intermediate-level representation in reading—namely, individual letters—that ordinarily seem to be identified automatically and without conscious access. A more likely possibility, however, is that the damage has forced the subject to process information in a way not ordinarily used in normal reading (Patterson and Albert 1982). In short we are seeing the emergence not of intermediate-level representations in the operation of a module but of a new strategy that probably depends on central processes that bypasses the modular route entirely. Indeed the same subjects who read letter-by-letter consciously seem able to pick up a great deal of lexical, even semantic, information about the word, at a preconscious level. This kind of recruitment of central processes to take over cognitive operations that may have been modular is not uncommon after brain damage. Processes that were once effortless and automatic now require conscious involvement and painstaking effort. Luria's (1972) book, *The Man with a Shattered World*, gives a good feel for what it means to depend on central processes to make perceptual sense of a world with distorted input from defective modules. Similar examples can be found in Brodal 1973 with regard to movement and in Moss 1972 with regard to speech. Yet it is intriguing to think that in many of these patients, the perceptual, input modules still operate normally—only their output is prevented from reaching consciousness.

4. One additional criterion of modularity, computational autonomy, was not listed among the critical ones because no one, even Fodor, mentions it explicitly. Computational autonomy implies that computations that a processor carries out cannot be altered. Thus if a processor applies a particular algorithm to its input, that algorithm will not change in response to external influences.

5. Under some circumstances central systems may be as computationally autonomous and informationally encapsulated as modules. This is particularly noticeable when one falls into a set way of solving problems and making stereotypic social attributions. Because it is possible to alter performance or social perception by knowledge outside the specific domains involved, the processes are deemed to be central.

6. Such highly specific deficits have yet to be reported in humans, but there is no reason to believe that they cannot be found if a person with a highly restricted lesion is properly tested.

7. These processes may also be involved in setting up expectancies and as such may affect perception at a postmodular level.

8. We are aware that all phenomena that have been explained by invoking resource limitations can be explained equally well by alternative, sometimes simpler accounts

(Navon 1984). Nor is it clear how the concept of resources is translated in neurological terms. Ideally one would want to specify the cognitive operations and neural structures that are typically affected by conditions such as depression, fatigue, heightened motivation, aging, and dementia and that are believed to alter cognitive resources. This goal has not yet been attained. In the meantime we find it useful to retain the concept of cognitive resources for its heuristic value.

References

Alivisatos, B., and Milner, B. (1989). The effects of frontal or temporal lobectomy on the use of advance information in a choice reaction time task. *Neuropsychologia* 27: 495–503.

Anderson, J. R. (1978). Arguments concerning representations for mental imagery. *Psychological Review* 85: 249–277.

Baddeley, A. D. (1986). *Working Memory*. Oxford: Oxford University Press.

Baddeley, A. D., Lewis, V. J., and Vallar, G. (1984). Exploring the articulatory loop. *Quarterly Journal of Experimental Psychology* 36: 233–252.

Bauer, R. M. (1984). Autonomic recognition of names and faces in prosopagnosia: A neuropsychological application of the guilty knowledge test. *Neuropsychologia* 22: 457–469.

Bauer, R. M., and Rubens, A. B. (1985). Agnosia. In K. M. Heilman and E. Valenstein (Eds.) *Clinical Neuropsychology*. Oxford: Oxford University Press, pp. 187–241.

Behrmann, M., Moscovitch, M., Black, S. E., and Mozer, M. (in press). Perceptual and conceptual mechanisms in neglect dyslexia: Two contrasting case studies. *Brain*.

Bender, M. B. (1983). Selected papers. New York: Raren Press.

Benson, D. F. (1985). Aphasia. In K. M. Heilman and E. Valenstein (Eds.) *Clinical Neuropsychology*. Oxford: Oxford University Press, pp. 17–47.

Bentin, S. and Moscovitch, M. (in press). Psychophysiological indices of implicit tests of memory: Skin-conductance responses (SCR) and event-related potentials (ERP) in normal people. *Bulletin of the Psychonomics Society*.

Benton, A. (1985). Visuoperceptual, visuospatial, and visuoconstructive disorders. In K. M. Heilman and E. Valenstein (Eds.) *Clinical Neuropsychology*. Oxford: Oxford University Press, pp. 151–185.

Berlyne, N. (1972). Confabulation. *British Journal of Psychiatry* 120: 31–39.

Bianchi, L. (1922). *The Mechanism of the Brain and the Function of the Frontal Lobes*. Edinburgh: Livingstone.

Bisiach, E., and Vallar, G. (1988). Hemineglect in humans. In F. Boller and J. Grafman (Eds.) *Handbook of Neuropsychology, Volume 1*. Amsterdam: Elsevier, pp. 195–222.

Bisiach, E., Berti, A., and Vallar G. (1985). Analogical and logical disorders underlying unilateral neglect of space. In M. I. Posner and O. S. M. Marin (Eds.) *Attention and Performance XI: Mechanisms of Attention*. Hillsdale, N.J.: Erlbaum.

Bisiach, E., Bulgarelli, C., Sterzi, R., and Vallar, G. (1983). Line bisection and cognitive plasticity of unilateral neglect in space. *Brain and Cognition* 2: 32–38.

Blaxton, T. A. (1989). Investigating dissociations among memory measures: Support for a transfer appropriate processing framework. *Journal of Experimental Psychology: Learning, Memory, and Cognition* 15: 657–668.

Blount, J. (1979 Nov). The effect of depth cues and pictorial size on "sameness" judgments. Paper presented at the Psychonomic Society 20th Annual Meeting, Phoenix, Arizona.

Bowers, D., Bauer, R. M., Coslett, H. B., and Heilman, K. M. (1985). Processing of faces by patients with unilateral hemisphere lesions. *Brain and Cognition* 4: 258–272.

Brodal, A. (1973). Self observations and neuroanatomical considerations after a stroke. *Brain* 96: 675–694.

Bruce, V., and Young, A. (1986). Understanding face recognition. *British Journal of Psychology* 77: 305–327.

Butters, N. (1990). Dissociation of implicit memory in dementia. (Abst.) *Journal Experimental and Clinical Neuropsychology* 12: 79.

Butters, N., and Miliotis, P. (1985). Amnesic disorders. In K. M. Heilman and E. Valenstein (Eds.) *Chinical Neuropsychology*. Oxford: Oxford University Press, pp. 403–451.

Butters, N., and Cermak, L. S. (1986). A case study of the forgetting of autobiographical knowledge: Implications for the study of retrograde amnesia. In D. C. Rubin (Ed.) *Autobiographical Memory*. Cambridge: Cambridge University Press.

Butters, N., Salmon, D. P., Heindel, W., and Granholm, E. (in press). Episodic, semantic, and procedural memory: Some comparisons of Alzheimer's and Huntington's disease patients. In R. Terry (Ed.) *Aging and the Brain*. New York: Raven Press.

Campbell, R., Landis, T., and Regard, M. (1986). Face recognition and lipreading: A neurological dissociation. *Brain* 109: 509–521.

Case, R., Kurland, M., and Goldberg, J. (1982). Operational efficiency and the growth of short-term memory span. *Journal of Experimental Child Psychology* 33: 386–404.

Cermak, L. S. (1982). The long and short of it in amnesia. In L. S. Cermak (Ed.) *Human Memory and Amnesia*. Hillsdale, N.J.: Erlbaum.

Cermak, L. S. (1984). The episodic semantic distinction in amnesia. In L. R. Squire and N. Butters (Eds.) *Neuropsychology of Memory*. New York: Guilford Press.

Cermak, L. S., Butters, N., and Moreines, J. (1974). Some analysis of the verbal encoding deficits in alcoholic Korsakoff patients. *Brain and Language* 1: 141–150.

Cermak, L. S., and Reale, L. (1978). Depth of processing and retention of words by alcoholic Korsakoff patients. *Journal of Experimental Psychology: Human Learning and Memory* 4: 165–174.

Cheesman, J., and Merikle, P. M. (1985). Word recognition and consciousness. In D. Besner, T. G. Waller, and G. E. MacKinnon (Eds.) *Reading Research: Advances in Theory and Practice* (Vol. 5). New York: Academic Press.

Cohen, L. B., and Salapatek, P. (Eds.) (1975). *Infant Perception: From Sensation to Cognition*. New York: Academic Press.

Coltheart, M., Patterson, K. E., and Mashall, J. C. (Eds.) (1980). *Deep Dyslexia*. London: Routledge.

Coltheart, M. (1985). Cognitive neuropsychology and the study of reading. In M. I. Posner and O. S. M. Marin (Eds.) *Attention and Performance X*. Hillsdale, N.J.: Erlbaum, pp. 3–37.

Craik, F. I. M. (1977). Age differences in human memory. In J. E. Birren and K. W. Schaie (Eds.) *Handbook of the Psychology of Aging*. New York: Van Nostrand.

Craik, F. I. M., and Byrd, M. (1982). Aging and cognitive deficits: The role of attentional resources. In F. I. M. Craik and S. Trehub (Eds.) *Aging and Cognitive Processes*. New York: Plenum.

Damasio, A. R., Damasio, H., and Van Hoesen, G. W. (1982). Prosopagnosia: Anatomic basis and behavioral mechanism. *Neurology* 32: 331–341.

Damasio, A. R. (1985). The frontal lobes. In K. M. Heilman and E. Valenstein (Eds.) *Clinical Neuropsychology*. Oxford: Oxford University Press, pp. 339–375.

Daneman, M., and Carpenter, P. A. (1980). Individual differences in working memory and reading. *Journal of Verbal Learning and Verbal Behavior* 19: 450–466.

Daneman, M., and Green, I. (1986). Individual differences in comprehending and producing words in context. *Journal of Verbal Learning and Verbal Behavior* 25: 1–18.

Daneman, M., and Tardif, T. (1987). Working memory and reading skill re-examined. In M. Coltheart (Ed.) *Attention and Performance XII: The Psychology of Reading*. Hove and London: Erlbaum.

De Haan, E. H. F., Young, A., and Newcombe, F. (1987). Face recognition without awareness. *Cognitive Neuropsychology* 4: 385–415.

De Renzi, E. (1982). *Disorders of Space Exploration and Cognition*. New York: Wiley.

De Renzi, E. (1986). Current issues on prosopagnosia. In H. D. Ellis, M. A. Jeeves, F. Newcombe, and A. Young (Eds.) *Aspects of Face Processing*. Dordrecht: Nijhoff, pp. 243–252.

De Renzi, E., Liotti, M., and Nichelli, P. (1987). Semantic amnesia with perseveration of autobiographic memory: A case report. *Cortex* 23: 575–597.

De Renzi, E., and Lucchelli, F. (1988). Ideational apraxia. *Brain* 111: 1173–1185.

de Schonen, S., Gil de Diaz, M., and Mathivet, E. (1986). Hemispheric asymmetry in face processing in infancy. In H. D. Ellis, M. A. Jeeves, F. Newcombe, and A. Young (Eds.) *Aspects of Face Processing*. Dordrecht: Nijhoff, pp. 243–252.

de Schonen, S., and Mathivet, E. (1989). First come, first served: A scenario about the development of hemispheric specialization in face recognition during infancy. *European Bulletin of Cognitive Psychology* 9: 3–31.

Dixon, N. F. (1971). *Subliminal Perception: The Nature of a Controversy*. London: McGraw-Hill.

Dixon, N. F. (1981). *Preconscious Processing*. New York: Wiley.

Duncan, J. (1986). Disorganization of behaviour after frontal-lobe damage. *Cognitive Neuropsychology* 3: 271–290.

Fodor, J. (1983). The modularity of mind. Cambridge, MA: MIT Press.

Fodor, J. A. (1985). Multiple review of *The Modularity of Mind*. *Behavioral and Brain Sciences* 8: 1–42.

Forster, K. I., and Davis, C. (1984). Repetition priming and frequency attenuation in lexical access. *Journal of Experimental Psychology: Learning, Memory and Cognition* 10: 680–695.

Fowler, C. A., Wolford, G., Slade, R., and Tassinary, L. (1981). Lexical access with and without awareness. *Journal of Experimental Psychology: General* 110: 341–362.

Frank, H. S., and Rabinovitch, M. S. (1974a). Auditory short-term memory: Developmental changes in precategorical acoustic storage. *Child Development* 45: 522–526.

Frank, H. S., and Rabinovitch, M. S. (1974b). Auditory short-term memory: Developmental changes in rehearsal. *Child Development* 45: 397–407.

Freedman, M., and Oscar-Berman, M. (1986). Bilateral frontal lobe disease and selective delayed-response deficits in humans. *Behavioral Neuroscience* 100: 337–392.

Frisk, V. (1988). Comprehension and recall of stories following left-temporal lobectomy. Doctoral dissertation, McGill University, Montreal, Quebec, Canada.

Gabrielli, J. (1989). Paper persented at the meeting of the Memory Disorders Research Society.

Geschwind, N., Quadfasel, F. A., and Segarra, J. M. (1966). Isolation of the speech area. *Neuropsychologia* 6: 327–340.

Goldberg, E. (1989). The gradiental approach to neocortical functional organization. *Journal of Clinical and Experimental Neuropsychology* 11: 489–517.

Goldberg, E., and Costa, L. D. (1986). Qualitative indices in neuropsychological assessment: An extension of Luria's approach to executive deficit following prefrontal lesions. In G. I. Grant and K. M. Adams (Eds.) *Neuropsychological Assessment of Neuropsychiatric Disorders*. New York: Oxford University Press.

Goldberg, E., and Bilder, R. M. (1986). Neuropsychological perspectives: Retrograde amnesia and executive deficits. In L. W. Poon (Ed.) *Clinical Memory Assessment of Older Adults*. Washington, D.C.: APA Press.

Goldberg, E., and Bilder, R. M., Jr. (1987). The frontal lobes and hierarchical organization of cognitive control. In E. Perecman (Ed.) *The Frontal Lobes Revisited*. New York: IRBN Press.

Goldman-Rakic, P. S. (1987). Circuitry of primate prefrontal cortex and regulation of behavior by representational memory. In F. Plum (Eds.) *Handbook of Physiology—The Nervous System*. Volume 5. Bethesda, MD: The American Physiological Society.

Guitton, D., Buchtel, H. A., and Douglas, R. M. (1985). Frontal lobe excisions in man cause difficulties in suppressing reflexive glances and in generating goal-directed saccades. *Experimental Brain Research* 58: 455–472.

Graf, P., and Schacter, D. L. (1985). Implicit and explicit memory for new associations in normal and amnesic subjects. *Journal of Experimental Psychology: Learning, Memory, and Cognition* 11: 501–518.

Hanson, V. L. (1977). Within-category discrimination in speech perception. *Perception and Psychophysics* 21: 423–430.

Harlow, J. M. (1868). Recovery from the passage of an iron bar through the head. *Publication of the Massachusetts Medical Society* 2: 327–346.

Hécaen, H., and Albert, M. L. (1978). *Human Neuropsychology*. New York: Wiley.

Hécaen, H., Angelergues, R., Bernhard, C., and Chiarelli, J. (1957). Essai de distinction des modalitées cliniques de l'agnosie des physionomies. *Revue Neurologique* 96: 125–144.

Heilman, K. M., Watson, R. T., and Valenstein, E. (1985). Neglect and related disorders. In K. M. Heilman and E. Valenstein (Eds.) *Clinical Neuropsychology*. Oxford: Oxford University Press, pp. 243–293.

Heilman, K. M., and Gonzales Rothi, L. J. (1985). Apraxia. In K. M. Heilman and E. Valenstein (Eds.) *Clinical Neuropsychology*. Oxford: Oxford University Press, pp. 131–150.

Heindel, W., Salmon, D., Butters, N., and Shults, L. (1988). Implicit memory in patients with Parkinson's disease (abstract). *Journal of Clinical and Experimental Neuropsychology* 10: 54.

Huberman, M., Freedman, M., and Moscovitch, M. (1988). Performance on implicit and explicit tests of memory in patients with Parkinson's and Alzheimer's disease. Paper presented at the International Society for the Study of Parkinson's Disease, Jerusalem, Israel.

Huppert, F. A., and Piercy, M. (1976). Recognition memory in amnesic patients: Effect of temporal context and familiarity of material. *Cortex* 12: 3–20.

Jackson, J. H. (1932). *Selected Writings*, J. Taylor (Ed.). London: Hodder and Stoughton.

Johnson-Laird, P. N. (1983). *Mental Models*. Cambridge: Cambridge University Press.

Johnson-Laird, P. N. (1988). A computational analysis of consciousness. In A. J. Marcel and E. Bisiach (Eds.) *Consciousness in Contemporary Science*. Oxford: Oxford University Press, pp. 357-368.

Jonides, J. (1981). Voluntary versus automatic control over the mind's eye's movement. In J. B. Long and A. D. Baddeley (Eds.) *Attention and Performance IX*. Hillsdale, N.J.: Erlbaum, pp. 187–203.

Jonides, J., and Yantis, S. (1988). Uniqueness of abrupt visual onset in capturing attention. *Perception and Psychophysics* 43: 346–354.

Kanizsa, G. (1979). *Organization in Vision*. New York: Praeger.

Kapur, N., and Coughlan, A. K. (1980). Confabulation and frontal lobe dysfunction. *Journal of Neurology, Neurosurgery, and Psychiatry* 43: 461–463.

Keele, S. W., Pokorny, R. A., Corcos, D. M., and Ivry, R. I. (1985). Do perception and production share common timing mechanisms? A correlation analysis. *Acta Psychologica* 60: 173–191.

Kimura, D. (1977). Acquisition of a motor skill after left-hemisphere damage. *Brain* 100: 527–542.

Kimura, D. (1982). Left-hemisphere control of oral and brachial movements and their relation to communication. *Philosophical Transactions of the Royal Society of London*, B 298: 135–149.

Kimura, D., Hahn, A., and Barnett, H. J. M. (1989). Attentional perseverative impairment in two cases of familial fatal parkinsonism with cortical sparing. *Neuropsychologia* 19: 491–503.

Klatzky, R. L. (1984). *Memory and Awareness*. New York: Freeman.

Kolb, B., and Milner, B. (1981). Performance of complex arm and facial movements after focal brain lesions. *Neuropsychologia* 19: 491–504.

Kolb, B., and Whishaw, I. Q. (1984). *Fundamentals of Human Neuropsychology*. San Francisco: W. H. Freeman & Co.

Kolers, P. A. (1968). Some psychological aspects of pattern recognition. In P. A. Kolers and M. Eden (Eds.) *Recognizing Patterns*. Cambridge, MA: MIT Press.

Landis, T., Regard, M., and Serrant, A. (1980). Iconic reading in a case of alexia without agraphia caused by a brain tumor: a tachistoscopic study. *Brain and Language* 11: 45–53.

Levin, H. S. (1990). Memory deficit after closed-head injury. *Journal of Clinical and Experimental Neuropsychology* 12: 129–153.

Liberman, A. M., and Mattingly, I. G. (1985). The motor theory of speech perception revised. *Cognition* 21: 1–36.

Liberman, A. L., and Mattingly, I. G. (1989). A specialization for speech perception. *Science* 243: 489–494.

Light, L. L., and Singh, A., (1987). Implicit and explicit memory in young and older adults. *Journal of Experimental Psychology: Learning, Memory, and Cognition* 13: 531–541.

Linebarger, M. C., Schwartz, M. F., and Saffran, E. M. (1983). Sensitivity to grammatical structure in so-called agrammatic aphasics. *Cognition* 13: 361–392.

Linebarger, M. C. (in press). Neuropsychology of sentence parsing. In A. Caramazza (Ed.) *Advances in Cognitive Neuropsychology and Neurolinguistics, Vol. 1.*

Logan, G. D. (1978). Attention in character classification: Evidence for the automaticity of component states. *Journal of Experimental Psychology: General* 107: 32–63.

Logan, G. D. (1985). Executive control of thought and action. *Acta Psychologica* 60: 193–210.

Luria, A. R. (1966). *Higher Cortical Functions in Man*. New York: Basic Books.

Luria, A. R. (1972). *The Man with a Shattered World: The History of a Brain Wound*. New York: Basic Books.

Marcel, A. J. (1983). Conscious and unconscious perception: Experiments on visual masking and word recognition. *Cognitive Psychology* 15: 197–237.

Marr, D. (1982). *Vision*. San Francisco: Freeman.

Marr, D., and Nishihara, H. K. (1978). Representation and recognition of the spatial organisation of three-dimensional shapes. *Proceedings of the Royal Society of London*, B 200: 269–294.

Marshall, J. C., and Halligan, P. W. (1988). Blindsight and insight in visuo-spatial neglect. *Nature* 336: 766–767.

54 Moscovitch and Umilta

Marshall, J. C. (1984). Multiple perspectives on modularity. *Cognition* 17: 209–242.

Marslen-Wilson, W. D., and Teuber, H. -L. (1975). Memory for remote events in anterograde amnesia: Recognition of public figures from news photographs. *Neuropsychologia* 13: 347–352.

Massaro, D. W. (1986). Review of "The Modularity of Mind." *American Journal of Psychology* 99: 435–442.

McIntyre, J. S., and Craik, F. I. M. (1987). Age differences in memory for item and source information. *Canadian Journal of Psychology* 41: 175–192.

McGurk, H., and MacDonald, J. (1976). Hearing lips and seeing voices. *Nature* 264: 746–748.

Mesulam, M.-M. (1981). A cortical network for directed attention and unilateral neglect. *Annals of Neurology* 10: 309–325.

Michaels, C. F., and Turvey, M. T. (1979). Central sources of visual masking: Indexing structures supporting seeing at a single, brief glance. *Psychological Research* 41: 1–61.

Millberg, W., and Blumstein, S. E. (1981). Lexical decision and aphasia: Evidence for semantic processing. *Brain and Language* 14: 371–385.

Millberg, W., Blumstein, S. E., and Dworetzky, B. (1987). Processing of lexical ambiguities in aphasia. *Brain and Language* 31: 138–150.

Miller, G. A. (1988). The challenge of universal literacy. *Science* 241: 1293–1298.

Milner, B. (1982). Some cognitive effects of frontal-lobe lesions in man. *Philosophical Transactions of the Royal Society of London* 298: 211–226.

Milner, B. (1974). Hemispheric specialization: Scope and limits. In F. O. Schmitt and F. G. Worden (Eds.) *The Neurosciences: Third Research Program*. Cambridge, MA: MIT Press.

Milner, B. (1966). Amnesia following operation on the temporal lobe. In C. W. M. Whitty and O. L. Zangwill (Eds.) *Amnesia*. London: Butterworth.

Milner, B., and Scoville, W. B. (1957). Loss of recent memory after bilateral hippocampal lesions. *Journal of Neurology, Neurosurgery, and Psychiatry* 20: 11–21.

Mishkin, M. (1982). A memory system in the monkey. *Philosophical Transactions of the Royal Society of London, B* 298: 85–96.

Morris, R. G. (1984). Dementia and the functioning of the articulatory loop system. *Cognitive Neuropsychology* 1: 143–157.

Morris, R. G. (1986). Short-term forgetting in senile dementia of the Alzheimer's type. *Cognitive Neuropsychology* 3: 77–97.

Morris, R. G., and Kopelman, M. D. (1986). The memory deficit in Alzheimer-type dementia: A review. *Quarterly Journal of Experimental Psychology* 38A: 575–602.

Moscovitch, M. (1982a). Multiple dissociations of function in amnesia. In L. S. Cermak (Ed.) *Human Memory and Amnesia*. Hillsdale, N.J.: Erlbaum.

Moscovitch, M. (1982b). A neuropsychological approach to perception and memory in normal and pathological aging. In F. I. M. Craik and S. Trehub (Eds.) *Memory and Cognitive Processes in Aging*. New York: Plenum Press.

Moscovitch, M. (1984). The sufficient conditions for demonstrating preserved memory in amnesia: A task analysis. In N. Butters and L. R. Squire (Eds.) *The Neuropsychology of Memory*. New York: Guilford Press.

Moscovitch, M. (1985). Memory from infancy to old age: Implications for theories of normal and pathological memory. *Annals of the New York Academy of Sciences* 444: 78–96.

Moscovitch, M. (1989). Confabulation and the frontal system: Strategic vs. associative retrieval in neuropsychological theories of memory. In H. L. Roediger III and F. I.

M. Craik (Eds.) *Varieties of Memory and Consciousness: Essays in Honor of Endel Tulving*. Hillsdale, N.J.: Erlbaum.

Moscovitch, M., Winocur, G., and McLachlan, D. (1986). Memory as assessed by recognition and reading time in normal and memory impaired people with Alzheimer's disease and other neurological disorders. *Journal of Experimental Psychology: General* 115: 331–347.

Moss, C. S. (1972). *Recovery with Aphasia*. Urbana, Ill.: University of Illinois Press.

Navon, D. (1984). Resources—a theoretical soup stone? *Psychological Review* 91: 216–234.

Norman, D. A., and Shallice, T. (1986). Attention to action: Willed and automatic control of behavior. In R. J. Davidson, G. E. Schwartz, and D. Shapiro (Eds.) *Consciousness and Self-Regulation: Advances in Research*. Vol. 4. New York: Plenum Press, pp. 1–18.

Patterson, K. E., and Coltheart, V. (1987). Phonological processes in reading: A tutorial review. In M. Coltheart (Ed.) *Attention and Performance, XII: The Psychology of Reading*. Hillsdale, N.J.: Erlbaum.

Patterson, K. E., Coltheart, M., and Marshall, J. C. (Eds.) (1985). *Surface Dyslexia*. London: Erlbaum.

Patterson, K. E., and Kay, J. (1982). Letter-by-letter reading: Psychological descriptions of a neurological syndrome. *Quarterly Journal of Experimental Psychology* 34: 411–442.

Petrides, M., and Milner, B. (1982). Deficits on subject-oriented tasks after frontal- and temporal-lobe lesions in man. *Neuropsychologia* 20: 249–262.

Pisoni, D. B., and Tash, J. (1974). Reaction times to comparisons within and across phonetic categories. *Perception and Psychophysics* 15: 285–290.

Posner, M. I. (1980). Mental chronometry and the problem and consciousness. In R. Klein and R. Jusczeck (Eds.) *Structure of Thought: Essays in Honor of D. O. Hebb*. Hillsdale, N.J.: Erlbaum, pp. 95–113.

Posner, M. I., Cohen, Y., and Rafal, R. D. (1982). Neural system control of spatial orienting. *Philosophical Transactions of the Royal Society of London, B* 298: 187–198.

Posner, M. I., Walker, J. A., Friedrich, F. J., and Rafal, R. D. (1984). Effects of parietal injury and covert orienting of attention. *Journal of Neurosciences* 4: 1863–1874.

Posner, M. I., Inhoff, A. W., Friedrich, F. J., and Cohen, A. (1987). Isolating attentional mechanisms: A cognitive-anatomical analysis. *Psychobiology* 15: 107–112.

Ratcliffe, G., and Newcombe, F. (1982). Object recognition: Some deductions from the clinical evidence. In A. W. Ellis (Ed.) *Normality and Pathology in Cognitive Functions*. London: Academic Press.

Rees-Nishio, M. (1984). The relation between skin conductance and memory for emotional and neutral words in normal young and elderly people and in amnesic patients. Doctoral dissertation, University of Toronto, Toronto, Ontario, Canada.

Riddoch, M. J., and Humphreys, G. W. (1987). Visual object processing in optic aphasia: A case of semantic access agnosia. *Cognitive Neuropsychology* 4: 131–186.

Rizzolatti, G., and Camarda, R. (1987). Neural circuits for spatial attention and unilateral neglect. In M. Jeannerod (Ed.) *Neurophysiological and Neuropsychological Aspects of Spatial Neglect*. Amsterdam: North Holland.

Rizzolatti, G., and Gallese, V. (1988). Mechanisms and theories of spatial neglect. In F. Boller and J. Grafman (Eds.) *Handbook of Neuropsychology, Volume 1*. Amsterdam: Elsevier, pp. 223–246.

Roediger, H. L., Srinivas, K., and Weldon, M. S. (1989). Dissociations between implicit measures of retention. In S. Lewandowsky, J. C. Dunn, and K. Kirsner (Eds.) *Implicit Memory: Theoretical Issues*. Hillsdale, NJ: Erlbaum.

Roy, E. A. (1983). Neuropsychological perspectives on apraxia and related action disorders. In R. A. Mugill (Ed.) *Advances in Psychology, Vol. 12: Memory and Control of Action*. Amsterdam: North Holland Press.

Rozin, P. (1976). The evolution of intelligence and access to the cognitive unconscious. In J. M. Sprague and A. N. Epstein (Eds.) *Progress in Physiological Psychology (Vol. 6)*. New York: Academic Press.

Rubin, D. C. (Ed.) (1986). *Autobiographical Memory*. Cambridge: Cambridge University Press.

Saffran, E. M. (1984). Acquired dyslexia: Implications for models of reading. In G. E. Mackinnon and T. G. Waller (Eds.) *Reading Research: Advances in Theory and Practice*. (Vol. 4) New York: Academic Press.

Saffran, E. M. (1982). Neuropsychological approaches to the study of language. *British Journal of Psychology* 73: 317–337.

Sagar, J. J. Cohen, N. J., Sullivan, E. V., Corkin, S., and Growdon, J. H. (1988a). Remote memory in Alzheimer's disease and Parkinson's disease. *Brain* 111: 185–206.

Sagar, J. J., Sullivan, E. V., Gabrielli, J. D. E., Corkin, S., and Growdon, J. H. (1988b). Temporal ordering and short-term memory deficits in Parkinson's disease. *Brain* 111: 525–540.

Saint-Cyr, J. A.: Taylor, A. E., and Lang, A. E. (1988). Procedural learning and neostriatal dysfunction in man. *Brain* 111: 941–959.

Schacter, D. L. (1985). Priming of old and new knowledge in amnesic patients and normal subjects. *Annals of the New York Academy of Sciences* 444: 41–53.

Schacter, D. L. (1987a). Memory, amnesia, and frontal lobe dysfunction. *Psychobiology* 15: 21–36.

Schacter, D. L. (1987b). Implicit memory: History and current status. *Journal of Experimental Psychology: Learning, Memory, and Cognition* 13: 501–518.

Schacter, D. L. (1990). Toward a cognitive neuropsychology of awareness: Implicit knowledge and anosagnosia. *Journal of Clinical and Experimental Neuropsychology* 12: 155–178.

Schacter, D. L. (in press). Perceptual representational systems and implicit memory: Toward a resolution of the multiple memory systems debate. In A. Diamond (Ed.) *Development and neural bases of higher cognition: Annals of the New York Academy of Sciences*.

Schacter, D. L., Eich, J. E., and Tulving, E. (1978). Richard Semon's theory of memory. *Journal of Verbal Learning and Verbal Behavior* 17: 721–743.

Schacter, D. L., McAndrews, M. P., and Moscovitch, M. (1988). Access to consciousness: Dissociations between implicit and explicit knowledge in neuropsychological syndromes. In L. Weiskrantz (Ed.) *Thought without Language*. Oxford: Oxford University Press, pp. 242–278.

Schlotterer, G., Moscovitch, M., and Crapper-McLachlan, D. (1983). Visual processing deficits as assessed by spatial frequency contrast sensitivity and backward masking in normal aging and Alzheimer disease. *Brain* 107: 309–325.

Schneider, W., Dumais, S. T., and Shiffrin, R. M. (1984). Automatic and control processing and attention. In R. Parasuraman and D. R. Davies (Eds.) *Varieties of Attention*. New York: Academic Press.

Schwartz, M. F., Marin, O. S. M., and Saffran, E. M. (1979). Dissociations of language function in dementia. A case study. *Brain and Language* 7: 277–306.

Schwartz, M. F., Saffran, E. M., and Marin, O. S. M. (1980). Fractionating the reading process in dementia: Evidence for word-specific print-to-sound associations. In

M. Coltheart, K. E. Patterson, and J. C. Marshall (Eds.) *Deep Dyslexia*. London: Routledge and Kegan Paul.

Schwartz, M. F., and Schwartz, B. (1984). In defence of organology. *Cognitive Neuropsychology* 1: 25–42.

Semon, R. (1921). *The Mneme*. London: George Allen & Unwin.

Shallice, T. (1981). Neurological impairment of cognitive processes. *British Medical Bulletin* 37: 187–192.

Shallice, T. (1982). Specific impairments of planning. *Philosophical Transactions of the Royal Society of London, B* 298: 199–209.

Shallice, T. (1984). More functionally isolable subsystems but fewer "modules"? *Cognition* 17: 243–252.

Shallice, T. (1988). *From Neuropsychology to Mental Structure*. Cambridge: Cambridge University Press.

Shallice, T., and Saffran, E. M. (1986). Lexical processing in the absence of explicit word identification: evidence from a letter-by-letter reades. *Cognitive Neuropsychology* 3: 429–458.

Shallice, T., and Warrington, E. (1970) Independent functioning of verbal memory stores: A neuropsychological study. *Quarterly Journal of Experimental Psychology* 22: 261–273.

Sherry, D. F., and Schacter, D. L. (1987). The evolution of multiple memory systems. *Psychological Review* 94: 439–454.

Shimamura, A. D. (1986). Priming effects in amnesia: evidence for a dissociable memory function. *Quarterly Journal of Experimental Psychology* 38A: 619–644.

Shimamura, A. P., Janowsky, J. S., and Squire, L. R. (1988). Memory of temproal order in patients with frontal lobe lesions and patients with amnesia. *Society for Neuroscience Abstracts* 418: 8.

Shimamura, A. P., Salmon, D. P., Squire, L. R., and Butters, N. (1987). Memory dysfunction and word priming in dementia and amnesia. *Behavioral Neuroscience* 101: 347–351.

Smith, M. L., and Milner, B. (1984). Differential effects of frontal lobe lesions on cognitive estimation and spatial memory. *Neuropsychologia* 22: 697–705.

Squire, L. R. (1987). *Memory and Brain*. New York: Oxford University Press.

Squire, L. R., and Cohen, N. (1982). Remote memory, retrograde amnesia, and the neuropsychology of memory. In L. S. Cermak (Ed.) *Human Memory and Amnesia*. Hillsdale, N.J.: Erlbaum.

Squire, L. R., Cohen, N. J., and Nadel, L. (1984). The medial temporal region and memory consolidation: A new hypothesis. In H. Weingartner and E. Parker (Eds.) *Memory Consolidation: Towards a Psychobiology of Cognition*. Hillsdale, N.J.: Erlbaum.

Stuss, D. T., Alexander, M. D, Liberman, A., and Levine, H. (1978). An extraordinary form of confabulation. *Neurology* 28: 1166–1172.

Teuber, H.-L. (1955). Physiological psychology. *Annual Review of Psychology* 9: 267–296.

Teuber, H.-L., Battersby, W. S., and Bender, M. B. (1960). *Visual Field Defects After Penetrating Missile Wounds of the Brain*. Cambridge, Mass.: Harvard University Press.

Tranel, E., and Damasio, A. R. (1985). Knowledge without awareness: An autonomic index of facial recognition by prosopagnosics. *Science* 228: 1453–1454.

Treisman, A., and Gelade, G. (1980). A feature integration theory of attention. *Cognitive Psychology* 12: 97–136.

Treisman, A., and Souther, J. (1986). Illusory words: the roles of attention and of top-down constraints in conjoining letters to form words. *Journal of Experimental Psychology: Human Perception and Performance* 12: 3–17.

Tulving, E. (1972). Episodic and semantic memory. In E. Tulving and W. Donaldson (Eds.) *Organization of Memory*. New York: Academic Press, pp. 382–404.

Tulving, E., Schacter, D. L., McLachlan, D., and Moscovitch, M. (1988). Priming of semantic autobiographical knowledge: A case study of retrograde amnesia. *Brain and Cognition* 8: 3–20.

Tulving, E. (1983). *Elements of Episodic Memory*. Oxford: Oxford University Press.

Turvey, M. T. (1973). On peripheral and central processes in vision: Inferences from an information-processing analysis of masking with patterned stimuli. *Psychological Review* 80: 1–52.

Umiltà, C. (1988a). The control operations of consciousness. In A. J. Marcel and E. Bisiach (Eds.) *Consciousness in Contemporary Science*. Oxford: Oxford University Press, pp. 334–356.

Umiltà, C. (1988b). Orienting of attention. In F. Boller and J. Grafman (Eds.) *Handbook of Neuropsychology, Volume 1*. Amsterdam: Elsevier, pp. 175–193.

Underwood, G. (1982). Attention and awareness in cognitive and motor skills. In G. Underwood (Ed.) Aspects of Consciousness: Awareness and Self-Awareness, Volume 3. New York: Academic Press, pp. 111–145.

Vallar, G., and Baddeley, A. D. (1984a). Fractionation of working memory: Neuropsychological evidence for a phonological short-term store. *Journal of Verbal Learning and Verbal Behavior* 23: 151–161.

Vallar, G., and Baddeley, A. D. (1984b). Phonological short-term store, phonological processing and sentence comprehension: A neuropsychological case study. *Cognitive Neuropsychology* 1: 121–141.

Volpe, B. T., LeDoux, J. E., and Gazzaniga, M. S. (1979). Information processing visual stimuli in an "extinguished" field. *Nature* 282: 722–724.

Walsh, K. W. (1988). *Neuropsychology: A Clinical Approach*. 2nd ed. London: Churchill Livingston.

Warrington, E. K. (1982). Neuropsychological studies of object recognition. *Philosophical Transaction of the Royal Society of London, B* 298: 15–33.

Warrington, E. K., and Shallice, T. (1969). The selective impairment of auditory verbal short-term memory. *Brain* 92: 885–896.

Warrington, E. K., and Sanders, H. I. (1971). The fate of old memories. *Quarterly Journal of Experimental Psychology* 23: 432–442.

Warrington, E. K., and Shallice, T. (1972). Neuropsychology evidence of visual storage in short-term memory tasks. *Quarterly Journal of Experimental Psychology* 24: 30–40.

Warrington, E. K., and Taylor, A. M. (1973). The contribution of the right parietal lobe to object recognition. *Cortex* 9: 152–164.

Warrington, E. K., and Taylor, A. M. (1978). Two categorical stages of object recognition. *Perception* 7: 695–705.

Warrington, E. K., and Shallice, T. (1980). Word-form dyslexia. *Brain* 103: 99–112.

Warrington, E. K., and Shallice, T. (1984). Category specific semantic impairments. *Brain* 107: 829–853.

Weiskrantz, L. (1986). *Blindsight*. Oxford: Clarendon Press.

Weiskrantz, L. (1988). Some contribution of neuropsychology of vision and memory to the problem of consciousness. In A. J. Marcel and E. Bisiach (Eds.) *Consciousness in Contemporary Science*. Oxford: Oxford University Press, pp. 183–199.

Wickens, C. D. (1984). Processing resources in attention. In R. Parasuraman and D. R. Davies (Eds.) *Varieties of Attention*. New York: Academic Press, pp. 63–102.

Winocur, G. (1982a). Learning and memory deficits in institutionalized and non-institutionalized old people: An analysis of interference effects. In F. I. M. Craik and S. Trehub (Eds.) *Aging and Cognitive Processes*. New York: Plenum.

Winocur, G. (1982b). The amnesic syndrome: A deficit in cue utilization. In L. S. Cermak (Ed.) *Human Memory and Amnesia*. Hillsdale, N.J.: Erlbaum.

Yin R. K. (1970). Face recognition by brain-injured patients: A dissociable ability *Neuropsychologia* 8: 395–402.

Chapter 2

Clinicopathological Models of Alzheimer's Disease and Senile Dementia: Unraveling the Contradictions

Myrna F. Schwartz and Jacqueline A. Stark

In April 1976 an editorial in Archives of Neurology, *written by Robert Katzman, proclaimed the unity of Alzheimer's disease and senile dementia. There was, Katzman declared, no compelling evidence for the distinction between the two conditions—not on clinical, pathological, or genetic grounds —and much to support the identity of the two. Katzman wrote, "Today, the majority of workers in the field accept the identity of the two diseases. We believe that it is time to drop the arbitrary age distinction and adopt the single designation, Alzheimer disease" (p. 217).*

Katzman's editorial marked the end of what might be called the dark ages in the study of degenerative dementia. For about a century confusion had surrounded the relation between senile dementia and Alzheimer's disease, leading to contradictory claims concerning the "organicity" of the condition, its neuropathological characteristics, and its clinical course. In this chapter Schwartz and Stark explore the areas of confusion, tracing their origin in the two major traditions of geriatric psychiatry. One of these traditions has given rise to the now-discredited notion that senile demantia represents inevitable intellectual decay in old age. This notion, the authors argue, continues to exert an insidious influence on contemporary writings on Alzheimer's disease, even within the medical-scientific community. Indeed we might think of this as the tenacious straw man against which much of the argumentation of this book is targeted.

M.F.S.

Today's ideas about dementing disorders in the aged are informed and influenced by two related but distinct traditions in medical psychology and psychiatry: The first of these has its roots in ancient philosophical views of mind and mental disorders, and second in nineteenth-century views of brain structure and brain disease. We refer to the first as the medicophilosophical school and the second as the neuropsychiatric school, although the lines between these are not actually as distinct as these labels suggest. The important point about these traditions, from the perspective of this chapter, is that they gave rise to two quite contradictory accounts of senile dementia, both of which continue to influence popular and scientific beliefs. It is this, we believe, that accounts for the inconsistencies in content and terminology that characterize the relevant literatures. In this chapter we examine the inconsistencies and trace their origin in these two major psychiatric traditions.

The Medicophilosophical View

From the philosophers and physicians of ancient Greece came the equation of *mind* with *reason* (intellect) and the view of dementia—the deterioration of the mind—as the loss of the capacity to reason and to act reasonably (reviews of this early history are available in Lipowski 1981 and Torack 1983). The ancients did not differentiate between the variety of organic and functional psychotic states manifesting in impaired reasoning, although they did distinguish between dementia and the emotional disorders *mania* and *melancholia*. And, as we read in this verse from Lucretius (BC 99–55) (cited in McMenemey 1963), they viewed advanced age as one of the conditions disposing to dementia:

> . . . when the mighty force of years
> Their frame hath shaken, and their limbs collapse
> With blunted strength, the intellect grows dim.
> The tongue talks nonsense and the mind gives way
> And all things fail, and altogether go.

These notions carried over into second-century Rome, where both Aretaeus of Cappadocia and Galen wrote of a form of chronic disease that started during old age and was marked by "a torpor of the senses and a stupefaction of the gnostic and intellectual faculties" (from Arataeus, as quoted in Lipowski 1981).

When modern psychiatry began to emerge in nineteenth-century France, it strongly reflected this ancient medicophilosophical perspective. For example, Esquirol's influential 1838 monograph, *Mental Maladies: A Treatise on Insanity*, describes dementia as "a weakening of the sensibility, understanding and will." This condition, indicated by "incoherence of ideas and a want of intellectual and moral spontaneity," is different from mania: "Maniacs and monomaniacs are drawn away by errors of sensation, by false perceptions, hallucinations, and the abundance and fixedness of the ideas and affections. He who is in a state of dementia imagines not, nor indulges in thought. He has few or no ideas. He neither wills nor determines, but yields; the brain being in a weakened state." (p. 419). Esquirol goes on to enumerate the variety of factors that dispose to dementia. Among the physical factors are apoplexy, falls upon the head, menstrual disorders, progress of age, abuse of wine, and masturbation. Various "moral causes" are also cited, including domestic trials and political shocks. He notes that dementia in young people is more common among the higher classes of society, where "the abuse of pleasures, inordinate passions, and errors of regimen destroy man, wear out the brain from early youth, dispose him to dementia, and urge him into a premature old age" (p. 423). The theme of dementia as the natural consequence of old age is sounded several times in the monograph. At one point dementia is described as "a malady which is so often the termination of a great many others, which is, so to speak, *the constitutional condition of old age*" (p. 424; our emphasis). Subsequently Esquirol distinguishes three varieties of dementia, the third of which (after acute and chronic) is senile dementia. "Senile dementia," Esquirol asserts, "results from the progress of age. Man, passing insensibly into the vale of years, loses his sensibility, along with the free exercise of his understanding, before reaching the extreme of decrepitude. This form of mental disease is gradually established. It commences with a weakening of the memory, especially with respect to recent impressions. Sensations are feeble. Attention is uncertain and without impulse; and the movements are slow or impracticable" (p. 435).

The view that Esquirol was espousing in these latter passages, that senile dementia is not a disease but rather a manifestation of the aging process, was to take firm hold on the emerging geriatric psychiatry. This orientation was propelled by the studies of morbid anatomy and especially histopathology, which revealed the effects of aging on the bodily organs and tissue systems, including the central nervous system. Charcot, lecturing in Paris in 1867, commented, "We shall have to remark, among other things, that the changes of texture impressed on the organism by old age sometimes become so marked that the physiological and pathological states seem to merge into one another by insensible transitions and cannot be clearly distinguished" (Charcot 1881, W. S. Tuke, trans., p. 27). To illustrate, he provided a detailed description of atrophic and atherosclerotic processes arising in the brain and elsewhere in the aged patient.

In Britain these same themes were being articulated—that senile dementia is continuous with the intellectual decline of advanced age and that the pathological basis for this condition is a set of age-related destructive processes in nerve cells and cerebral vessels. Henry Maudsley's *The Pathology of Mind* (1879) summarized the prevailing widsom on what he calls *senile insanity*: "It is in this form of insanity that we are most likely to find atheromatous cerebral arteries, which, if they are not directly the cause, are at any rate the mark of a real decay of brain . . . With the decay of brain goes a corresponding decay of mind, the symptoms of which are characteristic. They may be described as the exaggeration of the natural decline of mental faculties which often accompanies the bodily decline of old age" (pp. 472–473).

Throughout much of the nineteenth century, arteriosclerosis was looked upon as a primary disease mechanism and as a cause of many of the pathologic changes of old age (Beach 1987). Most authorities subscribed to the view that arteriosclerosis caused senile dementia by depriving cerebral tissue of essential nutrients and that cortical atrophy was a manifestation of cell death resulting from this "brain anemia," and this view persisted well into the next century. The fact that between 1900 and 1920 there were numerous reports of senile dementia in which neither cerebral arteriosclerosis nor generalized atrophy was observed at autopsy (for example, McGaffin 1910, Southard 1910; see also citations in Beach 1987) did little to undermine this presumed linkage between brain anemia, atrophy, and intellectual decay. Conceivably the persistence of this idea reflects the lingering influence of the pseudoscience of craniotomy, which had been so enormously popular in the preceding decades. Stephen Jay Gould (1981) has described how, in the latter half of the nineteeth century, the linking of intelligence to brain size was propounded by the most influential scientists of the day and used to promote and perpetuate existing prejudices pertaining to race and class structure. His quote from the great physician-anthropologist Paul Broca illustrates the tie to geriatrics: "In general, the brain is larger in mature adults than in the elderly, in men than in women, in eminent men than in men of mediocre talent, in superior races than in inferior races. . . . Other things being equal, there is a remarkable relationship between the development of intelligence and the volume of the brain" (quoted in Gould 1981, p. 83).

Craniotomy is remembered today primarily as an adjunct of the theory of phrenology, which held as one of its basic tenets that organ size was directly proportional to functional energy. On the other hand the phrenologists were not in sympathy with the equating of brain size with intellectual function. They viewed the brain as divided into multiple organs, each of which performed a basic function, and each of which was subject to the doctrine relating size to function. For the phrenologists intelligence was itself decomposable into several faculties, each served by its own organ, which together were located in the anterior lobes of the brain. Nevertheless when it came to considerations of the effects of advanced age on the mind, phrenologists too tended to think in terms of general decay:

In old age . . . the brain has lost so much of its activity by natural decay, and the vivacity of feeling and energy of thinking are thereby so much subdued, that exciting causes of any kind have no longer the same hold, and no longer make the same impressions that they would have done in earlier life. (Combe 1934, p. 137)

The geriatric psychiatry that emerged in early twentieth-century England and America was firmly rooted in the medicophilosophical tradition and perpetuated its emphasis on the characterization of intellectual changes in normal and abnormal senescence. This enterprise received a great boost with the advent of the science of mental measurement (psychometrics) in the early decades of the century. Here, for the first time, subjective impressions could be replaced by hard numbers. The age-related decline in intelligence-test performance was easily and reliably documented. More important, however, was the fact that not all measures were equally affected. The resilience of vocabularly scores was already well-recognized when Babcock (1930) hit upon the idea of using it as a measure of premorbid intelligence. The basic idea of contrasting those measures that "hold" in aging with those that don't hold (Wechsler 1944) and using the result to measure intellectual deterioration was, and continues to be, a favored means of diagnosing early dementia. The underlying assumption will by now be familiar: senile dementia represents an exaggeration of normal aging and hence shows the same pattern of intellectual deterioration, but in a more extreme fashion. Pearce and Miller, writing in 1973, were able to find only one study that tested this assumption directly, and with negative results. According to the findings of Botwinick and Birren (1951), WAIS subtests most affected in senile dementia are *not* those that showed the greatest drop-off in normal aging. (Note that from the contemporary perspective, and especially from the perspective of this book, any generalization about test scores in senile dementia is suspect, given the wide diversity of clinical manifestations of that condition.)

Perhaps more important than the test batteries themselves were the mathematical procedures that were developed to guide their construction and interpretation. Based on correlation analysis, these procedures yielded "factors" underlying observed scores—constituents common to some test measures but not others. The first factor analytic procedures were developed by the eminent British psychologist and statistician Charles Spearman to determine whether there was a single factor underlying all mental abilities or a finite and limited set corresponding to the formal faculties proposed by philosophers and psychologists as far back as Plato. Spearman's important result isolated a single general factor encompassing much of the variance in the matrix of correlation coefficients for a large number of mental tests. The remaining "residual" variance was specific to each test. From this result Spearman articulated the famous *two-factor theory*, according to which all aspects of intellectual functioning reduce to a common element ("g" for general factor or general intelligence) plus elements unique to it ("s" for specific factor or specific intelligence) (Spearman 1904, 1927).

The two-factor theory had important implications for geriatric psychiatry. Vocabulary, the paradigmatic hold index, was also one that loaded most heavily on the "g" factor. According to Spearman, this led to the conclusion that "g" was not affected by age and that the age-related decline in test scores was due entirely to "s," especially the *retentivity* component of "s" (Spearman 1927, pp. 371–375). But on the other hand Spearman's speculative characterization of "g" as the mental energy that fueled the specific engines (that is, "s") and that was related to cortical mass action, provided the ideal construct to support the traditional account of the decline in normal and pathological aging. Thus the evidence for the existence of "g" was used by many clinicians to promote the notion that there exists a single general intellectual capacity, that this capacity is substantially damaged only in cases of diffuse cerebral disease, and that there is a clear relation between the extent of the brain damage and the weakening of intelligence.

This clinical extrapolation from psychometrics was soundly criticized by psychologist Oliver Zangwill, who wrote in 1964 that "The central issue in dementia is that of intelligence, about which psychologists are often supposed to know more than they actually do. In fact we know very little" (p. 32). Zangwill went on to argue against the idea of a general intellectual capacity and against the thesis of mass action. He was no more sympathetic to the various dichotomy theories that were being propounded, according to which dementia affects abstract but not concrete reasoning, or fluid but not crystallized intelligence, or new learning but not old facts. Zangwill cited the body of evidence from neuropsychology in support of the idea that human intelligence is multifaceted. And he posed this critical question: "Is it possible, then, to fractionate dementia, that is, to isolate its central components and relate them to mechanisms of a more specific kind?" (1964; p. 915). Such a question could not even arise, let alone be answered, from within the philosophical school of psychiatry. It stems from an altogether different approach to mind and mental disorders.

The Neuropsychiatric View

Zilboorg has recorded how German psychiatry in the latter decades of the nineteenth century turned away from its philosophical roots to fully embrace the newly emerging brain sciences. In the words of Griesinger, the early leader of this materialist school, "Psychiatry and neuropathology are not merely two closely related fields, they are but one field in which one language is spoken and the same laws rule" (cited in Zilboorg and Henry 1941, p. 436). Consistent with this principle, German psychiatrists of the late nineteenth century underwent strong training in neurology and neuropathology and worked side by side with the leading researchers in these fields.

The dominant figure of this era in German psychiatry was the eminent Emil Kraepelin. Kraepelin sought to discover distinct clinical-pathological correlations for each of the major psychiatric symptom-complexes (*Krankheitseinheit*), and in pursuit of that goal he brought together many of the leading neuropathologists of Europe. Among these were Franz Nissl and Alois Alzheimer, two pioneers in the development of histological staining techniques for the elucidation of cellular pathology. Alzheimer (figure 2.1) contributed enormously to the differentiation of the organic dementias. For example, in 1894 and 1902 he provided a complete description of arteriosclerotic dementia, and in 1904 he provided the first full histologic description of paralytic dementia (general paresis), an important link in the chain of scientific discoveries that eventually tied this condition to the syphilitic spirochete (Henry 1941).

The acceptance of paralytic dementia as a distinct clinicopathologic entity in the late nineteenth century marked the beginnings of neuropsychiatry. It is with paralytic dementia that the subdivision of the organic dementias began, and here too that the recognition took hold that focal clinical symptoms could arise in conditions of generalized brain disease. Before that time localizing symptoms in the context of a progressive dementia were taken to be either manifestations of the generalized intellectual disorder (this was the standard account of amnestic aphasia, "asymbolia," and agnosia, for example) or the result of complicating vascular accidents.

In exploring focal manifestations of diffuse brain diseases, the early neuropsychiatrists had a rich theoretical framework to draw on. Theirs was the era in which the great German neuroanatomists were elaborating the basic principles of development and functional organization of the cerebral cortex (Meynert 1884, Flechsig 1900, 1920), giving rise to the neuroanatomically based theories of the aphasias (Wernicke 1874, Lichtheim 1885), alexias (Dejerine 1892), apraxias

Figure 2.1
Alois Alzheimer. Portrait courtesy of Dr. F. H. Lewey, Philadelphia, Pennsylvania.
Reproduced with permission from Haymaker's *The Founders of Neurology*. Springfield,
IL: Charles C. Thomas.

(Liepmann 1905, 1920), and agnosias (Lissauer 1890). These theories
expanded the universe of localizing symptoms beyond those bearing
on sensation and motility, to include as well diverse aspects of cognition, including language. In addition they provided a vocabulary that
could be used to distinguish among the various clinical presentations
of dementia.

In this regard the work of Arnold Pick (figure 2.2) is especially important. An 1892 report by Pick set out to demonstrate that the
atrophic changes associated with senile dementia could give rise to
focal symptomatology, including aphasia. Pick described a 71-year-
old man with a three-year history of progressive memory loss and
speech disorder:

> The patient possesses a considerable vocabulary and speaks a lot;
> however, although sentences are sometimes correct when deal-

Figure 2.2
Arnold Pick. Portrait courtesy of Prof. F. Jahnel and Lt. Col. H. Sprinz, M. C., Munich, Germany. Reproduced with permission from Haymaker's *The Founders of Neurology*. Springfield, IL: Charles C. Thomas.

ing with simple matters, they generally are nonsensical, partly because of the incorrect arrangement of words, partly because the words themselves are unintelligible. This is due at times to transposition of consonants, e.g., he says "colmotive" instead of "locomotive". . .

Since our main concern is with the pathological anatomical diagnosis of the secondary symptom, namely, the speech disorder, the primary diagnosis, that of senile dementia, will not be discussed. In observing the speech disorder we lay greatest emphasis on the fact that we are not dealing with a disorder which can be exclusively, or even primarily, attributed to the simple amnestic effects of the senile process, but, rather, it more closely parallels those which are the result of focal lesions; it resembles those disorders which Wernicke-Lichtheim described as transcortical sensory aphasia. (Pick 1892, trans. Rottenberg and Hochberg 1977, pp. 36, 37)

Pick considers the possibility that this language disturbance is secondary to a complicating stroke, but rejects this on the basis of the autopsy findings: generalized atrophy of the cerebral hemispheres with narrowing of the gyri, *especially prominent in the left hemisphere temporal lobe*, and no evidence of focal softenings.

Pick concludes that simple progressive brain atrophy can lead to symptoms of local disturbance through local accentuation of the diffuse process, and he adds, "In passing, it should be mentioned that this evidence will significantly improve the understanding of other manifestations caused by the diffuse process" (1892; p. 40). Prophetic words, but poorly heeded.

A few years later, in a paper that is generally cited for the first identification of neuritic plaques in the brain of a patient dying with senile dementia, Redlich (1898) described a rapidly progressing dementia with pronounced focal manifestation in the form of expressive and receptive aphasia, apraxia, and seizures. The autopsy findings in this patient showed very pronounced atrophy of the whole brain, more impressive in the frontal and temporal lobes than in the parietal and occipital lobes. There were no focal softenings or hemorrhagic foci, but microscopic examination did reveal the numerous sites of sclerotic plaques, which Redlich took to be specifically proliferated glial cells. These plaques were concentrated in the granular layer of the cortex and were especially numerous in the left frontal convolutions on the convexity, including Broca's area, and in the first left temporal convolution. In summarizing this and a similar patient, Redlich comments on the severity of the dementia, particularly the language defects, "which reached an intensity that we otherwise only find with anatomically localized lesions of the language centers" (our trans.). Redlich points to the extensive histopathological changes in the language centers as providing the explanation.

Over the next decade this finding was to be replicated again and again. In his 1913 article in *Brain*, Mingazzini concluded his own case report with a review of 18 other reported patients in whom specific aphasic symptoms associated with dementia were referable to extreme accentuation of the degenerative or atrophic process in circumscribed areas with the temporal, frontal, and/or parietal lobes of the left hemisphere.

Alzheimer was undoubtedly familiar with some of these results when he published the case for which he is best known today (Alzheimer 1907). A few years earlier, speaking before the Society of

German Psychiatrists in Munich, he had discussed the difficulty of clinically differentiating arteriosclerotic dementia from the senile dementia with focal symptoms. The latter, he noted, "comes to a particularly intensive localization of the senile degenerative process in circumscribed parts, mainly in the posterior pallium (*Mantelhälfte*). . . The clinical effect is in addition to the senile dementia, often epileptic and apoplectic attacks and the development of pronounced focal symptoms, differing according to the localization of the most severe disease. These cases have nothing at all to do with arteriosclerosis of the brain"(1902, p. 709, our trans.).

Thus when Alzheimer five years later described his celebrated case as demonstrating a special illness that he had never seen or heard of before, it is doubtful that he was referring to the flagrant focal symptomatology—aphasia and apractagnosia—that stood out against the global mental deterioration. Perhaps he was referring to the pronounced psychotic symptoms: intense jealousy, disorientation, hallucinations, fits of screaming. Or perhaps it was the combination of all these, progressing so rapidly in a woman of just 51 years. In any case the histopathology was new; in addition to an abundance of the sclerotic plaques described by Redlich, Alzheimer identified here for the first time the alteration of the neurofibrils in ganglion cells that caused them to have peculiar staining properties. Under silver staining these neurofibrils appeared to be twisted in intricate tangles, which in some places merged into dense bundles. In the most advanced stage, he observed, the cell nucleus and cell body disintegrated, leaving only a tangled bundle of fibrils at the site of a former ganglion cell.

Alzheimer could not have remained impressed for long with the centrality of these neurofibrils to the dementia presentation he had observed; just a few years later he studied a similar patient who proved to have abundant plaques, but no fibrillary tangles (Perusini 1910). As to the plaques, these had received the most careful examination at the hands of Oskar Fischer, working in Pick's laboratory in Prague. Using staining techniques more advanced than Redlich's, Fischer (1910) was able to demonstrate that these plaques were not proliferated glial cells but rather a particular type of deposit, of indeterminate nature. (Today we know that the plaques consist of an outer region of degenerating neuritic processes, a middle zone of swollen axons and dendrites, and a central amyloid core.)

As to the clinical implications of these necrotic plaques, Fischer reported that of the 16 patients with senile dementia, 12 had plaques in abundance, and 4 did not. Those with plaques showed evidence of severe memory disorder with confabulation, a presentation that

Fischer (after Wernicke) identified as presbyophrenia. The remaining were, he claimed, "simple senile dements" with a "simple decrease of the psychological and intellectual capacities." Fischer concludes with the suggestion that the necrotic plaques are the patho-logical-anatomical substrate for presbyophrenia.

In the interim, however, Alzheimer had published the case report on his patient, who also showed abundant plaques, and Alzheimer's patron Kraepelin lost no time in pointing out the incompatibility between the clinical presentation of presbyophrenia and the serious dementia with focal manifestations that Alzheimer had described (Kraepelin 1910, trans. Bick et al. 1986, p. 79). Amaducci, Rocca, and Schoenberg (1986) have noted how, in light of the rivalry between his laboratory and Pick's (wherein Fischer carried out his studies), Kraepelin certainly would have been concerned to see that Alzheimer received the proper credit for his important observations. Certainly Kraepelin did over the years continue to promote the distinctiveness of "Alzheimer's disease" in his textbook, even while pointing out that both clinically and pathologically Alzheimer's disease was indis-tinguishable from severe cases of senile dementia.

And in fact by 1910 there had already been several demonstrations that not just Fischer's necrotic plaques but also Alzheimer's neurofib-rillary tangles were consistent features of senile dementia and that both could be found as well, though in lesser numbers, in the brains of normal aged individuals. According to his coworker Perusini (1910), Alzheimer appears to have succumbed to the view that the disease he had described was in fact a severe form of senile dementia, and Perusini himself put forth the thesis that both are associated with senile involution of the brain. Kraepelin retained doubts, however, as expressed in the following passage taken from the 1922 edition of his textbook: "Although the anatomic findings in this disease (i.e., Alzheimer's disease) would speak for it being an especially severe type of senile dementia, the fact that at times the onset occurs in the early forties would be against such an assumption. Under such cir-cumstances we would have to speak at least of a precocious senility, if indeed we are not dealing with a process more or less independent of the senium" (Kraepelin 1922, cited in Malamud and Lowenberg 1929).

That the process is indeed more or less independent of the senium has been established in subsequent years by evidence showing that neurofibrillary tangles and so-called senile plaques are found both alone and together in a variety of pathological conditions not gener-ally associated with aging, for example, posttraumatic dementia and Down's syndrome. In view of this evidence, most authorities have come to accept the notion that in Alzheimer's disease too the etiological basis is other than aging. But then what does this say about senile dementia? Might senile dementia represent Alzheimer's disease, a disease *sui generis*, in older persons?

For psychiatrists of the twentieth century to answer yes to these questions required that they abandon firmly entrenched views on the continuity of aging and dementia. Understandably there was a great deal of resistance to this move. Hence the literature of the twentieth century is a mass of contradictions on these fundamental questions: Do Alzheimer's disease and senile dementia represent variants of the same morbid entity? If so, what is the proper characterization of this entity?

Alzheimer's Disease and Senile Dementia

The literature up through 1975 is replete with arguments for the distinctiveness of Alzheimer's disease and senile dementia. One set of arguments draws on the microscopic features, contending that in Alzheimer's disease the neuritic plaques and/or neurofibrillary tangles are more numerous than in senile dementia (for example, Critchley 1931, Rothschild and Kasanin 1936, Sourander and Sjogren 1970), or that they are distributed differently (Simchowicz 1911), or that they are histologically distinct (Hannah 1936, cited in Newton 1948).

Among these proposed indices only severity of pathology has proved reliable in differentiating early- from late-onset forms of the disease (see reviews by Jervis and Soltz (1936) and Newton (1948)). Most investigators agree that the distribution of early-onset cases is skewed in the direction of more severe neuropathology. This is not limited to the morphological changes (that is, plaques and tangles), but is true also of the more recently identified neurotransmitter alterations (Bondareff 1983, Rossor et al. 1984). Does it follow that the early- and late-onset forms are etiologically distinct? Most would argue no (but see Bondareff 1983 and Seltzer and Sherwin 1983).

For one thing recent population-based studies that estimate age-specific incidence rates of Alzheimer's disease have tended to show a smooth exponential increase after age 40, rather than the bimodal curve predicted by the two-diseases account (for review, see Amaducci, Rocca, and Schoenberg 1986). Moreover an important study by Heston and colleagues showed that with respect to clinical course and outcome for families, the relation between Alzheimer's disease and senile dementia parallels that between severe and milder forms of many other medical conditions that have a genetic component (Heston, Mastri, Anderson, and White, 1981). The evidence bearing on severity is thus consistent with a unified account of Alzheimer's disease and senile dementia.

Among those authorities who accept that Alzheimer's disease is indistinguishable from senile dementia on pathological grounds, there are some who have nevertheless argued for its distinctiveness based on what they take to be its unique clinical presentation. Recall that from the outset the reports of cases of Alzheimer's disease emphasized the florid and focal symptomatology (see, for example, Fuller's (1912) review of the first 12 patients reported in the literature). This was in marked contrast to the traditional characterization of senile dementia, although not, as we have stressed, to that of the early neuropsychiatrists, especially Arnold Pick.

Recall that Pick's general thesis was that senile dementia is a highly differentiated clinicopathologic entity, reflecting the distribution of cortical atrophy. In making this case, Pick called attention to the aphasia associated with circumscribed atrophy of the left temporal lobe (1892), visuoperceptual disorders referable to atrophy of the occipital lobes (1908, 1923), and disorders of praxis bearing on object use (1905). Unfortunately subsequent events blunted the force of his arguments. In 1911 Alzheimer discovered some distinctive nerve cell changes—swollen nerve cells with eccentric nuclei, and agyrophilic inclusions in the cytoplasm—in a case of circumscribed left temporal lobe atrophy of the sort Pick had described. A few years later Onari and Spatz reported that the cellular distribution of the atrophic changes in a series of such cases was too consistent and too selective to have arisen from random accentuation of a generalized process. Instead Onari and Spatz hypothesized a specific pathologic condition, which they named *Pick's disease*, with a particular predilection for frontal and temporal cytoarchitectonic zones that are, phylogenetically speaking, the most recent to develop and that serve as the substrate for the most integrative behaviors (Onari and Spatz 1926). Thus did Pick's name become associated with focal atrophy of specifically anterior distribution. Later writers added further conditions: the presence of either swollen nerve cells or argyrophilic inclusion bodies in the affected areas, onset in the presenium. The general point argued by Pick, that focal atrophies are common elements of senile dementia and influence how that disorder is expressed clinically, was largely lost. And with Pick's disease relegated to the status of a rare presenile condition, there was little to challenge the traditional wisdom that senile dementia produced diffuse intellectual deterioration, without the focal manifestations of Alzheimer's disease.

By 1970 this had become the accepted wisdom. In that year, however, in a book summarizing the proceedings of a Ciba-sponsored symposium on Alzheimer's disease (Wolstenholme and O'Connor 1970), that wisdom was seriously questioned in one of the group discussions. The eminent geriatrician Sir Martin Roth had this to say:

> Traditionally the distinction between Alzheimer's disease and senile dementia was a clear one. It rested on the occurrence in Alzheimer's disease of focal phenomena: the parietal lobe group of features, the characteristic mixture of apraxia, agnosia, aphasia, spatial disorientation, and so on. In senile dementia, on the other hand, a simple amnestic dementia was held to be the principal ingredient of the clinical picture. The condition progresses from amnesia for recent events to more general intellectual deficiencies and personality deterioration without definable focal symptoms or signs. The German workers have recently called this distinction into question. Lauter and Meyer (1968) claim to have demonstrated focal phenomena in the senile cases. In the light of these findings is the distinction valid clinically or pathologically, or are we left with age criteria alone? (p. 33)

Roth's citation was to a large-scale clinical investigation carried out in Germany by Lauter and Meyer and published in English two years earlier. As part of that investigation 40 women who had independently been given the clinical diagnosis "senile dementia" were examined by Lauter and Meyer for the presence of *Werkzeugstörungen*: higher level cognitive disturbances. Of the 40 patients studied, 32 showed amnestic aphasia, 26 showed disturbances of spatial orientation, and 30 showed apraxia or agnosia. Only 3 of the 40 were free of *Werkzeugstörungen*. According to Lauter and Meyer (1968, p. 17), "The clinical symptoms of senile dementia and Alzheimer's disease show many more similarities than is usually assumed," leading to the conclusion that "senile dementia and Alzheimer's disease are simply different manifestations of one disease entity."

Roth's question, is the distinction valid clinically and pathologically? was answered negatively by his fellow discussants, and that verdict was echoed over the next few years in a succession of influential writings and conference proceedings (for example, Katzman 1976, Katzman, Terry, and Bick 1978, McKhann et al 1984). By 1985 the identity of Alzheimer's disease and senile dementia had become the accepted wisdom.

The Clinicopathological Model of Alzheimer's Disease

Quite aside from the issue of the identity of Alzheimer's disease and senile dementia, there was, and continues to be, considerable confusion surrounding the clinicopathological model of Alzheimer's disease. The founding neuropsychiatrists, whose work we extensively cited, emphasized clinicopathological correlations and showed a readiness to attribute focal symptomatology, including aphasic, agnosic, and apractic symptomatology, to local degenerative processes in cortical gray or white matter.

In subsequent years the opposing viewpoint came to be espoused, namely, that focal cognitive symptoms do not reflect the locus of pathological processes but rather arise as consequences of diffuse pathology and/or as manifestations of a central psychological deficit. In the German literature this position is most closely associated with Stertz. In a 1921 article entitled "Concerning the question of Alzheimer's disease," Stertz declared that the psychological core of the disorder is a global impairment of memory ("reproduction") alongside a preserved self-awareness, leading to embarrassment and perplexity. The agnosic, apractic, and aphasic disorders are not localizable symptoms in the usual sense, but are rather "partial signs of the general mnestic associative failure and thus an integral part of the basic disorder." To explain his patient's bouts of stuttering and logoclonia, Stertz appealed to the conflict between "initiation mutism" and the will to respond. Motor stereotypes (rubbing, wiping) arose as "embarrassment responses." Even the increased muscle tension was denied an organic base and was attributed instead to "psychic responses" growing out of the basic condition.

Sterz's thesis was cited with approval by many subsequent investigators, among them Kahn (1925), who described his patient's "pronounced word-finding difficulties and apractic deficits" as "due to his severe memory impairment" (p. 733) and Grünthal (1926), who affirmed that in general the focal deficits of Alzheimer's disease are an expression of general damage and not tissue changes in specific localizations. Grünthal's paper, which reported clinical-pathological correlations in 14 patients, all of whom had been diagnosed clinically by Kraepelin, received a good deal of attention outside of Germany. It is unfortunate that subsequent investigators seem to have overlooked the fact that these postmortem examinations sometimes sampled from quiet restricted regions of cortex. In view of the fact that critical areas of frontal, parietal, and temporal lobes were rarely examined, Grünthal's negative findings with respect to local tissue changes certainly warrants skepticism.

In America a variant of this same thesis was put forth by Rothschild and his colleagues, who were familiar with the work of Stertz and his supporters in Germany. These passages from Rothschild (1934) on the nature of the speech disorder, which emerged in his clinicopathological study of five Alzheimer's patients, conveys the general tenor of the argument:

> The disorder of speech did not conform to any of the classical types of aphasia. It was characterized chiefly by perseveration and paraphasia. In some instances there was also a tendency to mispronunciation of words that was probably due to dysarthric defects. As a rule the perseveration first revealed itself as a tendency for the same thoughts to recur frequently. Later it took the form of a repetition of phrases or words. Finally, in the severest cases syllables or meaningless sounds were continually repeated. Analysis of the paraphasia during the earliest stages of the disorder indicated that this condition consisted in the replacement of the proper words by material which, though incorrect, belonged to the same general category as the appropriate responses . . . These symptoms, taken by themselves, do not point to a disease of any particular part of the brain. They are to be regarded as indications of a lowering of function which may occur following any severe cerebral lesion . . . Apparently the disturbance of speech is merely one manifestation of a general reduction to a lower level of nervous function. (pp. 504–505)

In general Rothschild was ambivalent on the issue of focal deficits and their pathoanatomical basis:

> The widespread nature of the pathologic process renders it difficult to determine the anatomic substratum of particular symptoms. There was some evidence that certain symptoms found in individual cases owed their origin to variations in the localization of the chief changes. For example, the unusual affective changes noted in case 3 might perhaps be correlated with the extensive involvement of the frontal lobes. In case 4 the visual agnosia and apraxia probably arose from damage to the parieto-occipital region. On the other hand, the disorder of speech was apparently based on the diffuse rather than focal alterations. This was indicated not only by the character of disturbance, but also by the absence of excessive changes in the areas particularly concerned with speech. (p. 510)

With respect to this last point, it is worth pointing out that the staining methods used by Rothschild did not allow him to compare corresponding areas of the left and right hemispheres.

For present purposes the importance of the above-cited works is that they had the effect of obscuring the cogent clinical model that had emerged in the preceding decades in the works of Redlich,

Alzheimer, Pick, and others. In asserting a "core" psychological deficit from which diverse "focal" manifestations arise, in choosing to emphasize dubious negative findings relating to the symptom-substrate correlations in the face of much positive evidence, and in making unsupported claims about the psychological consequences of diffuse brain damage, these investigators incorporated into the model of Alzheimer's disease older ways of thinking, harkening back to the traditional (that is, medicophilosophic) account of dementia.

This blurring of the lines between what was, and should be, two distinct clinicopathological models has persisted into the contemporary literature on Alzheimer's disease and has, in our view, stood in the way of genuine understanding of this morbid entity. As evidence of the problem we point to the continued promulgation of the notion that the clinical progression of Alzheimer's disease takes a predictable, stagewise course. This idea is familiar from the older literature on senile dementia. For example, Pritchard's 1837 *A Treatise on Insanity* enumerated four stages in the clinical course of senile dementia: the first stage marked by impairment of recent memory with intact remote memories, the second by loss of reason, the third by incomprehension, and the fourth by loss of instinctive action (cited in Lipowski 1981). That the deterioration should proceed in stages is consistent with the notion that there is a single entity (that is, general intelligence, mental energy, or reproductive memory) that is being progressively eroded. But this notion is not and never has been consonant with the facts about Alzheimer's disease.

Still it continues to be promoted by respected authorities in the field. For example, a group of prominent researchers at New York University have constructed The Global Deterioration Scale (GDS) for Age-Associated Cognitive Decline and Alzheimer's disease (Reisberg, Ferris, deLeon, and Crook 1982), which presupposes a continuum of decline from the normal senile forgetfulness to severe dementia. GDS scores have been shown to correlate significantly with the extent of anatomic brain changes visualized on computed tomographic scans (deLeon et al. 1980) and with metabolic changes as determined by positron emission tomography (Ferris et al. 1980). But the cost of establishing these large-scale statistical correlations is obfuscation of the particular patterns of cognitive decline that vary so much from patient to patient and of the relation between these symptom patterns and the specifics of the neuroanatomic and neurophysiologic changes. For example, the clinical descriptions associated with each of the seven GDS stages are presented as lists of disjunctive criteria, only some of which need be present to identify a patient with that stage. Thus two patients at the same stage may show, indeed are likely to show, fundamentally different cognitive impairments. That this is considered irrelevant by the creators of the scale presumably reflects their belief that these disparate cognitive manifestations merely serve as pointers to a general underlying factor. From our reading this looks suspiciously like the general intelligence of an earlier generation of geriatricians.

Conclusion

For the most part contemporary research is proceeding on the notion that Alzheimer's disease is the major cause of primary degenerative dementia in adults from middle to advanced years, that Alzeimer's disease results from degenerative processes in nervous elements that are related to genetic factors, and that the aging process increases the likelihood that these degenerative changes will arise, but does not cause them directly. It is also part of the contemporary wisdom that the way in which the disease expresses itself clinically is a function at least in part of the density and locus of the degenerative changes and the pace and pattern of their development and spread. Most important from the perspective of this book is the fact that the various degenerative changes may be quite selective in their sites of action, targeting the neural networks and neurochemical systems that form the fundamental "modules" of the brain in relation to cognition. If this is true, there is a great deal to be gained from the close study of the clinicopathological correlations within and among patients. The remaining chapters of this book endorse and exemplify this point of view.

Acknowledgment

Otto Schlogl, librarian at the University of Vienna, assisted in the literature search.

References

Alzheimer, A. (1894). Die arteriosclerotische Atrophie des Gehirns. *Neurologisches Centralblatt* 113: 765–767.

Alzheimer, A. (1902). Die Seelenstörungen auf arteriosclerotischer Grundlage. *Allgemeine Zeitschrift für Psychiatrie und psychisch-gerichtliche Medizin* 59: 695–711.

Alzheimer, A. (1907). A characteristic disease of the cerebral cortex. In Bick, K., Amaducci, L., and Pepeu, G. (Eds. and Trans.) (1986). *The Early Story of Alzheimer's Disease*. Padua, Italy: Liviana Press.

Alzheimer, A. (1911). Über eigenartige Krankheitsfälle des späteren Lebens. *Zeitschrift für die gesamte Neurologie und Psychiatrie: Originalien* 4: 356–385.

Amaducci, L. A., Rocca, W. A., and Schoenberg, B. S. (1986). Origin of the distinction between Alzheimer's disease and senile dementia: How history can clarify nosology. *Neurology* 36: 1497–1499.

Babcock, H. (1930). An experiment in the measurement of mental deterioration. *Archives of Psychology* 117:105.

Beach, T. G. (1987). The history of Alzheimer's disease: Three debates. *Journal of the History of Medicine and Allied Sciences, Inc.* 42:327–349.

Bondareff, W. (1983). Age and Alzheimer disease. *Lancet* 1: 1447.

Botwinick, J., and Birren, J. E. (1951). Differential decline in the Wechsler-Bellevue subtests in the senile psychoses. *Journal of Gerontology* 6: 365.

Charcot, J. M. (1867). Leçons sur les maladies des viellards et les maladies chroniques. Translated by W. S. Tuke (1881). *Clinical Lectures on Senile and Chronic Diseases*. London: New Sydenham Society.

Combe, A. (1834). *Observations on Mental Derangement*. 1972 facsimile reproduction of the first American edition. Delmar, N Y: Scholars' Facsimiles and Reprints.

Critchley, M. (1931). The neurology of old age, part III. *The Lancet* 1: 1331–1337.

deLeon, M. J., Ferris, S. H., George, A.E. et al. (1980). Computed tomography evaluations of brain-behavior relationships in senile dementia of the Alzheimer's type. *Neurobiology of Aging* 1: 69–79.

Dejerine, J. (1892). Contribution a l'étude anatomoclinique et clinique des différentes varietiés de cécité verbale. *Compte Rendu Hebdomadaire des Scénances et Memoires de la Société de Biologie* 4: 61–90.

Esquirol, J. E. D. (1838). *Traite des Maladies Mentales*. Translation by E. K. Hunt (1845). *Mental Maladies—A Treatise on Insanity*. Philadelphia: Lea & Blanchard. Reprinted 1965, New York: Hafner.

Flechsig, P. (1900). Uber Projections- und Associations-Zentren des menschlichen Gehirns. *Neurologisches Centralblatt* 19.

Flechsig, P. (1920). *Anatomie des menschlichen Gehirns und Rückenmarks auf myelogenetischer Grundlage*. Leipzig: Thieme.

Ferris, S. H., deLeon, M. J., Wolf, A. P., et al. (1980). Positron emission tomography in the study of aging and senile dementia. *Neurobiology of Aging* 1: 127–131.

Fischer, O. (1910). Miliary necrosis with nodular proliferation of the neurofibrils, a common change of the cerebral cortex in senile dementia. In Bick, K., Amaducci, L., and Pepeu, G. (Eds. and Trans.) (1986). *The Early Story of Alzheimer's Disease*. Padua, Italy: Liviana Press.

Fuller, S. C. (1912). Alzheimer's disease (senium praecox): The report of a case and review of published cases. *Journal of Nervous and Mental Diseases* 39: 440–536.

Gould, S. J. (1981). *The Mismeasure of Man*. New York: Norton.

Grünthal, E. (1926). Uber die Alzheimersche Krankheit. Eine histopathologisch-klinische Studie. *Zeitschrift für die gesamte Neurologie und Psychiatrie* 101: 128–157.

Henry, G. W. (1941). Organic mental diseases. In G. Zilboorg and G. W. Henry, *History of Medical Psychology*. New York: Norton.

Heston, L. L., Mastri, A. R., Anderson, V. E., and White, J. (1981). Dementia of the Alzheimer type: Clinical genetics, natural history, and associated conditions. *Archives of General Psychiatry* 38: 1085–1090.

Jervis, G., and Soltz, S. E. (1936). Alzheimer's disease—The so-called juvenile type. *American Journal of Psychiatry* 93: 39–56.

Kahn, E. (1925). Demonstration präseniler Verblödungsprozesse. *Zentralblatt für die gesamte Neurologie und Psychiatrie* 40: 733–735.

Katzman, R. (1976). The prevalence and malignancy of Alzheimer's disease. *Archives of Neurology* 33: 217–218.

Katzman, R., Terry, R. D., and Bick, K. L. (Eds.) (1978). *Alzheimer's Disease: Senile Dementia and Related Disorders*. New York: Raven.

Kraepelin, E. (1910). Senile and pre-senile dementias. In Bick, K., Amaducci, L., and Pepeu, G. (Eds. and Trans.) (1986). *The Early Story of Alzheimer's Disease*. Padua, Italy: Liviana Press.

Kraepelin, E. (1922). *Ein Lehrbuch für Studierende und Arzte* (8th ed.). Leipzig: Johann Ambrosius Barth.

Lauter, H., and Meyer, J. E. (1968). Clinical and nosological concepts of senile dementia. In C. Muller and L. Ciompi (Eds.) *Senile Dementia: Clinical and Therapeutic Aspects*. Bern: Hans Huber.

Liepmann, H. (1905). Die linke Hemisphare und das Handelm. *Münch. Med. Wschr.* 49: 2375–2378.

Liepmann, H. (1920). Apraxie. *Ergon der ges Med.* 1: 516–543.

Lichtheim, L. (1885). On aphasia. *Brain* 2: 433–484.

Lipowski, Z. J. (1981). Organic mental disorders: Their history and classification with special reference to DSM-111. In N. E. Miller and G. D. Cohen (Eds.) *Clinical Aspects of Alzheimer's Disease and Senile Dementia* (Aging, Vol. 5). New York: Raven.

Lissauer, H. (1890). Ein Fall von Seelenblindheit nebst einem Beiträge zur Theorie derselben. *Archivr für Psychiatrie und Nervenkrankheiten* 21: 222–270.

McGaffin, C. G. (1910). An anatomical analysis of seventy cases of senile dementia. *American Journal of Insanity* 65: 649–656.

McKhann, G., Drachman, D., Folstein, M., et al. (1984). Clinical diagnosis of Alzheimer's disease: Report of the NINCDS-ADRDA work group. *Neurology* 31: 939–944.

McMenemey, W. H. (1963). Alzheimer's disease: Problems concerning its concept and nature. *Acta Neurologica Scandinavica* 39: 369–380.

Malamud, W., and Lowenberg, K. (1929). Alzheimer's disease: A contribution to its etiology and classification. *Archives of Neurology and Psychiatry* 21: 805–827.

Maudsley, H. (1879). *The Pathology of Mind* (3rd edition of the second part of *Physiology and Pathology of Mind*). London: Macmillan & Co.

Meynert, T. (1884). *Psychiatry: A Clinical Treatise on Diseases of the Forebrain. Based upon a Study of its Structure, Functions, and Nutrition. Part 1. The Anatomy, Physiology, and Chemistry of the Brain.* Trans. B. Sachs. New York: Putnam.

Mingazzini, G. (1913–1914). On aphasia due to atrophy of the cerebral convolutions. *Brain* 36: 493–524.

Newton, R. D. (1948). The identity of Alzheimer's disease and senile dementia and their relationship to senility. *Journal of Mental Science* 94: 225–249.

Onari, K., and Spatz, H. (1926). Anatomische Beiträge zur Lehre von der Pickschen umschriebenen Grossrindenatrophie. *Zeitschrift für die gesamte Neurologie und Psychiatrie* 101: 470–511.

Pearce, J., and Miller, E. (1973). *Clinical Aspects of Dementia*. London: Bailliere-Tindall.

Perusini, G. (1910). Histology and clinical findings of some psychiatric diseases of older people. In Bick, K., Amaducci, L., and Pepeu, G. (Eds. and Trans.) (1986) *The Early Story of Alzheimer's Disease*. Padua, Italy: Liviana Press.

Pick, A. (1892). On the relation between aphasia and senile atrophy of the brain. In Rottenberg, D. A., and Hochberg, F. H. (Eds.) (1977) *Neurological Classics in Modern Translation*. New York: Hafner.

Pick, A. (1905). Uber einen weiteren Symptomenkomplex im Rahmen der Dementia senilis, bedingt durch umschriebene stärkere Hirnatrophie (gemischte Apraxie). *Monatsschrift für Psychiatrie* 19: 97–108.

Pick, A. (1908). Zur Symptomatologie des atrophischen Hinterhauptslappens. Studien zur Hirnpathologie und Psychologie. Sonderabdruck aus der deutschen psychiatrischen Universitatsklinik in Prag.

Pick, A. (1923). Zur Zerlegung der "Demenz." *Monatsschrift für Psychiatrie und Neurologie* 54: 3–10.

Redlich, E. (1898). Uber miliare Sklerose der Hirnrinde bei seniler Atrophie. *Jahrbücher für Psychiatrie und Neurologie* 17: 208–216.

Reisberg, B., Ferris, S. H., deLeon, M. J., and Crook, T. (1982). The Global Deterioration Scale (GDS): An instrument for the assessment of primary degenerative dementia (PDD). *American Journal of Psychiatry*, 139: 1136–1139.

Rossor, M. N., Iversen, L. L., Reynolds, G. P., Mountjoy, C. Q., and Roth, M. (1984). Neurochemical characteristics of early and late onset types of Alzheimer's disease. *British Medical Journal* 288: 961–964.

Rothschild, D. (1934). Alzheimer's disease: A clinicopathologic study of five cases. *American Journal of Psychiatry* 91: 485–518.

Rothschild, D., and Kasanin, J. (1936). Clinicopathologic study of Alzheimer's disease. *Archives of Neurology and Psychiatry, Chicago* 36: 293–321.

Seltzer B., and Sherwin, I. (1983). A comparison of clinical features in early- and late-onset primary degenerative dementia: One entity or two? *Archives of Neurology* 40: 143–146.

Simchowicz, T. (1911). Histologische Studien über die senile Demenz. In Nissl, F., and Alzheimer, A. (Eds.) *Histologische und histopathologische Arbeiten über die Grosshirnrinde mit besonderer Berücksichtigung der pathologischen Anatomie der Geisteskrankheiten.* Volume 4. Jena: Verlag.

Southard, E. E. (1910). Anatomical findings in senile dementia: A diagnostic study bearing especially on the group of cerebral atrophies. *American Journal of Insanity* 66: 571–577.

Sourander, P., and Sjogren, H. (1970). The concept of Alzheimer's disease and its clinical implications. In *Alzheimer's Disease and Related Conditions: A Ciba Foundation Symposium* London: Churchill.

Spearman, C. (1904). General intelligence objectively determined and measured. *American Journal of Psychology* 15: 201–293.

Spearman, C. (1927). *The Abilities of Man.* New York: MacMillan.

Stertz, G. (1921). Zur Frage der Alzheimerschen Krankheit. *Allgemeine Zeitschrift für Psychiatrie und psychisch-gerichtliche Medizin* 77: 336–339.

Torack, R. M. (1983). The early history of senile dementia. In B. Reisberg (Ed.) *Alzheimer's Disease.* New York: The Free Press.

Wechsler, D. (1944). *The Measurement of Adult Intelligence* (3rd ed.). Baltimore: Williams & Wilkins.

Wernicke, C. (1874). The aphasia symptom complex: A psychological study on an anatomical basis. Reprinted in G. H. Eggert (Ed. and Trans.) (1977). *Wernicke's Works on Aphasia.* The Hague: Mouton.

Wolstenholme, G. E. W., and O'Connor, M. (1970). *Alzheimer's Disease and Related Conditions: A Ciba Foundation Symposium.* London: Churchill.

Zangwill, O. L. (1964). Psychopathology of dementia. *Proceedings of the Royal Society of Medicine* 57: 914.

Zilboorg, G., and Henry, G. W. (1941). *History of Medical Psychology.* New York: Norton.

Chapter 3

Reflections on the Selectivity of Neuropathological Changes in Alzheimer's Disease

Antonio R. Damasio, Gary W. Van Hoesen, and Bradley T. Hyman

Although the degenerative pathology in Alzheimer's disease is often described as diffuse, it is well known that the pathological markers of the disease are not uniform in their distribution within the brain, or even within the cerebral cortex. Recent studies have confirmed what was long suspected, namely, this regional specificity derives from the selective vulnerability of certain cell types and cellular layers. It is this finding that establishes the relevance of this disease to cognitive neuroscience.

In this chapter Damasio, Van Hoesen, and Hyman review the evidence regarding the cellular distribution of neurofibrillary tangles in the brain of the patient with Alzheimer's disease and suggest some tantalizing hypotheses concerning the relation between neuropathological findings and cognitive symptomatology. These hypotheses make numerous points of contact with the formulation of Moscovitch and Umilta (chapter 1), especially regarding the memory disorders of dementia. For example, the "deafferentation" of hippocampus documented in the meticulous neuropathological studies of the Damasio group should, on Moscovitch and Umilta's account, seriously compromise the associative (automatic) component of encoding and retrieval and the sense of familiarity attached to a recalled event. In addition such damage should effectively preclude strategic (effortful, deliberate) learning and recall because the latter also depend on an intact hippocampal network to retrieve the encoding and retrieval cues it generates.

Damasio and colleagues have long maintained, as do Moscovitch and Umilta, that episodic memory traces do not reside in the hippocampal and forebrain structures implicated in human memory disorders, but rather exist in distributed cortical networks responsible for encoding and interpreting events. Here Damasio and colleagues discuss the breakdown in the retrieval process (which on their view is actually more a process of reconstruction) that arises in Alzheimer's disease as a consequence of the disruption of cortico-cortical connectivity. The importance of these ideas to the understanding of the memory disorders of degenerative dementia cannot be overstated.

Among the other important features of the Alzheimer's symptom complex that Damasio and colleagues discuss are the disorder of generic (conceptual or semantic) memory and the lexical retrieval disorder. Recent evidence suggests that these two are related; the chapter by Chertkow and Bub (chapter 7) presents compelling evidence to this effect.

M.F.S.

The Neuropathology of Alzheimer's Disease

The neuropathology of Alzheimer's disease is characterized by two major signature phenomena: the neurofibrillary tangle and the neuritic plaque. The neurofibrillary tangle results from a transformation of a once viable neuron whose cell body loses cytoplasm, organelles, cytoskeleton, and eventually function (figure 3.1 shows the appearance of neurofibrillary tangles, as stained by thioflavin S). The development of neurofibrillary tangles leads to neuronal loss and to a disruption of the normal cellular anatomy of cortical layers (laminae) or nuclei. Naturally, as neural somata die, their axons degenerate, and the normal patterns of connectivity among cortical regions are disrupted. The genesis of neuritic plaques and their role in the disruption of normal anatomy are less clear. Plaques may signal the degeneration of axon terminals or may spring into existence due to some other cause, but it is not apparent that they are a decisive factor in modifying normal functional brain anatomy. Less-understood pathological accompaniments of Alzheimer's disease include Hirano bodies, granulovacuolar degeneration, and cell loss.

It is reasonable to say that the critical aspect of neuropathology in Alzheimer's disease is the disease of many neurons whose cell bodies and axons die away. This causes disruption of the intricate cortical architecture on which, it so happens, cognitive processes depend. Stained neurofibrillary tangles should be viewed as a useful way of marking the pathological process that leads to neuronal death.

It is conceivable that a disease randomly affecting many neurons in the telencephalon might lead, after enough neurons became damaged, to multiple signs of cognitive impairment. Such a characterization, however, does not apply to Alzheimer's disease. Not only has it long been known that the accrual of neuropathological defects is gradual, over a fairly long period of years, it is also now clear that the disease affects neural structures selectively, in terms of (1) the brain regions, (2) the laminae within the regions, and even (3) the cell types within the laminae. The following is a brief account of pathological selectivity based on studies that use the neurofibrillary tangle, as stained by Congo red or thioflavin S, as the signature markers of the disease.

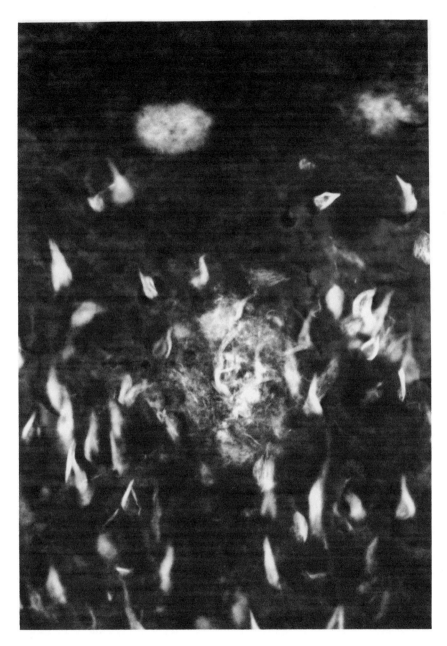

Figure 3.1
Neurofibrillary tangles and neuritic plaques are illustrated from the subiculum of a patient with Alzheimer's disease. The section is stained by thioflavin S and viewed under fluorescent conditions. Neurofibrillary tangles are often flame-shaped and occupy the cytoplasm of these pyramidal neurons. Neuritic plaques are spherical and occur in the neuropil.

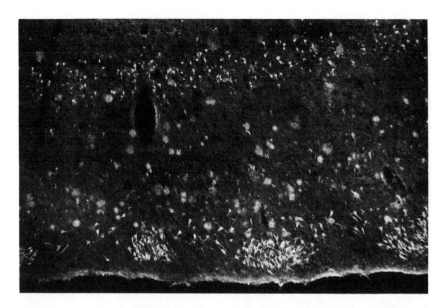

Figure 3.2
This figure shows the involvement of layer II and layer IV in entorhinal cortex by neurofibrillary tangles, stained with thioflavin S and viewed under fluorescent conditions. The clusters of large neurons in layer II are replaced by neurofibrillary tangles, although some neuritic plaques occur in this lamina. Layer IV is a thin layer of pyramidal neurons that also is susceptible to neurofibrillary degeneration.

Damage to Limbic System

The notion that Alzheimer's disease strikes temporal lobe structures to a greater extent than other telencephalic structures is part of classical teaching. Recent studies, however, not only have confirmed that notion but have revealed a striking selectiveness and magnitude for such lesions. Perhaps the most significant finding is that the entorhinal cortex, the pivotal way station for input to and from hippocampus, is disrupted by neurofibrillary tangles in layers II and IV (figure 3.2). The normal layer II of entorhinal cortex contains numerous clusters of neurons that give rise to the perforant pathway, the main avenue of entry into the hippocampal formation. In Alzheimer's disease layer II is filled massively with neurofibrillary tangles (Hyman et al. 1984, Ball et al. 1985, Pearson et al. 1985). As a consequence a major part of the perforant pathway is destroyed (Hyman et al. 1986). It has also been shown that the neurotransmitter used by this pathway, glutamate in all likelihood, is drastically reduced in the terminal zone of the projection within the dentate gyrus of the hippocampal formation (Hyman, Van Hoesen, and Damasio 1987). The end result of such pathology is that as more and more neurons in the layer II clusters of the entorhinal cortex become diseased and inoperative, lesser and lesser signaling of cortical activity is available to the hippocampal formation. In some of our patients, studied in collaboration with Robert Terry at the University of California, San Diego, it appears that more than 85 percent of such neurons are lost. A virtual deafferentation of the hippocampus from cortical inputs must certainly obtain in those instances. One can only guess as to what proportion of neurons would be necessary to maintain viable function in the entorhinal cortex to hippocampus system. The issue of magnitude of pathology required to cause dysfunction and induce symptomatology is discussed further in the last section of this chapter.

As if it were not enough to produce deafferentation of the hippocampal system, the disease eventually also breaks the efferent linkage of the hippocampus back to cerebral cortex. It achieves this by severe pathological changes at two sites: One is the subiculum, the hippocampal formation structure from which efferents both from hippocampus to cerebral cortex and from hippocampus to subcortical structures take their origin. In many patients with Alzheimer's disease, presence of neurofibrillary tangles in the subiculum is such that it is difficult to imagine any effective output from hippocampus to any cortical or subcortical station. The other site of effective deafferentation is layer IV of the entorhinal cortex. This layer is a critical pivot in the projections from hippocampus to cerebral cortex and is often involved in Alzheimer's disease to a degree comparable to the involvement of layer II and of the subiculum. In short, regardless of the relatively modest presence of neuritic plaques in the hippocampal formation itself, the presence and distribution of neurofibrillary tangles in its input-output staging areas ensures that normal communication between cerebral cortex and hippocampus is precluded. The selectivity of these lesions and their functional consequence are indeed noteworthy. There are layers in the entorhinal cortex—for example, layer III, layers V and VI—that appear spared by the disease, as far as disease is identifiable by neurofibrillary tangles, and the same applies to the Ammonic fields in the hippocampus.

Limbic neuropathology in Alzheimer's disease is not confined to the entorhinal cortex and the hippocampus. Equally noteworthy is the involvement of the amygdala, a key component of the subcortical limbic system. Many nuclei of the amygdala are also heavily disrupted by neurofibrillary tangles, and others contain prodigious quantities of neuritic plaques. It is curious to note, however, that the brunt of the damage is received by those nuclei that are closely interconnected with the hippocampal formation (Van Hoesen and Damasio 1987).

Neuropathologic involvement in basal forebrain is also unquestionable. The nucleus basalis of Meynert is compromised (Whitehouse et al. 1981), as are other cholinergic nuclei of the region (Van Hoesen and Damasio 1987). The fact that these cortical neurons are the main purveyors of acetylcholine to the cerebral cortex and hippocampal structures is of some pertinence because it is known that in most brains of patients with Alzheimer's disease, enzymatic indicators of acetylcholine indicate a marked reduction in the neurotransmitter (Davies and Maloney 1976). But it should be pointed out that several dementias, of the degenerative type or of other types, show no deficiency whatsoever in acetylcholine, whereas some illnesses not associated with dementia do show an acetylcholine deficiency. This certainly means that acetylcholine deficiency is not the critical element in the mechanisms leading to cognitive impairment. Furthermore disruption in basal forebrain nuclei might influence cortical function through mechanisms unrelated to acetylcholine. Finally, it is conceivable that changes in the basal forebrain might be secondary to primary changes in cerebral cortex.

Damage in Cerebral Cortices
Damage in cerebral cortices, as seen from the point of view of neurofibrillary tangles, is most marked in the higher-order association cortices (Van Hoesen and Damasio 1987, Lewis et al. 1957, Pearson et al. 1985, Esiri, Pearson, and Powell 1986). There is a clear trend toward diminution of the magnitude of pathology in cortices that sit progressively closer to primary sensory cortices. For example, the higher-order visual cortices within areas 20 and 21 are more heavily invested with neurofibrillary tangles than are cortices in areas 18 and 19. Area 17, the primary visual cortex, is virtually free of neurofibrillary tangles, although it can contain a considerable number of neuritic plaques. A similar pattern of pathology can be noted for the auditory cortex with changes being far more marked in fields within area 22 than in the primary cortices of area 41 and 42. The so-called multimodal cortices of areas 37 and 39 are heavily involved in this manner, and so are the frontal association cortices. But perhaps the most significant aspect of this pattern of pathology is that the laminar distribution is remarkably different from that found in entorhinal cortex. In association cortices, layers III and V are the primary recipients of the damage (figure 3.3) (Van Hoesen and Damasio 1987). Considering that these are pivotal layers for cortico-cortical projections, it is apparent that just as pathology in layers II and IV of the entorhinal cortex

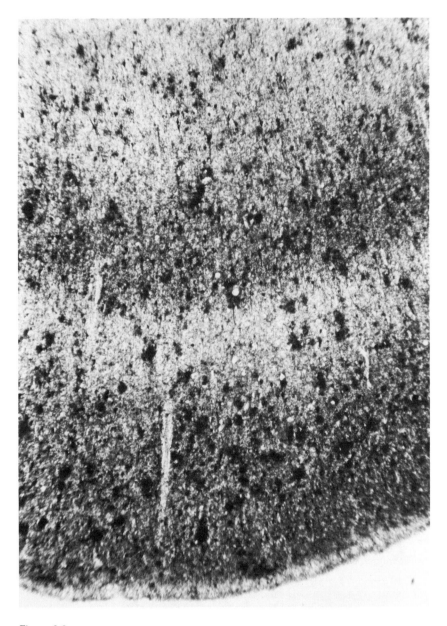

Figure 3.3
Involvement of layers III and V in association cortex. This section is stained with the monoclonal antibody Alz-50, and visualized with a peroxidase-linked secondary anti-body and 3,3'-diaminobenzidine as developing agent. Abnormal neurons and their processes, as well as the neuritic portion of neuritic plaques, are recognized by Alz-50.

disrupts input and output of the hippocampus, pathology in layers III and V of association cortices disrupts the input and output of each area, that is, feedforward and feedback projections that conjoin cortical areas of different hierarchies. In our view the presence of these lesions is no less important than the presence of lesions in the medial temporal sector of the brain, as far as the genesis of cognitive impairment is concerned. Several neuropsychological defects appear to be related to dysfunction in cortices outside the medial temporal sector. In turn such dysfunction could easily be caused by feedforward-feedback disruption. Furthermore in a new model of neural architectural and cognitive operation that we have recently proposed, feedback projections from higher-order cortices toward "earlier" cortices in the system are critical for the normal operations of recall, recognition, and consciousness (Damasio 1989a, b). In this perspective Alzheimer's disease disrupts the systems-level networks on which the higher operations of the telencephalon are founded.

Motor System
The naked eye inspection of an Alzheimer's brain often reveals a discrepancy between the atrophy of temporal, parietal, and frontal gyri and the normal appearance of the rolandic gyri, which contain the motor and somatosensory cortices. This appearance suggests the preservation of neural structures concerned with motor control, and that is indeed confirmed by the histological study of virtually all motor structures (Terry and Katzman 1983). Areas 4 and 6, areas 3, 1, 2, as well as the basal ganglia and cerebellum, are certainly less affected by neurofibrillary tangles than other aspects of the telencephalon (Van Hoesen and Damasio 1987). This neuropathological finding has a cognitive counterpart: The learning and performance of motor-related skills are largely intact in Alzheimer's disease, in clear distinction from the learning and recognition of information that requires internal representation as the primary type of response.

The Investigation of Alzheimer's Disease Pathology Using Immunohistologic Techniques
The availability of monoclonal antibodies raised against specific neural tissue targets has opened new possibilities for the identification of pathological changes in degenerative diseases. Wolozin and Davies and colleagues have developed a monoclonal antibody against Alzheimer's disease brain tissue (Wolozin et al. 1986). The antibody, known as Alz-50, recognizes neurons affected by Alzheimer's disease. It marks a protein with a molecular weight of 68 Kd which likely is related to the development of the condition. From the point of view

of mapping diseased neurons, the importance of Alz-50 is that it reveals an extent of pathological involvement greater than that identified by neurofibrillary tangles. The cell types and laminae marked by Alz-50 are the same as those marked by neurofibrillary tangles (figure 3.3). In other words Alz-50 does not identify an abnormal protein in neurons outside the territories where neurofibrillary tangles are prominently found. However, it does show that neurons not yet transformed into tangles at these sites do contain an abnormal protein. Such neurons may well still be functional, but they appear to be undergoing changes that eventually lead to their demise (Hyman et al. 1988). The findings add to the picture of gradual development that we now have for this disease.

The Neuropathological Diagnosis of Alzheimer's Disease
The diagnosis of Alzheimer's disease in life never goes beyond the level of possible or probable. The confirmation of the diagnostic hypothesis is a matter of histologic study of the post-mortem brain specimen. It is important to note, however, that as knowledge about the neuropathology of the condition changes, so must the criteria for neuropathologic diagnosis change.

In addition to the exclusion of a host of processes that cause dementia and that have distinctive neuropathological characteristics, the current objective diagnostic criteria proposed by Khachaturian (1985) for a microscopic field encompassing 1 mm^2 (100× field) are as follows:

> 1. In any patient less than 50 years of age, the number of senile or neuritic plaques and neurofibrillary tangles anywhere in the neocortex should exceed two to five per field. This enables the anatomical pathologist to establish a firm diagnosis, even in medicolegal cases and in the absence of any helpful clinical history.
> 2. In any patient between the ages of 50 and 65 years, there may be some neurofibrillary tangles, but the number of senile plaques must be eight or greater per field.
> 3. For any patient between 66 and 75 years of age, some neurofibrillary tangles may be present, but the number of senile plaques must be greater than 10 per field.
> 4. In any patient over 75 years old, neurofibrillary tangles may sometimes not be found in the neocortex, but the number of senile plaques should exceed 15 per microscopic field.

These criteria do not take into account the plotting of the anatomical distribution of neurofibrillary tangles and plaques in relation to different neuroanatomical systems. In the future anatomical distribution is likely to play a greater role in the classification. Also the diagnosis is often based on a narrow sampling of brain regions. Even when samples are taken from several regions of neocortex (frontal, temporal, and parietal lobes), amygdala, hippocampal formation, basal ganglia, substantia nigra, cerebellar cortex, and spinal cord, there is a considerable gap between the judgment of pathology based on a few sampled microscopic fields and the systematic and fairly comprehensive description of the anatomical position of lesions within a neuroanatomical ·system. An optimal diagnostic study should include morphometric analysis such as practiced by Terry and coworkers (Terry and Katzman 1983, Terry et al. 1981). Clearly some balance between the desirable and the practically feasible must be struck, but the point remains that finer criteria no doubt need to be developed.

The Cognitive Defects of Alzheimer's Disease

Cognitive Profile

It is no doubt true that in the advanced stages of Alzheimer's disease, nearly all cognitive systems break down, as befits the term dementia. On the other hand throughout the course of disease in most patients, it is possible to recognize a relatively selective involvement of some cognitive processes pitted against the relative sparing of others. A different rate of accrual of severity within involved systems is also clearly manifest, so that at any given point, for any given patient, the profile of impaired and intact functions is individual and ragged. Furthermore in some patients with Alzheimer's disease, the selectivity appears to be such that only one or very few systems are involved, for a long period of the evolution, thus rendering the cognitive dissection of the condition even easier to define.

It is too soon to describe the typical picture of Alzheimer's disease in cognitive terms, both from the point of view of all the constituent components of the impairment as well as in terms of their relative severity. It may turn out that after a significant number of patients are systematically studied over long periods, in vivo, and later confirmed neuropathologically, the disease process will appear so individualized that little may ever be said about the "standard" cognitive profile beyond the fact that it always involves (1) an impairment of learning and retrieval of memory in verbal and nonverbal domains, (2) an eventual impairment in problem solving, and (3) an eventual impairment of emotion and affect.

In our experience the defect in the learning of information at episodic level is always present and always early, that is, the defective learning of entities and events that have a unique temporal and spatial placement in the individual's autobiography is a hallmark of the condition. The inability to solve day-to-day problems and to plan activities correctly might be entirely secondary to the episodic learning defect. A defect in retrieval of information at episodic level, especially of information that ought to have been acquired recently rather than in the more distant past, is always present, and its magnitude probably parallels the episodic learning defect. The autobiographical update needed for the appropriate acquisition of new information at episodic level is gradually disrupted in Alzheimer's disease, to a point that only autobiographical highlights—for example, the patient's name, the spouse's name, or the main activity in which the patient was engaged before the disease—remain reliably accessible.

Memory processing at nonepisodic level—that is, the forms of memory generally referred to as semantic or generic—is also disrupted in Alzheimer's disease. In most instances the breakdown of memory at the generic level occurs later than that at the episodic level and covers both acquisition of new items (a predictable finding considering that acquisition of memory at generic level is not possible when there is a primary defect in acquisition at episodic level) and the retrieval of items previously acquired. The full meaning of a large range of objects of different categories, natural or manufactured, progressively eludes patients with Alzheimer's disease. It is important to note that the defect for this particular level of memory processing assumes proportions never seen with amnesic syndromes caused by cerebrovascular disease or herpes encephalitis, for example, when they involve anterior temporal structures bilaterally. Furthermore it is important to note that the defective performance in retrieval of generic memory has its own special nature. The responses of patients with Alzheimer's disease are far more erratic than those of patients with other kinds of amnesia, and these responses are far less stable and richer in a peculiar way: The items offered as a response to a given stimulus are more likely to be an unrelated derailment across semantic fields than a mere "don't know" response or off-target but related response. The picture that a physiologically minded observer might construct is that the activation of records pertinent to given stimulus is occurring fleetingly and that the patient is unable to experience enough of those passing and out-of-register reactivations to generate a set of remembrances capable of yielding the meaning of a given object.

An important aspect of the retrieval defect at episodic level is the inability to recognize topographic locations, uniquely or categorically, and to determine the relations of objects or persons to those topographic locations. The phenomenon generates the look of bewilderment often noted in the face of patients with early Alzheimer's disease when they are confronted with rapidly changing scenes and locations. Patients develop greater and greater difficulty in relating objects and persons to novel places.

All patients with Alzheimer's disease have an impairment of language that should be viewed as a special form of memory disorder. For the most part of the disease's course, the language impairment does not compromise processing of syntax, the appropriate use of phonemic information, or the correct phonetic implementation. The defect sets in at lexical level and might be best described as an inability to retrieve lexical entries that denote specific nonverbal entities or events. As a result, for long periods into the evolution of the disease, patients harbor a virtual anomic or amnestic aphasia as a key component of their cognitive impairment. In some rare patients this type of language defect has been noted in progressive and circumscribed fashion with little or no accompanying decline of other cognitive operations for a good number of years (Mesulam 1982). It is entirely possible that some of those patients are indeed a variant of Alzheimer's disease. However, two patients of ours who died (out of a large group with seemingly "selective" language defects), turned out to have Pick's disease instead.

It is noteworthy that, just as is the case with amnesic syndromes of other causes, patients with Alzheimer's disease maintain the ability to learn new perceptuomotor skills (Eslinger and Damasio 1986). It is striking indeed to note the dissociation between the complete inability to learn the identity of new faces or new names and the preserved ability to perform as control subjects do in mirror tracing or rotor pursuit tasks. Only in the very late stages of the disease is the dissociation no longer noted.

Possible Neural Substrates
The defective acquisition of episodic memory is attributable to impairments in a bilateral network that includes the amygdala, the hippocampal formation, their input and output staging areas in the entorhinal cortex, and their projections to higher-order association cortices, for example, the polar, anterolateral, and anteroinferior temporal cortices, and the insular cortices. Given the profile of development of the episodic learning defect, it is reasonable to hypothesize that the primary site of damage within the network is in the

hippocampal formation itself (for instance, in the dentate gyrus) or in the entorhinal cortices, at the level of layer II. Damage in the nuclei of the basal forebrain (septal nuclei, nucleus accumbens, nucleus basalis) and in the midline nuclei of the thalamus (nonspecific nuclei) —both groups that project heavily to the hippocampus—probably contributes to the episodic learning defect.

The rationale for relating the hippocampal complex to memory comes primarily from the study of amnesia in humans (Scoville and Milner 1957, Damasio 1984). Experimental neuropsychological studies in nonhuman primates also support this relation (Mishkin et al. 1982). The rationale for linking midline structures and memory comes from the analysis of patients in whom amnesia developed after lesions in basal forebrain (Alexander and Freedman 1983, Damasio et al. 1985a, b) and in medial thalamus (Butters and Cermak 1980, Graff-Radford et al. 1985).

The defect in episodic retrieval is attributable not only to dysfunction in the hippocampal complex but largely to dysfunction in higher-order association cortices within fields 37, 39, 20, and 21. The study of patient Boswell (Damasio et al. 1985a, b, 1987) and the contrast with patients HM (Scoville and Milner 1957) and RB (Zola-Morgan, Squire, and Amaral 1986) provide the rationale for assigning the anterior temporal nonlimbic cortices a role in the retrieval of episodic level knowledge. This is because both HM and RB appear capable of some episodic retrieval, despite their extensive medial temporal damage, whereas Boswell has a virtually complete retrograde amnesia for episodic material. Our working hypothesis has been, for several years, that this massive retrograde defeat derives from the damage to cortices in which the combinatorial codes for episodes have been recorded and without which the reconstitution of episodic level experiences is no longer possible (see Damasio et al. 1985a, b, Damasio 1989a, b).

The impairment of memory at generic level, however, cannot be accounted for by dysfunction to this system. On the basis of current knowledge of the anatomical basis of the agnosias in humans and animals (Damasio 1985a, b, Mishkin et al. 1982) and again on the contrast between HM and Boswell (Damasio 1984, Damasio et al. 1985a, b, 1987), the defect should be related to a network that includes the modal sensory cortices and some higher-order association cortices located in (1) occipitotemporal and occipitoparietal regions (areas 18, 19, part of 37, 36, 35, and 39) and (2) part of the anterior temporal cortices (areas 20, 21, 22, 38) and insular cortices. This network is more caudally located than the network hypothesized for retrieval of memory at episodic level, but partly overlaps with it. In both of these overlapping networks, the disruption of feedforward-feedback circuitry alone might well explain the defects and probably is at the root of the peculiarly rich and detailed nature of recognition responses by patients with Alzheimer's disease. (Damasio 1989a, b).

The likely neural network responsible for the ability to acquire new motor skills must include not only motor and somatosensory cortices (area 6, 4, 3, 1, 2, 5) but also structures in the neostriatum, cerebellum, and thalamus. Motor structures in general and the basal ganglia and cerebellum in particular are known to be remarkably preserved in Alzheimer's disease (Terry and Katzman 1983). It is interesting to note that conditioning of motor responses can be disrupted by specific cerebellar lesions in experimental animals (McCormick and Thompson 1984). On the other hand damage to cortical structures, limbic and nonlimbic, fails to interfere with motor learning in non-human primates (Mishkin and Bachevalier 1983).

The neural systems responsible for the prevailing form of language disorder in Alzheimer's disease can now be pinpointed. The lack of impairments in phonemic programming and reception, in phonetic implementation, and in any type of syntactic processing that characterizes the early to middle periods of Alzheimer's disease exonerate the classic language areas of the frontal operculum (areas 44 and 45), the posterior region of superior temporal gyrus (area 22), and the supramarginal gyrus (area 40). Support for this functional distinction can be found in many recent studies on the anatomical correlates of the aphasias (see Damasio 1988). On the other hand a new set of neuropsychological and neuroanatomical findings in our laboratories indicates that the severe defect in naming is caused by dysfunction in the *dominant* temporal cortices of areas 20, 21, and 38 and in the adjoining dominant hippocampal system (Tranel, Damasio, and Damasio 1988, Damasio, Tranel, and Damasio 1988).

On the basis of current knowledge of cognitive disturbances caused by dysfunction in frontal cortices (Damasio 1985a, b, Eslinger and Damasio 1985, Goldman-Rakic 1984), the network related to defects in executive control (monitoring, higher-level problem solving, goal development, planning, judgment) includes a variety of areas in prefrontal cortex working in concert with parietal and temporal cortical regions.

Concluding Remarks

It is clear from the descriptions of neuropathologic and cognitive findings in Alzheimer's disease that once both sets of data are appropriately dissected, the selective or modular nature of the defects is unquestionable. Given the strong evidence for the association between certain cognitive impairments and certain components of neural networks, it is reasonable to hypothesize that some of the brain sectors damaged by Alzheimer's disease are at the root of the relatively separable cognitive impairments that we have described. And yet it is important to note that in our view focal and simultaneous damage to all the loci mentioned, but caused by a pathological process other than Alzheimer's disease (for instance, cerebrovascular disease), would fail to produce the cognitive profile of Alzheimer's disease. The point is that the manner in which deficient neuropathological processes disrupt neural tissue, cause dysfunction, and determine the emergence of disturbances, cognitive or noncognitive, generate symptoms with a unique nature.

We have noted the importance of the disruption of feedforward and feedback circuitry within association cortices and between association cortices and limbic structures. We believe it is this disruption that gives Alzheimer's disease its special neuropsychological profile. For long periods into the course of the disease, the affected cortical regions are allowed to operate *defectively* rather than not at all. The gradual loss of the neuron elements in the cortical circuits, along with the gradual loss of nonspecific neuronal projections from subcortical loci, distorts the regular operation of these regions. The result is both a partial suspension of the usual functions and the addition of atypical functions. The situation is indeed different with other pathologic processes. For instance, damage to all of the limbic cortices and subcortical limbic structures, such as the amygdala, combined with damage to all of the anterotemporal neocortices and basal forebrain, if caused by complete tissue destruction of the type seen in herpes encephalitis, certainly does not produce Alzheimer's disease, but rather a pervasive amnesic syndrome.

Our final comment is reserved for the issue of onset of Alzheimer's disease and its relation to the amount of pathology accrued by the time of onset. It is our view that the symptoms associated with Alzheimer's disease come out only gradually and insidiously but after many years of silent addition of cellular damage and disruption of neural circuitry in all the territories within which damage becomes highly notable later on. We believe that as more brains of patients with recognized Alzheimer's disease as well as age-matched control subjects are studied systematically, more instances will be found in which cognitively normal or near-normal subjects do have evidence of considerable amounts of pathology in some of the territories where damage hallmarks the disease. The issue is that it likely takes an extensive amount of cell destruction, within each unit, for symptomatology to emerge. In some parts of the system, the damage may well compromise more than half of local neuron availability before any manifestation of dysfunction ensues. In some instances, either independently or prompted by intervening factors such as head injury, infections, stroke, depression, or mere additional aging, the onset of symptomatology may appear precipitous. In other instances it will simply be gradual. The issue of when enough impairment is enough is important and unresolved.

Acknowledgment

This work was supported by NINCDS Grant P01 NS19632 and Kiwanis International (Illinois–Eastern Iowa District) Spastic Paralysis Research Foundation.

References

Alexander, M. P., and Freedman, M. (1983). Amnesia after anterior communicating artery aneurysm rupture. *Neurology* 33 (Suppl. 2): 104.

Ball, M. J., Hachinski, V., Fox, A., et al. (1985). A new definition of Alzheimer's disease: A hippocampal dementia. *Lancet* 1: 14–16.

Butters, N., and Cermak, L. S. (1980). *Alcoholic Korsakoff's Syndrome*. New York: Academic Press.

Damasio, A. R. (1984). The anatomic basis of memory disorders. *Seminars in Neurology* 4: 223–225.

Damasio, A. R. (1985a). Disorders of complex visual processing. In M.–M. Mesulam (ed.) *Principles of Behavioral Neurology*. Philadelphia: Davis, pp. 259–288 (Contemp. Neurol. Ser. 26).

Damasio, A. R. (1985b). Prosopagnosia. *Trends in Neuroscience* 8: 132–135.

Damasio, A. R. (1989a). The brain binds entities and events by multiregional activation from convergence zones. *Neural Computation* 1: 123–132.

Damasio, A. R. (1989b). Time-locked multiregional retroactivation: A systems-level proposal for the neural substrates of recall and recognition. *Cognition* 33: 25–62.

Damasio, A. R., Eslinger, P. J., Damasio, H., Van Hoesen, G. W., and Cornell, S. (1985a). Multimodal amnesic syndrome following bilateral temporal and basal forebrain damage. *Archives of Neurology* 42: 252–259.

Damasio, A. R., Graff-Radford, N., Eslinger, P. J., Damasio, H., and Kassell, N. (1985b). Amnesia following basal forebrain lesions. *Archives of Neurology* 42: 263–271.

Damasio, A. R., Damasio, H., Tranel, D., Welsh, K., and Brandt, J. (1987). Additional neural and cognitive evidence in patient DRB. *Society for Neuroscience* 13: 1452.

Damasio, H. (1988). Anatomical and neuroimaging contributions to the study of aphasia. In H. Goodglass (Ed.) *Handbook of Neuropsychology*. Volume on *Language*. Amsterdam: Elsevier.

Damasio, H. (1988). Anatomical and neuroimaging contributions to the study of aphasia. In H. Goodglass (Ed.) *Handbook of Neuropsychology*. Volume on *Language*. Amsterdam: Elsevier.

Damasio, H., Tranel, D., and Damasio, A. R. (1988). Isolated impairment of retrieval and learning of reference lexicon following left anterotemporal damage. *Society for Neuroscience* 14: 1289.

Davies, P., and Maloney, A. J. F. (1976). Selective loss of central cholinergic neurons in Alzheimer's disease. (Letter) *Lancet* 2(pt. 2): 1403.

Esiri, M. M. Pearson, R. C. A., and Powell, T. P. S. (1986). The cortex of the primary auditory area in Alzheimer's disease. *Brain Research* 366: 385–387.

Eslinger, P. J., and Damasio, A. R. (1985). Severe cognitive disturbance following bilateral frontal lobe ablation: Patient EVR. *Neurology* 35: 1731–1741.

Eslinger, P. J., and Damasio, A. R. (1986). Preserved motor learning in Alzheimer's disease. *Journal of Neuroscience* 6: 3006–3009.

Goldman-Rakic, P. S. (1984). The frontal lobes: Uncharted provinces of the brain. *Trends in Neuroscience* 7: 425–429.

Graff-Radford, N. R., Damasio, H., Yamada, T., Eslinger, P. J., and Damasio, A. R. (1985). Nonhemorrhagic thalamic infarction. Clinical, neuropsychological and electrophysiological findings in four anatomical groups defined by computerized tomography. *Brain* 108: 485–516.

Hyman, B., Van Hoesen, G. W., Damasio, A., and Barnes, C. (1984). Alzheimer's disease: Cell-specific pathology isolates the hippocampal formation. *Science* 225: 1168–1170.

Hyman, B., Van Hoesen, G., Kromer, L. J., and Damasio, A. (1986). Perforant pathway changes and the memory impairment of Alzheimer's disease. *Annals of Neurology* 20: 472–481.

Hyman, B., Van Hoesen, G. W., and Damasio, A. (1987). Alzheimer's disease: Glutamate depletion in the hippocampal perforant pathway zone. *Annals of Neurology* 22: 37–40.

Hyman, B. T., Van Hoesen, G. W., Wolozin, B. L., Davies, P., Kromer, L. J., Damasio, A. R. (1988). Alz-50 antibody recognizes Alzheimer-related neuronal changes. *Annals of Neurology* 23: 371–379.

Khachaturian, A. S. (1985). Diagnosis of Alzheimer's disease. *Archives of Neurology* 42: 1097–1105.

Lewis, D. A., Campbell, M. J., Terry, R. D., and Morrison, J. H. (1987). Laminar and regional distribution of neurofibrillary tangles and neuritic plaques in Alzheimer's disease: A quantitative study of visual and auditory cortices. *Journal of Neuroscience* 7: 1799–1808.

McCormick, D. A., and Thompson, R. F. (1984). Neuronal responses of the rabbit cerebellum during acquisition and performance of a classically conditioned nictitating-eyelid response. *Journal of Neuroscience* 4: 2811–2822.

Mesulam, M.–M. (1982). Slowly progressive aphasia without generalized dementia. *Annals of Neurology* 11: 592–598.

Mishkin, M., and Bachevalier, J. (1983). Object recognition impaired by ventromedial but not dorsolateral prefrontal cortical lesions in monkeys. *Society for neuroscience Abstract* 9: 29.

Mishkin, M., Spiegler, B. J., Saunders, R. C., and Malamut, B. J. (1982) An animal model of global amnesia. In S. Corkin, K. L. Davis, J. H. Growdon, E. Usdin, and R. J. Wurtman (Eds.) *Alzheimer's Disease: A Report of Progress. Aging* 19: 235–247. New York: Raven.

Pearson, R. C. A., Esiri, M. M., Hiorns, R. W., Wilcock, G. K., and Powell, T. P. S. (1985). Anatomical correlates of the distribution of the pathological changes in the neocortex in Alzheimer's disease. *Proceedings of the National Academy of Science* 82: 4531–4534.

Scoville, W. B., and Milner, B. (1957). Loss of recent memory after bilateral Hippocampal lesions. *Journal of Neurology, Neurosurgery and Psychiatry* 20: 249–262.

Terry, R. D., and Katzman, R. (1983). Senile dementia of the Alzheimer type. *Annals of Neurology* 14: 497.

Terry R. D., Peck, A., DeTeresa, R., Schechter, R., and Horoupian, D. S. (1981). Some morphometric aspects of the brain in senile dementia of the Alzheimer type. *Annals of Neurology* 10: 184–192.

Tranel, D., Damasio, H., and Damasio, A. R. (1988). Dissociated verbal and nonverbal retrieval and learning following left anterotemporal damage. *Neurology* 38: 322.

Van Hoesen, G. W., and Damasio, A. R. (1987). Neural correlates of cognitive impairment in Alzheimer's disease. In V. Mountcastle and F. Plum (Eds.) *Higher Functions of the Nervous System. Handbook of Physiology*. Bethesda, MD: American Physiological Society, pp. 871–898.

Whitehouse, P. J., Price, D. L., Clark, A. W., Coyle, J. T., and Delong, M. R. (1981). Alzheimer disease: Evidence for selective loss of cholinergic neurons in the nucleus basalis. *Annals of Neurology* 10: 122–126.

Wolozin, B.L., Pruchnichi, A., Dickson, D. W., and Davies, P. (1986). A neuronal antigen in the brains of Alzheimer patients. *Science* 232: 648–650.

Zola-Morgan, S., Squire, L. R., and Amaral, D. G. (1986). Human amnesia and the medial temporal region: Enduring memory impairment following a bitalteral lesion limited to the CA1 field of hippocampus. *Journal of Neuroscience* 6: 2950–2967.

Chapter 4

Positron Emission Tomographic Studies of Cerebral Metabolism in Alzheimer's Disease

John B. Chawluk, Murray Grossman, Julio A. Calcano-Perez, Abass Alavi, Howard I. Hurtig, and Martin Reivich

In this chapter Chawluk and colleagues review recent progress in correlating regional cerebral metabolism with neuropsychologic deficit profiles in patients with Alzheimer-type dementia. The evidence supports some broad generalizations: hypometabolism showing up early in the disease course in posterior association areas and somewhat later in frontal association areas, and greater variability in interhemispheric regional asymmetries in patients versus normal control subjects. The latter finding clearly relates to individual differences in neuropsychologic profile; at the very least the evidence from PET confirms that posterior temporal and parietal structures are implicated in the language disorders of Alzheimer's disease, and the right hemisphere parietal areas are implicated in the visuospatial impairments (and see Martin, chapter 57).

Chawluk and colleagues probe beyond these broad generalizations to the question that lies at the heart of this book: whether the deficit patterns in these patients can shed light on the functional organization of the brain. In a series of four case studies, they investigate the perceptual and lexical-semantic processes that contribute to confrontation naming performance and the distribution of metabolic changes associated with deficits in one or more of these processes. Their preliminary results support the thesis that distinct brain regions are involved in the perceptual and semantic categorization of objects, a thesis that is taken up in more detail in chapters 7 and 8.

M.F.S.

As scientific interest in dementing illnesses has increased over the past twenty years, we have grown to recognize the discrete nature of cognitive and behavioral abnormalities seen in patients with dementia of the Alzheimer type (DAT). The capability of correlating these behavioral changes with anatomic or physiologic alterations demonstrated in vivo should considerably enhance our understanding of this all-too-common degenerative disorder. Up to now anatomic imaging methods such as X-ray computed tomography (CT) and magnetic resonance imaging (MRI) have provided little data on focal structural changes that might underlie specific behavioral abnormalities characteristic of DAT. Surprisingly little work has been done correlating localized electroencephalographic abnormalities with behavioral derangements in DAT, despite the fact that EEG was the first tool available for such investigations.

The modern concept that brain functional activity is reflected by substrate utilization (glucose and oxygen metabolism), which is in turn strongly correlated with cerebral blood flow (CBF), can be traced to Roy and Sherrington's work at the end of the last century (1890). This rather radical idea was poorly supported by experimental evidence, and it was not until a half a century later that Kety and Schmidt's (1948) pioneering measurements of global CBF in awake humans led to a flood of investigations correlating altered mentation with changes in CBF. The finding that patients with severe dementia had significant reductions in global CBF was not startling and served to reinforce the widely held notion of DAT as a diffuse process. With the extension of the Kety-Schmidt principle by Lassen and Ingvar (1963), Obrist and colleagues (1967), and others, determinations of regional CBF were made possible. Continuing probes into CBF in dementia determined that specific association cortices (temporal, frontal) were predominantly affected by the underlying disease process (Ingvar and Gustavson 1970, Obrist et al. 1970). Moreover specific cognitive impairments could be correlated with these blood flow impairments (Hagberg and Ingvar 1976). These early regional CBF measurements, using stationary detectors with limited spatial resolution, although titillating did not lead to the same excitement generated by tomographic anatomic imaging (CT scanning) of other central nervous system disorders such as stroke and brain tumor. A logical and highly desirable advancement would be the development of tomographic methods for imaging brain physiology (CBF, metabolism, and so on). This aim was met by the development in the late 1970s of the PET (positron emission tomography) technique, which has proved valuable in studying the biological basis for altered behavior in DAT. Most of these PET studies have used 18 F-fluorodeoxyglucose (FDG) to measure local cerebral glucose metabolism (LCMRgl) (Reivich et al. 1979). In this chapter we critically review the current literature correlating PET results in DAT patients with their behavioral profiles. In general the neuropsychological approach in these studies has evolved from global assessments to attempts at isolating particular cognitive functions via standarized test batteries. More novel tasks designed to address specific hypotheses on behavioral disturbances in DAT should prove superior to methods implemented so far. We close this chapter by describing in detail some of our preliminary work using such less conventional approaches.

Cerebral Glucose Metabolism in Alzheimer's Disease

Early PET studies of patients with Alzheimer's disease failed to reveal consistently diminished CMRgl except in the most severely demented patients (Ferris et al. 1983, Frackowiak et al. 1981, DeLeon et al. 1983). Moreover these early studies, all using a cross-sectional design, were unable to document any statistically significant diminution of CMRgl on PET in the more severely demented patients when compared with less severely demented patients (Foster et al. 1984).

Several technical and methodological problems may have contributed to these inconclusive findings, and their resolution has left us with a much more reliable and detailed picture of brain glucose metabolism in dementia. For example, investigators noticed a large variance in absolute metabolic rates for glucose within both normal and dementing groups of subjects. By using a normalization ratio of regional metabolism to the same subject's average whole-brain metabolic rate or to the metabolic rate of a cortical area typically less involved histopathologically (such as primary visual or sensorimotor cortex), more reliable metabolic observations could be made with PET-FDG. By this strategy, researchers have been able to report reduced LCMRgl in parietal regions of the brains of patients with presumed mild to moderate degrees of dementia. (Cutler et al. 1985, Alavi et al. 1986, Duara et al. 1986, Haxby et al. 1985, McGeer et al. 1986a, b). These patients may also exhibit asymmetric reductions of LCMRgl in parietal regions, but one hemisphere does not appear to be more frequently involved than the other (Friedland et al. 1985b, Haxby et al. 1986). This issue requires further investigation, however, because preliminary data from our group (Jamieson et al. 1987) and Loewenstein and colleagues (1987) raise the possibility of greater left hemisphere involvement. Patients who are more severely demented, as determined by performance on a simple dementia rating scale such as the Mini Mental State Exam (MMSE) (Folstein et al. 1975), exhibit hypometabolism of frontal association regions as well (Benson et al. 1983, Chawluk et al. 1985, Cutler et al. 1985b, Duara et al. 1986, Friedland et al. 1985a, b, McGeer et al. 1986a). Thus, through the use of normalization ratios, reductions in LCMRgl, which can be imaged using PET-FDG, have been largely restricted to cortical association areas, involving primary sensory and motor areas only to a negligible degree (Foster et al. 1983, Haxby et al. 1985, Alavi et al. 1986).

Another difficulty concerns the validity of these reduced LCMRgl findings in DAT. The data suggest that there are reliable changes in regional glucose metabolic activity in the brains of patients with DAT that can be imaged using the PET-FDG method, yet these findings are not clearly diagnostic of DAT. Patients with other disease states also manifest hypometabolic indices on PET. These include multi-infarct dementia (for example, Kuhl et al. 1985), epilepsy (for example, Engel 1984, Theodore et al. 1986), schizophrenia (for example, Brodie et al. 1984, Buchsbaum et al. 1984), depression (for example, Phelps et al. 1984), Parkinson's disease and Huntington's chorea (for example, Kuhl et al. 1984), and progressive supranuclear palsy (for example, D'Antona et al. 1985). Few if any metabolic or infectious causes of dementia have been studied by PET, so that patterns of metabolic abnormalities in such conditions are unknown. Short of direct comparisons among these conditions that might reveal pathognomonic motifs of glucose hypometabolism, it would be important to determine that the regional distribution of hypometabolism on PET in DAT corresponds with the regional distribution of the microscopic pathological changes characteristic of Alzheimer's disease. In fact a suprisingly small number of patients have been subjected both to PET-FDG metabolic assessments during life and to the identification of histopathological abnormalities at autopsy (McGeer et al. 1986b). There does appear to be a correspondence between pathologically involved areas and imaged glucose hypometabolism (Friedland et al. 1985a).

Many questions can be raised concerning the clinical characteristics of the particular demented patients selected for examination. For example, it has been argued that dementia first noticed at a younger age may progress more rapidly and even manifest itself in a qualitatively different fashion when compared with DAT first noticed at an older age. Koss and her coworkers (1985) subdivided their dementing patients on the basis of the age of onset and found that younger dementing patients (less than 65 years old at onset) exhibited relative reductions in right temporoparietal LCMRgl, whereas older patients (65 years or older at onset) exhibited relative left frontal hypometabolism. Others (for example, Chui et al. 1985 Filley et al. 1986) have found by comparison that language impairments—and by implication left hemisphere dysfunction—occur at an earlier age than visuospatial deficits, which are associated traditionally with right hemisphere dysfunction. In the context of other PET-FDG studies documenting an increase in the variance of lateralization of metabolic abnormalities in DAT without a bias to the left or right hemisphere (for example, Friedland et al. 1985b, Haxby et al. 1985, 1986), it would be important to determine that claims of lateralization at some stage or in a particular subpopulation of patients with Alzheimer's disease do not merely represent a sampling error.

Some patients who are at risk for Alzheimer's disease due to an apparent genetic predisposition have been studied in an attempt to identify the earliest metabolic and behavioral manifestations of the disorder. Cutler and associates (1985a) found memory impairments in a 57-year-old man whose first PET scan was normal, but who manifested bilateral parietal lobe hypometabolism on a subsequent scan performed about 12 months later. Luxenberg and colleagues (1987) evaluated neuropsychological and glucose metabolic indices in the identical twin of a patient with probable Alzheimer's disease. They found intellectual deficits on visuoperceptual organization and verbal memory tasks in the unaffected twin despite normal glucose metabolic rates. Haxby and colleagues (1986), by comparison, found that 5 subjects with mild memory deficits had no apparent difficulties on their battery of language and visuospatial tests, but had metabolic abnormalities on PET scans. Similarly Polinsky and colleagues (1987) found that an asymptomatic individual at risk for familial DAT displayed reduced LCMRgl in the left supramarginal gyrus. Discrepancies in these findings may be attributable to incomplete neuropsychological evaluations, limited imaging resolution of the current generation of PET scanners, other technical limitations of the PET-FDG method, or greater clinical heterogeneity than expected even in this restricted area of study. Regardless of the specific explanation, future systematic studies of familial Alzheimer's disease may help resolve questions about the metabolic and behavioral characteristics of DAT at its onset.

A related problem is the cross-sectional design of most data collected. Although dementia of the Alzheimer type is a progressive disorder, only a few studies have actually attempted to assess the cerebral metabolism of a particular patient on several successive occasions. Some researchers have found reductions in LCMRgl on repeat PET scans (Cutler et al. 1985a, McGeer et al. 1986a, b), but others have failed to document changes in the cortical glucose metabolism of particular individuals over time (Duara et al. 1986, Grady et al. 1986). Indeed it has been argued that reductions of LCMRgl may precede clinical evidence for cognitive impairment in DAT and that LCMRgl does not change significantly despite clinical evidence for deterioration (Foster et al. 1984, Haxby et al 1986). Claims such as these are limited by the neuropsychological batteries that are administered and by the absence of histopathological correlates of the extent of the disease process at various stages.

In the same context there are also difficulties at the level of determining the severity of a dementia. Most studies use measures such as the MMSE or the Mattis Dementia Scale to stratify the degree of dementia. Unfortunately recent assessments of dementia scales indicate that they may not be reliable in their diagnosis of dementia, let alone their ability to determine the degree of a dementia (for example, Folstein et al. 1985, Huff et al. 1987, Nelson et al. 1986). This may be due in part to the variable presentations of DAT and to our limited appreciation of the natural history of the disease (for example, Martin et al. 1986, Neary et al. 1986; see also chapters 5 and 6).

Taken together, the findings suggest that PET-FDG studies may provide us with a characteristic profile of brain glucose metabolism in DAT. Certainly additional work is necessary. Nevertheless the picture that seems to be emerging is one of relatively selective hypometabolism in cerebral association areas, most prominently in parietal association areas early in the disease process, but later involving frontal association areas as well. Histopathological evidence seems to support the validity of the regional distribution of hypometabolism on PET in DAT. The relation between glucose metabolic findings and the clinical manifestations of DAT, however, is just beginning to be elucidated.

In the following section we review some salient behavioral observations in DAT that are crucial to a more detailed discussion of PET-neuropsychological correlations.

Behavioral Abnormalities in Alzheimer's Disease

An increasing number of careful behavioral studies have been conducted with patients suffering from Alzheimer's disease. Rather than conceiving of dementia as a more-or-less undifferentiated cognitive impairment, this body of work attempts to define the specific nature of the cognitive impairments in DAT. These studies have usually investigated one of three aspects of intelligence: language and other symbol systems used for communication, memory and learning, and visuospatial and visuoconstructional skills. Within each of these domains there is an emerging consensus that there are specific areas of compromised functioning, whereas other functions appear relatively preserved. It is possible to test the hypothesis then that the brain regions thought to subserve these compromised functions may correspond to the areas of regional glucose hypometabolism seen on PET studies.

Let us first consider language function. Recent studies of the performance of dementing patients on large clinical aphasia batteries

(Appell et al. 1982, Cummings et al. 1985) have generally confirmed the conclusions of earlier case studies (for example, Critchley 1964, Schwartz et al. 1979, Sjogren et al. 1952, Warrington 1975, Whitaker 1976) that naming and the comprehension of oral and written material are most severely compromised in DAT, particularly early in the disease process. Cross-sectional observations indicate that features of language use in DAT that may be compromised later in the disease may include logicogrammatical skills and the ability to edit out intrusions (Hier et al. 1985, Fuld et al. 1981). Areas of language functioning that seem relatively preserved throughout the course of the disease include phonologic processing, repetition, and automatic speech. From a localizationist perspective (for example, Benson and Geschwind 1986, Kertesz 1985) the earlier pattern of deficit might be expected in patients with focal insult to the inferior parietal and posterior temporal regions of the left hemisphere and would best correspond clinically to an anomic aphasia or a transcortical sensory aphasia. This localization moreover reflects just those areas that are hypometabolic on PET-FDG studies of midly to moderately demented subjects. If longitudinally structured studies confirm the cross-sectional findings, then the apparent logicogrammatical difficulty and frequent occurrence of intrusions could conceivably correspond to the later-appearing hypometabolism in left frontal association areas.

Deficits in appreciating visuospatial material are also evident in patients with DAT. Brouwers and colleagues (1984) found significant impairments on tests of visuospatial processing that require the appreciation of extrapersonal space, in contrast to their patients' somewhat better performance in visuospatial tasks requiring an appreciation of egocentric space. Others have also observed deficits on visuoconstructional tasks such as drawing pictures or copying stick figures (Moore and Wyke 1984, Rosen 1983). From a localizationist perspective impairments such as these would be expected after insult to the inferior parietal and posterior temporal portions of the right hemisphere. This again corresponds to the hypometabolism observed in the posterior association cortices of the right hemisphere in PET-FDG studies of DAT.

Impairments of memory functioning are most frequently cited as a manifestation of dementia of the Alzheimer type and are in fact a sine qua non for establishing this diagnosis. Deficits on tasks assessing short-term memory for a variety of verbal and visuospatial material are frequently observed (for example, Corkin 1982, Kopelman 1985, Morris 1986). Assessments of longer-term memory, often spanning decades, have also revealed deficits for an equally varied range of material (for example, Corkin 1982, Corkin et al. 1984, Moscovitch

1982, Rosen 1983, Wilson et al. 1981). On the other hand it has been observed that patients allowed to learn a certain quantity of new material up to a criterion level equal to that of control subjects (through multiple exposures, for example) are later able to recall the new material as well as the control subjects (for example, Becker et al. 1987, Corkin et al. 1984, Kopelman 1985). Findings such as these suggest that the memory deficit in DAT may in some instances occur at the point of acquisition and in others at the recall stage. Others have argued that patients with DAT exhibit relatively compromised acquisition of factual information, as demonstrated in the above studies, although the acquisition of new procedures or implicit information is relatively preserved (for example, Eslinger and Damasio 1986, Knopman and Nissen 1987, Morris et al. 1983). This factual/procedural distinction in DAT has not been replicated in other laboratories (for examples, Grober 1985, Shimamura et al. 1987). Although the localization of clinical memory functioning is far from clear (for example, Squire 1986), structures frequently implicated in memory functioning include the hippocampus and the dorsomedial nucleus of the thalamus (Charness and DeLa Paz 1987, Gebhardt et al. 1984, Milner 1974, Squire and Moore 1979, Victor et al. 1987). These regions are small and paramedian, therefore difficult to image accurately by PET, which may account in part for the observation of clinical deficits without corresponding regional PET hypometabolism (although compare McGeer et al. 1986a, b).

Regional Glucose Hypometabolism in Demented Patients with Behavioral Impairments

Several studies have been conducted that test the hypothesis that regional hypometabolic indices on PET-FDG examination correspond to the anatomic localization thought to account for specific compromised intellectual functions. Such investigations require that individual patients with DAT be evaluated both behaviorally and metabolically. Although serving as valuable first steps, the studies that have been reported are open to criticism from both metabolic and behavioral perspectives.

Foster and colleagues (1984) administered a broad-based battery of clinical neuropsychological tests to 20 unselected patients with DAT. Their behavioral assessment was primarily designed to determine overall impairment, severity of mnestic difficulties, and hemisphere lateralization of cognitive dysfunction. Thus the Wechsler Adult Intelligence Scale (WAIS), the Wechsler Memory Scale (WMS), a collection of memory tests comprising a memory quotient (MQ), and the Mattis Dementia Scale were administered. They applied rigorous criteria for studying a patient. Patients averaged 60 years of age with a mean age of onset at 57 years. Scores on the Hachinski Ischemia Scale (Hachinski et al. 1975) were less than 4 for each subject, thus indicating that the patients were unlikely to be suffering from multi-infarct dementia. EEGs were generally free of localized abnormalities, and CT scans usually revealed generalized, nonspecific cerebral atrophy. In addition other systemic or neurological diseases were excluded, and patients were thought not to suffer from a primary major depression. Clinical features such as these have since been published by an NINCDS-ADRDA committee as research criteria for the diagnosis of probable Alzheimer's disease (McKhann et al. 1984). The results of behavioral testing were compared with the regional pattern of glucose metabolism obtained from PET-FDG studies. PET-FDG data were collected in a quiet, darkened room, and analysis of the metabolic results was performed without normalization (that is, absolute metabolic rates were used). Behavioral and metabolic data from patients with probable DAT were compared with similar findings in control subjects matched for age, sex, and education.

Scores on each of the behavioral tests were significantly depressed in the demented patients when compared with scores of the control subjects. Similarly LCMRgl was significantly reduced in patients with DAT when compared with LCMRgl in control subjects. The greatest metabolic reduction was found in posterior parietal cortex, although adjacent posterior temporal, anterior occipital, and superior parietal lobule cortices were also hypometabolic. When patients were subdivided according to the severity of their dementia, there were reductions in the levels of glucose metabolism in severely demented patients when compared with mildly demented patients, but these differences did not attain statistical significance. Severely demented patients performed at significantly inferior levels on all behavioral tests in comparison with the mildly demented subjects. Scores on general measures of intellectual ability such as the WAIS IQ, WMS, and Mattis Dementia Scale correlated with LCMRgl in all lobes of both hemispheres. Performance on the verbal subtests of the WAIS correlated with LCMRgl in all cortical regions except the right parietal lobe, whereas performance subtest scores correlated with LCMRgl in all cortical regions except the left frontal lobe. These results do not fit well with predicted functional localizations, such as an aphasia due to left hemispheric dysfunction. Indeed the ability to establish new insights into brain-behavior relations from such broad test batteries is limited.

Friedland and colleagues (1985b; also compare Koss et al. 1985) compared the behavioral and glucose metabolic data of 17 patients with probable Alzheimer's disease of moderate severity (according to the Mattis Dementia Scale) with the findings in 7 healthy aged subjects. Behavioral testing included the verbal and performance scales from the WAIS. Demented patients exhibited significantly reduced levels of FDG utilization in temporoparietal regions—but not frontal regions—when compared with controls. All of the patients with DAT exhibited relative hypometabolism in temporoparietal cortical areas when compared with frontal cortical areas, but the mean absolute rates of glucose utilization in these two regions did not differ significantly. Such a regional difference was not observed in age-matched control subjects. Assessments of hemispheric differences did not reveal a predominance of hypometabolism in one hemisphere or the other. Rather an increase in the variability of asymmetric metabolism was seen within the group of demented subjects when compared with that of control subjects. Demented subjects with predominantly right hemispheric hypometabolism performed at significantly inferior levels on the performance scale of the WAIS when compared with patients exhibiting predominantly left hemispheric hypometabolism.

Again the interest generated by this observed relation is restricted. On a more superficial level one could predict that difficulty with the performance portion of the WAIS should be associated with right hemisphere dysfunction on PET scanning. But the performance scale is far from homogeneous in the skills it assesses. Chase and his coworkers (1984a, b) attempted to "localize" the subtests of the WAIS by correlating PET-FDG measurements with scores on various aspects of the WAIS in 17 patients with probable Alzheimer's disease. These researchers found that the performance IQ correlated largely—but not exclusively—with metabolic measures in right temporoparietal regions, as might have been predicted. In detailed evaluations of the subtests contributing to the performance IQ, behavior-metabolic correlations for the object assembly and block design subtests resembled those for the performance IQ as a whole. Many correlations for the digit symbol and picture completion subtests also were found with left parietal LCMRgl, and the picture arrangement subtest correlated equally with left and right hemisphere metabolic values. Scores on the verbal IQ portion of the WAIS correlated with LCMRgl in left frontal and temporal regions, as might have been predicted. The similarities subtest had a similar distribution of LCMRgl correlations. Information, comprehension, arithmetic, and vocabulary subtests correlated with glucose metabolic indices in these left hemisphere regions as well as some right frontotemporal regions. The digit span subtest correlated equally with frontal and parietal regions of both left and right hemispheres. It is quite difficult then to "metabolically localize" such routinely used clinical tests, even those that have commonly been thought to tap the functions of a particular hemisphere.

What may account for this less-than-perfect correspondence between reduced regional cerebral glucose metabolism and the predictions of anatomically localizable dysfunction based on patterns of behavioral deficits? One possibility is that unanticipated brain-behavior correlations are due to statistical artifact, that is, false positive correlations emerging from a very large correlational matrix. This type of problem can be obviated through the use of appropriately conservative statistics and rigorous criteria for labeling a finding "abnormal." A second possibility is that the PET data are inaccurate in their reflection of reduced LCMRgl. Many studies have been unsuccessful in detecting metabolic abnormalities using absolute PET values, whereas the utilization of normalized values or other statistical techniques that reduce global absolute variability reveals consistent and clinically plausible patterns of abnormal metabolism (Chawluk et al. 1985, Durar et al. 1986, Rottenberg et al. 1987, Mazziotta et al. 1987). Another possibility is that the behavioral analysis is in error. Measures of intellectual functioning such as performance/verbal IQ score or a confrontation naming test may not "localize" to a particular region of the brain or even to a hemisphere. Thus the data cited may not be adequate to test the hypothesis that regions expected to account for intellectual deficits in DAT should evidence focal CMRgl abnormalities.

One approach to avoiding such pitfalls in a study of metabolism-behavior correlations is to preselect patients for more specific clinical deficits. Foster and colleagues (1983) studied three DAT patients with predominantly language problems, four patients with striking visuospatial deficits, and six patients whose memory disorder was most prominent. An extensive battery of psychometric tests was administered. This included the Mattis Dementia Scale, a lengthy questionnaire specifically designed to evaluate the severity of dementia; the Boston Diagnostic Aphasia Examination (BDAE), a collection of subjects assesssing various clinical aspects of language and communication; a test of simple reaction time; the Rey-Osterreith Figure test, where a complex geometric design must be reproduced from memory and then copied; the Benton Copy test, another visuoconstructional task; and the Mosaic Comparisons test, a complicated match-to-sample task using visuoperceptual material as stimuli. PET scans were performed on the awake subjects in a quiet, darkened room, and analysis of the metabolic results used absolute metabolic rates with their inherent higher coefficient of variation (as opposed to "normalized" ratios).

The patients in Foster's study who exhibited primarily language difficulties on clinical examination performed at significantly inferior levels on several language portions of the test battery when compared with the other patients. However, they did not differ from other patients in terms of their performance on broad-based tests of intellectual functioning such as the combined WAIS IQ score, the Mattis Dementia Scale, and simple reaction time. These patients also revealed 20 percent to 40 percent reductions in cortical glucose metabolism in their left parietal, temporal, and frontal association areas when compared with the homologous regions contralaterally. Performance on the naming subtest of the BDAE correlated with many metabolic measures in left temporal association areas, as would be predicted by a localizationist hypothesis for correspondence between an anomic impairment and regional brain dysfunction (for example, Benson and Geschwind 1985). Performance on the verbal fluency portion of the Mattis Dementia Scale correlated with LCMRgl in left frontal association areas, also corresponding to localizationist theories. Other findings in this study were not consonant with traditional aphasiological localization based on examinations of patients with language disorders after focal cerebral infarction. For example, verbal fluency correlated with left *temporal* metabolism, and naming performance with LCMRgl in left frontal association cortex. Moreover both verbal fluency and naming correlated with CMRgl measures in portions of the *right* hemisphere.

Patients in the Foster study with predominantly visuoconstructional deficits on clinical examination were significantly compromised in their ability to perform many of the visuoconstructional tasks in the test battery when compared with the aphasic DAT patients, although they did not differ in terms of their performance on tests of global intellectual ability. Moreover these patients exhibited significant reductions in right temporoparietal metabolism when compared with the homologous regions of the left hemisphere. Performance on visuoperceptual skills correlated with glucose metabolism in many regions of right parietal association cortex, but also with left frontal and left temporal glucose metabolic measures. As with the language fluency and naming measures, then, there is some correspondence between the predicted localization of dysfunction and the actual region of hypometabolism. However, the behavior-metabolic correlations do not adhere strictly to localizationist predictions of dysfunction restricted to the right hemisphere in patients with visuospatial difficulties.

In fact it is probably unreasonable to expect these complex cognitive tasks to conform to simple localizationist schema. Networks of interlacing region-to-region connections most likely cross lobar and hemispheric boundaries, providing the basis for complex behaviors. For example, a right hemisphere dominant network influencing left hemisphere as well as ipsilateral remote areas has been postulated for directed attention to environmental stimuli (Mesulam 1982). Even without invoking a network hypothesis, Metter and colleagues (1984) found significant intercorrelations among inferior frontal (including Broca's area), posterior temporal (including Wernicke's area), and inferior parietal regions in normal subjects aged 24 to 78. Metter and colleagues (1984) and Horwitz and associates (1984) also found significant correlations (in fact generally the highest partial correlation coefficients) between homotopic regions of the two hemispheres. Thus correlations between language functions and right hemisphere regional metabolism may be a result of normally high interhemispheric homotopic covariance or could represent a contributory role (for example, attentional) of right hemisphere structures to the specific language domains being studied.

Haxby and his coworkers (1985) attempted to deal with many of the problems of behavioral analysis in PET studies of dementia by designing tasks that they felt would be more specific than standarized tests in the evaluation of lateralized hemispheric functions. They collected behavioral and metabolic data on 10 subjects who met rigorous criteria for probable DAT, 10 neurologically intact volunteers matched for age, sex, and education who served as controls for the neuropsychological tests, and 26 normal subjects who served as controls for the PET study. The battery of neuropsychological tests included the WAIS; the Mini Mental State; the Mattis Dementia Scale; two delayed memory subtests taken from the WMS; the Syntax Comprehension Test, in which subjects were asked a simple question about a target sentence; and the Extended Range Drawing Test, a test of the ability to copy increasingly complex geometric figures. Pairs of tests were taken from this battery to generate two behavioral measures of hemispheric asymmetry: The first was a difference between the ranks of performance on the Syntax Comprehension Test and the Extended Range Drawing Test; the second consisted of the factor score on the WAIS for visuospatial construction minus tests of mental arithmetic and verbal memory. PET data were collected with eyes closed and ears plugged with cotton, and metabolic data were expressed as laterality or asymmetry indices.

Patients with DAT were generally less demented than those evaluated in most earlier studies. Despite the relatively mild degree of dementia, statistically significant metabolic deficits were found in parietal and temporal association areas, when DAT patients were compared with nondemented elderly control subjects. Although significant metabolic asymmetries were not found in the demented group, the degree of variance in the demented patients' metabolic indices for left versus right frontal, parietal, and temporal association areas was significantly greater than was evident in control subjects. Both behavioral measures of asymmetry correlated significantly with the metabolic measure of hemispheric asymmetry, and the syntax/drawing ratio also correlated with metabolic asymmetry observed regionally in frontal and parietal association areas. Relatively impaired language function was apparently associated with hypometabolism in the left hemisphere, and compromised drawing performance was apparently found in patients with reduced LCMRgl in the right hemisphere. In a subsequent report assessing 22 patients with probable Alzheimer's disease who were stratified for severity (Haxby et al. 1986), the correlations between behavioral asymmetries and metabolic asymmetries were evident in moderately demented patients, but not mildly demented patients.

Martin and colleagues (1986) administered a large battery of neuropsychological tests to 42 patients with a mean age of about 60 years (the duration of the dementia is not provided) who met rigorous criteria for the diagnosis of probable Alzheimer's disease. Twenty-one neurologically intact individuals, matched for age, sex, and education, served as control subjects. Psychometric assessment included measurements of general intelligence such as the Mattis Dementia Scale, the WAIS, and the WMS; language assessments such as the Boston Naming Test (a standardized assessment of visual confrontation naming, which has been normed for the age of the subject), a word fluency test (the number of animals named in 60 seconds), and the easy version of the paired-associate learning subtest of the WMS; and visuo-perceptuo-constructional tasks such as the block design subtest of the WAIS, the "copy" portion of the Rey-Osterreith Complex Figure Test, and the Mosaic Comparisons Test. Nineteen of the 42 demented subjects and 7 of the 21 control subjects also were studied with PET-FDG.

A factor analysis was performed on the results of patients' behavioral test performance. This yielded two factors: the first thought to be visuoconstructional and the second thought to be word-finding. A cluster analysis was then performed on the individual patient's factor scores. This statistical procedure yielded five clusters: a group of patients with primarily a visuoconstructional impairment, another group with primarily a word-finding deficit, and three groups of patients with relatively mild, moderate, or severe levels of global impairment. The PET studies revealed reduced LCMRgl in the left temporal regions of the patients with word-finding difficulties, hypometabolic indices in the right temporoparietal regions of the patients with impaired visuoconstructional skills, and bilateral temporoparietal hypometabolism in the globally impaired patients, which was somewhat more severe in the patients with greater cognitive impairments.

These studies of Haxby (1985, 1986) and Martin and colleagues (1986) represent significant improvements on earlier work from both behavioral and PET/metabolic perspectives. Through normalization techniques tighter metabolic data could be used to perform a differential analysis of patients based on the severity of dementia. Their behavioral data characterized the salient cognitive features of DAT in a manner more suitable for correlation with the metabolic data. Nevertheless further methodological improvements could help provide greater insights into brain-behavior interrelationships during normal aging and with DAT. Group data are important for establishing reliability and generalizablity, but reliance solely on group data may overlook important relations between behavior and metabolism in individual patients. Moreover the behavioral tasks used by Haxby and Martin are still very complex, tapping multiple levels of processing, any one of which may be compromised, thus leading to obvious difficulties with localization of brain functions. This may in part explain the frequent correlations observed between performance on one neuropsychological test and metabolism in multiple topographically disparate brain regions. The correlations described by Haxby and Martin conform well with traditional localizationist views, for example, anomia as result of left temporal lobe demage (Benson and Geschwind 1986). Indeed in a clinical setting this traditional approach to language assessment has stood the test of time well. It has brought very little explanatory power to the study of language deficits in brain-damaged adults, however. Nor has this approach been particularly helpful in constraining models of normal language processing.

An attempt may be made to infer the role played by a cerebral region after its destruction, but the clinical picture emerging after focal brain damage may not correspond with psychologically determined elements thought to be necessary for performing cognitive tasks. As we have noted, the performance of most clinical tests is highly complex, probably requiring the contribution of multiple cortical regions for successful completion. Tests of "verbal fluency" such as category naming, for example, require an appreciation of the definition of the target category, the retrieval of semantically accurate tokens, their translation into appropriate phonologic shapes, and finally their oral production through an executory motor plan. Consider for instance the clinical observation of nonfluent speech. Localizationist-based analyses of speech impairments frequently associate nonfluent speech with left frontal lesions, a *Broca's aphasia*. However nonfluent speech can also be seen following left temporal or right frontal lesions. It would be a serious analytical error to believe that an observed clinical failure to speak fluently following each of these three lesions carries the same psychological significance. A linguistic analysis of the speech in each case may reveal very different levels of language dysfunction—an agrammatism in one patient, a word-finding impairment in another, or an aprosodia in yet another. Furthermore adequate performance on any linguistic task presupposes sustained attention to the test at hand and continuous recall of the task's demands during its performance.

In summary any difficulties with the brain-behavior hypotheses examined by the studies reviewed here may not be inaccuracies in the measurement of LCMRgl, but may be due to the behavioral analyses used. This conclusion is underlined by a study of Foster and his coworkers (1986). Seventeen patients with probable Alzheimer's disease and 6 age-matched control subjects were asked to perform various gestures both to verbal command and to visual imitation. The results of this testing were correlated with regional glucose metabolic rates obtained from PET-FDG studies.

Demented patients' praxis performance was significantly inferior to that of control subjects, regardless of the manner of testing. Despite being asked to perform the identical gestures under the two presentation conditions, correlations with LCMRgl for each testing condition differed radically. Praxis testing to imitation correlated with metabolic measures in right posterior and temporal regions, whereas praxis testing to verbal command correlated with left temporal metabolic measures. In each case one metabolic data point in the contralateral prefrontal region correlated with praxis performance, presumably related to the execution of the target gesture. These findings suggest then that the particular manner of processing a cognitive task like executing a gesture may radically influence the cerebral regions brought to bear in such performance.

An Information Processing Approach to Naming Deficits in Dementia

Preliminary Data
One alternative to the localizationist approach to brain-behavior relations begins with an analysis of the psychological processes thought

to be necessary for the performance of a cognitive task. This strategy then attempts to determine the role played by various cortical regions in realizing the cognitive process.

Consider the task of confrontation naming, where the subject is asked to name a visually presented target. Naming has proved very difficult to localize because all naming failures appear quite similar clinically, regardless of the locus of the lesion with which the anomia is associated. This has led to the familiar clinical adage that "naming failures are not localizing." Some progress may be made in our understanding of naming deficits in pathological states if we begin by analyzing the processing elements that may contribute to naming. This would be especially valuable in dementia, where naming deficits are a prominent feature of the clinical presentation of the disease. A highly simplified analysis of confrontation naming might find that the subject engages first in a low-level visual analysis of the target. A higher-level visuoperceptual analysis interfacing with functional information may then be used as the input to a mental dictionary, where the lexical entry corresponding best to the semantic interpretation of the ongoing perceptual-functional processing can be found. The phonological shape of the target's name can then be accessed, and the vocal apparatus can finally articulate the word. In contrast to the behavioral approaches reviewed in the preceding section, we would not necessarily expect that this naming process would be localized to a single cerebral region. Our goal instead would be to identify the group of brain areas that may contribute to the performance of confrontation naming tasks. We could then proceed to design specific tests that would attempt to evaluate each individual processing component. Studies of patients with dementia have in fact suggested that naming deficits may occur for any number of reasons, possibly corresponding to some of the basic elements in this processing model. Thus Kirshner and colleagues (1984) have found that confrontation naming failures in demented patients vary as a function of the perceptual complexity of the target. Rochford (1971) believed that 55 percent of the naming errors in his patients with DAT were due to visual misperceptions. Lawson and Baker (1968) found that confrontation naming improves when the demented patient is allowed to handle the objects. Findings such as these have been taken to support the claim that naming may break down at the level of visuoperceptual analysis.

Others have argued, by comparison, that naming deficits in DAT may be due to a problem at the level of processing the semantic information contained in the mental dictionary. Thus Bayles and Tomoeda (1983), Martin and Fedio (1983), and Wilson and colleagues

(1981) have analyzed patients' naming errors and have found that misnamings are often semantically related to the target (for example, "dog" in response to a picture of a cat). Martin and Fedio (1983) and Ober and coworkers (1986) have also noted that demented patients often provide related but inaccurate items on a category naming task (such as "apple" in response to a request for the names of vegetables). Huff and colleagues (1986) examined naming in demented patients who were prescreened to minimize visuoperceptual problems. They found that impaired confrontation naming correlates with errors in selecting a picture's correct name from among several semantically related alternatives and with difficulties on a semantically based category naming task. Grober and her coworkers (1985) found that patients with DAT can identify attributes related to target words, but are impaired in their ability to rank the attributes in terms of their importance for the concept.

Still other researchers (for example, Miller and Hague 1975, Miller 1984, Rosen 1980) have noted that confrontation naming failures occur despite the demented patient's ability to recognize the target picture. These investigators found correlations between confrontation naming errors and performance on tests of verbal fluency such as category naming. Such data could be offered as support for the claim that the naming failure occurs at the level of word retrieval.

The traditional approach has been to view possibilities such as these as competing alternatives to explain naming deficits in dementia. This may be appropriate for patients who manifest a single focal lesion. Indeed much of the basic data underlying a processing-based analysis of naming failures has derived from studies of patients with strokes (for example, Caramazza and Berndt 1978, Geschwind 1967, Grossman, in press). However, this approach may not be appropriate for the study of dementia, where the functioning of multiple cortical regions may be impaired and correspondingly more than one processing element may be compromised. In assessments of naming deficits in patients with DAT, then, we would expect correlations between naming performance and metabolic indices in several cortical regions. Moreover it is possible that relative impairments of different aspects of naming would be reflected in corresponding degrees of regional hypometabolism on PET-FDG studies. To test this hypothesis, a variety of tasks assessing particular aspects of naming have been administered to patients with Alzheimer's disease who have also been studied with PET-FDG. Specifically we administered separate tasks that would evaluate patients' ability to (1) bring higer-level perceptual and semantic information to bear in the recognition of a word's referent, (2) superimpose reliable category boundaries on arrays of material taken from meaningful (fruits and vegetables) and nonmeaningful (colored shapes) domains, and (3) express their knowledge of a word's referents using both words and drawings.

Subjects
Four consecutive patients were evaluated at our laboratory during October 1987. They met rigorous criteria for the diagnosis of probable Alzheimer's disease. One of these patients (CON) in fact had definite Alzheimer's disease on the basis of a brain biopsy performed several months before evaluation. All patients had modified Hachinski ischemic scores of less than 4 (Rosen et al. 1980), were free of systemic or neurological diseases that could potentially interfere with intellectual functioning, were not thought to have primary major depression, had EEGs that revealed diffuse nonspecific background slowing, and had CT scans and MRIs that showed nonspecific ventricular and sulcal atrophy. The following is a brief description of each patient's clinical course, mental status assessment, and neurological examination.

CON
This 53-year-old right-handed man was admitted to evaluate a two-year history of progressive visual and memory disturbances. About eighteen months before admission the patient noted inability to construct a set of redwood furniture for his backyard, some difficulty putting on his clothes, and trouble finding his way around the area around his house. About six months before admission he began to notice difficulty understanding and remembering what he was reading. At this time his wife began to notice word-finding difficulty and an increasing frequency of literal paraphasias in the patient's spontaneous speech. Lightninglike jerks of any of his extremities, usually provoked by stress, were observed during the several months before admission. The patient had been hypertensive in the past, but his medication had been stopped during the year before admission. He had suffered a drug withdrawal reaction about eight years before admission, which had resulted in a seizure, transient myoglobinuria, and transient acute renal failure. He had consumed significant amounts of alcohol in the past, but had abstained for at least six years before admission.

General physical examination was unremarkable. Mental status assessment revealed reduced fluency in spontaneous speech due to word-finding pauses, with rare literal paraphasias. Oral reading was performed fluently. Writing to dictation and spontaneous writing were executed with mild difficulty. Written language comprehension was more impaired than oral language comprehension and was limited by grammatical complexity. Confrontation naming was mildly to moderately impaired and was frequently helped by semantic and phonological cues. Repetition was unimpaired. He was able to recall one out of three items after 5 minutes, but readily recognized the other two items. Memory for random shapes was noticeably impaired and improved minimally with a recognition procedure. Digit span was 5 forward, and pointing span was 3 forward. Visual constructions were performed poorly, and difficulty was encountered on a match-to-sample task using simple visual geometric shapes as stimuli. Calculations were poorly performed. Ideomotor apraxias were not detected. Neurologic examination revealed a mild increase in tone with minimal weakness in the left-upper extremity, some decrease of associated arm movements while walking, a left plantar reflex that was equivocal to extensor, and relatively impaired graphesthesia in the left palm. Many so-called frontal release signs were evident bilaterally. One or two brief myoclonic jerks were noticed during the patient's hospital admission.

DAL

This 62-year-old right-handed man was admitted for evaluation of a two-year history of gradually progressive forgetfulness, which limited his ability to shop for groceries or introduce his friends, spatial disorientation including difficulty walking in the area around his house without getting lost, and word-finding problems in spontaneous speech. His past medical history was significant for rheumatic fever as a child. He had taken dapsone for dermatitis herpetiformis, discontinued several months before admission. General physical examination was unremarkable. Mental status evaluation was remarkable for spontaneous speech, which was mildly halting due to some word-finding pauses. Deficits in language comprehension were more notable in oral than written modalities, and in neither case was comprehension obviously limited by grammatical complexity. Confrontation naming errors were evident, but occasionally could be circumvented through the use of semantic and phonologic cues. Repetition was not impaired. A digit span of 5 forward was attained, but he achieved a pointing span of only 3. Verbal memory was severely compromised, with an inability to retrieve any of three items after 5 minutes. Memory was somewhat better for geometric shapes. Long-term memory was also quite compromised. The patient had significant difficulty on constructional tasks, including poor production of geometric figures to copy or to command. He also had difficulty with a simple match-to-sample visuoperceptual task. Acalculia and apraxia were not detected. Neurologic examination was significant for some decreased graphesthesia on the left palm, a left plantar reflex that was equivocal to extensor, and some decreased associated movement of the right arm when walking.

PAR

This 66-year-old right-handed woman was admitted because of progressive deterioration in mental status beginning 18 months earlier. At that time she and her husband first noticed some word-finding problems in her spontaneous speech. About a year before admission she began to notice difficulty in getting dressed, negotiating moderately familiar areas of her hometown, and remembering the shopping list or remembering the route to the store from her recently acquired winter home. These limitations had forced her to stop working. She was taking no medications at admission.

General physical examination was unremarkable. Mental status testing revealed halting spontaneous speech attributable to word-finding pauses with multiple literal and verbal paraphasias. Oral reading was much more fluent. Comprehension of oral and written material was fair and did not appear to be limited by grammatical complexity. Confrontation naming was somewhat impaired, but improved in response to both semantic and phonologic cues. Digit span was 6 forward, but pointing span was only 2 forward. Short-term memory was mildly to moderately impaired. One out of 3 verbal or geometric items was recalled after 5 minutes, but a second item was readily recognized in each case. Constructional abilities were markedly impaired, although the patient performed simple match-to-sample visuoperceptual tasks accurately. Calculations were poorly performed. There was no finger agnosia. An apraxia was not found. There was a suggestion of left-sided neglect during double simultaneous stimulation in both visual and tactile modalities. Neurologic examination was significant for some minimal left-upper extremity weakness, a mild high-frequency postural tremor, a plantar reflex on the left that was extensor and on the right that was equivocal.

DUE

This 65-year-old right-handed man was admitted because of a three-year history of progressive difficulty with verbal memory, which limited his shopping, word-finding impairments, which prevented him from introducing his friends; and deterioration in his penmanship and spelling. These difficulties had required the patient to change his job to one that was less demanding. His past medical history was significant for rheumatic fever as a child. He had a 60-pack-year smoking history. He was taking no medication on admission.

Physical examination was unremarkable. Mental status assessment revealed spontaneous speech that was mildly halting due to word-finding pauses. Literal and verbal paraphasias were noted. Oral reading was more fluent, but paralexias were noted. Oral language comprehension was mildly impaired, but did not seem to be limited by grammatical complexity. Confrontation naming was impaired, and there was greater response to semantic cues than phonologic cues. Repetition was performed well. Only one of three verbal items was recalled after 5 minutes, and an additional item was recognized. Memory for random geometric shapes was equally impaired. Digit span was 4 forward, and pointing span was 4 forward. Long-term memory was moderately impaired. Mild difficulties were also evident in performing calculations and praxis testing. Neurologic examination was significant for a slight increase in tone and some minimal weakness in the right-upper extremity, some decrease in associated arm movements on the right while walking, a plantar reflex that was equivocal on the right, and a Hoffmann sign that was positive only on the right.

Materials for Behavioral Assessments

All patients were evaluated on a comprehensive battery of tasks designed to bring out deficits in perceptual, semantic, and lexical aspects of the confrontation naming process. The tasks were presented in a predetermined order in an attempt to minimize the likelihood that information from a previous task could be used to assist patients in their performance on a subsequent task. Tasks requiring the presentation of similar material but in two different modalities were presented in alternating order for each successive patient tested and were separated by other tests evaluating perfomance on tasks not pertinent to the specifically targeted test material. An order effect was not evident in the results. Following are brief descriptions of the tasks. More detailed descriptions can be obtained from the references provided.

Category Recognition (Grossman 1981)   Patients were asked to determine whether each stimulus presented to them was a member of the target superordinate category *vegetable*. Stimuli were either colored cartoonlike pictures or words printed in upper-case block letters. An identical list of category members, ranging from highly representative instances (for example, *carrot*) to less representative instances (for example, *avocado*), was used in both presentation modalities. Foils in the picture modality included equal numbers of semantic distractors (that is, members of other superordinate categories) and perceptual distractors (that is, errors in the color or shape of the depicted items). In each case half of each type of foil was semantically related to the target, whereas the other half was not related semantically. Foils in the verbal modality included semantic distractors or phonologic distractors (that is, nonmembers of the target category that sounded like and resembled orthographically the names of category members). We noted both the total number of errors and the types of errors made.

Category Borders (Grossman and Wilson 1987)   Patients were asked to determine whether a stimulus item was a highly representative, moderately representative, or less representative member of one of two related categories or was equally a member of both categories. The categories included pictures taken from a continuum of fruits and vegetables, printed names of the same fruits and vegetables, and the continuum of colored shapes between green/circle and blue/square. For each continuum, moreover, portions of the entire set were presented in a blocked fashion, with groups composed of items taken predominantly from one of the categories, from the other of the categories, or from a more equal distribution of items from both categories. Because items were presented on several occasions, but in different contexts, we could assess the stability of a category judgment by observing the degree of bias exerted on the judgment by the associated items. We scored the number of classification errors and the number of reclassifications when an item was presented in more than one context.

Hierarchical Relationships (Grossman 1978)   Patients were asked to make quantitative judgments about whether a word contains more items of a superordinate category or more of one of the category's members (for example, "Are there more vegetables or more cucumbers?"). We scored the number of incorrect responses.

Category Naming (Grossman 1981)   Patients were asked to name as many fruits and as many vegetables as they could in 60 seconds. We scored the number of responses, the number of noncategory members provided, and the relatedness of an error to the target category.

Category Drawing (Grossman, in press)   Patients were asked to use eight colored pens to draw as many members of a target category (for example, fruits or vegetables) as they could in 180 seconds. We scored the number of responses, the number of noncategory responses provided, and the recognizability of a picture on a scale devised for this task ranging from 1.00, or highly recognizable, to 7.00, unrecognizable.

Materials for Metabolic Assessments
After an overnight fast patients were given FDG (0.1 miC/kg) by catheter placed in an antecubital vein. They rested quietly with eyes and ears unoccluded during the 40-minute period of FDG uptake into the brain before PET scanning, during which time blood samples were obtained from a radial artery catheter. Images were obtained using a PETT V tomograph, which has an effective in-plane resolution of 16.5 mm (full width at half maximum). Seven cross-sectional brain images (17.4 mm thick) were obtained simultaneously, and two sets of scans were obtained, yielding 14 images per session. Between scanning sets each patient was displaced cephalad half of the thickness of a slice, so that slices from the two scans were intercalated. A minimum of one million counts per slice were collected. Metabolic rates were calculated using the operational equation of Sokoloff and colleagues (1977), as modified by Phelps and colleagues (1979), to include k_4. Lumped constant and average rate constants were determined in our laboratory from 9 young normal subjects (Reivich et al. 1985). Anatomic regions of interest (ROIs) were placed automatically on the PET images, as described by Alavi and coworkers (1986), using a dedicated image analysis system. These ROIs were determined from average anatomic locations based on four cadaver brains. A normalization ratio method of data analysis for LCMRgl was used, the denominator being a weighted average of LCMRgl from all ROIs included in the anatomic atlas overlay (an approximate whole-brain value). The results for the demented patients were compared with PET data obtained from 18 nondemented control subjects matched for age and education. We report only hypometabolic abnormalities in our patients' PET scans that differ from the same region of control patients' PET scans by at least 3 standard deviations (a conservative significance level allowing for multiple comparisons).

Results
Clinical mental status assessment of the four patients suggests that they have deficits consistent at least with a bilateral temporoparietal syndrome. Thus constructional and visuoperceptual tasks are performed poorly, praxis testing and calculations are occasionally impaired, and several aspects of language function are compromised,

Table 4.1
Patient Test Results—Components of Confrontation Naming

Test	Score			
	CON	DAL	PAR	DUE
Mini Mental State Examination (30 = perfect score)	20	26	20	28
Confrontation naming[a]	55	65	70	60
Category recognition[a]				
Pictures	62	78	84	76
Foils-related	25	30	70	70
Foils-unrelated	85	90	80	90
Words	98	87	91	93
Foils-related	100	100	90	100
Foils-unrelated	100	100	100	100
Category borders				
Perceptual[b]	88	100	94	82
Reclassifications[c]	56	47	29	41
Semantic Pictures[b]	75	90	95	95
Reclassifications[c]	30	40	55	25
Semantic words[b]	95	80	95	100
Reclassifications[c]	25	30	30	20
Category naming				
Oral[d]	38	38	56	50
Errors[e]	12	0	0	13
Drawing[d]	29	38	33	46
Errors[e]	0	11	13	28
Perceptual accuracy	fair to poor	fair	poor	fair

[a] percent correct
[b] percent not misclassified
[c] percent reclassifications of appropriately classified items
[d] percent of expected production per unit time
[e] percent of items that are semantically inaccurate
See text for further description of tests and results.

including oral and written comprehension, confrontation naming, spelling, and writing. Our patients also exhibit memory impairments. Taken together, these deficits are typical of a patient with early features of Alzheimer's disease. Indeed in all patients the MMSE was greater than 20, a level of impairment taken by most investigators to indicate a mild dementia.

The preliminary data from our confrontation naming battery are presented in table 4.1 for each patient. Control subjects matched for age and education almost never made any errors on our tasks. The category drawing output of most neurologically intact adults approached 10 over a 3-minute period, and their pictures were quite recognizable, attaining a recognizability score of 2.35 on our 1.00-to-7.00 scale. The category naming output of our controls was a little less than 15 over a 60-second period. Pictures or names that were not members of the target category were rarely provided as responses.

CON performed at random levels, according to the binomial test, on the picture version of the category recognition task. His greatest impediment to recognizing members of the target category was in his failure to reject perceptual distractors, regardless of their relation to the target category. This is in sharp contrast to his category recognition performance when the stimuli consisted of printed words, where he recognized members of the target category almost flawlessly. When asked to use this visuoperceptual information to judge the degree of a pictured item's category membership in one of two related categories on the category borders task, CON made several classification errors. Moreover his categories were quite unstable when asked to judge pictures because he reclassified several items when they were presented again amidst a different set of items. By comparison he made no classification errors when asked to classify printed words, and he reclassified only one printed word upon second presentation. CON also made one error when asked to classify colored geometric shapes, the only control or demented subject to make such an error. He reclassified one of these stimulus items when presented again among different items. CON produced a very small number of drawings (on average 3.5 per target category) on the category drawing task. The drawings that he did produce were poorly recognizable (about 4 on our scale of 1.00 to 7.00). By comparison he produced 6 names for each category on the category naming task, and only one of these was not a category member. CON was accurate in his responses to questions about sentences describing semantic hierarchical relations. In summary these findings suggest difficulty at the level of the perceptuosemantic interpretation of pictures, with his lexical access to printed words relatively intact.

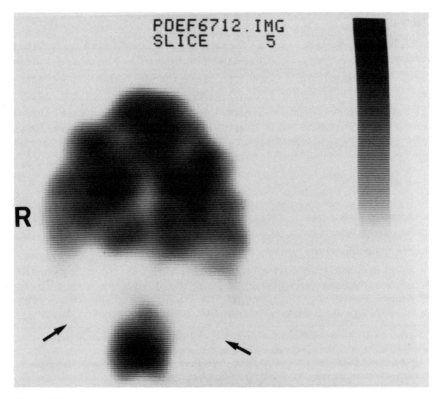

Figure 4.1
Patient CON's PET scan of local cerebral glucose metabolism at level of basal ganglia and thalamus, demonstrating marked bilateral parietal and lateral occipital hypometabolism (arrows). This is somewhat more extensive on the right. (See table 4.2 for quantitative data.)

Visual inspection of CON's PET scan revealed reduced glucose metabolism in parietal and some occipital brain regions bilaterally, although the primary visual cortex was largely spared (figure 4.1). Quantitative LCMRgl measures, provided in table 4.2, revealed hypometabolism differing in magnitude from control subjects by at least 3 standard deviations in the right inferior parietal lobule, left calcarine visual association cortex, and bilateral superior parietal and parietooccipital junction (visual association) cortices.

DAL, like CON, encountered difficulty with the picture version of the category recognition task, approaching random levels of performance. He differed from CON, however, because his errors were not predominantly in the realm of perceptual appreciation, but rather consisted of difficulty in discriminating between actual members of

Table 4.2
Summary of Quantitative Normalized PET Metabolic Rates for Glucose (CMRgl)

Region	Controls (SD)		CON	DAL	PAR	DUE
L post. sup. temporal gyrus	111	(8)	94[a]	81[b]	109	111
R	111	(9)	89[a]	82[b]	102	99
L Heschel's gyrus	118	(13)	90[a]	89[a]	114	117
R	118	(7)	112	97[a]	113	114
L inferior parietal lobule	76	(10)	51[a]	73	64	83
R	77	(7)	41[d]	54[b]	45[c]	74
L parietal visual association cortex	98	(9)	53[c]	123	73[a]	112
R	100	(9)	55[c]	89	52[d]	102
L superior parietal lobule	139	(10)	90[c]	143	141	145
R	139	(9)	109[b]	117[a]	120	152
L anterior calcarine cortex	140	(18)	101[a]	154	121	145
R	142	(19)	104[a]	147	120	138
L calcarine association cortex (Brodmann area 18)	106	(10)	57[d]	130	100	110
R	109	(9)	88[a]	97	90[a]	102

Metabolic rates are normalized to a computed whole-brain CMRgl determined by averaging the rates for all regions defined by the anatomic atlas.
Superscripts indicate number of standard deviations (SD) below the mean metabolic rate for the control group: [a] $\geq$ 2 SD; [b] $\geq$ 3 SD; [c] $\geq$ 4 SD; [d] $\geq$ 5 SD.

the target category and related nonmembers. He had less difficulty in making category recognition judgments with verbal stimuli, but any errors that were made again consisted of failures in discriminating between category members and related nonmembers. DAL also made errors when asked to determine the degree of a picture's category membership in one of two related categories. Unlike CON he also made many errors when classifying printed words, but no errors when classifying colored shapes. For all three types of stimuli, DAL's judgments were quite stable because he never reclassified a stimulus when presented again amidst a different set of items. Sentences describing semantically based hierarchical relationships were answered correctly. DAL was able to draw 4.5 items on average for each category in the category drawing task, and one of his items was not a member of the target category. His recognizability score was 2.75. DAL also offered 6 names on average for each category in the category naming task, all of the items being members of the targeted category. This pattern of findings suggests that DAL's difficulty may be at the level of appreciating the appropriate meaning of concepts such as vegetable.

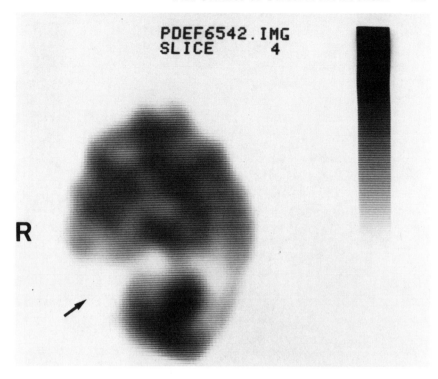

Figure 4.2
Patient DAL's PET scan of local cerebral glucose metabolism at level of basal ganglia-thalamus. Note asymmetric hypometabolism affecting predominantly the right inferior parietal lobule at this level (arrow).

Visual inspection of the PET scan performed on DAL revealed hypometabolism in posterior temporal and parietal regions bilaterally. As can be seen in figure 4.2, this is pronounced in the right hemisphere. Quantitative LCMRgl indices that differed from those of control subjects by at least 3 standard deviations included the right inferior parietal lobule and posterior superior temporal cortices bilaterally (table 4.2).

PAR performed at better-than-random levels on the category recognition task with words and pictures, with any errors consisting mostly of perceptual difficulties. Despite this adequate level of performance on a task requiring visuoperceptual appreciation, which would eventually contribute to a semantic judgment, PAR's performance on a match-to-sample task involving geometric shapes was random. Unlike CON then there was an apparent dissociation in PAR's performance between meaningless visuoperceptual judgments

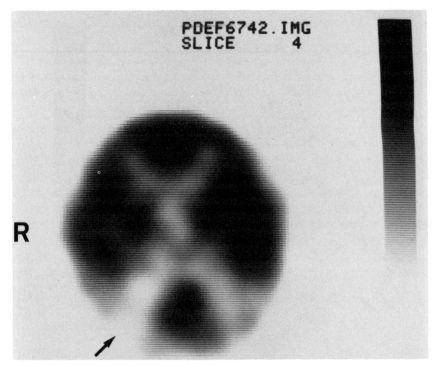

Figure 4.3
Patient PAR's PET scan of local cerebral glucose metabolism at level of basal ganglia, showing asymmetric hypometabolism affecting primarily the right inferior parietal-visual association areas (arrow).

and visuoperceptual judgments that might be required for subsequent semantic decisions. PAR made no errors when judging the degree to which a picture is a member of one or the other related categories and also did not err when judging printed words or colored shapes. For the most part her category judgments were also quite stable in that she rarely reclassified an item upon second presentation. Semantically based hierarchical relationships were well appreciated. PAR produced on average 4 items for each category on the category drawing task, one of the items in total being not a member of the category. Her recognizability score was about 6, consistent with her impaired visuoperceptual performance. PAR named 9 items for each category on the category naming task, and none of these items were errors. We interpret these results as suggesting a visuoperceptual processing deficit that does not interfere with other aspects of naming.

Visual inspection of PAR's PET scan revealed hypometabolism predominantly in inferior parietal regions of the right hemisphere, although subtle deficits in left inferior parietal glucose metabolism were also evident (figure 4.3). A quantitative comparison of her PET scan with the results of age-matched nondemented control subjects revealed significantly reduced LCMRgl indices in the right inferior parietal lobule and right visual association cortex (table 4.2).

DUE encountered mild levels of difficulty with the picture version of the category recognition task, his errors usually being due to difficulty in discriminating between category members and related nonmembers. He encountered less difficulty in judging printed words. DUE made no errors on the category borders task, where he was asked to determine the degree of a picture's membership in one of two related categories. Although he also did not err when judging printed words, he reclassified colored shapes on 3 occasions. He responded accurately to questions about sentences describing semantically based hierarchical relationships. DUE produced 5.5 pictures on average for each target category on the category drawing task, and 3 items in total were not members of the target category. The recognizability score of DUE's pictures was about 3. He named on average 8 items for each category on the category naming task, and offered 2 items in total that were not members of the target category.

Visual inspection of DUE's PET scan revealed minimal regional hypometabolism. Quantitative of LCMRgl indices, when compared with the PET results from age-matched control subjects, failed to reveal any significantly reduced metabolic levels.

Discussion: The Relation between Behavioral and Metabolic Assessments in Patients with Alzheimer's Disease

We have reviewed the literature on PET-glucose metabolic studies in patients with DAT and the attempts to correlate these results with behavioral observations of the same patients. The level of behavioral analysis used in these PET studies has often failed to capture an appropriate perspective on the clinical deficits evident in the patients. This is not because of a lack of care or expertise on the part of investigators, but rather because of a natural evolution in the level of sophistication brought to these studies. Nevertheless one consequence of this shortcoming is that clinical deficits in areas such as naming often seem forced into expected brain regions, even when there might be evidence that the clinical deficit correlates with other cortical regions as well.

We have taken the view that tasks such as confrontation naming are highly complex and that they should not be expected to be localized to a single brain region. Certainly there may be a critical region of the brain that may preclude naming if compromised. We felt it likely, however, that other brain regions would also contribute to the naming process. Therefore we have developed a very simple model of naming to test the hypothesis that a network of brain regions subserves tasks like naming and that relative degrees of hypometabolism in different cortical regions might reflect corresponding degrees of difficulty, with each step contributing to the process of confrontation naming.

Our results offer some preliminary support for our hypothesis. CON, for example, encountered considerable difficulty in using the information derived from his visuoperceptual analysis of the target to help in the naming process. Correspondingly he exhibited the greatest degree of glucose hypometabolism in his right inferior parietal lobule. DAL exhibited a moderate degree of hypometabolism in right parietal cortex, and he also manifested some impairments in visuoperceptual aspects of naming, but to a lesser degree than CON. CON also exhibited considerable hypometabolism in right parietooccipital association cortex, but there are other findings that suggest that this region may not be critical to the visuoperceptual processing required particularly for naming. For example, PAR was found to have significant hypometabolic indices in right parietooccipital association cortex, but did not exhibit the same difficulty with visual versions of the category judgment and category borders tasks. Both CON and DAL encountered difficulty with a visuoperceptual match-to-sample task. This right parietooccipital visual association area may therefore play a critical role in perceptual processing at a level other than that directly needed for accurate confrontation naming.

Let us now consider the semantic judgments that are made on the basis of this visuoperceptual information. DAL exhibited significant difficulty in making accurate categorization judgments, often misclassifying items. He clearly made many more of this type of error than did other patients, and he was also the only patient to have significant glucose metabolic deficits in left posterior superior temporal cortex. CON had a lesser degree of hypometabolism in the same cortical region, but he also had a less severe impairment in semantic aspects of categorization. Just as there are aspects of visuoperceptual processing that may contribute to confrontation naming only indirectly, there also appear to be aspects of lexical semantics that are not necessarily compromised in DAT, even though processing components pertinent to naming may be impaired. The appreciation of lexical semantics in the context of sentence comprehension (that is, sentences probing hierarchical relationships) was relatively preserved in both CON and DAL.

It is also of interest that DUE exhibited an inconsistent behavioral profile on our battery. His deficits did not seem to respect our hypothesized model for confrontation naming. He was also the only patient who failed to manifest any focal glucose metabolic abnormalities.

Certainly our data are not free of problems. The most obvious difficulty is the small sample. Our thesis is that it is important to relate the behavioral findings in *individuals* to their metabolic patterns. But it is equally important to document the reliability of these findings in a larger number of subjects. We wish to emphasize the preliminary and exploratory nature of our findings. Indeed it is the approach that we wish to underline. Moreover we are not using the PET scan as another expensive tool for identifying a structural lesion already detected by CT or MRI. Rather, we hope to portray the multifocal breakdown of a complex process such as naming by identifying an interactive metabolic network that may be selectively compromised. It could be argued that we are simply localizationists in PET clothing, attributing particular aspects of complex behavior to discrete cortical regions. However, we believe that we are adopting a somewhat different approach. In this context we are striving to achieve an appropriate level of behavioral analysis. One might criticize our selection of superordinate categories (fruits and vegetables) because items in these classes may have a special status in the mental dictionary (for example, Hart et al. 1985). Consequently we would not want to claim that our findings are necessarily applicable to all semantic domains until there is corroborating empirical evidence from other sources. Nevertheless we strongly believe that traditional characterizations of behavioral deficits, tightly yoked to clinical observations, have not adequately advanced our knowledge of the physiological basis of language competence and performance. Adopting a structuralist approach to linguistics and the information-processing techniques used to analyze behavior, we can attempt to test the hypothesis that particular elements of specific language-processing tasks are associated with particular nodes in a network of brain regions. Our approach makes no specific claims with respect to rigidly defined connectionist requirements for lesion localization, but allows for some empirical variation in the anatomical substrate of a process from individual to individual and for changes within a given individual over time. Through careful observations of both cognitive and metabolic activity, we hope to fashion a model of brain functioning that is compatible with our knowledge of cognition and to describe cognitive functioning in a fashion that respects opposing constraints implied by physiological studies of the normal and diseased human brain.

Acknowledgment

This work was supported by USPHS Program Project Grant NS 14867, NIA Teaching Nursing Home Award AG-03934, and NIH Clinical Research Center Grant 5-M01-R00040.

References

Appell, J., Kertesz, A., and Fisman, M. (1982). A study of language functioning in Alzheimer patients. *Brain and Language* 17: 73–91.

Alavi, A., Dann, R., Chawluk, J., Alavi, J., Kushner, M., and Reivich, M. (1986). Positron emission tomography of regional cerebral glucose metabolism. *Seminars in Nuclear Medicine* 16: 2–34.

Bayles, K., and Tomoeda, C. (1983). Confrontation naming impairment in dementia. *Brain and Language* 19: 98–114.

Becker, J., Boller, F., Saxton, J., and McGonigle-Gibson, K. (1987). Normal rates of forgetting of verbal and non-verbal material in Alzheimer's disease. *Cortex* 23: 59–72.

Benson, D., and Geschwind, N. (1985). Aphasia and related disorders: A clinical approach. IN M.-M. Mesulam (Ed.) *Principles of Behavioral Neurology*. Philadelphia: Davis.

Benson, D., Kuhl, D., Hawkins, R., Phelps, M., Cummings, J., and Tsai, S. (1983). The fluoro-deoxyglucose 18-F scan in Alzheimer's disease and multi-infarct dementia. *Archives of Neurology* 40: 711–714.

Brodie, J., Christman, D., and Corona, J. (1984). Patterns of metabolic activity in the treatment of schizophrenia. *Annals of Neurology* 13 (Supplement): S166–S169.

Brouwers, P., Cox, C., Martin, A., Chase, T., and Fedio, P. (1984). Differential perceptuo-spatial impairment in Huntington's and Alzheimer's dementias. *Archives of Neurology* 41: 1073–1076.

Brun, A., and Englund, E. (1986). Brain changes in dementia of Alzheimer's type relevant to new imaging diagnostic methods. *Progress in Neuropsychopharmacology and Biological Psychiatry* 10: 309–321.

Buchsbaum, M., DeLisi, L., and Holcomb, H. (1984). Anteroposterior gradients in cerebral glucose use in schizophrenia and affective disorders. *Archives of General Psychiatry* 41: 1159–1166.

Caramazza, A., and Berndt, R. (1978). Syntactic and semantic processes in aphasia: A review of the literature. *Psychological Review* 85: 898–918.

Charness, M. E., and DeLaPaz, R. L. (1987). Mamillary body atrophy in Wernicke's encephalopathy: Antemortem identification using magnetic resonance imaging. *Annals of Neurology* 22: 595–600.

Chase, T., Fedio, P., Foster, N., Brooks, R., DiChiro, G., and Mansi, L. (1984a). Weschler adult intelligence scale performance: Cortical localization of fluorodeoxyglucose F-18 positron emission tomography. *Archives of Neurology* 41: 1244–1247.

Chase, T., Foster, N., Fedio, P., Brooks, R., Mansi, L., and DiChiro, G. (1984b). Regional cortical dysfunction in Alzheimer's disease as determined by positron emission tomography. *Annals of Neurology* 15 (Supplement): S170–S174.

Chawluk, J. B., Alavi, A., Hurtig, H., Dann, R., Rosen, M., Kushner, M., Silver, F., and Reivich, M. (1985). Altered patterns of regional cerebral glucose metabolism in aging and dementia. *Journal of Cerebral Blood Flow and Metabolism* 5 (Supplement 1): 121–122.

Chui, H., Teng, E., Henderson, V., and Moy, A. (1985). Clinical subtypes of dementia of the Alzheimer type. *Neurology* 35: 1544–1550.

Corkin, S. (1982). Some relationships between global amnesia and the memory impairments in Alzheimer's disease. In S. Corkin, K. Davis, J. Growdon, E. Usdin, and R. Wurtman (Eds.) *Alzheimer's Disease: A Report of Progress in Research.* New York: Raven Press.

Corkin, S., Growdon, J., Nissen, M., Huff, F., Freed, D., and Sagar, H. (1984). Recent advances in the neuropsychological study of Alzheimer's disease. In R. Wurtman, S. Corkin, and J. Growdon (Eds.) *Alzheimer's Disease: Advances in Basic Research and Therapies.* Cambridge: Center for Brain Sciences and Metabolism Trust.

Critchley, M. (1964). The neurology of psychotic speech. *British Journal of Psychiatry* 40: 353.

Cummings, J., Benson, D., Hill, M., and Read, S. (1985). Aphasia in dementia of the Alzheimer type. *Neurology* 35: 394–396.

Cutler, N., Haxby, J., Durar, R., Grady, C., Moore, A., Parisi, J., White, J., Heston, L., Margolin, R., and Rapoport, S. (1985a). Brain metabolism as measured with positron emission tomography: Serial assessment in a patient with familial Alzheimer's disease. *Neurology* 35: 1556–1561.

Cutler, N., Haxby, J., Duara, R., Grady, C., Kay, A., Kessler, R., Sundaram, M., and Rapoport, S. (1985b). Clinical history, brain metabolism and neuropsychological function in Alzheimer's disease. *Annals of Neurology* 18: 298–309.

D'Antona, R., Baron, J.-C., Samson, Y., Serdaru, M., Viader, F., Agid, Y., and Cambier, J. (1985). Subcortical dementia: Frontal cortex hypometabolism detected by positron tomography in patients with progressive supranuclear palsy. *Brain* 108: 785–799.

Dastur, D., Lane, M., Hansen, D., Kety, S., Butler R., Perlin, S., and Sokoloff, L. (1963). Effects of aging on cerebral circulation and metabolism in man. In Birren, Butler, Greenhouse, Sokoloff, and Yarrow (Eds.) *Human Aging: A Biological and Behavioral Study.* U. S. Dept. HEW, PHS Publication No. 986. Washington: U. S. Govt. Printing Office.

DeLeon, M., Ferris S., George, A., Reisberg, B., Christman, D., Kricheff, I., and Wolf, A. (1983). Computed tomography and positron emission transaxial tomography evaluations of normal aging and Alzheimer's disease. *Journal of Cerebral Blood Flow and Metabolism* 3: 391–394.

Duara, R., Grady, C., Haxby, J., Ingvar, D., Sokoloff, L., Margolin, R., Manning, R., Cutler, N., and Rapoport, S. (1984). Human brain glucose utilization and cognitive function in relation to age. *Annuals of Neurology* 16: 702–713.

Duara, R., Grady, C., Haxby, J., Sundaram, M., Cutler, N., Heston, L., Moore, A., Schlageter, N., Larson, S., and Rapoport, S. (1986). Positron emission tomography in Alzheimer's disease. *Neurology* 36: 879–887.

Duara, R., Margolin, Robertson-Tschabo, E., London, E., Schwartz, M., Renfrew, J., Koziarz, B., Sundaram, M., Grady, C., Moore, A., Ingvar, D., Sokoloff, L., Weingartner, H., Kessler, R., Manning, R., Channing, M., Cutler, N., and Rapoport, S. (1983). Cerebral glucose utilization as measured with positron emission tomography in 21 resting healthy men between the ages of 21 and 83 years. *Brain* 106: 761–775.

Engel, J., Jr. (1984). The use of positron emission tomographic scanning in epilepsy. *Annals of Neurology* 15(suppl.): S180–S191.

Engel, J., Kuhl, D., Phelps, M., and Mazziotta, J. (1982). Interictal cerebral glucose metabolism in partial epilepsy and its relation to EEG changes. *Annals of Neurology* 12: 510–517.

Eslinger, P., and Damasio, A. (1986). Preserved motor learning in Alzheimer's disease: Implications for anatomy and behavior. *Journal of Neuroscience* 6: 3006–3009.

Ferris, S., DeLeon, M., Wolf, A., George, A., Reisberg, B., Brodie, J., Gentes, C., Christman, D., and Fowler, J. (1983). Regional metabolism and cognitive deficits in aging and senile dementia. In D. Samuel, S. Algeri, S. Gershon, V. Grimm, and G. Toffano (Eds.) *Aging of the Brain.* NY: Raven Press.

Filley, C., Kelly, J., and Heaton, R. (1986). Neuropsychologic features of early- and late-onset Alzheimer's disease. *Archives of Neurology* 43: 574–576.

Folstein, M., Anthony, J., Parhad, I., Duffy, B., and Gruenberg, E. (1985). The meaning of cognitive impairment in the elderly. *Journal of the American Geriatric Society* 33: 228–235.

Folstein, M., Folstein, S., and McHugh, P. (1975). Mini Mental State: A practical method for grading the cognitive state of patients for the clinician. *Journal of Psychiatry Research* 12: 189–198.

Foster, N., Chase, T., Fedio, P., Patronas, N., Brooks, R., and DiChiro, G. (1983). Alzheimer's disease: Focal changes shown by positron emission tomography. *Neurology* 33: 961–965.

Foster, N., Chase, T., Mansi, L., Brooks, R., Fedio, P., Patronas, N., and DiChiro, G. (1984). Cortical abnormalities in Alzheimer's disease. *Annals of Neurology* 16: 649–654.

Foster, N., Chase, T., Patronas, N., Gillespie, M., and Fedio, P. (1986). Cerebral mapping of apraxia in Alzheimer's disease by positron emission tomography. *Annals of Neurology* 19: 139–143.

Frackowiak, R., and Gibbs, J. (1983). Cerebral metabolism and blood flow in normal and pathological aging. In Magistretti (Ed.) *Functional Radionuclide Imaging of the Brain.* New York: Raven Press.

Frackowiak, R., Lenzi, G., Jones, T., and Heather, J. (1980). Quantitative measurement of cerebral blood flow and oxgyen metabolism in man using 15O and positron emission tomography. *Journal of Computer Assisted Tomography* 4: 727–736.

Frackowiak, R., Pozzillic, C., Legg, N., Duboulay, G., Marshall, J., Lenzi, G., and Jones, T. (1981). Regional cerebral oxygen supply and utilization in dementia: A clinical and psychological study with oxygen-15 and positron tomography. *Brain* 104: 752–778.

Frackowiak, R., Wise, R., Gibbs, J., and Jones, T. (1984). Positron emission tomographic studies in aging and cerebrovascular disease at Hammersmith Hospital. *Annals of Neurology* 15 (Supplement): S112–S118.

Friedland, R., Brun, A., and Budinger, T. (1985a). Pathological and positron emission tomographic correlations in Alzheimer's disease. *Lancet* 1: 228.

Friedland, R., Budinger, T., Koss, E., and Ober, B. (1985b). Alzheimer's disease: Anterior-posterior and lateral hemispheric alterations in cortical glucose utilization. *Neuroscience Letters* 53: 235–240.

Fuld, P., Katzman, R., Davies, P., and Terry, R. (1981). Intrusions as a sign of Alzheimer dementia: Chemical and pathological verification. *Annals of Neurology* 11: 155–159.

Gebhardt, C., Naeser, M., and Butters, N. (1984). Computerized measures of CT scans of alcoholics. *Alcohol* 1: 133–140.

Geschwind, N. (1967). The varieties of naming errors. *Cortex* 3: 97–112.

Grady, C., Haxby, J., and Schlageter, N. (1986). Stability of metabolic and neuropsychological asymmetries in dementia of the Alzheimer type. *Neurology* 36:

Grober, E. (1985). Encoding of item-specific information in Alzheimer's disease. *Journal of Clinical and Experimental Neuropsychology* 7: 614.

Grober, E., Buschke, H., Kawas, C., and Fuld, P. (1985). Impaired ranking of semantic attributes in dementia. *Brain and Language* 26: 276–286.

Grossman, M. (1978). The game of the name: An examination of linguistic reference after brain damage. *Brain and Language* 5: 112–119.

Grossman, M. (1981). A bird is a bird is a bird: Marking reference within and without a superordinate category. *Brain and Language* 12: 313–331.

Grossman, M. (1982). Reversal operations after brain damage. *Brain and Cognition* 1: 331–359.

Grossman, M. (1988). Drawing deficits in brain-damaged patients' freehand pictures. *Brain and Cognition* 8: 187–213.

Grossman, M. (submitted). Seeing and believing: Perceptual and semantic contributions to recognizing category membership in focal brain damage.

Grossman, M., and Wilson, M. (1987). Stimulus categorization by brain-damaged patients. *Brain and Cognition* 6: 55–71.

Gustafson, L., Hagberg, B., and Ingvar, D. H. (1978). Speech disturbances in presenile dementia related to local cerebral blood flow abnormalities in the dominant hemisphere. *Brain and Language* 5: 102–118.

Hachinski, V., Iliff, L., Zilkha, E., DuBoulay, G., McAllister, V., Marshall, J., Russell, R., and Lindsay, S. (1975). Cerebral blood flow in dementia. *Archives of Neurology* 32: 632–637.

Hagberg, B., and Ingvar, D. H. (1976). Cognitive reduction in presenile dementia related to regional abnormalities of the cerebral blood flow. *British Journal of Psychiatry* 128: 209–222.

Hart, J., Berndt, R. S., and Caramazza, A. (1985). Category-specific naming deficit following cerebral infarction. *Nature* 316: 439–440.

Haxby, J., Duara, R., Grady, C., Cutler, N., and Rapoport, S. (1985). Relations between neuropsychological and cerebral metabolic asymmetries in early Alzheimer's disease. *Journal of Cerebral Blood Flow and Metabolism* 5: 193–200.

Haxby, J., Grady, C., Duara, R., Schlageter, N., Berg, G., and Rapoport, S. (1986). Neocortical metabolic abnormalities precede nonmemory cognitive defects in early Alzheimer's-type dementia. *Archives of Neurology* 43: 882–885.

Haxby, J., and Rapoport, S. (1986). Abnormalities of regional brain metabolism in Alzheimer's disease and their relation to functional impairment. *Progress in Neuropsychopharmacology and Biological Psychiatry* 10: 427–438.

Hier, D., Hagenlocker, K., and Shindler, A. (1985). Language disintegration and dementia: Effects of etiology and severity. *Brain and Language* 25: 117–133.

Hochanadel, G., and Kaplan, E. (1983). Neuropsychology of normal aging. In M. Albert (Ed.) *Aging and Dementia*. New York: Oxford University Press.

Horwitz, B., Duara, R., and Rapoport, S. I. (1984). Intercorrelations of glucose metabolic rates between brain regions: Application to healthy males in a state of reduced sensory input. *Journal of Cerebral Blood Flow and Metabolism* 4: 484–499.

Horwitz, B., Duara, R., and Rapoport, S. (1986). Age differences in intercorrelations between region cerebral metabolic rates for glucose. *Annuals of Neurology* 19: 60–67.

Huff, F., Becker, J., Belle, S., Nebes, R., Holland, A., and Boller, F. (1987). Cognitive deficits and clinical diagnosis of Alzheimer's disease. *Neurology* 37: 1119–1124.

Huff, F., Corkin, S., and Growdon, J. (1986). Semantic impairment and anomia in Alzheimer's disease. *Brain and Language* 28: 235–249.

Ingvar, D. H., and Gustafson, L. (1970). Regional cerebral blood flow in organic dementia with early onset. *Acta Neurologica Scandinavica* 43: 42–73.

Jamieson, D. G., Chawluk, J. B., Alavi, A., Hurtig, H. I., Rosen, M., Bais, S., Dann, R., Kushner, M., and Reivich, M. (1987). The effect of disease severity on local cerebral glucose metabolism in Alzheimer's disease. *Journal of Cerebral Blood Flow and Metabolism* 7 (Supplement 1): S410.

Kertesz, A. (1985). Aphasia. In J. Frederiks (Ed.) *Handbook of Clinical Neurology*. Vol. 45. Le Hague: Elsevier/North Holland Press.

Kety, S. (1956). Human cerebral blood flow and oxygen consumption as related to aging. *Research Publications for the Association for Research in Nervous and Mental Disease* 35: 31–45.

Kety, S., and Schmidt, C. F. (1948). The nitrous oxide method for the quantitative determination of cerebral blood flow in man: Theory, procedure, and normal values. *Journal of Clinical Investigation* 27: 476–483.

Kirshner, H., Webb, W., and Kelly, M. (1984). The naming disorder of dementia. *Neuropsychologia* 22: 23–30.

Knopman, D., and Nissen, M. (1987). Implicit learning in patients with probable Alzheimer's disease. *Neurology* 37: 784–788.

Kopelman, M. (1985). Rates of forgetting in Alzheimer-type dementia and Korsakoff's syndrome. *Neuropsychologia* 23: 623–638.

Koss, E., Friedland, R., Ober, B., and Jagust, W. (1985). Differences in lateral hemispheric asymmetries of glucose utilization between early- and late-onset Alzheimer-type dementia. *American Journal of Psychiatry* 142: 638–640.

Kuhl, D., Metter, E., and Riege, W. (1985). Patterns of cerebral glucose utilization in depression, multiple infarct dementia, and Alzheimer's disease. *Research Publications of the Association for Research in Nervous and Mental Disease* 63: 211–226.

Kuhl, D., Metter, E., Riege, W., and Markham, C. (1984). Patterns of cerebral glucose utilization in Parkinson's disease and Huntington's disease. *Annuals of Neurology* 15 (Supplement): S119–S125.

Lassen, N. A., and Ingvar, D. H. (1963). Regional cerebral blood flow measurement in man. *Archives of Neurology* 9: 615–622.

Lawson, J., and Baker, M. (1968). The assessment of nominal dysphasia in dementia: The use of reaction time measures. *British Journal of Medical Psychology* 41: 411–414.

Loewenstein, D., Yoshii, F., Barker, W. W., Apicella, A., Emran, A., Chang, J. Y., and Duara, R. (1987). Predominant left hemisphere metabolic deficit predicts early manifestation of dementia. *Journal of Cerebral Blood Flow and Metabolism* 7 (Supplement 1): S416.

Luxenberg, J., May, C., Haxby, J., Grady, C., Moore, A., Berg, G., White, B., Robinette, D., and Rapoport, S. (1987). Cerebral metabolism, anatomy, and cognition in monozygotic twins discordant for dementia of the Alzheimer's type. *Journal of Neurology, Neurosurgery, and Psychiatry* 50: 333–340.

Martin, A., Brouwers. P., and Lalonde, F. (1986). Towards a behavioral typology of Alzheimer's disease. *Journal of Clinical and Experimental Neuropsychology* 8: 594–610.

Martin, A., and Fedio, P. (1983). Word production and comprehension in Alzheimer's disease: The breakdown of semantic knowledge. *Brain and Language* 19: 124–141.

Mazziotta, J. C., Phelps, M. E., Pahl, J. J., Huang, S.-C., Baxter, L. R., Riege, W. H., Hoffman, J. M., Kuhl, D. E., Lanto, A. B., Wapenski, J. A., Markham, C. H.

(1987). Reduced cerebral glucose metabolism in asymptomatic subjects at risk for Huntington's disease. *New England Journal of Medicine* 316: 357–362.

McGeer, P., Kamo, H., Harrop, R., Li, D., Tuokko, H., McGeer, E., Adam, M., Ammann, W., Beattie, B., Calne, D., Martin, W., Pate, B., Rogers, J., Ruth, T., Sayre, C., and Stoessl, A. (1986a). Positron emission tomography in patients with clinically diagnosed Alzheimer's disease. *Canadian Medical Association Journal* 134: 597–607.

McGeer, P., Kamo, H., Harrop, R., McGeer, E., Martin, W., Pate, B., and Li, D. (1986b). Comparison of PET, MRI, and CT with pathology in a proven case of Alzheimer's disease. *Neurology* 36: 1569–1574.

McKhann, G., Drachman, D., Folstein, M., Price, D., and Stadlan, E. (1984). Clinical diagnosis of Alzheimer's disease: Report of an NINCDS-ADRDA Work Group under the auspices of Department of Health and Human Services Task Force on Alzheimer's disease. *Neurology* 34: 939–944.

Mesulam, M.-M. (1982). Slowly progressive aphasia without generalized dementia. *Annals of Neurology* 11: 592–598.

Mesulam, M.-M., Mufson, E., and Rogers, J. (1987). Age-related shrinkage of cortically projecting cholinergic neurons: A selective effect. *Annals of Neurology* 22: 31–36.

Metter, E. J., Riege, W. H., Kuhl, D. E., and Phelps, M. E. (1984). Cerebral metabolic relationships for selected brain regions in healthy adults. *Journal of Cerebral Blood Flow and Metabolism* 4: 1–7.

Miller, E. (1984). Verbal fluency as a measure of verbal intelligence and in relation to different types of cerebral pathology. *British Journal of Clinical Psychology* 23: 53–57.

Miller, E., and Hague, F. (1975). Some characteristics of verbal behavior in presenile dementia. *Psychologic Medicine* 5: 255–259.

Milner, B. (1974). Hemispheric specialization: Scope and limits. In F. Schmitt and F. Worden (Eds.) *The Neurosciences Third Program*. Cambridge: MIT Press.

Moore, V., and Wyke, M. (1984). Drawing disability in patients with senile dementia. *Psychologic Medicine* 14: 97–105.

Morris, R. (1986). Short-term forgetting in senile dementia of the Alzheimer's type. *Cognitive Neuropsychology* 3: 77–97.

Morris, R., Wheatley, J., and Britton, P. (1983). Retrieval from long-term memory in senile dementia: Cued recall revisited. *British Journal of Clinical Psychology* 22: 141–142.

Moscovitch, M. (1982). A neuropsychological approach to perception and memory in normal and pathological aging. In F. Craik and S. Trehub (Eds.) *Aging and Cognitive Processes*. New York: Plenum Press.

Neary, D., Snowden, J., Bowen, D., Sims, N., Mann, D., Benton, J., Northen, B., Yates, P., and Davison, A. (1986). Neuropsychological syndromes in presenile dementia due to cerebral atrophy. *Journal of Neurology, Neurosurgery, and Psychiatry* 49: 163–174.

Nelson, A., Fogel, B., and Faust, D. (1986). Bedside cognitive screening instruments. *Journal of Nervous and Mental Disease* 174: 73–83.

Ober, B., Dronkers, N., Koss, E., Delis, D., and Friedland, R. (1986). Retrieval from semantic memory in Alzheimer-type dementia. *Journal of Clinical and Experimental Neuropsychology* 8: 75–92.

Obler, L., and Albert, M. (1983). Language in aging. In M. Albert (Ed.) *Aging and Dementia*. New York: Oxford University Press.

Obrist, W. D., Thompson, H. K., Jr., King, C. H., and Wang, H. S. (1967). Determination of regional cerebral blood flow by inhalation of 133-xenon. *Circulation Research* 20: 124–135.

Obrist, W. D., Chivian, E., Cronquvist, S., and Ingvar, D. H. (1970). Regional cerebral blood flow in senile and presenile dementia. *Neurology* 20: 315–322.

Pearson, R., Esiri, M., Hiorns, R., Wilcock, G., and Powell, T. (1985). Anatomical correlates of the distribution of the pathological changes in the neocortex in Alzheimer disease. *Proceedings of the National Academy of Sciences USA* 82: 4531–4534.

Phelps, M. E., Huang, S.-C., Hoffman, E. J., Selin, C., Sokoloff, L., and Kuhl, D. E. (1979). Tomographic measurement of local cerebral glucose metabolic rate in humans with (F-18)2-fluoro-2-deoxyglucose-D-glucose: validation of method. *Annals of Neurology* 6: 371–388.

Phelps, M., Mazziotta, J., Baxter, L., and Gerner, R. (1984). Positron emission tomographic study of affective disorders: Problems and strategies. *Annals of Neurology* 15 (Supplement): S149–S156.

Polinsky, R., Noble, H., DiChiro, G., Nee, L., Feldman, R., and Feldman, R. (1987). Dominantly inherited Alzheimer's disease: Cerebral glucose metabolism. *Journal of Neurology, Neurosurgery, and Psychiatry* 50: 752–757.

Rapoport, S. (1986). Positron emission tomography in normal aging and Alzheimer's disease. *Gerontology* 32 (Supplement 1): 6–13.

Reivich, M., Alavi, A., Wolf, A., Fowler, J., Russell, J., Arnett, C., MacGregor, R. R., Shiue, C. Y., Atkins, H., Anand, A., and Greenberg, J. H. (1985). Glucose metabolic rate kinetic model parameter determination in humans: The lumped constants and rate constants for [18F]fluorodeoxyglucose and [11C]deoxyglucose. *Journal of Cerebral Blood Flow and Metabolism* 5: 179–192.

Reivich, M., Kuhl, D., Wolf, A., Greenberg, J., Phelps, M., Ido, T., Casella, V., Fowler, J., Hoffman, E., Alavi, A., Som, P., and Sokoloff, L. (1979). The [18F]fluorodeoxyglucose method for the measurement of local cerebral glucose utilization in man. *Circulation Research* 44: 127–137.

Rochford, G. (1971). A study of naming errors in dysphasic and demented patients. *Neuropsychologia* 9: 437–443.

Rosen, W. (1980). Verbal fluency in aging and dementia. *Journal of Clinical Neuropsychology* 2: 135–146.

Rosen, W., Terry, R. D., Fuld, P. A., et al. (1980). Pathological verification of ischemic score in differentiation of dementias. *Annals of Neurology* 7: 486–488.

Rosen, W. (1983). Neuropsychological investigation of memory, visuoconstructional, visuoperceptual, and language abilities in senile dementia of the Alzheimer type. In R. Mayeux and W. Rosen (Eds.) *The Dementias.* New York: Raven Press.

Rottenberg, D. A., Moeller, J. R., Strother, S. C., Sidtis, J. J., Navia, B. A., Dhawan, V., Ginos, J. Z., and Price, R. W. (1987). The metabolic pathology of the AIDs dementia complex. *Annals of Neurology* 22: 700–706.

Roy, C. S., and Sherrington, M. B. (1890). On the regulation of the blood supply of the brain. *Journal of Physiology* 11: 85–108.

Schwartz, M., Marin, O., and Saffran, E. (1979). Dissociations of language function in dementia. *Brain and Language* 7: 277–309.

Shimamura, A., Salmon, D., Squire, L., and Butters, N. (1987). Memory dysfunction and word priming in dementia and amnesia. *Behavioral Neuroscience* 101: 347–351.

Sjogren, T., Sjogren, H., and Lindgren, A. (1952). Morbus Alzheimer and morbus Pick: A genetic, clinical, and patho-anatomical study. *Acta Psychiatrica et Neurologica Scandinavica* 82 (Supplement): 1–152.

Sokoloff, L., Reivich, M., Kennedy, C., DesRosier, M., Patlak, C., Pettigrew, D., and Sakurada, M. (1977). The [14C]deoxyglucose method for the measurement of local cerebral glucose utilization: Theory, procedure and normal values in the conscious and anesthetized albino rat. *Journal of Neurochemistry* 28: 897–916.

Squire, L. (1986). Mechanisms of memory. *Science* 232: 1612–1619.

Squire, L., and Moore, R. (1979). Dorsal thalamic lesion in a noted case of chronic memory dysfunction. *Annals of Neurology* 6: 503–506.

Terry, R., DeTeresa, R., and Hansen, L. (1987). Neocortical cell counts in normal human adult aging. *Annals of Neurology* 21: 530–539.

Theodore, W., Dorwart, R., Holmes, M. (1986). Neuroimaging in refractory partial seizures: Comparison of PET, CT, and MRI. *Neurology* 36: 750–759.

Victor, M., Adams, R., and Collins, G. (1971). *The Wernicke-Korsakoff Syndrome*. Philadelphia: Davis.

Warrington, E. (1975). The selective impairment of semantic memory. *Quarterly Journal of Experimental Psychology* 27: 635–657.

Whitaker, H. (1976). A case of isolation of the language function. In H. Whitaker and H. Whitaker (Eds.) *Studies in Neurolinguistics*. Vol. 2. New York: Academic Press.

Wilson, R., Bacon, L., Fox, J., and Kaszniak, A. (1983). Primary memory and secondary memory in dementia of the Alzheimer type. *Journal of Clinical Neuropsychology* 5: 327–334.

Wilson, R., Kaszniak, A., and Fox, J. (1981). Remote memory in senile dementia. *Cortex* 17: 41–48.

Young, A., Penney, J., Starosta-Rubinstein, S., Karkel, D., Berent, S., Giordani, B., Ehrenkaufer, R., Jewett, D., and Hichwa, R. (1986). PET scan investigations in Huntington's disease: Cerebral metabolic correlates of neurologic features and functional decline. *Annals of Neurology* 20: 296–303.

Zurif, E., and Caramazza, A. (1976). Algorithmic and heuristic processes in sentence processing in aphasia. *Cortex* 12: 149–155.

Chapter 5

Neuropsychology of Alzheimer's Disease: The Case for Subgroups

Alex Martin

Virtually all students of behavior who come into contact with numbers of Alzheimer patients are impressed by the differences between them. Each patient presents a landscape of eroding cognitive and functional capacities, but the landscape contains peaks and valleys. One patient may be seen with particularly severe visuospatial confusion and little language disturbance; another patient may show the reverse. Patients may be "frontal" to a greater or lesser extent. They may have marked extrapyramidal motor signs, or they may remain free of these until the very end. In some patients the impairments in the domain of memory, language, perception, or action may be so well circumscribed at the outset that it is years before the presence of a dementing condition is recognized. More typically patients show simultaneous dissolution across several domains.

In this chapter Alex Martin discusses the heterogeneous presentation of Alzheimer-type dementia and the implications this has for nosology, research methodology, and clinical interventions. He attempts to characterize subgroups of patients based on the prominence of one or another cognitive component, and he considers what an adequate taxonomy of subgroups would look like.

Martin is well qualified to be engaging in these far-ranging speculations. He is the major investigator in a series of studies that proved that the linguistic and visuospatial components of the Alzheimer's symptom complex can be doubly dissociated and that the degree of involvement of one or the other component predicts the pattern of regional hypometabolism on PET studies. These studies went a long way toward convincing investigators that the diverse clinical presentations are an essential feature of Alzheimer's disease and revealing of underlying pathological processes.

M. F. S.

At the Clinical Center of the National Institutes of Health (NIH), the research patients often shared a room on the ward. During one of my earliest encounters with an individual who was assigned the diagnosis of probable Alzheimer's disease, the patient expressed concern about his roommate and wanted to know what was wrong with him. One response would have been to explain to the patient that he and his roommate had the same thing wrong with them; they were both suffering from Alzheimer's disease (AD). That answer, although correct, would have clearly missed the intent of the question. What the patient was referring to was the fact that his roommate had particular difficulty expressing what he wanted to say and, apparently as a result, was often frustrated and irritable. In contrast the patient I was interviewing had no such word-finding difficulty. He did, however, have considerable difficulty in finding his way around in space and manipulating objects, so that he was now unable to perform many tasks and chores that he used to accomplish with ease. His roommate had none of these problems. As it turned out, these patients did have certain cognitive deficits in common, including severely impaired ability to learn and recall both verbal material and spatial arrays. Nevertheless their language and spatial impairments were clearly their most prominent symptoms. The qualitatively different and relatively focal presentations of these patients was subsequently documented by neuropsychological investigation and cerebral metabolism studies (see Martin 1987 for a detailed description of similar patients). More recently the possibility that at least some of these patients were suffering from AD, and only AD, has been verified by neuropathological evidence obtained at autopsy. Thus as was readily apparent to this patient, one level of analysis, namely, neurological disease state, does not map directly, or in a simple one-to-one fashion, onto a neuropsychological level of analysis.

In this chapter I argue that for Alzheimer's disease, as well as for all other dementing disorders, the mapping relation is, and in fact must be, one to many. That is, especially during the early stages, such disorders will not be reducible to a single neuropsychological profile, but rather will manifest as a family or subgroupings of qualitatively distinct profiles of impaired and preserved cognitive ability. Moreover recognition of this state of affairs has critical implications for a wide range of issues, including early diagnosis, assessment of therapeutic interventions, and for furthering our understanding of the nature of dementing disorders and their concomitant cognitive impairments.

The Argument

The mid- to late 1970s was marked by a heightened awareness among the scientific community of the devastating medical, social, and economic consequences of AD (Katzman 1976). The causal and pathophysiological mechanism(s) responsible for this disease were unknown, and no biological marker had been identified. As a result confirmation of this diagnosis depended on neuropathological criteria. Thus AD was a diagnostic category, the assignment of which depended largely on a process of exclusion. (These conditions of course remain true today.) Given the diagnostic uncertainty that surrounded this disorder, and the critical importance of distinguishing it from treatable forms of dementia, a pressing need was identified for the discipline of neuropsychology to address. Because the central feature of AD was cognitive deterioration, it was clear that the identification of a specific profile of impaired and preserved functions would be of great significance for improving the accuracy of early diagnosis and advancing our understanding of this disorder. Given the potential payoff to be reaped if this goal could be accomplished, it is rather easy to understand the efforts that were, and continue to be, directed toward uncovering the "signature" profile of AD (see, for example, Gainotti et al. 1980, Pillon et al. 1986).

The typical approach to this problem has been to assess the performance of AD patients on a test battery of choice, average the data from each measure, and then compare the results to the average performance of patients with other forms of dementia and/or normal individuals. There are two difficulties inherent in this approach: one methodological and the other conceptual. First, the issue of diagnostic uncertainty is a double-edged sword. On the one hand it provides the central rationale for performing these studies and gives them their particular importance and relevance. On the other hand, however, one is forced to acknowledge that there is no way of knowing, short of brain tissue biopsy, how many of the patients in the AD group are in fact suffering from AD. As a result there is no way to determine to what extent the group profile is distorted by the inclusion of patients who do not have this disease.

One way around this difficulty would be to use more stringent exclusionary criteria. This is reasonable solution as long as the criteria do not include assessment of cognitive functioning. To the extent that they do (for example, all AD patients must have progressive impairments of functions A, B, C, and so on), then the group will be preselected for the presence of certain deficits or combinations of deficit and not others. Thus, for example, Alzheimer's initial patient with the disease that would later bear his name was seen with personality change as the most prominent initial symptom. It was only later that deterioration of memory and other cognitive functions became apparent (Alzheimer 1907). If it is preordained that AD is not seen in this manner, then obviously such patients will never appear for study until further deterioration is evident.

The second difficulty is more conceptual and underlies the central potential pitfall of the previously defined approach. Specifically the practice of averaging patient data based solely on diagnostic category depends on the proposition that homogeneity with regard to one category—disease state—will ensure homogeneity with regard to another category—cognitive functioning (Martin 1988).

To begin, I take it as given that what we are seeking to accomplish, on the most general level, is to provide an accurate description of the cognitive abilities of patients afflicted with a common disorder. The problem is to generate a description that on the one hand is not so broad that it does violence to (that is, obscures) distinct patterns of impairment and on the other hand is not so specific that generalizations cannot emerge. The central thesis being advanced is simply that individual patients with the same disease will vary with regard to their cognitive deficits. Before proceeding, it is necessary to clarify the type of variability under discussion. Variability in this context is not meant to refer to the fact that because AD is a progressive disorder, some patients will have more severe dificits across a set number of domains of functioning than others. Nor is it meant to refer to the fact that some individuals will have impairments in more domains than others will have. Thus individual differences in depth or breadth of impairment as a function of disease progression is not at issue. In addition I am not referring to the fact that individuals at roughly the same stage of progression may have differing degrees of impairment across a set number of domains. Therefore the fact that a group of patients may all have deficits in learning, word finding, and visuospatial functions, but some patients have relatively more severe memory impairments relative to their word-finding and spatial deficits, and others have more severe spatial impairment relative to memory and word finding and the like is of little interest. After all the same could be said about normal individuals, given that their overall level of performances and the discrepancies between them are all within the normal range. Rather the type of variability I am alluding to refers to fact that individuals with the same disease, and at a comparable stage of impairment, may show *qualitatively* different profiles of impaired and preserved ability. That is, some patients may be seen with an impairment in one domain, yet performing normally in another, whereas other patients may have the opposite arrangement. In other words a single disease may produce doubly dissociated deficits. Finally, to the extent that clusters of individuals with common profiles of this type can be identified, we can assert that neuropsy-chologically defined *subgroups* have been identified.

Following a suggestion by Jorm (1985), these clusters will be referred to as *subgroups*. The term *subtypes* will be reserved for groupings that indicate differences in etiology. For our purposes a subgroup be defined as a cluster of individuals meeting established criteria for the diagnosis of probable AD who are seen with a common impairment in one domain of functioning, although performing normally, or near normally, on measures of another domain that is usually impaired during the relatively early stages of the disease process. Subgroup membership is thus defined by both the presence and absence of certain types of deficits. Because the current criteria for assigning the diagnosis of the probable AD require deficits in two or more areas of cognition (McKhann et al. 1984), the patients comprising a single subgroup may vary with regard to the presence of other impairments. For example, a group of patients who all have spatial dysfunction, but intact language abilities, may be hetero-geneous with regard to different types of memory, attention, or mood disorders. Moreover the nature of the spatial deficit may vary so that the patients comprising a single subgroup may differ with regard to the specific processing deficit responsible for their spatial difficulty. As a result of these possibly confounding factors, certain questions, especially those directed at understanding the nature of specific cog-nitive mechanisms, may be addressable only by detailed, single-case analyses.

The reason why such subgroups must occur is quite straightfor-ward. For the sake of argument let us assume that we are confronted with a group of patients with "pure AD" who are at a relatively equivalent stage of progression. That is, these patients' brains at autopsy will show the cardinal features of AD, and only AD. Therefore by definition the group is homogeneous with regard to its central de-fining characteristic, that is, a predetermined, minimum number of neurofibrillary tangles and neuritic plaques in the hippocampus and neocortex without evidence of vascular disease or other dementing disorder (Tierney et al. 1988). Our main goal would be to describe the cognitive and affective changes that characterize this group of pa-tients and possibly distinguishes them from patients with other de-menting disorders. The primary determinant of such change is, however, not the mere presence of neuropathology but rather its location. The extensive literature on the effects of focal brain damage attests to the fact that relatively small changes in the primary locus of pathology can have vastly different consequences for cognitive func-tioning. Moreover as our models of brain function become increasing sophisticated and our test instruments increasing sensitive, the greater will be the likelibood that even subtle differences in location of pathology will be related to differences in functional impairment. Therefore for our patient group to be homogeneous with regard to their pattern of neuropsychological deficit would require, at minimum, severe constraints on the location of initial pathology as well as on its progression through the central nervous system.

This would be the minimum requirement in recognition of the fact that the mapping between specific anatomic loci and cognitive function is itself frought with a host of conceptual difficulties that remain to be resolved (see, for example, Caplan 1981, Phillips, Zeki, and Barlow 1984). In fact what would be required would be the neuropathology associated with AD disrupting function within the same set of cognitive domains, and the same components of those domains, in all of our patients. Documentation of this possibility would in turn require a case-by-case comparison of each patient in our group. Therefore the mapping between disease state and neuropsychological profile includes all of the difficulties inherent in the problem of functional localization plus the variable relation that may exist between disease and the location of pathology in one individual in comparison with another.

In essence then the argument that a single disease maps onto a single profile of cognitive impairment must require an intervening step—specifically that the disease produces an invariant pattern of anatomical/neurochemical dysfunction. To the extent that this is untrue, the notion of an invariant profile must be equally false. It should also be clear that the present argument would hold even if, for example, the neuropathology of AD had an exclusive predilection for association cortex, unless it could be demonstrated that the disease affected the same cortical tissue and produced the same type or types of deficit in each patient. If not, then one would be no more justified in averaging the data from these patients because they all had plaques and tangles limited to association cortex than one would be to average the data from patients with the same type of tumor regardless of variability in tumor location from one patient to another.

The fact that this conceptual issue is commonly disregarded likely stems from the fact that there is considerable evidence that AD is highly selective for certain brain regions and neurochemical systems and not others. In particular the hippocampus (Hyman et al. 1984), amygdala (Herzog and Kemper 1980), select regions of the neocortex (Brun and Gustafson 1976), and the basal forebrain cholinergic system (Whitehouse et al. 1982), are commonly, and may in fact be universally, involved by disease end-stage. However, it is critical to note that the fact that the pathological changes associated with AD are selective does not mean that they are invariably present in every affected individual *at a given point in time*. First, we have almost no knowledge about disease progression with regard to location of pathology (Mann and Esiri 1988). Are all of these structures affected simultaneously, or does the disease progress from one to another? If so, is this order of progression the same for all individuals? Second, the above list is not exhaustive. Thus, for example, some but not all patients have substantial cell loss in the locus ceruleus noradrenergic system (Bondareff, Mountjoy, and Roth 1982) and dorsal raphe serotonergic system (Curcio and Kemper 1984, Yamamoto and Hirano 1985). Moreover reduction of other neurotransmitters (for example, glutamate, Greenamyre et al. 1985; γ-aminobutyric acid, Rossor et al. 1982) as well as several neuropeptides (for example, somatostatin, Beal et al. 1985; vasopressin, Fujiyoshi et al. 1987) have been reported. Finally, cell loss in other anatomical structures and regions has been found (for example, the olfactory bulb, Esiri and Wilcock 1984; cerebral white matter, Brun and Englund 1986).

Although it remains to be determined which of these anatomical lesions and neurochemical deficits are primary versus which are secondary consequences of AD, it is clear that quite a number of cortical regions and subcortical structures can be involved in this disease. Therefore these structures and neurochemical systems should be viewed as being at risk for developing pathology. As such, they provide important constraints on the types of deficits that one may expect to be associated with this disorder. At risk, however, does not equal invariant.

Having argued that the relation between a neurological disease and pattern of neuropsychological functioning must be one to many, in the next section I review evidence that this is in fact the case for Alzheimer's disease.

The Evidence

At autopsy the brains of patients with AD often show relatively circumscribed cerebral atrophy. These changes affect primarily temporal, parietal, and perhaps to a lesser extent frontal association cortex. In contrast the motor, sensory, and visual primary projection regions are commonly spared. A similar pattern of spatial distribution occurs for the neurofibrillary tangles and neuritic plaques that are the cardinal features of AD. This pattern thus defines the constraints on neocortical involvement. However, embedded within this general picture, it has also been established that individual brains may exhibit varying degrees of hemispheric and lobular asymmetries (for example, Tariska 1970, Brun and Gustafson 1976). Thus even at disease end-stage differing patterns of relatively focal degeneration can be observed in at least some patients with AD. If we assume that before death these patients were at their most globally demented state, then these autopsy findings raise the possibility of even more focal patterns of pathology earlier in the disease process. This possibility has now been well documented by detailed neuropsychological investigation coupled with cerebral metabolic studies using positron emission tomography (PET), and verified by findings at autopsy.

The Breakdown of Sematic Knowledge and Visuospatial Skill: Temporal and Parietal Lobe Dysfunction

In a series of PET studies at the NIH, Foster, Chase, and colleagues found that patients meeting established criteria for the diagnosis of AD exhibited a relatively distinct pattern of hypometabolism. The posterior parietal and temporal regions were most severely affected, whereas the frontal lobes were relatively spared (Chase, Foster, and Mansi 1983, Foster et al. 1984). In addition some patients exhibited lateral hemispheric differences in glucose utilization that roughly corresponded to the patients' most prominent symptom (greater left-sided hypometabolism in patients with more severe language deficits relative to their visuosconstructive difficulties; greater right-sided hypometabolism in patients with the converse cognitive profile; Foster et al. 1983). Although several of these patients were selected for study because of their relatively focal symptomatology, it is noteworthy that similar PET findings have been reported by other laboratories using unselected samples (for example, Friedland, Brun and Budinger 1985, Haxby et al. 1985 and see Chawluk et al., chapter 4).

In a more detailed report on the neuropsychological status of the NIH patients, Martin and colleagues (1984, 1986) provided evidence for the existence of qualitatively distinct subgroups defined by profile of cognitive deficit. The patients (n = 42) were relatively young (mean = 59.3 years), well educated (mean = 14.5 years), and most were in the early stages of the disease process (average reported symptom duration of approximately 3 years). Based on previous clinical and

---

Figure 5.1

Examples of copies of the Rey-Osterrieth complex figure by patients with (A) relatively focal word-finding deficits and (B) relative focal visuospatial and construction impairment. The number in parentheses under each drawing indicates the number of line-drawn objects from the Boston Naming Test that the patient was able to name before phonemic cuing (maximum score = 85, normal range = 50–85). (From Martin 1987)

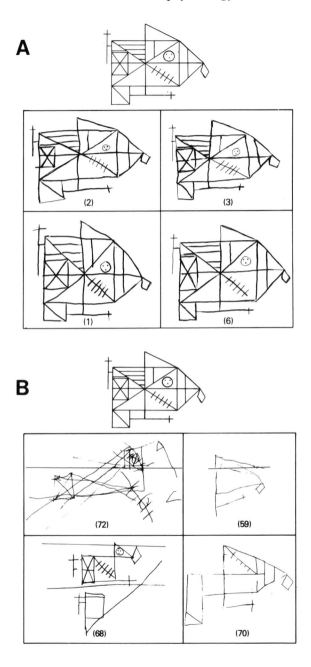

experimental evaluations (Brouwers et al. 1984, Martin and Fedio 1983, Martin et al. 1985a); it was apparent that the most prominent impairments exhibited by these patients encompassed primarily three domains of functioning: episodic memory, as assessed by tests requiring recall and recognition of newly presented material; semantic knowledge or memory, especially as measured by object naming and category fluency tasks; and visuospatial and constructional skill, as assessed by block design, complex figure copying, and other spatial tasks. Although most of these patients had deficits in all domains, some demonstrated normal access to semantic/lexical knowledge and others intact visuospatial skills. In fact because of their apparently atypical, circumscribed symptomatology, these patients were excluded from the previously noted experimental reports (Martin et al. 1985b). Clinical evidence of the extent to which these domains of functioning were independently disrupted in these patients is provided in figure 5.1.

To statistically document and verify these clinical differences, three measures of semantic knowledge and three measures of visuospatial and constructional skill were submitted to a factor analysis, using varimax rotation of the principal-components solution. This analysis revealed two relatively independent factors, each characterized by high loadings for one set of the tests and low loadings for the other set. The factor scores assigned to each patient were then used to plot the individuals in the two-dimensional space defined by the independent factors. Cluster analysis indicated essentially three qualitatively distinct groupings. The accuracy of cluster membership was verified by a linear discriminant analysis, which successfully reclassified the patients based on their factor scores. The majority of the patients (n = 25) exhibited relatively equal impairment of word-finding ability and visuospatial and constructional skill. These patients could be further subdivided into groups of mildly, moderately, and severely impaired individuals. In addition 9 patients were identified with severe word-finding difficulties concurrent with intact, or relatively intact, spatial and constructional ability, whereas 8 individuals showed the opposite cognitive profile (figure 5.2A). These subgroups did not differ with respect to age, education, or reported duration of symptoms.

Consistent with these contrasting patterns of deficit, estimates of cortical glucose utilization obtained via PET from select patients in each group revealed corresponding differences with regard to region of maximal pathology. Patients with deficits in both cognitive domains had relatively symmetrical, bilateral hypometabolism of the temporal and parietal lobes. Patients with primarily word-finding difficulties had significantly greater hypometabolism in the left temporal

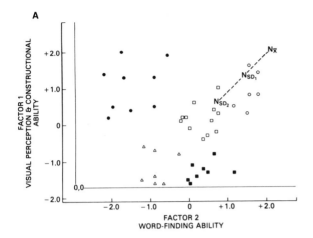

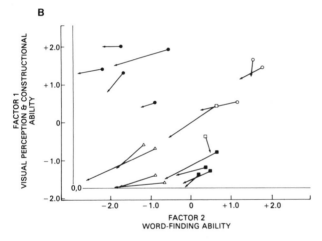

Figure 5.2
(A) Plot of 42 AD patients according to their factor scores. Also included is a point indicating the mean score achieved by the normal subjects on all measures ($N_{\bar{x}}$), points representing 1 (N_{SD_1}) and 2 (N_{SD_2}) standard deviations below this mean, and a point indicating the position of a hypothetical patient who scored 0 on all six tests (0,0). Cluster analysis identified five patient groupings. Patients comprising groups 1A (○), 1B (□), and 1C (△) clustered along the diagonal line connecting point $N_{\bar{x}}$ to 0,0, indicating relatively equal impairment in both cognitive domains. The positions of patients assigned to groups 2 (●) and 3 (■) illustrate their contrasting patterns of impaired and peserved abilities with respect to word-finding and visuoconstructive functions. (From Martin et al. 1986) (B) Plot of 18 of the patients depicted in part A. Symbols indicate position at initial testing. Arrows indicate direction and extent of cognitive deterioration after a one- to two-year follow-up interval. Patients exhibited significantly different patterns of deterioration as a function of initial subgroup membership. (From Martin et al. 1987)

lobe relative to all other cortical regions. Patients with severe visuo-constructional deficits, but normal naming and category fluency scores, exhibited significantly greater hypometabolism in the right parietal and, to a lesser degree, temporal regions. As noted previously, frontal regions were relatively better preserved, and the rate of glucose metabolism in the frontal zones did not distinguish between these patients groupings (Foster et al. 1984, Martin et al. 1984, 1986). Thus, the PET data provided external validation of these neuro-psychologically defined subgroupings.

Reevaluation of a subset of these patients after a one- to two-year interval indicated significantly different patterns of deterioration as a function of initial subgroup membership. The patients were retested on the six measures included in the original analysis, and these scores were transformed to factor scores based on the results of the initial factor analysis. As illustrated in figure 5.2B, patients who were seen initially with relatively equal impairment of both semantic knowledge (word finding) and spatial and constructional skill showed continued symmetrical decline. In contrast most patients with relatively focal patterns of deficit exhibited significantly greater deterioration within the domain that was most impaired at initial evaluation. Overall rate of deterioration was not related to initial subgroup membership (Martin et al. 1987). Finally, autopsy studies have verified the diagnosis of AD, and only AD, in at least one member of each of these subgroups.

Taken together, these findings suggest that during the early stages of AD, neuropathology may be restricted to a relatively circumscribed cortical region resulting in relatively focal impairment of either semantic knowledge or visuospatial functions. Moreover these patients may show continued deterioration within one of these domains before the onset of more global cognitive deterioration. These data therefore suggest that cortical neuropathology limited to one area may progress to functionally adjacent tissue before other regions become affected (for example, continued progression within left temporal regions before involvement of the parietal lobes).

Additional evidence for the presence of these subgroups has been provided by a replication of Martin and colleagues' study using a larger cohort from the Alzheimer's Research Program at the University of Pittsburgh (86 patients, average symptom duration of approximately three years; Becker et al. 1988). Six measures—three assessing access to semantic/lexical knowledge and three tests of visuo-constructive ability—that were similar, but not identical, to those used by Martin and colleagues were submitted to a principal-components factor analysis using varimax rotation. The analysis yielded a two-factor solution that was nearly identical to the one reported in the NIH study. Composite scores based on these clusters of tasks were created to try and identify patients with impairment in one domain and normal performance in the other. Eleven patients were identified with semantic, but not visuoconstructive, impairment. Four others were identified with the opposite pattern. This study was of particular importance because, in contrast to the NIH report, none of the patients were initially selected for study because of the presence of focal cognitive impairment (J. Becker, personal communication). Thus over 17 percent of this unselected sample had a severe deficit in one domain concurrent with normal ability in the other domain of functioning.

In addition to these group studies, a number of patients have been reported on who had either focal language or visual perceptual and/or spatial and constructional impairments. For several of these patients the diagnosis of AD has been confirmed by neuropathological examination of brain tissue obtained via biopsy or autopsy.

Neary and colleagues (1986) report on 18 patients with biopsy-proved AD. All of the patients were classified as amnesic. The majority of patients (11) also had language and visuospatial impairments and were thus similar to the "globally" impaired patients in the studies by Martin and colleagues (1986) and Becker and colleagues (1988). Five of the remaining patients had severe perceptual-spatial or constructional impairments, but normal language abilities on formal testing. Crystal and coworkers (1982) reported on a patient with biopsy-proved AD who was seen with an even more focal constellation of symptoms. Their patient exhibited a right parietal lobe syndrome including severe constructional difficulty, decreased position sense, two-point discrimination, and stereognosis on the left hand, and extinction of the left visual field to double simultaneous stimulation (left-sided extinction was also present in 3 of the 8 patients without language impairment in Martin and colleagues 1986 report). Although the left-sided position sense and sensory changes were the earliest symptoms, memory problems were documented at the time of formal examination. Language processes, however, were spared.

Autopsy data are now available on 2 of the 8 patients with visuoconstructive, but not language, impairment in Martin and colleagues' study. Both of these patients had AD. One of these patients has been previously described in detail because of his highly specific spatial deficit and clues it provided about the normal organization of spatial processes and constructional skill (see discussion of patient C in Martin 1987).

The visual difficulties of these patients appeared to be limited to spatial processes. Object recognition was intact as documented by normal performance on tests of object naming. Other patients have been reported with more widespread visual disturbances involving both spatial and object recognition processes, but without language, or in some cases memory deficits. DeRenzi (1986) reported on two patients with what he termed "progressive visual agnosia without dementia." These patients were markedly impaired on tests of line and angle discrimination, copying, and visual closure. Naming was impaired for objects presented visually, but not tactilely. Color naming was preserved. Memory functions were mildly impaired in one patient and more severely impaired in the other. Cogan (1985) reported an autopsy-verified case of AD in which the patient was seen with severe spatial and constructional difficulties, neglect of left hemispace, and impaired visual, but not tactile, object recognition. Again color naming ability was intact. Memory was not assessed. Before the patient's death a dense left homonymous hemianopsia and progressive decline of all cognitive functions developed. An even more severe loss of visual functioning was reported by Faden and Townsend (1976). Their patient experienced a progressive loss of vision that resulted in complete blindness within four months. This was rapidly followed (over a six-month period) by confusion, memory loss, language difficulties, and myoclonus. AD was confirmed at autopsy, which also revealed mild diffuse cortical atrophy that was most prominent in the occipital lobes. Spongiform changes, which would have been indicative of Creutzfeldt-Jacob disease, were not present.

Thus there have been reports on at least 22 patients with probable of possible AD with varying degrees of visuospatial, constructional, and visual recognition deficits, without expressive or receptive language problems or evidence for impaired access to, or loss of knowledge of, semantic/lexical information. Of these the diagnosis has been verified by autopsy or biopsy for 10 individuals.

In contrast a number of patients have been reported who were seen with relatively severe and progressive language impairments without deficits in visual spatial or perceptual processes. However, unlike the patients reviewed previously, the relation between this pattern of presentation and the neuropathology of AD is less clearly established. Detailed reports of patients with progressive and relatively isolated deterioration of the semantic system have been presented by Warrington (1975), Coughlan and Warrington (1981; 3 patients), Schwartz, Marin, and Saffran (1979; 1 patient), Marin, Glenn, and Rafal (1983; 1 patient), and Martin (1987; 1 patient). An additional patient with similar features, although not described in detail, was reported by Shuttleworth (case 3; 1984). Although neuropathological confirmation was not available for any of these patients, Pogacar and Williams (1984) reported a case of autopsy-verified AD in a patient with naming and word-finding deficits as the most prominent initial symptom. Within a year of the first symptoms, other cognitive deficits emerged, including speech, reading, and writing problems, apraxic and constructional difficulties, calculation problems, and left-right confusion. All of these difficulties are consistent with a progressive process limited to the left hemisphere (Benson, Cummings, and Tsai 1982). This picture progressed over a relatively short period of time (three months after the initial evaluation and approximately two year since the onset of naming difficulties), to include deficits in memory, spatial analysis, and myoclonus.

If we include the 9 patients in Martin and colleagues' study (1986) and the 11 patients identified by Becker and colleagues (1988), a total of 27 patients have been reported who showed a fluent, anomic aphasia coupled with normal visuospatial and constructional skills. Autopsy data have been obtained from 2 of the 9 patients identified in the NIH series. One patient had neuropathological changes consistent with the diagnosis of AD. In the other patient marked cortical atrophy was noted. However, neither neuritic plaques, neurofibrillary tangles, nor Pick bodies were present. Therefore, including the patient reported on by Pogacar and Williams (1984), 2 of 3 patients who have come to autospy have had AD.

A number of other patients with progressive and focal impairment of language abilities have been reported. These patients, however, seem to differ in several important ways from the previously described patients with probable AD. In 1982 Mesulam studied six patients with what he has termed "progressive aphasia without dementia" or "primary progressive aphasia" (Mesulam 1987). A similar patient was reported on by Heath, Kennedy, and Kapur (1983). Initially questions were raised concerning the degree to which other cognitive processes were compromised in these patients (Foster and Chase 1983, Gordon and Selnes 1984). However, a subsequent report indicated progressive deterioration limited to specific language, praxic, and arithmetic functions consistent with pathology limited to the left perisylvian region (Mesulam and Weintraub 1983). Additional patients with progressive aphasia without dementia have been reported on by Kirshner and associates (1984; 6 patients), Morris and associates (1984; 2 patients, IV-4, IV-6), and Mehler and colleagues (1987; 2 patients). From these 17 patients neuropathologic evidence has been reported for 5 patients (1 via biopsy from Mesulam's original series, 2 from Kishner and colleagues' series (1987), 1 from Morris and associates' series, and 1 from Mehler and colleagues' series).

Of the four brains available for examination, all had focal atrophy and spongiform change of the frontotemporal region of the left hemisphere. Cortical cell loss was most focal in Kirshner and colleagues' patients. Atrophy was more widespread in Mehler and colleagues' patient and included posterior regions of the left hemisphere and most of the right hemisphere as well. Morris and associates also reported cell loss in the hippocampus, substantia nigra, and locus ceruleus, whereas Mehler and colleagues reported cell loss in the substantia nigra and basal ganglia. Mehler and colleagues also documented a marked reduction of somatostatinlike immunoreactivity, but not of choline acetyltransferase activity as commonly seen in AD. In none of these patients was evidence obtained to support a diagnosis of either AD or Pick's disease.

Mesulam (1987) has suggested several differences between this group of patients and AD patients who initially experience language symptoms. These include a slower and considerably more circumscribed pattern of progression, PET evidence of focal hypometabolism of the left perisylvian region, and agrammatical and nonfluent speech similar to the type seen in Broca's aphasia. It is noteworthy that patients with Pick's disease may also show a similar pattern of progressive nonfluent speech impairment (Holland et al. 1985, Wechsler et al. 1982). In this regard the patient with focal language impairment from the NIH series who did not have neuropathological evidence of AD may be of particular interest. Marked cortical neuronal loss and gliosis were present bilaterally, especially in the frontal and temporal regions and the hippocampus. Spongiform changes were also visible in the more severely affected areas. Therefore the neuropathology of this patient was most similar to that of others who initially showed progressive aphasia without dementia, except that heimispheric differences were not noted. Clinically this patient differed from the other 8 patients in the NIH language-impaired group in that his spontaneous speech was markedly nonfluent—again more similar to the symptomatology of progressive aphasia than to AD. However, he experienced a considerably faster rate of progression, and his cognitive deterioration was more widespread than that reportedly associated with primary progressive aphasia. For example, although his memory difficulties were limited to verbal material when he was first seen for evaluation, he was amnesic for both verbal and nonverbal material when retested after a 16-month interval. Visual spatial and other nonverbal processing abilities, however, remained intact (for details, see Martin et al. 1985b. This patient was designated as patient 1 in that report). The patient continued to become more globally impaired and died only seven and half years after initial onset of symptoms. Thus this patient had certain clinical features consistent with primary progressive aphasia (nonfluent speech) and others that were not (relatively quick and more widespread deterioration).

Taken together, the available evidence suggests several possibilities regarding the presence of relative focal and progressive language disturbance: One possibility, as suggested by Mesulam (1987), is that primary progressive aphasia may be clinically and neuropathologically distinct from AD. Whereas both patients would be expected to perform poorly on naming and fluency tasks, this difficulty may reflect an underlying semantic impairment in AD patients, but not in progressive aphasia patients (but see Schwartz and Chawluk, chapter 8). Thus AD patients would be expected to make semantic errors on test of confrontation naming and perform worse on semantic category than on letter fluency tasks. Impaired fluency in patients with primary progressive aphasia, in contrast, would be expected to be characterized by limited output and perseveration, as often seen in patients with frontal lobe involvement. Alternatively this clinical distinction may be more apparent than real. It may well turn out that both types of neuropathology (neuritic plaques and neurofibrillary tangles versus focal atrophy and spongiform change) are associated with overlapping spectrums of clinical presentations that vary from focal to more generalized or global cognitive dysfunction. Support for either of these, or other, alternatives must await additional detailed, longitudinal studies linking clinical presentation and pattern of deterioration to findings at autopsy.

Regardless of final outcome the existence of this nosological controversy serves to underscore the importance of carefully documenting the clinical presentation of patients with progressive cognitive disorders, regardless of the nature of the presenting symptoms. Nevertheless, based on the above evidence, it appears safe to conclude that at least some, but certainly not all, patients initially seen with a relatively focal and progressive cognitive disorder will be found at autopsy to have had AD. Moreover the available evidence strongly suggests that at least some of these patients will have preserved language or visuospatial abilities concurrent with severe impairments in the constrasting domain of functioning.

Perseverative Behavior, Personality, and Mood Change: Is There a "Frontal Lobe" Subgroup?
The evidence I have reviewed suggests that temporal and parietal regions are commonly affected in AD. In addition these regions may

be selectively involved, thus leading to the types of relatively focal clinical presentations previously discussed. However, neuropathological study of the neocortex has consistently revealed that atrophy and neuritic plaques and neurofibrillary tangles have a predilection for association cortex, including the frontal lobes. Because some patients have relatively focal involvement of temporal areas and others of the parietal lobes, it would seem likely that frontal regions and/or their subcortical connections should also be selectively involved in at least some patients. In other words one would expect to find group of AD patients with clinical and neuroimaging evidence for markedly greater involvement of anterior zones.

There is, however, little evidence to support this possibility. First, although neuropathology is evident in frontal areas at autopsy, this region has been reported to be less severely affected than the temporal and parietal cortex in some studies (Brun and Gustafson 1976, Brun and Englund 1986). Second, imaging studies using PET (Foster et al. 1984), single photon emission computed tomography (SPECT; Jagust, Budinger, and Reed 1987), and cerebral blood flow (Prohovnik et al. 1988) have consistently documented temporal and parietal dysfunction with relative sparing of the frontal lobes, especially during the earlier stages (and see Chawluk et al., chapter 4). The apparent discrepancy between autopsy studies and the neuroimaging data suggest that anterior association cortex may not be compromised until the later stages of the disease process. A similar suggestion has been made by Rossor and colleagues based on studies of age-related changes in the cortical distribution of the cholinergic marker enzyme choline acetyltransferase (Rossor et al. 1981, Rossor 1983).

Alternatively it may be argued that a "frontal" subgroup exists, but remains undetected because the subtle changes in cognitive flexibility, problem solving, personality, and mood that often accompany damage to prefrontal cortex and/or its subcortical connections are difficult to assess and quantify (Stuss and Benson 1984). In addition these individuals may be misdiagnosed. Thus, for example, an individual who is seen with personality and affective changes may be referred to psychiatry and not to neurology until memory and other cognitive deficits become clinically apparent. Therefore the lack of behavioral and neuroimaging evidence for a group of AD patients who initially are seen with relative focal involvement of frontal lobes may reflect a sampling bias resulting from the types of dysfunction that we are willing to accept as early manifestations of AD. Thus although the currently available evidence suggests that the frontal lobes are typically relatively unaffected until the latter stages of the disease process, this issue will remain unresolved pending detailed, longitudinal study of patients with progressive disorders, regardless of the nature of the initial symptomatology.

Is There an Amnesic Subgroup?
Impaired ability to learn and recall newly presented information has traditionally been considered one of the universal characteristics of AD. This view stems in part from the observation that patients and especially their families commonly cite memory failure as a chief complaint. Moreover it is often maintained that memory difficulties were the first indication that something was amiss. These observations, however, must be tempered by the fact that the lay use of the term *memory* does not distinguish between the nature of the to-be-learned material (day-to-day events, faces and names, spatial routes, motor and other types of skills) or whether the difficulty involves only new learning and/or failures to retrieve different types of previously acquired knowledge. Nevertheless it is beyond question that AD patients typically have learning impairments and that these difficulties are often disproportionately severe in comparison with the status of other cognitive process (for example, Corkin 1982). The central questions for our present discussion are, however, first, Do at least some AD patients show an isolated amnesia? and, conversely, Are there other patients who show progressive cognitive impairments, but normal learning ability?

The presence of hippocampal neuropathology is one of the defining features of AD (for example, Teirney et al. 1988). Therefore determining whether a memory impairment for at least some types of newly presented material is a universal, early feature of AD may be of critical importance for understanding the pathogenesis of this disease and its route of progression. Evidence in support of the possibility that AD patients can experience a selective amnesia has been provided by Neary and colleagues (1986). These investigators identified two patients with five- and six-year histories of isolated and progressive memory impairment, but no evidence of visuospatial, perceptual, language, or other cognitive or motor difficulties on formal testing. Social behavior and mood were appropriate. The diagnosis of AD was verified by biopsy in both patients.

In contrast, as noted previously, several investigators have claimed that some early AD patients may have intact memory abilities. Psychometric evidence in support of this claim has, however, typically not been included in these case reports. In two of the subgrouping studies that did include formal memory testing (Martin et al. 1986,

42 patients; Neary et al. 1986, 18 patients), impaired ability to learn at least some types of newly presented material was verified in every patient. There are two likely sources for this discrepancy: One possibility is that it reflects a sampling bias in the larger studies with regard to an unwillingness to assign a diagnosis of probable AD to patients who do not have memory deficits. The second possibility is that patients with relatively focal cognitive impairment may have a material-specific learning deficit corresponding to their primary domain of cognitive dysfunction. Thus, for example, anomic patients may also have a selective verbal memory deficit that is overshadowed by the patients' naming difficulty and that therefore remains clinically undetected in the absence of formal testing.

Evidence for this possibility was provided by Martin and colleagues (1985b), who reported a material-specific, verbal memory deficit in 5 patients who were seen with relatively focal word-finding difficulty. The poor recall and recognition abilities of these patients were apparent even when full credit was given for the retrieval of appropriate descriptions or semantically related names on an object memory task (Martin 1987). In contrast reproduction of previously presented nonverbal material was considerably better preserved. On follow-up testing after a one- to two-year interval 4 of these 5 individuals were found to be amnesic for both verbal and nonverbal material. However, their ability to process the nonverbal information that they were now unable to recall remained intact (for example, stable and normal ability to copy the Rey-Osterrieth complex figure coupled with a severe decline in their ability to reproduce the figure from memory). These findings suggest that AD patients can in fact have a material-specific memory deficit corresponding to their primary domain of cognitive dysfunction. Moreover impaired learning may precede decline in the related cognitive domain. The recent findings of marked left/right asymmetries in the density of neurofibrillary tangles, muscarinic receptors, and choline acetyltransferase activity in the entorhinal cortex of the hippocampus add further support for the possibility of material-specific learning and memory deficits in AD (Moossy et al. 1988, Zubenko et al.1988).

There is then some evidence that AD patients may experience a selective and isolated amnesia, but little evidence that AD patients may be seen without impaired learning for at least some types of material. If so, then the anatomic structures necessary for normal learning of verbal and nonverbal material (for example, hippocampus and amygdala) may be universally involved, and also among the earliest, if not the earliest, region to be affected in AD.

Disturbances of Attention, Arousal, and the Sleep-Wake Cycle:
Involvement of the Locus Ceruleus and Raphe Nuclei
Clinical observation and anecdotal reports suggest that even during the early stages some AD patients seem to have particular difficulty in selectively focusing and maintaining attention. Disruption of the sleep-wake cycle and a nocturnal confusional state referred to as *sundowning* has also been described (for example, Loewenstein et al. 1982). These observations may be of particular significance in light of recent neuropathological and neurochemical evidence indicating disruption to the ascending noradrenergic and serotonergic pathways in some, but not all, AD patients. As noted previously, a subgroup of patients with extensive loss of noradrenergic neurons in nucleus locus ceruleus has been identified (Bondareff, Mountjoy, and Roth 1982, Bondareff et al. 1987, Mann, Yates, and Marcyniuk 1984). Loss of serotonergic neurons and the presence of neurofibrillary tangles in the nucleus raphe have been documented as well (Yamamoto and Hirano 1985). As would be expected, significant reductions of noradrenaline and serotonin in cerebral cortex have also been found (Rossor and Iversen 1986).

Although attentional processes and sleep phenomena in AD patients have been relatively neglected areas of investigation, the available evidence does suggest impairment in these domains. For example, Prinz and colleagues (1982) reported a reduction of both REM and slow-wave sleep and increased wakefulness in "late-stage" AD patients (approximately six-year duration of symptoms), and Loewenstein and colleagues (1982) found a marked reduction of slow-wave sleep time and percentage in more moderately impaired individuals (approximately two-year symptom duration). No information concerning the percentage of subjects who manifested these changes was reported. Therefore although these findings are intriguing, systematic study is needed to determine whether there is a subgroup of patients who suffer from a specific disruption of circadian rhythms or whether these changes simply reflect a nonspecific disruption as a consequence of more widespread pathology during the later stages of the disease process.

The possibility that at least some AD patients may suffer from limited attentional capacity during the relatively early stages of the disease process is suggested by reports of reduced digit span in some studies (Kazniak, Garron, and Fox 1979, Kopelman 1985, Morris 1986), but not others (Corkin 1982, mild cases; Martin et al. 1985a; Weingartner et al. 1981). More direct evidence of an attentionally impaired subgroup has been provided by a recent series of studies by Freed and coworkers (1988; 1989). These investigators identified a group of AD patients with impaired performance on a test of visual selective attention. These same patients were also found to have a significantly greater reduction of MHPG, the major metabolite of noradrenaline, in their cerebral spinal fluid in comparison with AD patients who performed normally on the attention task. The subgroups were matched for severity of "dementia," as assessed by the Blessed Dementia Scale. These findings suggest that patients at a relatively comparable stage of disease progression may differ with regard to the status of specific aspects of attention and that this difference may be directly related to the integrity of the noradrenergic system. Thus one would expect that the patients identified by these behavioral procedures will be found at autopsy to have extensive damage to nucleus locus ceruleus.

Although these findings are extremely interesting, a critical issue for our present purposes is to determine whether these patient differences are a reflection of disease duration. For example, it would be necessary to demonstrate that the attentional impairment can precede the deterioration of other cognitive domains that are commonly affected in AD. Further study will be needed to clarify the relation between these findings, length of illness, and pattern and severity of other cognitive impairments.

Implications
Although a number of issues remain to be resolved, the studies I have reviewed confirm that AD patients many be seen with a variety of different patterns of impaired and preserved cognitive abilities and skills. Therefore AD must be viewed as heterogeneous with regard to the principal target of neuropsychological investigation, namely, the integrity of cognitive systems. This fact has in turn critical implications for a number of issues.

Early Diagnosis
Perhaps most important these data should serve to alert the clinical community to the varied and relatively focal symptomatology that may be associated with the early onset of AD. They should also serve to underscore the importance of carefully evaluating and documenting the cognitive and behavioral status of patients across a large number of domains and of following their evolution over time, regardless of the nature of these deficits and changes.

Pharmacological Intervention
Neuropathological study has firmly established that a variety of neurochemical systems can be affected by this disorder. Moreover

some of these systems will be affected in some patients and not others. Therefore the success of palliative interventions will depend on increasing our knowledge of relation between specific cognitive deficits and their underlying neuropathology. Related, greater care will be needed in quantifying each patient's pattern of deficit for both the assignment of patients to appropriate drug trials and determining appropriate study end-points.

Research Methodology
The evidence reviewed here constitutes a strong case against the practice of averaging data across patients simply because they were all assigned the same diagnostic label. The reason for this, as argued previously, is that data averaging, based solely on diagnostic classification, may yield a distorted profile of deficits because of the possibility of obscuring relatively focal and qualitatively different patterns of impairment. The central question for clinical research is not What is the profile of cognitive deficit associated with the early manifestations of AD? but rather How many subgroups are there? What are their frequencies of occurrence? How stable and they? and What are their patterns and rates of deterioration? If one insisted on disregarding this evidence, arguing instead that all AD patients present a common set of symptoms, follow an invariant pattern and sequence of deterioration, and so forth then one should be able to demonstrate these universal characteristics case by case. This argument should not be interpreted to mean that it is inappropriate to do group studies, but rather that in performing such studies subjects must be grouped in a "rational, theoretically revealing fashion" (Marshall and Newcombe 1984).

This caveat also applies to experimental investigations directed toward furthering our understanding the nature of specific types of cognitive impairment. For the sake of argument assume that AD will invariably result in highly specific disruption of semantic/lexical knowledge that follows a universal sequence of progression. However, although the underlying disorder may be pure, the tests and procedures used to evaluate them are not (for example, object-naming tasks depend on a number of processes, including visuoperceptual as well as semantic/lexical processes). When during the course of illness this semantic deficit occurs in a given individual, it may appear in the context of a variety of other impairments. Moreover the nature and severity of these other impairments will vary from patient to patient. As a result misleading conclusions may be drawn about the nature of the underlying problem, depending on the prevalence of these unrelated deficits in the experimental group (for example, see studies by

Barker and Lawson (1968) and Rochford (1971), which concluded that the object-naming deficit in AD was primarily due to misperception). Averaging data in this fashion provides no way of determining which of the patients' current impairments are obligatory for the occurrence of the phenomena of interest (for example, anomia), versus those that are merely incidental, but confounding, variables (Weiskrantz and Warrington 1975).

Understanding of the Neuropathological Progression of AD
Based on our knowledge of behavior/brain relations, specification of the variety of clinical presentations and their patterns of progression should provide valuable clues for determining the universal or invariant versus optional neuroanatomic loci of AD from its initial onset through its terminal stages. That is, neuropsychological investigation should provide evidence for the site or sites of the initial lesion(s) in AD and the variety of paths of progression through the brain that may be associated with this disorder.

As an illustrative example consider the following "minimal" model, which is, at least in part, consistent with much of the evidence reviewed in this chapter:

1. The amygdala and the hippocampus are the initial sites of pathology. These structures in turn may be at high risk because of their rich connections with the olfactory bulb; they are a proposed point of entry for the AD "pathogen" (Mann and Esiri 1988, Pearson et al. 1985, Reyes et al. 1987). Initial involvement of the medial temporal region is supported by (1) autopsy evidence of severe and perhaps universal involvement of this region, (2) the established role of these structures in new learning and remembering, which in turn is consistent with the common early complaint of forgetfulness, and (3) reports of an isolated amnesic syndrome, documented by formal testing, in biopsy-proved patients with AD. The affective and behavioral changes that reportedly occur as the earliest symptom in some patients would not be an unexpected consequence of bilateral damage to this region, especially if amygdala is primarily involved (for example, Rosvold, Mirsky, and Pribram 1954).

2. The neuropathology associated with the disease then progresses to posterior parietal and temporal cortex.

3. Further progression is characterized by posterior-to-anterior spread to frontal cortex and also to select subcortical nuclei (nucleus basalis, locus ceruleus, raphe).

Thus, typical AD patient would be expected to show increasing difficulty in learning and recalling newly presented information, closely followed by the development of the types of semantic/lexical, visuoperceptual, and visuospatial dysfunctions reviewed previously.

To account for subgroups, we need to add to this model a factor or set of factors, as yet to be identified, that would render certain of these regions at greater risk for or, conversely, more protected from pathology in a given individual. These factors, for example, would be responsible for lateralized medial temporal asymmetries (and therefore material-specific memory disorders) and inter- and intrahemispheric asymmetries (thus accounting for focal patterns of cognitive dysfunction) in the early expression of AD. For some individuals the pathology may therefore initially invade only the left or right medial temporal region, followed by asymmetric involvement of either the temporal or parietal lobes.

Within the context provided by this model, a number of predictions can be generated. For example:

> 1. All AD patients should initially have olfactory detection deficits and/or other deficits consistent with focal pathology of the medial temporal region (for example, a learning deficit, which may be material specific, in the absence of other cognitive impairments).
> 2. Cognitive deficits or deficit consistent with pathology of the temporal and/or parietal association cortex of either hemisphere should follow and never precede the developments listed in 1.
> 3. Cognitive and behavioral changes consistent with involvement of the frontal lobes and select subcortical structures should never precede the developments listed in 2.

The degree to which patients conform to this pattern of progression would provide clues to the severity of constraints placed on the distribution of pathology and its evolutionary sequence. For example, the minimal model argues for severe constraints on both the types of subgroups that will occur and their pattern of progression. In contrast evidence against this sequence of events (for example, onset of cortically based cognitive impairment before memory dysfunction) would suggest that the constraints were considerably less severe.

Understanding of the Organization of Cognitive Systems
Finally, as exemplified by several chapters in this book, patients with relatively focal and progressive disorders constitute a unique natural experiment that can provide valuable information concerning the normal organization of cognitive systems. As a working hypothesis it may

be that in some individuals the progression of the neuropathology of AD follows a path of least resistance defined by neuronal pathways or networks subserving a single domain of functioning. Therefore in these patients the disease may literally carve out functionally related tissue before progressing to other cognitive systems. In the process the hierarchical organization of these systems may be revealed sequentially.

As I have previously suggested (Martin 1987), the subgroups identified in the NIH study—namely, contrasting patterns of impaired and preserved semantic/lexical knowledge and visuospatial functions and corresponding patterns of left temporal or right parietal hypometabolism—were consistent with selective involvement of either one or the other of the two cortical visual systems proposed by Mishkin and colleagues (see, for example, Mishkin, Ungerleider, and Macko 1983). First, the deficits associated with these patient differences is consistent with a large body of evidence on the distinctive roles of temporal and parietal regions. Second, there is evidence suggesting that the semantic disorder in AD progresses from the loss of knowledge of specific object attributes to disruption of specific category and finally higher levels of category knowledge. This pattern of deterioration was noted to be consistent with electrophysiological evidence obtained from nonhuman primates of increasingly higher levels of integration of visual properties, from simple physical attributes to complex objects and categories, as revealed by single-cell recording proceedings from posterior to anterior regions of the inferior temporal lobe (Desimone et al. 1984). This possible correspondence is illustrated in figure 5.3, in which the two cortical visual system pathways are superimposed over the cortical regions of maximal pathology at autopsy (Brun and Englund 1986). Thus the what/where visual system model may provide a useful framework and foundation for conceptualizing some of the grosser cognitive dissociations that can occur in AD. Within this framework the component processes and structures of these and related domains may be revealed by longitudinal study of select patients.

Final Comment

In this chapter I have reviewed the available evidence on the variety of qualitatively distinct clinical presentations associated with AD. It is probably safe to assume that many additional atypical patients would have been revealed if the overwhelming majority of previous investigations had not limited the depth of their analyses to group data. I have also tried to clarify why these types of subgroups should be the

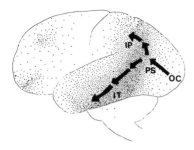

Figure 5.3
The distribution and severity of cortical degeneration in "typical" AD patients, as reported and illustrated by Brun and Englund (1986). The arrows indicate the two cortical visual pathways for object and spatial vision as schematized in Mishkin, Ungerleider, and Macko (1983). OC = occipital cortex; PS = perstriate cortex; IP = inferior parietal lobule; IT = inferior temporal lobe. Mishkin and colleagues have presented considerable evidence to support the role of the prestriate-inferior temporal pathway in object vision and of the prestriate-inferior parietal pathway in spatial processes.

expected finding for AD as well as for all other progressive neurological disorders. Finally, I have delineated some of the implications of these varied clinical presentations for advancing our understanding of this disorder and normal cognitive systems.

A central point has been that our understanding of AD will be hampered if we insist on maintaining research practices that, by their very nature, can potentially obscure fundamental characteristics of entity that they seek to describe. It is likely that in the not too distant future, a biological marker for identifying individuals at risk for AD will be discovered. At that time efforts will be directed toward detecting subtle cognitive or affective changes that would indicate the first signs of this dementing process. This in fact is the task that currently confronts investigators studying individuals infected with the human immunodeficiency virus (HIV). In this situation we know who has the virus, but do not know when, or even if, it will infect the brain before the onset of overt disease. If HIV-seropositive individuals vary with regard to type of initial deficit, then comparison of groups of individuals with and without the virus may yield negative results even though a proportion of individuals in the infected group may be impaired. This possibility has recently been demonstrated by Grant and colleagues (1987), who reported that although 44 percent of the seropositive individuals in their study were impaired on at least one of the nine tasks in their battery, no statistically significant differences were found on any of these measures when asymptomatic seropositive and seronegative control groups were compared. The lesson here should be clear: Data averaging may not only obscure distinct patterns of deficit but also prevent the detection of any impaired individuals when these deficits are relatively subtle and varied.

It should also be clear that the subgrouping and case study approach does not, in and of itself, prevent discovery of universal or invariant features. If commonalities exist, they should be readily apparent from subgroup to subgroup and case to case. For those in need of global generalizations, I offer the following: All dementing disorders will result in subgroups. The degree to which the subgroups within a single disorder (for example, AD) share common features will depend on the degree to which the individuals comprising these groups share common loci of pathology. The same holds for the degree of similarity between one dementing disorder and another (for example, AD versus Parkinson's versus Huntington's dementias).

Figure 5.2 illustrates the position and direction of deterioration for individual patients within a two-dimensional cognitive space. In reality we are dealing with an n-dimensional space, with n equal to the number of cognitive, affective, and motor systems that are independently represented in the brain. If they had been represented singularly, normal individuals would have comprised a cluster in the upper-right-hand sector. The boundaries of that cluster, the forces that hold it together, would be the normal limits of performance on the measures used to assess each domain of functioning. The consequence of progressive dementing disorders would be to remove individuals from this cluster and send them on a path toward the lower-left corner. That is, to the terminal stage of zero performance on all of our measures. The path that an individual took through this multidimensional cognitive space would largely depend on the initial location of pathology and its progression through the brain of that individual subject. Thus commonalities both within and across disorders would be represented by the formation of new clusters during the course of the journey. Our ability to sort out complex relations between cognitive deficits, the development of other types of impairments (for example, myoclonus), biological parameters, subject characteristics (age of onset, sex, family history, prior neurological insult and so on), and type of neuropathology will directly depend on our ability to accurately chart each patient's course.

Acknowledgment

I would like to thank my colleagues, Pim Brouwers, Christiane Cox, and Francois Lalonde, who participated in all phases of the NIH studies, and Thomas N. Chase and

Norman Foster for allowing study of their patients, access to the positron emission tomography data, and permission to cite the autopsy findings.

References

Alzheimer, A. (1907). A peculiar disease of the cerebral cortex (National Library of Medicine trans.). *Allgemeine Zeitschrift fuer die Psychiatrie* 64: 146–148.

Barker, M. G., and Lawson, J. S. (1968). Nominal aphasia in dementia. *British Journal of Psychiatry* 114: 1351–1356.

Beal, M. F., Mazurek, M. F., Tran, V. T., Chattha, G., Bird, E. D., and Martin, J. B. (1985). Reduced numbers of somatostatin receptors in the cerebral cortex in Alzheimer's disease. *Science* 229: 289–291.

Becker, J. T., Huff, F. J., Nebes, R. D., Holland, A., and Boller, F. (1988). Neuropsychological function in Alzheimer's disease: Pattern of impairment and rate of progression. *Archives of Neurology* 45: 263–268.

Benson, D. F., Cummings, J. L., and Tsai, S. Y. (1982). Angular gyrus syndrome simulating Alzheimer's disease. *Archives of Neurology* 39: 616–620.

Bondareff, W., Mountjoy, C. Q., and Roth, M. (1982). Loss of neurons of origin of the adrenergic projection to cerebral cortex (nucleus locus ceruleus) in senile dementia. *Neurology* 32: 164–168.

Bondareff, W., Mountjoy, C. Q., Roth, M., Rossor, M. N., Iversen, L. L., and Reynolds, G. P. (1987). Age and histopathologic heterogeneity in Alzheimer's disease: Evidence for subtypes. *Archives of General Psychiatry* 44: 412–417.

Brouwers, P., Cox, C., Martin, A., Chase, T. N., and Fedio, P. (1984). Differential perceptual-spatial impairment in Huntington's and Alzheimer's dementias. *Archives of Neurology* 41: 1073–1076.

Brun, A., and Englund, E. (1986). A white matter disorder in dementia of the Alzheimer type: A pathoanatomical study. *Annals of Neurology* 19(3): 253–262.

Brun, A., and Gustafson, L. (1976). Distribution of cerebral degeneration in Alzheimer's disease. A clinico-pathological study. *Archives of Psychiatry and Neurological Sciences* 233: 15–33.

Caplan, D. (1981). On the cerebral localization of linguistic functions: Logical and empirical issues surrounding deficit analysis and functional localization. *Brain and Language* 14: 120–137.

Chase, T. N., Foster, N. L., and Mansi, L. (1983). Alzheimer's disease and the parietal lobe. *The Lancet* 2: 225.

Cogan, D. G. (1985). Visual disturbances with focal progressive dementing disease. *American Journal of Ophthalmology* 100: 68–72.

Corkins, S. (1982). Some relationships between global amnesia and the memory impairments in Alzheimer's disease. In S. Corkin, K. L. Davis, J. H. Growdon, and R. J. Wurtman (Eds.) *Alzheimer's Disease: A Report of Progress in Research*. Aging, Vol. 19. New York: Raven Press.

Coughlan, A. K., and Warrington, E. K. (1981). The impairment of verbal semantic memory: A single case study. *Journal of Neurology, Neurosurgery, and Psychiatry* 44: 1079–1083.

Crystal, M. A., Horoupian, D. S., Katzman, R., and Jotkowitz, S. (1982). Biopsy-proved Alzheimer's disease presenting as a right parietal lobe syndrome. *Annals of Neurology* 12: 186–188.

Curcio, C. A., and Kemper, T. (1984). Nucleus raphe dorsalis in dementia of the Alzheimer's type: Neurofibrillary changes and neuronal packing density. *Journal of Neuropathology and Experimental Neurology* 43: 359–368.

DeRenzi, E. (1986). Slowly progressive visual agnosia or apraxia without dementia. *Cortex* 22: 171–180.

Desimone, R., Albright, T. D., Gross, C. G., and Bruce, C. (1984). Stimulus-selective properties of inferior temporal neurons in the macaque. *The Journal of Neuroscience* 4: 2051–2062.

Esiri, M. M., and Wilcock, G. K. (1984). The olfactory bulbs in Alzheimer's disease. *Journal of Neurology, Neurosurgery, and Psychiatry* 47: 56–60.

Faden, A. I., and Townsend, J. J. (1976). Myoclonus in Alzheimer's disease: A confusing sign. *Archives of Neurology* 33: 278–280.

Foster, N. L., and Chase, T. N. (1983). Diffuse involvement in progressive aphasia. *Annals of Neurology* 13: 224–225.

Foster, N. L., Chase, T. N., Fedio, P., Patronas, N. J., Brooks, R. A., and Di Chiro, G. (1983). Alzheimer's disease: Focal cortical changes shown by positron emission tomography. *Neurology* 33: 961–965.

Foster, N. L., Chase, T. N., Mansi, L., Brooks, R., Fedio, P., Patronas, N. J., and Di Chiro, G. (1984). Cortical abnormalities in Alzheimer's disease. *Annals of Neurology* 16(6): 649–654.

Freed, D. M., Corkin, S., Growden, J. H., and Nissen, M. J. (1988). Selective attention in Alzheimer's disease: CSF correlates of behavioral impairments. *Neuropsychologia* 26: 895–902.

Freed, D. M., Corkin, S., Growden, J. H., and Nissen, M. J. (1989). Selective attention in Alzheimer's disease: Characterizing cognitive subgroups of patients. *Neuropsychologia* 27: 325–340.

Friedland, R. P., Brun, A., and Budinger, T. M. (1985). Pathological and positron emission tomographic correlation in Alzheimer's disease. *The Lancet* 1: 228.

Fujiyoshi, K., Suga, H., Okamoto, K., Nakamura, S., and Kemeyama, M. (1987). Reduction of arginine-vasopressin in the cerebral cortex in Alzheimer's type senile dementia. *Journal of Neurology, Neurosurgery, and Psychiatry* 50: 929–932.

Gainotti, G., Caltagirone, C., Masullo, C., and Miceli, G. (1980). Patterns of neuropsychological impairment in various diagnostic groups in dementia. In L. Amaducci, A. N. Davidson, and P. Antuono (Eds.) *Aging of the Brain and Dementia*. Aging, Vol. 13. New York: Raven Press.

Gordon, B., and Selnes, O. (1984). Progressive aphasia "without dementia": Evidence of more widespread involvement. *Neurology* 34: 102.

Grant, I., Atkinson, J. M., Messelink, J. R., Kennedy, C. J., Richman, D. D., Spector, S. A., and McCutchan, J. A. (1987). Evidence for early central nervous system involvement in the Acquired Immunodeficiency Syndrome (AIDS) and other human immunodeficiency virus (HIV) infections. *Annuals of Internal Medicine* 107: 828–836.

Greenamyre, J. T., Penney, J. B., Young, A. B., D'Amato, C. J., Hicks, S. P., and Shoulson, I. (1985). Alterations on L-glutamate binding in Alzheimer's and Huntington's disease. *Science* 227: 1496–1499.

Haxby, J. V., Duara, R., Grady, C. L., Cutler, N. R., and Rapoport, S. I. (1985). Relations between neuropsychological and cerebral metabolic asymmetries in early Alzheimer's disease. *Journal of Cerebral Blood Flow and Metabolism* 5: 193–200.

Heath, P. D., Kennedy, P., and Kapur, N. (1983). Slowly progressive aphasia without generalized dementia. *Annals of Neurology* 13: 687–688.

Herzog, A. G., and Kemper, T. L. (1980). Amygdaloid changes in aging and dementia. *Archives of Neurology* 37: 625–629.

Holland, A. L., McBurney, D. H., Moossy, J., and Reinmuth, O. M. (1985). The dissolution of language in Pick's disease with neurofibrillary tangles: A case study. *Brain and Language* 24: 36–58.

Hyman, B. T., Van Hoesen, G. W., Damasio, A. R., and Barnes, C. L. (1984). Alzheimer's disease: Cell-specific pathology isolates the hippocampal formation. *Science* 225: 1168–1170.

Jagust, W. J., Budinger, T. F., and Reed, B. R. (1987). The diagnosis of dementia with single photon emission computed topography. *Archives of Neurology* 44: 258–262.

Jorm, A. F. (1985). Subtypes of Alzheimer's dementia: A conceptual analysis and critical review. *Psychological Medicine* 15: 543–553.

Katzman, R. (1976). The prevalence and malignancy of Alzheimer's disease. *Archives of Neurology* 33: 217–218.

Kazniak, A. W., Garron, D. C., and Fox, J. (1979). Differential aspects of age and cerebral atrophy upon span of immediate recall and paired associate learning in older patients with suspected dementia. *Cortex* 15: 285–295.

Kirshner, H. S., Tanridag, O., Thurman, L., and Whetsell, W. O. (1987). Progressive aphasia without dementia: Two cases with focal spongiform degeneration. *Annals of Neurology* 22(4): 527–532.

Kirshner, H. S., Webb, W. G., Kelly, M. P., and Wells, C. E. (1984). Language disturbance: An initial symptom of cortical degenerations and dementia. *Archives of Neurology* 41: 491–496.

Kopelman, M. D. (1985). Rates of forgetting in Alzheimer's-type dementia and Korsakoff's syndrome. *Neuropsychologia* 23: 623–638.

Loewenstein, R. J., Weingartner, H., Gillin, C., Kaye, W., Ebert, M., and Mendelson, W. B. (1982). Disturbances of sleep and cognitive functioning in patients with dementia. *Neurobiology of Aging* 3: 371–377.

Mann, D. M. A., and Esiri, M. M. (1988). The site of the earliest lesions of Alzheimer's disease. *New England Journal of Medicine* 318: 789–790.

Mann, D. M. A., Yates, P. O., and Marcyniuk, B. (1984). Monoaminergic neurotransmitter systems in presenile Alzheimer's disease and in senile dementia of Alzheimer type. *Clinical Neuropathology* 3: 199–203.

Marin, O. S. M., Glenn, C. G., and Rafal, R. D. (1983). Visual problem solving in the absence of lexical semantics: Evidence from dementia. *Brain and Cognition* 2: 285–311.

Marshall, J. C., and Newcombe, F. (1984). Putative problems and pure progress in neuropsychological single-case studies. *Journal of Clinical Neuropsychology* 6: 65–70.

Martin, A. (1987). Representation of semantic and spatial knowledge in Alzheimer's patients: Implications for models of preserved learning in amnesia. *Journal of Clinical and Experimental Neuropsychology* 9: 191–224.

Martin, A. (1988). The search for the neuropsychological profile of a disease state: A mistaken enterprise? *Journal of Clinical and Experimental Neuropsychology* 10: 22–23.

Martin, A., Brouwers, P., Cox, C., and Fedio, P. (1985a). On the nature of the verbal memory deficit in Alzheimer's disease. *Brain and Language* 25: 323–341.

Martin, A., Brouwers, P., Lalonde, F., Cox, C., and Fedio, P. (1987). Alzheimer's patient subgroups: Qualitatively distinct patterns of performance and subsequent decline. In R. J. Wurtman, S. H. Corkin, and J. H. Growdon (Eds.) *Alzheimer's Disease: Advances in Basic Research*. Cambridge, MA: Center for Brain Sciences and Metabolism Charitable Trust.

Martin, A., Brouwers, P., Lalonde, F., Cox, C., Foster, N. L., Chase, T. N., and Fedio, P. (1984). Subgroups of Alzheimer's patients: Neuropsychological and cerebral metabolic profiles. *Society for Neuroscience Abstracts* 10: 318.

Martin, A., Brouwers, P., Lalonde, F., Cox, C., Teleska, P., and Fedio, P. (1986). Towards a behavioral typology of Alzheimer's patients. *Journal of Clinical and Experimental Neuropsychology* 8: 594–610.

Martin, A., Cox, C., Brouwers, P., and Fedio, P. (1985b). A note on different patterns of impaired and preserved cognitive abilities and their relation to episodic memory deficits in Alzheimer's patients. *Brain and Language* 26: 181–185.

Martin, A., and Fedio, P. (1983). Word production and comprehension in Alzheimer's disease: The breakdown of semantic knowledge. *Brain and Language* 19: 124–141.

McKhann, G., Drachman, D., Folstein, M., Katzman, R., Price, D., and Stadlan, E. M. (1984). Clinical diagnosis of Alzheimer's disease. *Neurology* 34: 939–944.

Mehler, M. F., Horoupian, D. S., Davies, P., and Dickson, D. W. (1987). Reduced somatostatin-like immunoreactivity in cerebral cortex in nonfamilial dysphasic dementia. *Neurology* 37: 1448–1453.

Mesulam, M.-M. (1987). Primary progressive aphasia: Differentiation from Alzheimer's disease. *Annals of Neurology* 22: 533–534.

Mesulam, M.-M. (1982). Slowly progressive aphasia without generalized dementia. *Annals of Neurology* 11: 592–598.

Mesulam, M.-M., and Weintraub, S. (1983). Diffuse involvement in progressive aphasia (reply). *Annals of Neurology* 13: 225.

Mishkin, M., Ungerleider, L. G., and Macko, K. A. (1983). Object vision and spatial vision: Two cortical pathways. *Trends in Neuroscience* 6: 414–417.

Moossy, J., Zubenko, G. S., Martinez, A. J., and Rao, G. R. (1988). Bilateral symmetry of morphologic lesions in Alzheimer's disease. *Archives of Neurology* 45: 251–254.

Morris, J. C., Cole, M., Banker, B. Q., and Wright, D. (1984). Hereditary dysphasic dementia and the Pick-Alzheimer spectrum. *Annals of Neurology* 16: 455–466.

Morris, R. G. (1986). Short-term forgetting in senile dementia of the Alzheimer's type. *Cognitive Neuropsychology* 3: 77–97.

Neary, D., Snowden, J. S., Bowen, D. M., Sims, N. R., Mann, D. M. A., Benton, J. S., Northen, B., Yates, P. O., and Davison, A. N. (1986). Neuropsychological syndromes in presenile dementia due to cerebral atrophy. *Journal of Neurology, Neurosurgery, and Psychiatry* 49: 163–174.

Pearson, R. C. A., Esiri, M. M., Hiorns, R. W., Wilcock, G. K., and Powell, T. P. S. (1985). Anatomical correlates of the distribution of the pathological changes in the neocortex in Alzheimer disease. *Proceedings the National Academy of Sciences* 82: 4531–4533.

Phillips, C. G., Zeki, S., and Barlow, H. B. (1984). Localization of function in the cerebral cortex: Past, present, and future. *Brain* 107: 327–361.

Pillon, B., Dubois, B., Lhermitte, F., and Agid, Y. (1986). Heterogeneity of cognitive impairment in progressive supranuclear palsy, Parkinson's disease and Alzheimer's disease. *Neurology* 36: 1179–1185.

Pogacar, S., and Williams, R. S. (1984). Alzheimer's disease presenting as slowly progressive aphasia. *Rhode Island Medical Journal* 67: 181–185.

Prinz, P. N., Peskind, E. R., Vitaliano, P. P., Raskind, M. A., Eisodorfer, C., Zemcuzniko, N., and Gerber, C. J. (1982). Changes in the sleep and waking EEG of nondemented and demented elderly subjects. *Journal of the American Geriatric Society* 30: 86–94.

Prohovnik, I., Mayeux, R., Sackeim, M. A., Smith, G., Stern, Y., and Alderson, P. O. (1988). Cerebral perfusion as a diagnostic marker of early Alzheimer's disease. *Neurology* 38: 931–937.

Reyes, P. F., Golden, G. T., Fagel, P. L., Fariello, R. G., Katz, L., and Carner, E. (1987). The prepiriform cortex in dementia of Alzheimer type. *Archives of Neurology* 44: 644–645.

Rochford, G. (1971). A study of naming errors in dysphasic and demented patients. *Neuropsychologia* 9: 437–443.

Rossor, M. N. (1983). Focal changes in Alzheimer's disease and cholinergic hypothesis. *The Lancet* 2: 465.

Rossor, M. N., Garrett, N. J., Johnson, A. L., Mountjoy, C. Q., Roth, M., and Iversen, L. L. (1982). A post-mortem study of the cholinergic and GABA systems in senile dementia. *Brain* 105: 313–330.

Rossor, M. N., Iversen, L. L., Johnson, A. L., Mountjoy, C. Q., and Roth, M. (1981). Cholinergic deficit in frontal cerebral cortex in Alzheimer's disease is age dependent. *The Lancet* 2: 1422.

Rossor, M., and Iversen, L. L. (1986). Non-cholinergic neurotransmitter abnormalities in Alzheimer's disease. *British Medical Bulletin* 42: 70–74.

Rosvold, H. E., Mirsky, A. F., and Pribram, K. M. (1954). Influences of amygdalectomy on social behavior in monkeys. *Journal of Comparative and Physiological Psychology* 47: 173–178.

Schwartz, M. F., Marin, O. S. M., and Saffran, E. M. (1979). Dissociation of language function in dementia: A case study. *Brain and Language* 7: 277–306.

Shuttleworth, E. C. (1984). Atypical presentations of dementia of the Alzheimer type. *Journal of the American Geriatric Society* 32: 485–490.

Stuss, D. T., and Benson, D. F. (1984). Neuropsychological studies of the frontal lobes. *Psychological Bulletin* 95: 3–28.

Tariska, I. (1970). Circumscribed cerebral atrophy in Alzheimer's disease: A pathological study. In G. E. Wolstenholme and M. O'Connor (Eds.) *Alzheimer's Disease and Related Conditions*. Ciba Foundation Symposium. London: Churchill.

Tierney, M. C., Fisher, R. H., Lewis, A. J., Zorzitto, M. L., Snow W. G., Reid, D. W., and Nieuwstraten, P. (1988). The NINCDS-ADRDA Work Group criteria for the clinical diagnosis of probable Alzheimer's disease: A clinicopathologic study of 57 cases. *Neurology* 38: 359–364.

Warrinton, E. K. (1975). The selective impairment of semantic memory. *Quarterly Journal of Experimental Psychology* 27: 635–657.

Wechsler, A. F., Verity, M. A., Rosenschein, S., Freid, I., and Scheibel, A. B. (1982). Pick's disease: A clinical, computed tomographic, and histopathological study with Golgi impregnation observations. *Archives of Neurology* 39: 287–290.

Weingartner, H., Kaye, W., Smallberg, S. A., Ebert, M. H., Gillin, J. C., and Sitaram, N. (1981). Memory failures in progressive idiopathic dementia. *Journal of Abnormal Psychology* 90: 187–196.

Weiskrantz, L., and Warrington, E. K. (1975). The problem of the amnesic syndrome in man and animals. In R. L. Isaacson and K. H. Pribram (Eds.) *The Hippocampus*. Vol. 2. New York: Plenum Press.

Whitehouse, P. J., Price, D. L., Struble, R. G., Clark, A. W., Coyle, J. T., and DeLong, M. R. (1982). Alzheimer's disease and senile dementia: Loss of neurons in the basal forebrain. *Science* 215, 1237–1239.

Yamamoto, T., and Hirano, A. (1985). Nucleus raphe dorsalis in Alzheimer's disease: Neurofibrillary tangles and loss of large neurons. *Annals of Neurology* 17: 573–577.

Zubenko, G. S., Mossy, J., Hanin, I., Martinez, J., Rao, G. R., and Kopp, U. (1988). Bilateral symmetry of cholinergic deficits in Alzheimer's disease. *Archives of Neurology* 45: 255–259.

Chapter 6

Symptomatology of Alzheimer-Type Dementia: Report on a Survey by Mail

Myrna F. Schwartz, Jonathan Baron, and Morris Moscovitch

This chapter takes up many of the same themes as chapter 5, in the context of a large-scale questionnaire sent out to members of the Alzheimer's Disease and Related Diseases Association. The questionnaire presented these caregivers of DAT patients with descriptions of 135 specific symptoms, asking that they rate those symptoms for severity both as current manifestations of the disease and as early manifestations. Factor analyses carried out on the symptom ratings identified orthogonal factors that largely conform to a priori expectations about the major symptom domains of DAT. Several of these factors succeeded in predicting certain clinical and demographic characteristics of the sample.

To examine what if any symptom-based subgroups existed in the sample, the investigators entered the individuals' factor scores into cluster analysis. This procedure yielded three patient groupings, but these groupings were differentiated primarily by factors bearing on affect and personality changes, not by the cognitive factors. Moreover, in contrast to the factors, the obtained clusters were not found to have clinical or demographic significance.

The authors use these results to argue for a multicomponential account of DAT, and against the idea of subgroups—where subgroups implies uniformity of symptom profile (not the sense intended by Martin, chapter 5). Patients who are judged to be alike by virtue of the prominence of the impairment in one symptom domain—for example, language or memory—need not, and do not in their sample, share a common profile apart from that domain.

M. F. S.

Descriptions of the clinical course of dementia of the Alzheimer type (DAT) generally make reference to a stagewise progression of symptoms: a first stage dominated by personality changes and amnesia; a second stage by the erosion of competence in the areas of language, praxis, and gnosis; and a third stage by the introduction of "hard" neurologic signs, including progressive immobility and the appearance of primitive reflexes (for example, Coblentz et al. 1973, Cummings 1982, Haase 1971). On the other hand several recent reports have called attention to patients whose progression of symptoms violates this typical pattern, patients in whom focal signs predominate from the outset or in whom the difficulties in one domain of cognitive function are dramatically disproportionate to the level of function in other domains (see Schwartz 1987 and references therein).

Whereas the stagewise characterization of DAT is consistent with an earlier conceptualization of global dementia as the clinical manifestation of progressive whole-brain dysfunction (Schwartz and Stark, chapter 2), the variety of atypical presentations are more in keeping with other evidence for specificity and multifocality. It is now apparent that the manner and degree of impairment in memory, language, visuospatial function, and so on is determined by the density and distribution of the underlying degenerative changes and that these changes can, in some patients at least, remain circumscribed (Brun and Englund 1981, Chase et al. 1984, Hagberg and Ingvar 1976, Tariska 1970).

Several investigators have responded to the heterogeneity in DAT by postulating subgroups or subtypes (for example, Chui et al. 1985, Mayeux, Stern, and Spanton 1985, Martin et al. 1986). The general tendency here is to identify the subtype with the presence of a particular symptom or with its disproportionate severity. Thus Alex Martin and his colleagues have presented data that they claim demonstrate the existence of at least two subtypes of DAT: one characterized by poor language and good visuospatial abilities, the second by the reverse pattern (Martin, chapter 5, Martin et al. 1986; see also Becker et al. 1988).

The essence of the subtypes model, as it has thus far been articulated, is the rejection of the notion of a homogeneous disintegration of function in DAT and the acceptance of the goal of delimiting a set of symptom domains that define and differentiate patients. We are in sympathy with this program, but we are not persuaded of the existence of true subtypes (also see Jorm 1986). As a preliminary to making the case, we believe that at least these questions need to be answered: What are the dimensions of variation that comprise the DAT symptomatology? Do quantitative differences in these dimensions have etiological significance, that is, are they predictive of clinical course, age at onset, or familial inheritance? Can groups of patients be identified who share common profiles with respect to these dimensions of variation? What, if anything, is the etiological significance of these groupings?

Answering questions like these requires access to extensive longitudinal data, gathered from a large number of subjects. Firsthand data of this sort is very hard to come by. We have elected to rely instead on secondhand reports, that is, on the insights and memories of those who live with and care for individuals with DAT. We report here on the findings of a questionnaire study conducted by mail, whose respondents were members of the national Alzheimer's Disease and Related Diseases Association (ADRDA).

Method

The Symptom Questionnaire

The questionnaire was organized into seven scales, identified by headings: Memory, Control of Movements, Practical Knowledge, Spatial Orientation, Perception, Language, and Emotion/Personality. Under each heading was enumerated a set of very specific symptoms, each followed by three questions:

> Was this a source of difficulty before the disease?
> Has this been a problem associated with the disease?
> If this has been a symptom, did it occur early on?

We call these questions *Prior*(P), *Current*(C), and *Early*(E), respectively. The Prior question was intended to provide information on whether premorbid strengths and weaknesses affect the manifestation of the disease and its course. We also anticipated that it might pick out very early symptoms not attributed by the respondent to the disease process.

Respondents indicated their answers to the three questions by circling one of series of letters—*Y, S, N, ?,* and *X*—corresponding to *yes, somewhat, no, don't know,* and *does not apply,* respectively. For data analysis a response of *yes* was coded as 1, *somewhat* as 2, *no* as 3, and *?* and *X* as missing data. It is important to remember, in the report of the data, that higher scores represent better (less impaired) clinical status.

In constructing the symptom items, we had in mind several things: first, the patterns of symptom associations and dissociations observed after focal insult to critical forebrain structures; second, the various claims in the literature concerning the clinical course of Alzheimer's disease and related dementing disorders; third, our own years of experience in the neuropsychological assessment of demented patients. Thus the memory scale, for example, included items designed to assess, among other things, the temporal dimension of a possible retrieval deficit:

Cannot recall things that happened years before or in childhood.

Cannot recall things that happened in the last few days.

Cannot recall things that happened a few minutes ago.

difficulties in the registration or acquisition of new information:

Cannot keep track of the events in the lives of family and close friends.

and visual versus verbal memory codes:

Cannot recognize close friends when he/she sees them.

Cannot recognize close friends by name.

Similarly the language scale queried the adequacy of expressive and receptive functions at word and sentence levels and in both the spoken and written domains.

These symptom scales formed the bulk of the questionnaire. In addition information was obtained concerning medical history, medications taken, family history of the disease, and when the onset of symptoms was first noticed and by whom.

Subjects

One thousand questionnaires were mailed in the spring of 1982 to the national membership of ADRDA. Approximately 500 were completed and returned.

Because the focus of this study was people with primary degenerative disorders, the returned forms were screened carefully on the basis of the personal and medical history. We excluded from all further analyses subjects with a past history of cerebrovascular accident or head trauma and those with any other neurological conditions that might directly, or through pharmacological intervention, compromise high cortical functions (for example, epilepsy, parkinsonism). Other criteria for exclusion were past history of alcoholism or of major psychiatric illness. One subject was excluded because of his career in professional boxing.

It should be noted that in applying these exclusion criteria, we attempted to distinguish between *premorbid* medical history versus the history of complications arising from the dementing condition. For example, seizure episodes occurring for the first time in clear association with other dementing signs were not considered grounds for exclusion. After the application of these exclusion criteria, we were left with 324 questionnaires to analyze. The sample includes slightly more males (176) than females (148), spanning the ages 34 through 92.

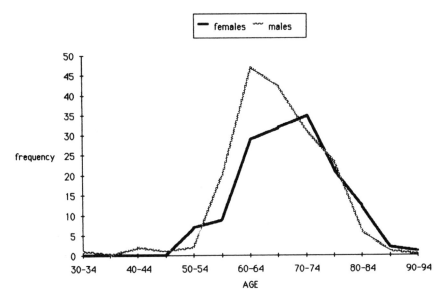

Figure 6.1
Age distribution for women (n = 148) and men (n = 176) in the sample.

Results

Subject Characteristics
These variables, which describe our sample, also enter into subsequent analyses:

Age   AGE means the age of the individual about whom the questionnaire was completed, specifically, the age during the year of the questionnaire or the age at death, whichever came first. In our sample the mean for AGE is 67.7, standard deviation (SD) 7.9, range 34 to 92. The AGE distribution is essentially comparable for males and females. In both sexes there is a single mode in the years 58 through 75 (see figure 6.1).

Onset   ONSET refers to the age of the subject when symptoms first became apparent, according to the respondent. Mean in our sample is 60.4, SD 8.9, range 30 to 88. ONSET is highly correlated with AGE ($r = .88$). As with AGE the distribution of ONSET is unimodal for both males and females, with a peak in the range 55 to 65 (see figure 6.2). Hence there is no basis in our sample for the distinction into presenile and senile forms of DAT.

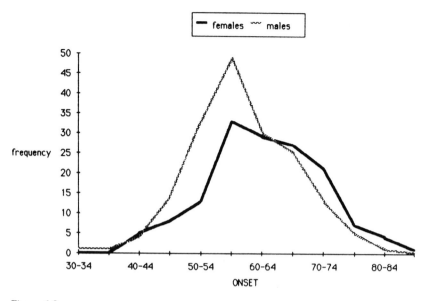

Figure 6.2
Distribution of estimated age of onset for women (n = 148) and men (n = 176).

Time Period TIME, the duration of the disease, was estimated for each subject from AGE minus ONSET. Mean TIME in our sample is 7.4 years, SD 4.3.

Medications The questionnaire queried informants as to the medications currently being taken by the subject. Based on their replies, five subject groups were formed:

> 1. Antipsychotics and major tranquilizers (for example, haloperidol, thioridazine, thiothixene): 69 subjects
> 2. Antidepressants and antianxiety agents (for example, imipramine hydrochloride, diazepam): 22 subjects
> 3. Anticonvulsants (for example, phenytoin, carbamazepine, phenobarbital): 6 subjects
> 4. Antispasmodics (for example, benztropine mesylate): 5 subjects
> 5. Other medications or no medication: 117 subjects

Subjects taking more than one drug were assigned to the lowest of the relevant groups. The remaining subjects, who were counted as missing data for medications analysis, were nevertheless included in all subsequent analyses.

Family   Respondents' replies to the family history query were coded on the FAMILY scale, in which 0 represents no known relatives with Alzheimer's disease (or "senility"), 1 represents one sibling or parent with the disease, and 2 represents more than one sibling or parent (cousins and grandparents alone were counted as missing data, as were cases in which this item was left blank). Code 0 was assigned to 153 subjects, code 1 to 60 subjects, and code 2 to 14 subjects. The correlation between FAMILY and ONSET is nonsignificant ($r = -.07$, $p > .10$). Thus positive family histories are as likely in late as in early onset cases.

Severity   A severity score, SUM, was computed for each subject by adding together all 135 current (C) symptom scores. In this and all other score-based calculations, missing items were replaced by item means across subjects. Because low numbers code for presence of deficit for individual symptom items, lower values of SUM indicate greater overall severity.

A central concern of this study was to determine whether severity level, SUM, was predictable from other variables, including Early symptom patterns. To determine the basic model for predicting SUM, we entered into a stepwise regression analysis the variables SEX, ONSET, FAMILY, TIME, and, to take account of any slowdown in the course of deterioration, TIMESQT, the square root of TIME.

The result showed that the best-fit model for SUM includes the variables TIME, TIMESQT, and SEX. The interaction terms do not enter into the model. Males and females show comparable deterioration over time, but females are judged more severe at all time periods. The coefficients for TIME and TIMESQT are $+10$ and -69, respectively. Because lower values of SUM indicate greater severity, this means that severity increases roughly as the square root of TIME (higher powers of TIME did not improve prediction).

Neither ONSET nor FAMILY contributes further to the prediction of SUM once TIME and TIMESQT have been entered.

Comment on Subject Characteristics

In the population at large there are many more women with dementia than men with dementia. This is mainly attributable to the fact that women tend to live longer, but it may also be true that DAT is more likely to develop in women (Mortimer and Hutton 1985, Rocca, Amaducci, and Schoenberg 1986). Nevertheless in our sample there are substantially more men than women. The most likely explanation for this is that wives of patients are more likely than husbands to join the

ADRDA support group and more willing to participate as respondents in our study.

This sampling bias undoubtedly influenced other demographic features of our data as well. For example, it is likely that the distribution of ONSET we obtained reflects the overrepresentation of early-onset patients among the ADRDA membership at that time. (Recall that until very recently cognitive deterioration in the very elderly was not considered evidence of pathology.) Thus whereas population studies tend to report a steep increase in age-specific incidence, at least up to age 90, our ONSET distribution peaks at 55 to 65 years and falls off sharply after age 75. The fact that our sample contains rather few subjects with late-onset dementia may account for the finding that ONSET does not contribute to the prediction of SUM, a finding that contradicts the well-supported generalization that early-onset patients deteriorate more rapidly (for example, Heston et al. 1981, Heston 1983, Seltzer and Sherwin 1983; but see Chui et al. 1985, Mayeux, Stern, and Spanton 1985).

The literature on genetic risk factors in DAT indicates that there are at least two forms of the disease: one aggregates in families in accordance with an autosomal dominant inheritance, and a second is sporadic. It was our a priori expectation, based again on preconceptions about the ADRDA membership, that our study would overrepresent patients with the familial form, but this is not what we found. Rather the percent of subjects with one or more first-degree relatives with dementia was 33 percent (74 of 227), which is well within the reported range (25 percent to 45 percent, as reported in Barclay et al. 1986, Chui et al. 1985, Fitch, Becker, and Heller 1988, Heston et al. 1981, Heyman et al. 1984, and Mayeux, Stern, and Spanton 1985).

The nonsignificant correlation between FAMILY and ONSET merits some discussion. Heston and colleagues (1981) found that the subjects with familial DAT tended to have more youthful onset; and this was confirmed in several studies involving large families with obvious autosomal dominant inheritance patterns (cited in Fitch, Becker, and Heller 1988). On the other hand the studies of Fitch, Becker, and Heller (1988), Chui and colleagues (1985), and Heyman and colleagues (1983) found no reliable association between age at onset and incidence of secondary dementia. Our findings support this lack of association, but here again the results might have been affected by paucity of late-onset cases.

The mean duration of illness in our sample is long (7.4 years), which implies that the sample contains many individuals who are severely deteriorated. We identified severely deteriorated subjects as those for whom at least 90 percent of the items (excluding those of the emotion/personality scale) were scored by the respondent as 1 (definite symptom). Sixty-two subjects met this criterion. In view of the fact that such deteriorated subjects cannot contribute to the definition of symptom patterns, their data were excluded from the various analyses performed on Current symptoms. These data were, however, entered into other analyses, including factor and cluster analyses performed on the Early question.

Symptoms

Current Symptoms   Table 6.1 lists the 20 most prevalent C-symptoms (items) in our sample, as measured by mean score across the 262 subjects (324 minus the 62 deteriorated cases). It is apparent that memory, and in particular recent memory symptoms, are especially prevalent. Indeed from the proximity of these obtained means to 1.0 (the response indicating definite impairment), it appears that recent memory impairments are ubiquitous in this subject pool.

In general the symptom listing in table 6.1 corresponds well with standard characterizations of DAT. This lends confidence in the validity of informants' judgments.

Early Symptoms   As shown in table 6.2, the most prevalent E-symptoms constitute a somewhat more heterogeneous array than was found with C-symptoms. Impairments of recent memory are evident, but so too are topographical disorientation and difficulties in the domain of practical knowledge and the performance of everyday tasks. This contradicts the general impression that onset of DAT is necessarily heralded by memory disturbance.

Prior Symptoms   The most common P-symptoms implicated memory and emotional lability; but the means of these are high, in the range 2.7 to 2.9. In fact most respondents checked off very few of these items. We disregard the data from the Prior question in subsequent discussion except where it helps to illuminate the evidence concerning Early and Current symptom patterns.

Factor Analysis

Current Symptoms   As a first step toward identifying salient symptom patterns, we performed exploratory factor analysis on the 135–C-item ratings for 262 subjects. We began with principal components (PC) analysis, a procedure that assigns to each item a loading on each of several factors, with the goal of explaining the item-item correla-

Table 6.1
Most Prevalent Current Symptoms

Rank	Scale	Current Symptom	Mean
1	Practical knowledge	Cannot keep track of finances	1.09
2	Memory	Cannot recall things from last few days	1.10
3	Memory	Cannot hold something (e.g., phone number) in mind for a few seconds	1.13
4	Memory	Cannot remember phone numbers, addresses of close friends and relatives	1.14
5	Language	Cannot write reports, letters, etc.	1.14
6	Spatial orientation	Cannot find way to new destinations	1.16
7	Memory	Cannot recall events from the past year	1.16
8	Memory	Cannot keep track of daily events	1.16
9	Memory	Cannot follow plot of TV show or movie	1.16
10	Memory	Cannot recall events from last few minutes	1.16
11	Memory	Cannot remember names of people recently met	1.18
12	Memory	Cannot keep track of month, year, or time of year	1.18
13	Memory	Cannot keep track of daily news events	1.18
14	Movement	Cannot perform complex tasks, like typing, carpentry, etc.	1.21
15	Memory	Cannot keep track of the lives of family and friends	1.23
16	Language	Cannot express ideas coherently	1.24
17	Language	Cannot maintain train of thought when speaking	1.24
18	Emotion/ personality	Tends to become confused or disoriented	1.24
19	Memory	Cannot remember events from 1 to 5 years ago	1.25
20	Practical knowledge	Cannot solve problems around house (e.g., source of a leak)	1.26

Table 6.2
Most Prevalent Early Symptoms

Rank	Scale	Current Symptom	Mean
1	Practical knowledge	Cannot keep track of finances	1.57
2	Spatial orientation	Cannot find way to new destinations	1.67
3	Memory	Cannot remember names of people recently met	1.71
4	Movements	Cannot perform complex tasks, like typing, carpentry, etc.	1.72
5	Memory	Cannot recall events from last few days	1.73
6	Emotion/ personality	Tends to become confused or disoriented	1.74
7	Memory	Cannot remember phone numbers, addresses of close friends and relatives	1.76
8	Language	Cannot write reports, letters, etc.	1.76
9	Memory	Cannot hold something (e.g., phone number) in mind for a few seconds	1.77
10	Language	Cannot write out checks	1.77
11	Memory	Cannot recall what happened in past year	1.79
12	Practical knowledge	Cannot pay for items purchased and keep track of change	1.79
13	Memory	Cannot keep track of what needs to be done during the course of the day	1.80
14	Practical knowledge	Cannot add and subtract simple figures	1.80
15	Memory	Cannot keep track of daily news events	1.81
16	Language	Cannot maintain a train of thought when speaking	1.82
17	Practical knowledge	Cannot solve problems around the house	1.82
18	Practical knowledge	Cannot make up a shopping list	1.87
19	Memory	Cannot remember events from 1 to 5 years ago	1.87
20	Practical knowledge	Cannot select needed food, clothes, etc. when shopping	1.88

tions in terms of loadings on common factors. Item loadings on the first PC accounts for the largest proportion of the variance expressed in the correlations. (Most of the variance in the first PC is due to overall severity; our first PC correlates .99 with SUM, the severity measure.) Each successive component is orthogonal to (not derivable from) other components and accounts for as much of the remaining variance as possible. In this case the first principal component accounts for 29 percent of the variance in the data. The first eight principal components together account for 56 percent of the variance, and there is little gain in resolving power with the addition of successive factors.

As step two these first eight principal components were subjected to rotation under the varimax criterion. Here the aim is to identify groups of symptoms that reveal the basic dimensions of symptom variation in our sample. In general the extracted varimax factors form psychologically cogent groupings:

Memory (11.8 per cent of the total variance) This factor closely parallels the memory scale as constructed on the questionnaire. It encompasses items dealing with anterograde and retrograde loss for all periods sampled, also the inability to keep track of ongoing events (including own behavior), loss of personal history and personal data. If there is a single psychological dimension identified here, it is a failure of information retrieval.

Movement (11.1 percent) The symptom items for this factor all deal with problems in the execution of movements. Most of these bear on difficulties orienting in space (for example, dressing), but other nonspatial acts of coordinated movement are also included (for example, walking at a normal pace). The items of this factor draw from two of our original scales: Control of Movements and Spatial Orientation.

Language (8.9 percent) This factor, drawing entirely on items from the Language scale of the questionnaire, implicates problems in speaking, understanding, reading, and writing.

Perception (5.4 percent) Symptoms of sensory/perceptual loss in the visual, auditory, and tactile modalities.

Affect (5.4 percent) These symptom items from the Emotion/Personality scale all deal with exaggerated affective responses: "Talks of suicide" and "inappropriate affect" items load most highly, also excessive concern over food, clothing, and personal hygiene, and inappropriate sexual behavior.

Agitated Depression (5.2 percent) Also drawing from the Emotion/Personality scale of the questionnaire, the symptoms constituting this factor are withdrawal, lethargy, sadness, emotional lability, outbursts of anger, distractibility, and nocturnal pacing.

Tasks (4.4 percent) Difficulties in the performance of complex tasks: driving, making purchases, planning, problem solving.

Withdrawal (3.8 percent) Mutism, unresponsiveness, altered eating behavior ("eats too quickly," "shows little interest in food").

Early Symptoms   A separate factor analysis was performed on the ratings for the Early question for all 343 subjects. Once again the first eight principal components, accounting for 61 percent of the total variance, were rotated by the varimax criterion. The composition of the extracted varimax factors is similar, but not identical, to the Current factors:

Activities (13.8 percent of total variance explained) This factor includes items from three different scales of the questionnaire: Practical Knowledge, Control of Movements, Spatial Orientation. A wide variety of daily activities are implicated: driving, dialing a telephone, making purchases, operating appliances, telling time, cooking, dressing.

Memory (11.6 percent) Once again the broad spectrum of memory symptoms brought together under the memory factor implicate a retrieval deficit. Memories for remote as well as recent time periods are affected, including even overlearned autobiographical facts (for example, own address and phone number).

Affect (7.3 percent) Exaggerated and inappropriate affective behavior reflecting depression, paranoid ideation, obsessional concerns, manic behavior, also incontinence of bladder and bowel.

Language (7.3 percent) As with the corresponding C-symptom factor, draws from items dealing with speaking, understanding, reading, and writing.

Agitated Depression (6.6 percent) Symptoms reflect distractibility, withdrawal, altered sleeping and eating patterns, neglect of personal hygiene, outbursts of hostility.

Motor Control (5.1 percent) Difficulties standing, sitting, walking, and chewing.

Discrimination (4.7 percent) Alterations in smell, taste, and color perception.

Sensory Loss (4.5 percent). Altered acuity in vision and audition.

Factor Correlations
Each subject was assigned a factor score on each factor: the standardized sum, across items, of the item loading multiplied by that

subject's item score. It is in the nature of the varimax factor analysis that these factor scores are orthogonal to one another; that is, the eight C-symptom factors are uncorrelated, as are the eight E-symptom factors. This orthogonality does not hold, however, across C and E factors. In table 6.3 we present the patterns of correlations that obtain across Current and Early symptom scores.

In most cases these correlations are easily understood in terms of the similarity of item loadings; this is true for the correlations of C-Memory and E-Memory (.28), C-Language and E-Language (.31), C-Perception and E-Sensory Loss (.62), C-Affect and E-Affect (.71), C-Agitated Depression and E-Agitated Depression (.55).

Other patterns are instructive for what they reveal about the impurity of certain of the factors. An example is the high positive correlation between the E-Activities factor and two C-factors: C-Movement (.35) and C-Tasks (.38). The first of these associations turns out to be accounted for entirely by those items in E-Activities that involve movement coordination and sequencing, in particular dressing, and not at all to those items relating to mental problem solving (for example, making purchases). Thus the E-Activities factor may be viewed as a combination of the C-Tasks and C-Movement factors, which may be less discriminable in E-symptoms (hence not separated by an analysis limited to eight factors).

The E-Language factor is a positive predictor of C-Withdrawal (.24) and a negative predictor of C-Agitated Depression (−.22). Presumably this reflects how serious an impediment to social interaction is the loss of communication skills. Note, however, that C-Withdrawal involves the altered responsiveness to food, in addition to mutism and lack of understanding, and as such is suggestive of the profile of late-stage Pick's disease. Early language involvement is also a common finding in Pick's disease, as is the blunting of affect. Conceivably then this association of factors could be a consequence of the presence in our sample of a group of patients with Pick's disease. This possibility is addressed further in the cluster analysis section.

Predictions from Factors

Onset Through multiple regression analysis it was determined that ONSET was predictable from the eight current factors ($R^2 = .12$, $p < .0003$). To determine which of the individual factor variables was responsible, we examined the standardized coefficients for the individual factors, equivalent to the partial correlation coefficient. Significant correlations were obtained for C-Affect ($−.16$, $p < .009$), C-Agitated Depression ($+.14$, $p < .01$), C-Tasks ($+.14$, $p < .02$), and

Table 6.3
Correlation Matrix for Early (E) and Current (C) Varimax Factors

C-Factors	E-Factors							
	ADL	Memory	Affect	Language	Agit.-Dep.	Motor	Discrim.	Sens. Loss
Memory	0.00	0.28	-0.11	-0.15	-0.08	-0.13	0.24	-0.05
Movement	0.35	-0.15	-0.05	-0.19	-0.15	0.34	0.08	0.06
Language	0.11	-0.09	-0.01	0.31	-0.05	-0.18	0.16	-0.04
Perception	0.06	0.06	0.00	0.01	-0.02	-0.03	0.21	0.62
Affect	-0.04	0.06	0.71	-0.06	-0.45	-0.08	-0.01	0.02
Agit.-Dep.	0.10	-0.06	0.27	-0.22	0.55	0.00	-0.06	0.09
Tasks	0.38	-0.13	0.05	0.00	0.08	0.00	-0.14	-0.08
Withdrawal	-0.24	0.06	0.20	0.24	0.15	0.22	0.00	-0.09

C-Movement $(+.12, p < .05)$. In interpreting the sign of these correlations it must be kept in mind that low factor scores are indicative of high severity. Hence early onset is associated with greater severity on Depression, Tasks, and Movement, and with less severity on Affect.

ONSET is also predicted by the eight Early factor scores $(R^2 = .11, p < .0001)$, and in particular by E-Agitated Depression (partial correlation $+.22, p < .0001$) and E-Memory $(-.12, p < .03)$. Hence the association of early onset with greater agitated depression holds for early presentation as well. On the other hand youthful onset is associated with *less severe* early memory symptoms.

A very similar pattern of results obtains when AGE is substituted for ONSET as the predicted variable (Recall that AGE and ONSET are highly correlated, $r = +.88$.)

Sex   The eight C-factors successfully differentiate women from men in this study $(R^2 = .14, p < .0008)$. The significant partial correlations are obtained for Memory $(+.25, p < .0003)$, Tasks $(+.14, p < .03)$, and Withdrawal $(-.19, p < .007)$; women are more impaired on the first two of these three factors; men are more impaired on the third. Regressing SEX on the eight Early factors did not yield significant results $(R^2 = .06, p > .05)$.

Family   Although family history was coded on a three-point scale (see Data Analysis), we treated FAMILY as a continuous variable in our analysis so as not to lose information. Regression analysis performed on the eight Current factors yielded overall significance $(R^2 = .09, p < .02)$, as did a second analysis on the early factors $(R^2 = .10, p < .002)$. Significant partial correlations obtained for C-Language $(+.18, p < .01)$ and C-Memory $(-.15, p < .03)$ and for E-Motor $(+.23, p < .0005)$ and E-Discrimination $(+.17, p < .009)$. The interpretation of these results is that severity on Memory predicts positive family history, whereas severity on Language, Motor, and Discrimination predicts negative family history.

Sum   The question posed here is whether Current severity level, indexed by SUM, is predicted by the pattern of Early symptom involvement. To answer this question, we normalized the Early factor scores for each subject around his or her mean Early factor score and entered these eight normalized Early factor scores into a regression analysis for SUM, along with the variables TIME, TIMESQT, and SEX. A multiple-partial F-test revealed that the normalized Early factor scores as a group contributed significantly to the prediction of SUM beyond those other variables ($F_{(7,224)} = 2.45$, $p < .05$). As for individual normalized factors only E-Language yielded a (minimally) significant partial correlation ($-.18$, $p = .05$), meaning that severe early language involvement predicts *better* overall status later on.

Cluster Analysis
Cluster analysis was performed to identify groups of subjects such that subjects within a group would be similar to one another in their pattern of factor scores. We used the S. A. S. Fastclus program, an iterative, nonhierarchical method that first assigns each subject to a cluster and then moves subjects iteratively from cluster to cluster so as to minimize the sum of the squared deviations of each subject from the middle of his cluster, for a prespecified number of clusters. Ten iterations were sufficient to allow the clusters to stabilize.

The inputs to this cluster analysis were the second through eighth principal components for the Current and Early symptoms. We eliminated the first principal component because we wanted the clusters to reflect the *pattern* of symptoms rather than overall severity. Combining Current and Early factors together into a single analysis was done to reduce the likelihood of error and to make possible the definition of disease patterns over longitudinal profile.

The cubic clustering criterion (CCC), a recommended index of the goodness of clusters, was maximized when the number of clusters was 3. We obtained a CCC of 18.05. On the null hypothesis the expected CCC for the number of clusters, variables, and observations we used is (conservatively) -6.6, SD 0.8. (Sarle 1983); thus it appears that our clusters are not due to chance. The three clusters contained 84, 106, and 153 subjects, respectively.

To determine which factor scores discriminated the clusters, we performed separate regression analyses for each pair of clusters, once using the varimax Current factors as predictors, and a second time with Early factors. The standarized coefficient for the individual factor scores, equivalent to the partial correlation coefficient, is the result of interest here, and the findings are easily summarized: The most robust correlations by far were seen for the factors reflecting affective involvement, and in particular C-Affect and E-Agitated Depression. In the following summary absolute values of these partial correlations are reported. The sign of the correlations is accounted for in the verbal summary (also see figure 6.3).

Clusters 1 and 2 are differentiated almost entirely by the factors C-Affect and E-Agitated Depression (partial correlations .90 and .86, respectively). Relative to cluster 2 cluster 1 is characterized by high severity on C-Affect and low severity on E-Agitated Depression.

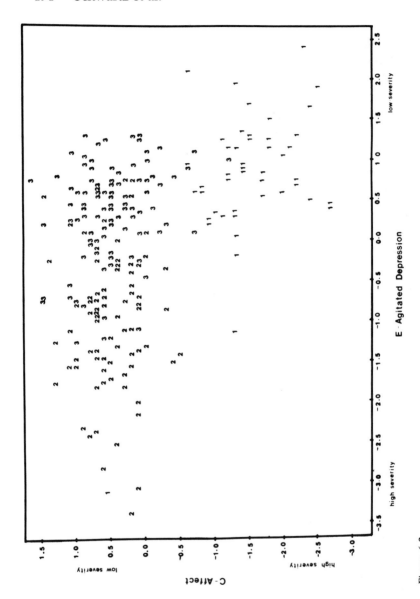

Figure 6.3
Standard scores for the factors C-Affect and E-Agitated Depression, according to cluster membership (26 observations are hidden)

The comparison of clusters 1 and 3 shows essentially the same result. C-Affect yields a partial correlation of .86, and E-Agitated Depression yields .26. Relative to cluster 3 too cluster 1 is characterized by high severity on C-Affect and low severity on E-Agitated Depression.

In the comparison of clusters 2 and 3, it is C- and E-Agitated Depression that yield the most robust correlations (.54 and .53, respectively). Relative to cluster 3 cluster 2 is characterized by high severity on Agitated Depression. In addition several of the other, nonaffective factors also yielded significant partial correlations ($p < .01$) with cluster 2, 3 membership. The significant Current factors are C-Movement (.30), C-Withdrawal (.25), and C-Tasks (.19). The significant Early factors are E-Activities (.27), E-Discrimination (.12), E-Motor (.12), E-Language (.10), and E-Memory (.11). Relative to cluster 3 membership in cluster 2 is associated with more severe memory loss and withdrawal (in addition to agitated depression) and with less severe task disruption, language loss, and sensory-motor involvement.

These results from cluster analysis suggest a differentiation of subjects in our sample based largely on the nature of their affective symptomatology. This impression is confirmed and supported by an analysis based on item scores rather than factor scores, for all three questions: Current, Early, and Prior. In particular we selected for consideration the 20 items with the highest (absolute) power to discriminate each pair of clusters, and then we categorized the items according to the direction of influence. An item was defined as *characterizing* the cluster that yielded lower values (higher severity) on that item.

Several items characterized cluster 1 for all three questions. These concerned talking of suicide, inappropriate happiness and energy, and problems with bowel and bladder control. Thus respondents are attributing to the subjects in the cluster *prior* as well as early and current difficulties in the domains of affect and excretory function. Whether these are in fact premorbid traits, symptomatic of other conditions (including advanced age) or alternatively very early signs of DAT (and not interpreted as such) cannot be determined.

Several other items also characterize cluster 1, but less consistently. Subjects in this category are more likely to pace at night, sleep little, and wander off without warning. They display both affective flattening and affective lability, and they are more likely to show affection toward strangers.

Turning now to cluster 2, we find that two items characterized this cluster on Prior, Early, and Current questions: (1) Tends toward violent outbursts of temper and (2) Is easily angered. Thus a tendency toward volatility may characterize those subjects whose clinical course is dominated by agitated depression. The significant Early and Current symptoms are excessive sleeping, loss of interest in former hobbies, inactivity, sadness, purposeless activity, confusion, distractibility.

It appears then that the affect and depression factors characterize clusters 1 and 2, respectively, and that some of the elements are present before the disease is recognized. All but one of the items that characterizes cluster 1 or 2 for Early or Current symptoms does so for *both* Early and Current symptoms. Thus the characteristics of the cluster 1 and 2 do not change much throughout.

Cluster 3 does not show this same stability. There were 10 items that characterized cluster 3 for Current symptoms only. These concerned dressing, driving, motor control, misuse of objects, finding one's way, reading clocks, and confusing left and right. In contrast to the pattern for clusters 1 and 2, only one item characterized cluster 3 for both Early and Current symptoms ("Cannot dial the telephone").

The question at this point is whether these clusters have etiological significance, that is, whether they are revealing of true subgroups in our sample (compare Martin, chapter 5). The alternative is that these clusters are telling us about differential affective responses to an Alzheimer-type dementia and possibly also the premorbid traits that predispose to those affective responses. To distinguish these possibilities, it is useful to determine the predictive significance of cluster membership with respect to the several etiological variables we have discussed. To this end we carried out a series of regression analyses in which the predictors were variables defined over cluster membership. Where this analysis yielded significant results, a multiple-partial F-test was conducted to determine whether cluster membership continued to contribute to the prediction of the dependent variable when Current factors were entered into the model. A summary of these analyses follows.

Predictions from Clusters
Cluster membership did not significantly predict ONSET ($R^2 = .02$, $p > .05$), SEX ($R^2 = .02$, $p > .05$), or FAMILY ($R^2 = .02$, $p > .05$). This is in contrast to the finding with factors as predictors, where both Early and Current factors yielded significant results. Clusters did predict AGE ($R^2 = .03$, $p < .02$), but the addition of cluster membership to a model containing the C-factors did not improve the prediction of AGE ($F_{(2,224)} = .58$, $p > .10$).

Regarding the severity index, SUM, the addition of cluster membership to the basic model containing the variables TIME, TIMESQT, and SEX yielded no further increase in the accuracy of the prediction of SUM ($F_{(2,229)}$ = 2.98, $p > .05$). Recall that the addition of the normalized Early factors did by contrast yield a significant increase in predictability over the basic model. As it turns out, this significant contribution of the Early factors is maintained even when the effects of cluster membership are removed ($F_{(7,222)}$ = 2.89, $p > .05$).

Cluster membership is associated with distinct medications history χ^2 = 21, degrees of freedom 10, $p = .02$). Over one-third of the patients in cluster 1 and approximately one-half of those in cluster 2 are currently taking one or another major tranquilizer. An additional 12 percent of both groups are on antidepressants. In cluster 3 by contrast the proportion of patients falling into one or another of these two medications categories is much smaller (27 percent).

Discussion

In the cluster analytic technique that we use, similarity across patients is defined on the overall pattern of symptoms and groups are formed such that the overall similarity of patients within each group is as high as possible and in particular higher than expected based on the magnitude of variation in the different symptoms making up the pattern. From the results obtained, we can conclude that our sample contains two subgroups distinguished from the remaining patients (cluster 3) largely by the extremity of their affective symptomatology. But these two groups basically do not differ from one another, or from the rest of the sample, in their clinical characteristics or in the other, nonaffective symptoms they display. The exception to this generalization arises in the comparison of clusters 2 and 3, where it was found that the patients of cluster 2 show, along with their severe depression, more memory loss and less sensory, motor, and language involvement. One possible interpretation of this finding is that it reflects the contribution to cluster 2 of non-DAT patients and in particular patients with so-called pseudodementia (Kiloh 1961, Wells 1979, 1982) or a dementia syndrome uniquely associated with depression (Folstein and McHugh 1978). Similarly we might speculate that cluster 1, which features frontal release signs, reflects the greater involvement of frontal lobes and related limbic structures, such as is commonly seen in Pick's disease.

If it were indeed true that the clusters reflect etiological differences along these lines, it should have been the case that cluster membership was predictive of at least some of the clinical variables we looked at, for example, ONSET, FAMILY, or SUM. Because no such associations were found, we are inclined to conclude that the clusters do not reveal true subgroups in our sample but rather reflect dichotomous affective reactions to the perceived loss of competence associated with the dementing condition, reactions conditioned by dispositional tendencies that predate the onset of dementia.

We have shown that cluster analysis did not yield subtypes characterized by distinct patterns of cognitive loss. But this does not imply an invariant or even "typical" cognitive profile among the patients in our sample. In fact the combined results from factor and cluster analyses are compatible with substantial variation in cognitive and behavioral presentation, and they help provide an account of that variation.

The results of the varimax factor analyses suggest that the major symptom domains—for example, language disturbance, memory loss, and loss of motor control—vary somewhat independently of one another. Impairment in any one of these areas is not an automatic consequence of impairment in others. From the extremely low mean values achieved by the items of the memory scale, and in particular those dealing with retrieval of recent memories (that is, on a time scale of minutes, days, and months; see table 6.1), we can justifiably assume that the probability of memory being affected at some time in the course of the disease is quite high, higher than for the other symptom domains. On the result obtained, however, memory involvement does not constitute a necessary condition for the emergence of those other symptoms, nor do those other symptoms constitute necessary conditions for one another.

To make these notions somewhat more concrete, it is useful to consider extreme presentation patterns in the form of double dissociations. For example, from the finding that C-Language and C-Movement constitute orthogonal factors, and that the means of items that constitute the two factors overlap substantially, it follows that some patients will be found who show severe involvement on Language but not Movement, and others will be found who show just the reverse pattern. To illustrate the existence of such dissociations in our sample, we used the following subsets of items, chosen for illustration because they loaded heavily and nearly exclusively on the factor in question and because the means of the two subsets were approximately the same:

from C-Movement:
Cannot execute the movements of dressing (for example, buttoning shirt, tying laces).
Cannot place arms properly in shirt or jacket.
Cannot coordinate knife, fork, and spoon during eating.

Cannot smoothly assume a sitting or standing position.
from C-Language:
Cannot understand instructions or simple commands.
Puts words together in speaking that don't make sense.
Stutters and stammers over words.
Cannot read and understand newspapers and magazines.

Nineteen of the 262 subjects (7 percent) obtained a mean score of 2.5 or more (no impairment) on the C-Movement subset, while simultaneously obtaining a mean score of 1.5 or less (severe impairment) on the language items. An additional 6 subjects showed precisely the reverse pattern: moderate to severe impairment on the movement items with no noticeable impairment on the language items. By contrast when dissociations are sought from combinations of these items that cross the factor boundaries, the number of dissociation cases turns out to be much smaller—a total of only 7.

This general finding is typical of other pairs of factors, with the exception of Memory, which is rarely spared. But note that we have set a very stringent dissociation criterion (mean score ≥ 2.5). With a somewhat less strict criterion, Memory can be doubly dissociated from the other factors, and of course the overall frequency of all dissociations increases.

Recent clinical studies support these data in showing that language, visuoperceptual, and motor components of the DAT symptom complex can and do doubly dissociate, even in histopathologically confirmed Alzheimer's disease patients (for example, Neary et al. 1986, Martin, chapter 5, Martin et al. 1986). With respect to the memory component, there is clear evidence for one-way dissociation—progressive amnesia without other cognitive deficits (Neary et al. 1986)—but to our knowledge no one has yet reported the sparing of memory in histologically verified Alzheimer's disease.

It is our contention that these various results point to a multicomponential account of DAT. The nature of this account, and how it differs from the alternative that features subtypes, can be illustrated with an analogy that associates each patient's symptom profile with a patchwork quilt, with the patch colors standing for symptoms differentiated by color into major symptom domains. On the multicomponential account there are no regularities in the quilt designs, that is, no repeatable geometric patterns. What commonalities there are among the quilts have to do with some aspect of the color scheme. The set of colors from which the quilts are constructed is not large, and certain colors (memory impairments) predominate in most if not all instances. Other colors vary in their prominence from quilt to quilt, but (this is the crucial point) there is no necessary relation between the presence or prominence of any one color and the presence or prominence of any other.

Having drawn this analogy, we are led to ask what exactly the colors represent, that is, what are the components that together yield the patchwork of impairments in Alzheimer-type dementia? Of course this is the question that the factor analysis was designed to address. That analysis attempts to account for observed intercorrelations by postulating a few underlying dimensions of variation (factors), which ideally correspond to distinct causal mechanisms. But factor analyses may yield results even if no distinct causal mechanisms exist (even random numbers may be factor analyzed). In addition factors may fail to capture those causal mechanisms that do exist, because factors are not uniquely determined by the data. Suppose one finds, as we do here, a set of eight factors that together account for the pattern of item correlations. It is the case that any other eight factors formed by different linear functions of the original eight will account for the item correlations just as well. Thus there is a need for independent confirmation from outside the technique. Our confidence in the analysis grows when we are able to show that the extracted factors (1) make sense, in terms of existing psychological and neuropsychological theories, and (2) have a clear differential relation to certain clinically and epidemiologically significant variables. Our evidence on these counts is mixed.

For the most part the extracted factors correspond well to the recognized symptom domains of DAT. Indeed the Current symptom factors follow quite closely the lines of the original scales. The correspondence of factors and scales was less obvious for the Early question, and this argues against the possibility that factors are mere artifacts of the questionnaire's organization.

Nevertheless the factor results were not entirely what we had expected. For one thing the widely recognized visuoperceptual and spatial impairments failed to emerge as distinct factors. And several of the factors that did emerge seemed overinclusive. Thus the factors relating to movement, language, and memory encompass functional deficits that turn out to be dissociable on single case or group studies (for example, Irigaray 1967, Morris and Kopelman 1986, Moscovitch 1982, Schwartz, Marin and Saffran 1979). In retrospect this is not surprising. The factor results are limited by both the informant methodology and the resolving power of the mathematical analysis. To illustrate the later: A separate varimax factor analysis performed on the C-ratings for just the 25 items of the memory scale turned up three factors reflecting three distinct aspects of memory function: the ability to keep track of recent and ongoing events, the recall of remote memories and autobiographical facts, and the recognition of individuals by name and sight. This suggests that these various aspects of memory function may in fact constitute distinct dimensions of variation, but the suggestion must be considered tentative, because the three factors actually accounted for very little of the variance in the correlation matrix of memory items: 5 percent, 4 percent, and 3 percent of the variance, respectively.

The fact that the original factors were shown to have etiological significance adds confidence in their biological reality. An example is the association found between youthful onset and low scores (high severity) on the Depression, Tasks, and Movement factors. Together these suggest the greater involvement of subcortical structures, and there is some neuropathological evidence to support this: Bondareff (1983), for example, argues that early-onset Alzheimer's disease is akin to Parkinson's disease in involving the selective degeneration of the transmitter-related neurons of the nucleus basalis, locus coeruleus, and substantia nigra.

Other investigators have suggested greater left hemisphere pathology in early-onset patients, based on their findings that language disorders are more prevalent and more profound in early-onset patients (for example, Chui et al. 1985, Filley, Kelly, and Heaton 1986, Seltzer and Sherwin 1983). Our evidence does not support this, neither does it support the notion that language involvement is predictive of a more rapid deterioration (compare Berg et al. 1984, Faber-Langendoen et al. 1988).

After Folstein and Breitner's (1981) report of a higher-than-expected incidence of secondary cases among DAT patients who were unable to write a sentence, several investigators sought to confirm an association between aphasia and familial DAT. Chui and colleagues (1985) and Heyman and colleagues (1983) found no such association, whereas Knesevich and associates (1985) found an association, but in the opposite direction, that is, aphasia predictive of nonfamilial DAT. Our results support those of Knesevich and associates in showing that C-Language (along with E-Motor control and E-Discrimination) predicted negative family history. The only factor predictive of positive family history was C-Memory.

The many findings from this study, and their correspondence or noncorrespondence with other reports, must be evaluated in light of the strengths and weaknesses of the methods used. Several of the weaknesses have already been noted: the sampling bias that resulted from drawing our subjects from the membership of ADRDA and the limitations and ambiguities inherent in the factor analytic approach.

What remains to be discussed is the potential for bias and inaccuracy that come with reliance on naive informants. One obvious example relates to the finding that women show greater severity on C-Memory and C-Tasks and men greater severity on C-Withdrawal. It is most likely that this result bears more on sex roles and sex role expectations than it does the biological processes underlying DAT.

It is of course true that the accuracy of obtained ratings is limited by informants' exposure to the subject in relevant circumstances, by their interpretation of the subjects' behavior, and by their understanding of the questions being asked. The inability of some raters to make fine-grained differentiations among the behaviors queried undoubtedly contributed to the noise in the data (recall that the eight symptom factors together account for little over half the variance in the data) and conceivably obscured the more refined symptom definition we had anticipated in constructing the various scales of the questionnaire.

Still the weaknesses of the questionnaire methodology do not negate its considerable advantages. It has given us access to a rich and highly detailed symptom characterization for 324 well-screened patients, far more than constitute the typical clinical or experimental sample, where strong selectional biases tend to operate and where unusual patients tend to be overrepresented. It has enabled us to make use of statistical techniques for summarizing and explaining the multiple sources of variability that enter into the clinical presentation of DAT and through these techniques has produced an account of that variability that should be of use in guiding future research.

To summarize this account: The many cognitive and behavioral signs and symptoms associated with DAT are reducible to a smaller number of dimensions of variation, at least some of which probably reflect the pathophysiologic involvement of distinct neural or pharmacologic systems. The clinical manifestation of the disease, both early in its course and later on, will be determined by which of these systems is implicated, to what degree, and in what order. Correlations between Early and Current factors suggest that those symptoms most severe at the outset are likely to continue to dominate the clinical picture. In addition, in a sizable proportion of patients the overall presentation picture will be colored by one of two extreme affective reactions: on the one hand depression with agitation and on the other hand an exaggerated acting-out coupled with lability of emotions and the alteration of personal habits. Concerning the underlying pathophysiologic systems, it is likely that some are more vulnerable to the disease process than others (for example, the hippocampal/cholinergic memory system may be especially vulnerable) and that this results in a characteristic order of symptom progression (memory symptoms occurring first). It may well be, however, that there is no necessity to this order of symptom progression, in that none of the implicated mechanisms sets a necessary condition for the others and none constitutes the sine qua non of the disease.

Acknowledgments

This research was supported by research grants from the MacArthur Foundation and the National Institutes of Health (#AG02231/06791). We wish to express our gratitude to Bobbie Glaze, Hilda Pridgen, and Terry S. Jenkins for their help with the distribution of questionnaires. Howard Hurtig assisted us in determining exclusion criteria and medications categories. Paul Rozin provided helpful suggestions at several stages in the preparation of the manuscript.

References

Barclay, L. L., Kheyfets, S., Zemcov, A., Blass, J. P., and McDowell, F. H. (1986). Risk factors in Alzheimer's disease. In A. Fisher, I. Hanin, and C. Lachman (Eds.) *Alzheimer's and Parkinson's Diseases: Strategies for Research and Development* (*Advances in Behavioral Biology*, Vol. 29). New York: Plenum.

Becker, J. T., Huff, J., Nebes, R. D., Holland, A., and Boller, F. (1988). Neuropsychological function in Alzheimer's disease. *Archives of Neurology* 45: 263–268.

Berg, L., Danziger, W. L., Storandt, M., Coben, L. A., Gado, M., Hughes, C. P., Knesevich, J. W., and Botwinick, J. (1984). Predictive features in mild senile dementia of the Alzheimer type. *Neurology* 34: 563–569.

Bondareff, W. (1983). Age and Alzheimer disease. *Lancet* 1: 1447.

Brun, A., and Englund, E. (1981). Regional pattern of degeneration in Alzheimer's disease: Neuronal loss and histopathological grading. *Histopathology* 5: 549–564.

Chase, T. N., Foster, N. L., Fedio, P., Brooks, R., Mansi, L., and Chiro, G. (1984). Regional cortical dysfunction in Alzheimer's disease as determined by positron emission tomography. *Annals of Neurology* 15 (Suppl): S170–S174.

Chui, H. C., Teng, E. L., Henderson, V. W., and Moy, A. C. (1985). Clinical subtypes of dementia of the Alzheimer type. *Neurology* 35: 1544–1550.

Coblentz, J. M., Mattis, S., Zingesser, L. H., Kasoff, S. S., Wisniewski, H. M., and Katzman, R. (1973). Presenile dementia. *Archives of Neurology* 29: 299–308.

Cummings, J. L. (1982). Cortical dementias. In D. F. Benson and D. Blumer (Eds.) *Psychiatric Aspects of Neurologic Disease. Vol. II*. New York: Grune & Stratton.

Faber-Langendoen, K., Morris, J. C., Knesevich, J. W., LaBarge, E., Miller, J. P., and Berg, L. (1988). Aphasia in senile dementia of the Alzheimer type. *Annals of Neurology* 23: 365–370.

Filley, C. M., Kelly, J., and Heaton, R. K. (1986). Neuropsychologic features of early- and late-onset Alzheimer's disease. *Archives of Neurology* 43: 574–576.

Fitch, N., Becker, R., and Heller, A. (1988). The inheritance of Alzheimer's disease: A new interpretation. *Annals of Neurology* 23: 14–19.

Folstein, M. F., and Breitner, J. C. S. (1981). Language disorder predicts familial Alzheimer's disease. *Johns Hopkins Medical Journal* 149: 145–147.

Folstein, M. F., and McHugh, P. R. (1978). Dementia syndrome of depression. In R. Katzman, R. D. Terry, and K. L. Bick (Eds.) *Alzheimer's Disease, Senile Dementia and Related Disorders (Aging, Vol. 7)*. New York: Raven.

Hasse, G. R. (1971). Disease presenting as dementia. In C. E. Wells (Ed.) *Dementia*. Philadelphia: F. A. Davis.

Hagberg, B., and Ingvar, D. H. (1976). Cognitive reduction in presenile dementia related to regional abnormalities of the cerebral blood flow. *British Journal of Psychiatry* 128: 209–222.

Heston, L. L. (1983). Dementia of the Alzheimer type: A perspective from family studies. *Banbury Report* 15: 183–191.

Heston, L. L., Mastri, A. R., Anderson, V. E., and White, J. (1981). Dementia of the Alzheimer type: Clinical genetics, natural history, and associated conditions. *Archives of General Psychiatry* 38: 1085–1090.

Heyman, A., Wilkinson, W. E., Hurwitz, B. J., Schmechel, D., Sigmon, A. H., Weinberg, T., Helms, M. J., and Swift, M. (1983). Alzheimer's disease: Genetic aspects and associated clinical disorders. *Annals of Neurology* 14: 507–515.

Heyman, A., Wilkinson, W. E., Stafford, J. A., Helmes, M. J., Sigmon, A. H., and Weinberg, T. (1984). Alzheimer's disease: A study of epidemiological aspects. *Annals of Neurology* 15: 335–341.

Irigaray, L. (1967). Approche psycho-linguistique du langage des dements. *Neuropsychologia* 5: 25–52.

Jorm, A. F. (1986). Subtypes of Alzheimer's dementia: A conceptual analysis and critical review. *Psychological Medicine* 15: 543–553.

Kiloh, I. G. (1961). Pseudodementia. *Acta Psychiatrica Scandinavica* 37: 336–351.

Knesevich, J. W., Toro, F. R., Morris, J. C., and LaBarge, E. (1985). Aphasia, family history, and the longitudinal course of senile dementia of the Alzheimer type. *Psychiatry Research* 14: 255–263.

Martin, A., Brouwers, P., Lalonde, F., Cox, C., Teleska, P., and Fedio, P. (1986). Towards a behavioral typology of Alzheimer's patients. *Journal of Clinical and Experimental Neuropsychology* 8: 594–610.

Mayeux, R., Stern, Y., and Spanton, S. (1985). Heterogeneity in dementia of the Alzheimer type: Evidence of subgroups. *Neurology* 35: 453–461.

Morris, R. G., and Kopelman, M. D. (1986). The memory deficits in Alzheimer-type dementia: A review. *Quarterly Journal of Experimental Psychology* 38A: 575–602.

Mortimer, J. A., and Hutton, J. T. (1985). Epidemiology and etiology of Alzheimer's disease. In J. T. Hutton and A. D. Kenny (Eds.). *Senile Dementia of the Alzheimer Type*. New York: A. R. Liss.

Moscovitch, M. (1982). Multiple dissociations of function in amnesia. In L. S. Cermak (Ed.) *Human Memory and Amnesia*. Hillsdale, NJ: Erlbaum.

Neary, D., Snowden, J. S., Bowen, D. M., Sims, N. R., Mann, D. M. A., Benton, J. S., Northen, B., Yates, P. O., and Davison, A. N. (1986). *Journal of Neurology. Neurosurgery and Psychiatry* 49: 163–174.

Rocca, W. A., Amaducci, L. A., and Schoenberg, B. S. (1986). Epidemiology of clinically diagnosed Alzheimer's disease. *Annals of Neurology* 19: 415–424.

Sarle, W. S. (1983). Cubic clustering criterion. *S. A. S. Technical Report A-108*. Cary, NC: S. A. S Institute Inc.

Schwartz, M. F. (1987). Focal cognitive deficits in dementia of the Alzheimer type. *Neuropsychology* 1: 27–35.

Schwartz, M. F., Marin, O. S. M., and Saffran, E. M. (1979). Dissociations of language function in dementia: A case study. *Brain and Language* 7: 277–306.

Seltzer, B., and Sherwin, I. (1983). A comparison of clinical features in early- and late-onset primary degenerative dementia: One entity or two? *Archives of Neurology* 40: 143–146.

Tariska, I. (1970). Circumscribed cerebral atrophy in Alzheimer's disease: A pathological study. In G. E. W. Wolstenholme and M. O'Connor (Eds.) *Alzheimer's Disease and Related Conditions*. London: J. & A. Churchill.

Wells, C. E. (1979). Pseudodementia. *American Journal of Psychiatry* 136: 895–900.

Wells, C. E. (1982). Pseudodementia and the recognition of organicity. In D. F. Benson and D. Blumer (Eds.) *Psychiatric Aspects of Neurologic Diseases*. Vol. II. New York: Grune & Stratton.

Chapter 7

Semantic Memory Loss in Alzheimer-Type Dementia

Howard Chertkow and Daniel Bub

This chapter by Chertkow and Bub takes as its starting point the suggestion we encountered in chapter 4 (Chawluk et al.) that among the factors that contribute to the widespread naming disorder of dementia is an impairment at the level of object semantics. The style of investigation comes out of cognitive neuropsychology: The investigators select from a large group of patients suspected of having Alzheimer's disease those whose test profiles implicate semantic loss as a primary determinant of the naming deficit. They then proceed to an in-depth analysis of what these patients know about concepts symbolized in picture and word and how that knowledge affects test performance with these types of materials. One finding merits special emphasis here, namely that degraded semantic representations more seriously affects word comprehension than picture comprehension because the latter, but not the former, has access to specialized "identification procedures" whose knowledge base is distinct from the amodal semantic core. The characterization of these identification procedures corresponds nicely to Moscovitch and Umilta's type II module, most notably with respect to the broad input domain over which they operate and the "shallow outputs" they deliver.

Chertkow and Bub's explorations of semantic memory impairments in DAT provide a model for investigators who seek to understand the nature of the functional deficits in DAT and how they interact with task demands to yield the behavioral measures that serve as our diagnostic signposts.

M. F. S.

Semantic Memory

Our knowledge of everyday concepts in the world must exist in some form of permanent storage in the brain. Such a knowledge base in long-term memory is an essential part of everyday cognitive activities like understanding the meaning of spoken words, identifying visual objects, and producing their corresponding names. This permanent conceptual store, termed *semantic memory* (Tulving 1983), has increasingly come to be viewed as a modular cognitive system with a structure and organization that are similarly maintained from one individual to the next. A great deal of evidence supports the distinction between levels of representation concerning the meaning of words and the grammatical role of words in sentences, and striking examples of this functional separability have been documented (Schwartz, Marin, and Saffran 1979).

Three basic elements in the structure of semantic memory that have emerged from studies in normal subjects concern its organization by categories, by hierarchies, and in terms of semantic association.

Rosch (1975) and others have argued that concept descriptions in memory are grouped together by their natural categories (that is semantic categories such as furniture, tools, animals, and so on). Within such groupings certain members are more prototypical, that is, more closely representative of the attributes common to the group.

Not all the knowledge pertaining to a concept is accessible at the same time in semantic memory. There is good evidence that a given concept (for example, *robin*) is more rapidly categorized as an instance of the immediate superordinate (*bird*) than a more distant one (*animal*) (Collins and Quillian 1969).

Finally, concepts, and the verbal labels denoting them, do not exist in isolation. Activation of one concept leads to some activation of related concepts, with the effect depending on the amount of semantic overlap between them (Collins and Loftus 1975).

Semantic Memory in Alzheimer's Disease

Crucial data regarding the nature of semantic memory may be obtained from brain-damaged individuals because the extreme (and often highly selective) conditions imposed by the deficit may reveal functional properties of the system more clearly than can be observed in normal subjects. Patients with dementia of the Alzheimer type (DAT) form a relevant clinical group in this regard—the prominence of anomia, which appears qualitatively diferent from the naming disorder of aphasic patients, its early manifestation in DAT, and its progression with the course of the disease have been attributed by some authors to the loss of conceptual knowledge in semantic memory (Appel, Kertesz, and Fisman 1982, Bayles 1982, Bayles and Kaszniak 1987). Other researchers have also taken decreased generation of word lists (Rosen 1980) and alteration in the pattern of word associations (Gewirth, Shindler, and Hier 1984) as further evidence in DAT of an impairment at the level of the semantic memory store.

Although a semantic deficit is now widely regarded as central to the communication problems of DAT patients (Bayles and Kaszniak 1987), the nature of the disturbance is not entirely clear. Some results are considered to indicate actual deterioration of conceptual representations in semantic memory. Other kinds of evidence, such as reports of retained semantic associative priming in DAT (Nebes, Martin, and Horn 1984, Nebes, Boller, and Holland 1986), are interpreted as proof that this store in fact remains intact and the task impairments reflect only an impaired ability to access these representations.

Until recently investigators used the approach of administering neuropsychological tests (for example, of visual perception, memory, and so forth) to groups of DAT patients and drew inferences regarding the importance of visual misperceptions, semantic impairment, and the like in DAT as a whole. Unfortunately DAT is clearly heterogeneous in terms of its presentation, its progression, and its neuropsychological deficit profile (chapters 5 and 6 and Martin and Fedio, 1983). Group studies that ignore this variability will certainly be unable to specify the particular ways in which DAT leads to deterioration within a single cognitive domain, nor will they be likely to provide relevant data concerning the normal functioning of any particular cognitive system. What is required is an approach that recognizes that within a heterogeneous group of DAT patients, there exist individuals with similar particular patterns of major cognitive impairment. In terms of the logic of cognitive neuropsychology, precise studies of carefully defined small groups of individual DAT patients with particular cognitive deficits will shed light on models of normal processing in that particular domain.

In this chapter we examine a group of patients with Alzheimer's disease who clearly are impaired in their ability to determine the full semantic description of pictures and words. In contrast to this the patients had no evidence of visual perceptual disturbance either at low or high levels of visual processing, nor did they have any alexia or aphasic comprehension disturbance. After determining that the impairment is semantic and not perceptual, we then proceeded to study the nature of the residual semantic description of object concepts to obtain information on their underlying structure. Our goal throughout this chapter is to elucidate the deficit as precisely as possible in functional terms, using a variety of current methods employed by researchers in the assessment of disturbed comprehension. One major focus is on automatic semantic priming as a possibly useful and important method of evaluating tacit knowledge of the associative relation between words without requiring the patient to make an explicit judgment concerning this relation. We then go on to investigate the disturbed semantic processing of pictures and words in the Alzheimer patients to clarify what functional differences, if any, might exist between verbal and nonverbal material with respect to the derivation of meaning. Finally, we make use of our findings to draw a distinction between the kind of semantic knowledge that enters specifically into the identification of visual objects and more general knowledge that does not form part of an identification procedure.

Defining the Test Population

Patients were first screened for anomia, considered as a crude marker for possible semantic memory loss. Anomic patients would then be tested on a detailed battery that looked for impairment of visual perception. Subjects with impairment of visual perception, whether low level or high level in nature, were excluded from further testing. A similar approach was used to exclude patients with impairment of auditory or written word perception, as well as impairment of phonological speech output.

Dementia patients with anomia who showed no impairment on tests of sensory input or speech output were tested for semantic impairment.

Subjects

We studied 42 patients with probable DAT. Data are presented only for the 10 subjects who demonstrated normal visual perception, with accompanying converging evidence of a semantic memory disturbance.

There 10 patients all had probable DAT by NINCDS-ADRDA criteria (McKhann et al. 1984). Seven women and 3 men met the following criteria: English-speaking, Hachinski scores less than 4 (Hachinski et al. 1975), no clinical evidence of focal brain disease on neurological exam, adequate vision and hearing, and cooperative and consenting. The patients were screened to exclude any patients with alexia, agnosia, or apraxia on mental status testing. A group of 10 normal elderly individuals served as control subjects (7 women and 3 men, aged 67 to 87, mean age 73).

Perceptual and Language Testing

A series of investigations, detailed elsewhere (Chertkow, Bub, and Seidenberg 1989, Chertkow, Bub, and Caplan, submitted, Chertkow and Bub, 1990), evaluated the perceptual and language abilities of these DAT patients. They all performed normally on tests of single-word recognition. They were all able to perform lexical decisions on words and nonwords. They scored normally on the Western Aphasia Battery (WAB) sections (Kertesz and Poole 1974) measuring comprehension and repetition, and the fluency rating on the spontaneous speech section were all in the range of normal control subjects.

The DAT group was impaired on the naming section of the WAB, scoring a mean of 7.9 (range 6.4 to 9.2, SD = 1.00), whereas control subjects scored mean 9.8. Eight of the 10 DAT patients would be classified as anomic aphasics, and 2 would be classified as normal on the WAB classification.

Basic tests of copying and visual perception were performed normally. Two further tests were performed to assess perceptual ability:

Perceptual Object Decision Task
Line drawings of 20 simple household objects and 20 nonobjects drawn from a group designed by Kroll and Potter (1984) were randomly presented. The nonobjects created by Kroll and Potter were designed to incorporate real object parts, although these parts were attached in a seemingly random fashion. Subjects were to answer yes or no in response to the question, Is this thing a real object or not? All stimuli were prescreened and selected so that at least 90 percent of normal subjects answered correctly for each item. Patients performed at the same level as control subjects on this test.

Mixed-Category (MC) Word-to-Picture Matching Test
Subjects were presented with line drawings of 150 items. These stimuli consisted of 150 concrete, picturable noun examplars, drawn from 8 semantic categories (15 items each) plus 30 miscellaneous objects. Categories were vehicles, clothing, furniture, tools, fruit, vegetables, animals, and body parts. Items in each category were drawn from Battig and Montague (1969) and Rosch (1975) and were chosen to include both high- and low-frequency values (Kucera and Francis 1967) and prototypicality. Line drawings were taken from the pictorial stimuli of Snodgrass and Vanderwart (1980). These pictures were displayed in groups of 5 items arranged vertically in a column on a card. The vertical arrangement was designed to eliminate any difficulties arising from visual inattention or neglect. Each item was drawn from a different semantic category or the miscellaneous category. An attempt was made to have the items on a card share basic perceptual features. For example, one card depicted a rocket (vehicle), screwdriver (tool), bean (vegetable), finger (body part), and belt (clothing).

Subjects were asked to point to the picture named by the examiner. All stimuli were selected and prescreened on normal subjects such that at least 95 percent of them identified each picture correctly. Patients performed at the same level as control subjects on this task also.

The normal performance of the 10 DAT patients on tests of object decision and mixed-category word-to-picture matching suggests that there is no significant deficit in visual processing. The normal WAB scores on comprehension, repetition, and fluency suggest that there was no deficit in phonological assembly that might account for the patient's anomia. Taken together, the test results of object decision and mixed-category matching of words to pictures provide evidence that these Alzheimer's disease patients had no problems in carrying out visual processing of pictorial stimuli up to and including its highest levels, but imply little about the state of semantic memory itself. Because distractors in the picture-matching test were all from different semantic categories, success on this task would be possible even if only superordinate category knowledge of the items was retained, which is the usual case even in dementia patients with relatively severe impairment of semantic memory (Warrington 1975). The results therefore provide converging evidence of adequate visual and auditory perceptual processing up to the level at which semantic memory is accessed in these patients.

Testing Object Concepts
We now document our patients' performance on tasks that directly measure the processing of object concepts. Picture-naming and word-comprehension tasks (measured by testing the ability of each patient to match an auditory word to its picture) were compared item by item. In addition probes questions were administered to test general and detailed knowledge of picture and their corresponding word labels.

Picture-Naming Task The 150 pictures used in the MC word-to-picture matching task were presented on cards at a separate session one week later to assess picture naming ability. The control subjects named 144 out of 146 items. The dementia patients showed a notable anomia on the picture items. They named a mean of 105 out of 146 items correctly and were significantly worse than the control group when compared on a t-test ($t = 8.54$, $p < .001$).

Same-Category (SC) Word-to-Picture Matching Test A second set of cards was created using the pictorial stimuli from the previous naming and matching tasks. Each card in this set contained 5 items from

Table 7.1
Picture Naming and Word-to-Picture Matching in DAT Patients and Control Subjects

Subjects	Picture Naming Score	Same-Category Word-to-Picture Matching Score
Control (n = 10)	144/146 (98.6%)	142/145 (98.0%)
DAT patients (n = 10)	105/146 (71.9%)	117/145 (80.8%)

within the same semantic category (SC), arranged vertically in a column (Butterworth, Howard, and McLoughlin 1984).

Results (table 7.1) suggest that DAT patients were much more impaired on SC matching than on the previous test of MC matching. Whereas control subjects performed well on the SC matching test, attaining 142 out of 145 correct, DAT patients were correct on mean 117 out of 145 and made considerably more errors than did control subjects. Statistical analysis confirms that the dementia group was significantly more impaired on this task than were control subjects ($t = 6.05$, $p < .001$). Because distractors are from within the same semantic category, this task demands complete identification of the target as an instance of a concept.

Analysis by Items   The relation between performance on the naming and the SC matching task (testing name recognition) was examined by comparing each patient's errors on corresponding items in the two tests (Huff, Corkin, and Growdon 1986). Similar to Huff and colleagues we found (table 7.2) that there was a clear correspondence between failure to demonstrate accurate name recognition and failure to name the item. The percentage of items named was much higher for items correctly matched on the SC matching task than for those items incorrectly matched. Results of a t-test ($t = 9.42$, $p < .001$) confirm that this difference was indeed significant, representing an item-specific correspondence.

This item-by-item correspondence in loss of name production and name comprehension represents an association of deficits at the level

Table 7.2
Naming Performance of DAT Patients and Control Subjects in terms of Performance on Same-Category (SC) Word-to-Picture Matching Test

Items on SC Match	Number of Items	Number Named	Percentage Named
Correct	1171	995	84.9%
Incorrect	280	60	21.4%

of individual concept items. The presence of such consistency may be taken as evidence that the disturbance is at a single functional level, that is, loss of information due to a storage disorder is responsible for failure on both tasks (Huff, Corkin, and Growdon 1986). The semantic impairment appears to be entirely different from the disturbance that is reported to yield inconsistent errors to the same items in aphasic patients (Butterworth, Howard, and McLoughlin 1984).

Semantic Knowledge Probes   To gain a more detailed knowledge of the extent of semantic loss, the probe technique of Warrington (1975) was adopted as a way of examining the items used on previous tests. The subject saw 130 of these picture items in a separate session one week after initial testing. At a second session the corresponding word, used in the previous reading task, was presented. Patients were asked not to name aloud the word or picture. They were given forced-choice questions regarding the item and instructed to answer each probe question.

One question was designed for each item on superordinate category membership (for example, Is this a tool or clothing?). Six more questions concerned knowledge of detailed attributes. Three questions concerned perceptual attributes (that is, [item = saw]; Is the tip made of metal or wood? Is it sharp or dull?). Three more questions were given regarding functional or contexual aspects of the item (that is, Do you cut things with it or lift with it? Is it used on a piece of wood or on stone?).

Questions were designed to be similar for most target items within each category. Different animals, for example, were assigned the same questions regarding size (Is it bigger or smaller than a person?) and habitat (Does it live in this country or is it a foreign animal?). Patients were given 6 attribute questions for each picture, and later the same questions were used for the corresponding word.

Patients were tested randomly on the items from all categories. Correct and incorrect answers were recorded. Patients were allowed to guess or to say "I don't know," the latter response being counted as errors. When perceptual questions were asked on picture presentation, the picture itself was turned over, to guard against any attempts to search the picture for clues. We also took pains to avoid testing physical attributes that were obviously visible in the picture.

Superordinate and Detailed Questions   When answers for the word and picture conditions are combined, questions regarding the *superordinate* category were anwered equally well by DAT patients and control subjects (table 7.3). Patients made few errors, responding correctly 96.5 percent of the time, whereas control subjects were correct

Table 7.3
Percentage of Probe Questions Answered Correctly

Subjects	Superordinate Questions	Subordinate Questions (all categories)	Subordinate Questions (only biological categories)
DAT patients (n = 10)	96.5%	87.3%	68.2%
Control (n = 10)	99.8%	98.4%	96.4%

99.8 percent of the time. Most errors were in differentiating fruits from vegetables.

Answers to probe questions of perceptual and functional attributes were more impaired in DAT patients than in control subjects. DAT patients were correct on 87.3 percent versus 98.4 percent in controls. A t-test confirms that the patients were significantly more impaired than control subjects in answering detailed probe questions ($t = 5.47$, $p < .001$).

The dementia patients appeared to be much more impaired on all tests for biological categories (animals, fruits, vegetables) than non-biological categories. Riddoch, Humphreys, Coltheart, and Funnell (1988) explain this pattern of results as being due to the greater structural and conceptual similarity between the items within a bio-logical category. If we consider only these three categories, the DAT patients were able to correctly answer only 68.2 percent of detailed questions, compared with 96.4 percent correct for control subjects.

Intact versus Degraded Items
As we have seen, the difficulty on probe questions was not spread evenly across all items or categories. Almost no errors were made regarding body parts, but errors were frequent on categories of ani-mals, fruits, and vegetables. Within a category some items seemed to show intact knowledge, and others showed deteriorated knowledge as measured by probe questions. The patients demonstrated a greater inability to answer probe questions concerning items for which they were anomic. This was to be expected because a semantic deficit is a primary cause for the naming disorder in dementia. On named items the 10 patients yielded a mean of 0.44 probe errors per item on the 12 detailed questions (range 0.09 to 0.75). On the unnamed items patients produced a mean of 3.7 errors per item (range 1.5 to 5.2). A t-test confirms that patients were significantly more impaired on items they were unable to name, $t(1,5) = 15.9$, $p < .005$.

The items were divided into intact and degraded lists, according to the answers on probe questions. If 3 or more errors were made in

Table 7.4
Naming of Items in DAT Patients Relative to their State of Probe Intactness (percentage of total items in brackets)

Items	Number of Items	Number Named	Number Unnamed
Intact	980	881 (89.9%)	99 (10.1%)
Degraded	311	37 (11.9%)	274 (88.1%)

answering the 12 detailed questions (6 for the word, 6 for the picture), the item was marked as degraded. Errors had to occur in both word and picture presentation conditions, and we assumed this to be a conservative estimate. Because 6 of the 12 questions could be answered correctly by simply guessing, a 50 percent loss of detailed knowledge would be required to result in a degraded item.

Out of 130 items thus probed, DAT patients showed degraded information by these criteria on a mean of 23.7 percent of items (range 14 to 56 items). Most (88.1 percent) of the items that were degraded were unnamed as well. DAT patients were anomic on a mean of 28.6 percent of items. Anomia (table 7.4) was therefore not entirely restricted to the items deemed to be degraded. Of interest 10.1 percent of the items assessed as being intact on probe questions were still unnamed.

Discussion   The results establish that a semantic processing deficit existed in these DAT patients. We demonstrated that the DAT patients had an item-specific loss of knowledge manifested by an item-to-item correspondence between loss of name comprehension (failure on same-category word-to-picture matching test) and name production (naming test). Our findings confirm those of Huff, Corkin, and Growdon (1986) for a similar DAT population.

Detailed probe questions showed that DAT patients fail on detailed questions, involving both perceptual and functional attrributes, but answer superordinate category questions accurately. This conforms to the pattern of deterioration found by Warrington (1975) in three patients with a progressive degenerative dementia, a pattern that we discuss further in the following section. The deficit cannot be restricted entirely to the comprehension of verbal material because degraded items were characterized by a failure to answer questions both for words and pictures. Rather we assume that the patients are displaying evidence of a loss of knowledge occuring within semantic memory that affects the categorization of verbal and nonverbal material as concepts.

Semantic Storage versus Semantic Access Disorders

Defining Criteria

Recently Warrington and Shallice (1979, Shallice 1987) have suggested a number of criteria that may serve to differentiate impaired semantic access from a loss of semantic knowledge:

1. If comprehension of the *same* items is affected on different occasions or in different tests, they argue, then it is reasonable to infer a permanent deterioration in the conceptual representation of these items. By contrast fluctuating performance over time (that is, correct understanding of an item on day 1 and failure to understand on day 2) must indicate an access disturbance rather than a breakdown in the semantic system. It is of interest here that Butterworth, Howard, and McLoughlin (1984) report no consistency across semantic tests for individual items in a group of aphasic patients with impaired verbal comprehension. The outcome in Alzheimer patients appears to be quite different: Huff, Corkin, and Growdon (1986) selected a group of Alzheimer's patients who showed no deficit on visual perceptual testing. They then measured the anomia of these patients and compared it with their loss of word comprehension (that is, inability to say whether a picture or word was an example of an X) for the same items. They demonstrated a clear item-to-item correspondence between loss of word comprehension and anomia for a particular concept. The result, the authors claim, provided strong evidence that their patients had sustained actual damage to semantic representations, a loss that would affect knowledge of the same item when tested in different ways.

2. Another measure of semantic breakdown is derived from a study by Warrington (1975) of three patients with diffuse dementia who showed marked anomia and an impaired ability to match words to pictures. When given probe questions about each item (animals, household objects, and birds were used as test items), it was clear that the patients were often unable to provide answers requiring detailed knowledge of each concept (*Is this a foreign animal?*), but they performed much better when asked to determine the general (superordinate) category (*Is this an object or an animal?*). Martin and Fedio (1983) and Schwartz, Marin, and Saffran (1979) also documented consistently preserved superordinate-level knowledge in Alzheimer's disease patients even in the presence of very limited ability to correctly answer more detailed probe questions. According to Warrington (1975), demage to the contents of semantic memory affects more detailed attribute information before more general superordinate descriptions. The retention of the concept's general category (for

example, that a dog is an animal) in association with a marked deterioration of specific attributes (that a dog can bark) therefore may be taken as further evidence for central damage to the representation of meaning.

3. A third criterion, suggested by Warrington and Shallice (1984; also see Shallice 1987), is that patients with semantic breakdown would not benefit from a priming event that occurs before the target item. Thus Shallice (1987, p. 118) argues: "If the representation no longer exists, one could not prime it."

There are a number of remarks that should be made about the possible influence of priming on word recognition and comprehension. First, the notion, as employed by Warrington and Shallice, appears to be rather ambiguous. Semantic *priming* usually refers to the passive spread of activation through semantic memory from a word or picture (the prime) and is measured by its effect on the recognition of a subsequent target bearing some relation to the prime. The word *lion*, for example, is identified more rapidly if *tiger* is displayed a short time—say 500 milliseconds—beforehand (Meyer, Schvaneveldt, and Ruddy 1975). The main point about the phenomenon is that it is largely automatic; the subject does not have to make any *explicit* judgment concerning the semantic relation between the prime and the target nor to *actively* use this information when making a response. Indeed there is good reason to believe that the effect can occur even when little attention is given to the word or picture occuring before the target (Posner and Snyder 1975) and, more dramatically perhaps, that the influence can persist under display conditions that prevent conscious identification of the prime (Carr et al. 1982, Marcel 1980).

The use of the term *priming* by Warrington and Shallice would seem to have a totally different implication, referring to a more voluntary, controlled procedure where the patient must actively employ a verbal or pictorial *cue* (or prompt) to facilitate the processing of a conceptually related item. For example, given the word *Egypt* as a cue, Warrington and Shallice found that a dyslexic patient had greater success at reading the word *pyramid* (a similar results was observed by Warrington (1981) for a patient with concrete-word dyslexia), leading these authors to conclude on the basis of this and other relevant criteria that the impairment was due to an access disorder.

The question of passive priming and its relation to degraded semantic representations and the further question of the relation between priming and cuing effects remain unanswered. We consider them in some detail later.

4. Finally, Warrington and Shallice (1979) have suggested that lower-frequency items (that is, less familiar) should be more susceptible to deterioration of the representations within semantic memory than high-frequency items. When impaired access is responsible for the comprehension disorder, however, "frequency would be expected to be a less important factor as the variability produced by specific access/information retrieval problems would tend to flatten any underlying 'normal' frequency function" (Shallice 1987, p. 118).

These indices are not without controversy (see Shallice 1988 for a discussion)—some of them (for example, the issue of priming) more so than others. We have taken as our defining criteria of semantic breakdown the facts that patients are *consistent* in the items they do not understand and that superordinate knowledge is preserved in the face of a clear impairment to attributes of the particular concept. We recognize that neither measure is entirely problem-free—there may be item-specific connections to meaning, for example, so that an access problem may yield consistent performance—but we have chosen them as a point of departure because they represent to us the most fundamental of the available criteria. As we proceed, we examine the relevance and possible convergence of other measures in analyzing the sematic deficit of Alzheimer patients.

To recapitulate, Warrington and Shallice (Warrington 1975, Warrington and Shallice 1979, Shallice 1987) argue that semantic storage disorders show a preservation of superordinate over detailed knowledge, which would not occur in access disorders. Second, storage disorders would show consistent item-specific errors, because concept items were truly lost, whereas access disorders would show inconsistent errors due to variable "noise." Third, storage disorders would display a clear frequency effect, with low-frequency items affected before high-frequency items. Access disorders would not show this frequency effect. Fourth, storage disorders would be marked by a loss of priming, whereas access disorders would not entail absent priming effects.

Thus far we have demonstrated the presence of item-by-item consistency and a distinction between knowledge of superordinate information and attributes in the DAT patients. We now explore a number of other measures, including the somewhat obscure claim that patients with semantic breakdown would no longer demonstrate sensitivity to priming. As we have argued, the prediction rests on evidence from *prompting* or *cuing* effects rather than passive priming on word recognition tasks. Our aim is to examine both cuing and priming in a larger group of patients, to determine the relevance of each as a marker of semantic impairment. We also provide further converging evidence that the comprehension disturbance is *item specific* by looking at consistency of naming errors over time rather than consistency between tasks.

Semantic Cuing

In the object naming test patients were successfully able to label a mean of 105.1 out of 146 items. In those cases where the patient was unable to produce the object's name, a semantic cue was offered while the patient studied the picture. The cue consisted of the imageable word, which was highly associated with the item, drawn from tables of word association norms (Postman and Keppel 1970). The word was embedded in a sentence (for example, picture of a lion— cue: It's like a tiger). Cuing results were recorded. No time limit was given.

Eight of the 10 patients were tested for semantic cuing. The 8 patients were anomic on a mean of 41.0 out of 150 items in the battery, giving a total of 328 unnamed items. Semantic cuing attempts for these items appeared to be largely ineffective in aiding performance, exerting a positive influence on only 43 responses (13.1 percent). This meant that in 285 cases (86.9 percent) semantic cuing was ineffective.

The anomic items for which cuing *was* effective were examined in relation to their semantic intactness according to verbal probes. Of the 43 items 25 were found to have been intact on verbal probe questions, and only 18 were degraded. Therefore if the 25 intact but anomic items are excluded, it becomes evident that semantic cuing was effective in only 5.4 percent of cases where the item was found to be semantically degraded. One is led to conclude that semantic cuing is indeed not effective in aiding naming in our patient group with semantic deterioration.

Consistency of Responses over Time

The 150 pictures used previously in the picture naming task were administered again one month later. Pictures were presented one at a time in a random order with semantic categories mixed together, and patients were asked to name the item. Results were compared with the previous naming task to examine consistency of correct and incorrect responses.

On the initial battery the 10 patients with Alzheimer's disease were anomic on a total of 409 items, mean 40.9, out of a battery of 146 items. When the test was repeated, the same items were unnamed in 378 of cases, representing 92.5 percent of the unnamed items. The coefficient of consistency, kappa, was calculated for each of the ten patients. Kappa measures may vary between −1 (complete inconsistency) to +1 (complete consistency), with kappa values greater than .65 indicating a high degree of consistency (Fleiss 1981). For each of our pateints kappa was found to lie in the range +.75 to +.91. This time-based reliability measure confirmed the high consistency of naming errors.

Discussion
Semantic cuing for unnamed items was found to be effective in less than 6 percent of cases when the item was semantically degraded. Loss of attribute knowledge, consistency of errors, and absence of semantic cuing effects therefore do coexist in DAT patients with suspected loss of conceptual information from semantic mémory (Shallice 1987). We may therefore suggest that some DAT patients do in fact satisfy the criteria of Shallice and Warrington for a semantic storage disorder.

The results of semantic cuing indicate that there are two sources to the anomia of these patients. We noted earlier that 10.1 percent of the semantically intact items remained unnamed in our patients. Here we find that of the 43 responses that demonstrated effective cuing, 58 percent were to items measured as semantically intact. This suggests that although most of the anomia in these patients occurred on the basis of a semantic memory disturbance, roughly 5 percent to 10 percent of the anomia was linked to an inability to access the spoken label for a particular picture. In such cases a semantic cue might be very effective, and the semantic probes would indicate intact semantic knowledge.

Semantic Priming

Meyer and Schvaneveldt (1971) were the first to show that the response latency (reaction times) to decide whether a pair of written stimuli are both words was less if the second word was a primary associate of the first (for example, bread-butter). This effect, now termed *semantic priming*, occurs if the words are presented simultaneously or if the first word precedes the second (Fischler 1977a), and it is obtained if the two words are semantically related (that is, within the same semantic category, such as *tools*), even if they are not highly associated (Fischler 1977b). Though generally a small effect (10 ms to 50 ms), the result has been found to occur reliably across other tasks such as naming, and semantic categorization as well.

We know little about semantic priming in patients with Alzheimer's disease. An initial study of 20 moderately impaired DAT patients by Nebes, Martin, and Horn (1984) found semantic priming to be equivalent for patients and matched controls. In a further study of sentence priming, Nebes, Boller, and Holland (1986) actually found a twofold increase in the priming to 18 unselected Alzheimer's disease patients when compared with normal control subjects. Nebes has continued to find variable results of semantic priming in unselected groups of patients (Nebes, Brady, and Huff 1989). He has interpreted the existence of priming as evidence that the structure of semantic memory remains relatively intact in Alzheimer's disease. Needless to say, we do not share this conclusion. Priming is a complex phenomenon that remains incompletely understood; it is entirely possible that the effect of semantic degradation might not be simply to abolish priming, but to alter it in subtle ways. Moreover because the semantic and perceptual status of Nebes's patients was not fully assessed, it is unclear whether these priming results reflected changes in semantic memory.

Present Priming Studies
We have carried out a detailed investigation of the extent of priming in our group of patients with DAT. (Chertkow, Bub, and Seidenberg 1989, Chertkow and Bub 1990). We wished to address two questions: (1) Did the items showing a partially degraded representation in semantic memory yield different (or absent) patterns of priming relative to items with a more precise semantic description? and (2) What is the relation between semantic priming and semantic cuing in our patients? To answer these questions, we designed an experiment of semantic priming on a speeded lexical decision task, using the same stimuli that had been chosen for the cuing experiment and the naming and semantic probe tests. Only 6 of the DAT patients were able to cooperate adequately to carry out a priming task, and data are therefore presented only for these 6.

Twenty-five words were selected as priming items. For each of the 25 priming words, an associatively related (AR) word pair was constructed, using published norms of word association (Postman and Keppel 1970). An additional semantically related (SR) word pair was also derived, using the same primes. The two words in the SR pair were semantically close (that is, another tool or animal), but not associated. For example, for item *hammer*, the AR pair was hammer-nail, and the SR pair was hammer-wrench. The stimuli for the priming experiment were linked to those of the previous tests, such that all words used for priming had also been used in the naming, read-

Table 7.5
Semantic Priming in DAT Patients and Control Subjects

Group	Mean Reaction Time on Unprimed Target (ms)	Priming Effect (ms)
Control (n = 10)	831.1 (SD = 227.9)	24.8 (SD = 22.4)
DAT patients (n = 6)	1255.1 (SD = 160.4)	140.6 (SD = 70.8)

ing, and probe tasks. There were altogether 200 stimulus pairs. Our results did not reveal significant differences between the priming of AR and SR pairs, so that we henceforth refer to the 50 word pairs as associated.

Reaction times for the lexical decision task were calculated, along with errors (the erroneous answers were not included in reaction time evaluation). The priming effect for each item was calculated by subtracting the response time for a particular target when preceded by an association word from the response time when preceded by a nonassociated word.

Latency Analysis   Our normal control subjects (table 7.5) displayed latency results similar to those obtained in previous series (Howard, McAndrews, and Lasaga 1981, Burke, White, and Diaz 1987). There was a notably wide range of reaction times for performing a lexical decision to an unassociated word target. Mean response time (RT) was 831.1 ms, with a range of 570 ms to 1183 ms. All 10 control subjects showed priming effects. The mean total priming effect was 24.8 ms (range 4 ms to 40.4 ms). Total priming as a percentage of the unprimed target RT ranged from 1.0 percent to 5.5 percent, with a mean of 2.9 percent. These results are comparable to previous results of priming in older populations, (Howard, McAndrews, and Lasaga 1981) and show little change relative to the many published studies of lexical decision priming in younger populations (for example, Fischler, 1977a, Neely 1977).

The 6 DAT patients also displayed a wide range of RT's on the unprimed targets, but were slower than normal subjects. Mean unprimed RT was 1255.1 ms, ranging from 1070 ms to 1428 ms. Note that there was considerable overlap between the reaction times of DAT patients and age-matched normal subjects. All DAT patients showed abnormally large priming effects. Total priming effect (TPE) for associated word pairs yielded a mean of 140.6 ms, ranging from 84.7 ms to 267.6 ms (figure 7.1).

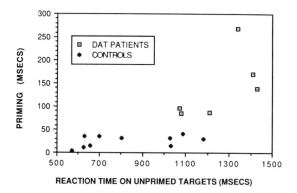

REACTION TIME ON UNPRIMED TARGETS (MSECS)

Figure 7.1
Total semantic priming for patients and control subjects versus unprimed reaction time on lexical decision task

When expressed as a percentage of the unprimed target RT, the TPE was 10.5 percent. There was no overlap between the DAT group and normal control subjects for TPE in terms of absolute times or percentages. Reaction time latencies were significantly shorter in the primed condition than the unprimed. Groups differed from each other in overall decision latency, with the demented group showing longer latencies than normal control subjects showed. A significant group x-prime interaction was found, confirming the finding that DAT patients showed abnormally *increased* TPE's, greater than expected relative to their slow reaction times. No speed-accuracy trade-off was evident from the error scores.

Semantic Priming of Intact and Degraded Items   To investigate the possible causes of our unexpected finding of increased semantic priming, the results were examined relative to previous comprehension scores. For each DAT subject priming word pairs were separated into those where the target item was found to be intact in terms of semantic knowledge (on probe recognition) versus pairs where the target item was degraded in terms of semantic knowledge. Priming effects were examined for the two groups of words (table 7.6).

For each of the 6 DAT patients, lexical decision speed in the unprimed condition (prime word being unassociated with target) was significantly longer for degraded items (mean 1551.8 ms) than for intact items (mean 1148.1 ms). Errors were excluded from reaction time measurements, but the error rate was also noted to be higher for the unprimed targets. There was thus no speed-accuracy trade-off. The priming effect is markedly increased for the degraded items (mean

Table 7.6
Semantic Priming on Intact versus Degraded Targets in DAT Patients

Patient	Intact Target			Degraded Target		
	No. of Items	Unprimed RT (ms)	Priming Effect (ms)	No. of Items	Unprimed RT (ms)	Priming Effect (ms)
SB	23	1212	72	10	1275	274
AT	24	1220	196	22	1795	435
JM	36	966	58	8	1298	236
AC	30	1211	65	15	1642	375
TA	37	1228	46	12	1943	402
KF	17	1051	−32	16	1358	206
Means (ms)	—	1148.1	67.5	—	1551.8	321.3

321.3 ms) than for the intact items (mean 67.5 ms). Statistical analysis confirms this impression. A two-way ANOVA shows a main effect of intactness, $F(1,5) = 15.2$, $p < .05$, including longer reaction times for degraded items. There was also a main effect of priming condition, $F(1,5) = 46.3$, $p < .005$.

Priming and Cuing   In designing the cuing task, care had been taken the cue words used would be identical to the words used as primes in the on-line semantic priming task. We therefore analyzed our results, searching for trials in which the target word was semanticaly degraded on verbal probes—the item had been unnamed on the naming task, semantic cuing had been carried out, and the identical words (that is, cue and target word) had been used as a priming pair. These conditions were satisfied on 73 trials. When we analyzed results on these trials (Chertkow and Bub 1990), we found no correlation between results of cuing and priming. In 61 of the 73 trials, a semantic cue was ineffective in aiding the subject's ability to name a picture of the item. Examing those items, we found positive semantic priming had occurred in 37 of the 73, and negative priming in 24 of them. Results on one test therefore did not predict results on the other test.

Discussion   The semantic priming experiment produced results in control subjects consistent with the literature. Elderly subjects appear to show priming on a lexical decision task similar to that of young subjects (Howard et al. 1981), even though their reaction times are slower (Benton 1977, Fischler and Goodman 1978).

In the DAT patients there was a quite unexpected result of increased priming effects compared with age-matched normal subjects (140.6 ms versus 24.8 ms in normal subjects). Reaction times for the DAT patients were much slower than normal subjects, although there was considerable overlap between the two groups. Fischler and Goodman (1978) observed that slower reaction times produce slightly increased priming effects, but not nearly of this magnitude. In addition there was no overlap between normal and DAT patients with respect to TPE, either in terms of quantitative TPE or percentage prime of the unassociated RT. This was true even relative to control subjects who were just as slow as the DAT patients.

A second phenomenon of interest is the marked difference between performance on semantically degraded and semantically intact targets in the DAT patients. Responses for degraded targets were significantly slower than for the intact targets (1551.8 ms versus 1148.1 ms) and were more influenced by semantic priming when preceded by an associated word (321.3 ms versus 67.5 ms). Analysis indicates this enhanced priming effect was unrelated to word frequency differences, but rather was linked to the semantic degradation of an item.

Previous researchers have assumed that deterioration of semantic knowledge would be associated with reduced or absent priming effects (Huff, Corkin, and Growdon 1986, Milberg and Blumstein 1981, Nebes, Martin, and Horn 1984). In fact the surprising finding we have documented is that despite evidence of clear impairment of semantic memory, they showed markedly *increased* semantic priming effects. Analysis shows that this hyperpriming is unlikely to be a trivial result of slower reaction times, but reflects the effect of semantic memory degradation in some way.

What is the functional locus of this unexpected outcome? If we assume that word recognition and semantic encoding proceed interactively, the effect of the prime may spread across a neighborhood of words, decreasing their activation threshold in the lexicon. Degraded items, with lower initial accessibility, would stand to gain more from this spreading activation than items with fuller semantic descriptions.

Another possibility is that the hyperpriming effect occurs at the level of response processes rather than stimulus encoding. In a lexical decision task there is evidence that priming exerts an influence on the decision mechanism as well as the stage of lexical access (Balota and Chumbley 1984, Seidenberg et al. 1984). This occurs perhaps by facilitating postlexical checks of semantic relatedness between the two items (that is, if the prime and target are related, they must both be words), which would speed performance of the lexical decision. If the patients consult semantic memory as a check before reaching a decision, their RT will be slower on items with an impaired representation. Exposure to a semantic prime may improve their evaluation of the related target by focusing their attention on the superordinate category. However, our recent investigations have revealed similar hyperpriming on naming tasks, which lack a postlexical stage, suggesting that the effect is not simply occurring at the level of response or decision processes. A detailed account of the abnormally large priming effect requires further investigation. What is evident, however, is that priming is a more complex phenomenon in brain-damaged patients than has previously been suspected. It is not simply present or absent, but may in fact become pathologically increased.

Finally, it should be noted that the results of semantic priming and semantic cuing in our chosen word pairs were markedly dissimilar in the presence of semantic deterioration. Although superficially similar tasks, the cognitive processing of off-line cues, and on-line semantic primes, is not identical. We must be careful not to generalize from the results of one task to another, particularly when the effects of a paradigm such as semantic priming remain only partially understood.

Single versus Multiple Semantic Systems

Thus far we have been occupied with the general semantic deficit affecting DAT patients and have made no distinction between verbal and nonverbal material. Our implicit assumption has been that semantic descriptions common to both kinds of material are damaged, placing equal constraints on the comprehension of pictures and words. A number of theorists have argued, however, that functionally distinct conceptual systems exist for different input channels, allowing for the possibility that the deficit in some or all of the patients may vary with respect to the sensory form of the target item. We briefly review the evidence for multiple semantic systems before we look for material-specific conceptual loss in our group of DAT patients with semantic impairment.

Intuition suggests that what we know about a object should be the same whether we encounter it as a spoken word, in pictorial form, or as a written label. Much of the experimental evidence from normal subjects is consistent with such a view. On speeded tasks of naming and lexical decision, for example, pictures can effectively prime words, and vice versa (Carr et al. 1982, Vanderwart 1984), an outcome that supports the claim that different modalities of input share a com-

mon representation at a semantic level. Certain experimental findings, however, indicate that the extraction of meaning from pictures
or words may be more complicated than is suggested by a theory of
amodal semantic representations. Investigations of semantic memory
using brain-damaged patients provide a powerful source of constraint
on attempts to develop a functional architecture of the semantic
mechanism.

Evidence for Multiple Stores

Evidence for multiple stores (reviewed in Shallice 1987) derives from
three sources involving the investigation of such patients: (1) Several
case studies describe cognitive deficits that may be characterized as
an impairment within a strictly verbal, or a strictly nonverbal, semantic memory store (Warrington 1975, Coughlan and Warrington 1978,
Warrington and Schallice 1979). (2) In one report (Warrington and
Shallice 1979) a patient with "semantic access dyslexia" was tested for
cuing effects in tests of naming, with pictures and words as cues. A
modality-specific insensitivity to cuing was found, and this was interpreted as evidence for multiple semantic stores. (3) Patients are found
on rare occasion who display a modality-specific aphasia (Beauvois
1982, Denes and Semenza 1975). In optic aphasia, the best described
of these syndromes, patients have a naming deficit primarily or exclusively for visually presented objects (Lhermitte and Beauvois 1973,
Riddoch and Humphreys 1987, Coslett and Saffran 1987). These patients are verbally intact; they can produce the name of objects when
supplied with a verbal definition. They are not obviously agnosic, in
that they demonstrate apparent understanding of the objects they
cannot name, through gesture or mime. These findings have been
taken to suggest that such patients demonstrate intact access to
semantic memory from vision. The anomia for visual objects has been
interpreted as the result of a disconnection between (intact) visual
and verbal semantic memory stores or subsystems, with object naming first requiring access to a verbal memory store (Beauvois 1982,
Shallice 1987). Optic aphasia is perhaps the most tantalizing neuropsychological evidence in support of the multiple semantic memory
model.

Nevertheless Riddoch, Humphreys, Coltheart, and Funnell (1988)
have strongly contested the arguments based on the performance of
brain-damaged patients. In the case of semantic access dyslexia, they
point out that some aspects of the patient's performance suggest that
he may have been impaired in his ability to access meaning from pictures as well as written words. If that was indeed the case, then "the
claim that he failed to show priming effects from pictures on word

naming is not particularly interesting and would be expected whether semantic information is modality specific or modality independent" (p. 7).

As for points 1 and 3, Riddoch and Humphreys criticize the original evidence on the grounds that what is interpreted as measures of visual semantic performance may in fact reflect only the patients' ability to extract information from a purely perceptual structural description of the visual object, a level of representation that is presemantic. They claim that patients may be capable of gesturing on objects' use or even answering detailed probe questions when shown a picture, simply by inferring some general properties from the physical description.

Warrington (1975), for example, interpreted the responses to verbal probe questions administered to her 3 demented patients as suggestive of a verbal/visual semantic dissociation. One of the patients demonstrated slightly superior performance on verbal probes for pictures than for words, leading Warrington to infer that for him visual semantics was less affected than verbal semantics. Riddoch and Humphreys have claimed that most of the questions used by Warrington could be answered accurately simply by inferring relevant attributes from physical cues in the structure of the object. Only one of her questions (*Is this animal foreign or local?*), they suggest, could not be answered this way and would therefore provide a legitimate test of semantic access from pictorial material.

As for the cases of modality-specific aphasias, such as optic aphasia (3), their criticism is similarly that normal entry to semantics has never been adequately demonstrated in most of these patients. The data, they propose, are more easily interpreted as a deficit in gaining access to meaning from the structural description of a picture than a disturbance within a semantic component.

Riddoch and Humphreys (1987) then conclude that intact access to semantics cannot be assumed on the basis of accurate gesturing to objects; intact gestures could be generated from presemantic structural descriptions that provide clues to the patient on the semantic properties of an object even when it has not been identified. They find no convincing evidence therefore to support the theory that there are multiple semantic memory stores.

Structural Descriptions and Object Identification
There are a number of comments that can be made regarding the view that functional and perceptual attributes may be derived or inferred directly from the structural description. First, the claim that miming the use of an object is generally posssible solely on the basis of its

structure ignores the specificity of many gestures. As Shallice (1988) points out, a vase structure may "afford" grasping, lifting, pouring, and drinking, but the most appropriate gesture requires correct retrieval of the typical use to which the object is put in our culture (that is, a container for flowers).

A second point is that the notion of presemantic visual categorization (yielding, among other forms of representation, the structural description of an object) needs to be clarified because it forms one major component of the puzzle surrounding material-specific conceptual breakdown. To begin with, let us assume that after a visual object is seen and matched to its corresponding structural description in memory, direct access occurs to a specific concept node within an amodal semantic memory store.

The structure of an object is a purely *physical* description, of course, and the task of locating the correct object concept in semantic memory would be simplified if we could define the concept itself in physical terms. Unfortunately there are good reasons for arguing that the semantic description of an object must include abstract and functional properties as well as perceptual features. Miller and Johnson-Laird (1976) emphasize that both kinds of information are required because any attempt to define an object in terms of perceptual features alone causes insurmountable difficulty. No matter how such a list is constructed, instances of a concept will be found that do not possess any of the defining features. In addition an object can alter its conceptual status under different circumstances, even though its structure remains unchanged. For example, the knowledge that a packing case makes a good table (although a drafting table generally does not) can never be represented directly in the physical structure of the object. It is linked to the *use* people get from a rigid, horizontal surface.

The argument that an object concept must contain both abstract and perceptual features generates a fundamental problem. At the level of structure the object itself must be encoded as a physical description consisting entirely of perceptual features that are then mapped onto semantic memory. If some features of the *concept* are abstract, but all features of the *object* are perceptual, the system must have a way of translating between the different kinds of representation at the two levels.

To illustrate with an example, taken from Smith and Medin (1981): The concept *boy* might include the abstract features *human, male,* and *young.* To determine whether a given person is an instance of the concept, the system would have to check for these features *perceptually,* using attributes like height, weight, and body proportion.

This requires ancillary knowledge about the perceptual features that instantiate abstract ones.

Smith and Medin (1981) therefore distinguish between the core of a concept, which permits the understanding of relations between objects (for example, between a boy and a kitten) and the identification procedure, a specialized component with both semantic and perceptual information needed to categorize particular instances (see Miller and Johnson-Laird 1976 for a very similar idea). Both of these semantic components would be accessed subsequent to the activation of a purely presemantic stored geometric listing of an object's perceptual properties, a representation that we would suggest is in fact the structural description of the object (Sutherland 1973).

Evidence for Two Components in Semantic Memory Processing
In previous work (Chertkow, Bub, and Seidenberg 1989) we examined semantic memory deterioration in our group of patients with Alzheimer's disease. One incidental finding was a dissociation in several patients between loss of ability of answer semantic questions of associative relationships (for example, Does a cat go more with a mouse or with a deer?) and preservation of the ability to answer perceptual probe questions (for example, Do cats have claws or hooves?). A possible explanation for this outcome is that knowledge of the relation between concepts depends on *core* aspects of meaning, which is more susceptible to deterioration in Alzheimer's disease than the knowledge required for the perceptual identification of an object as an instance of a concept. The fact that some Alzheimer's disease patients who were minimally anomic still showed impairment on questions that test associative relations also suggested to us that core knowledge might be functionally dissociable from the knowledge required for perceptual identification.

Is there a task that might test for the intactness of an identification procedure? Several researchers (Kroll and Potter 1984, Riddoch and Humphreys 1987) have utilized an object decision test, in which subjects were asked to discriminate real from nonsense objects or animals. The task may be relatively easy if nonobjects are chosen to be structurally improbable in the real world (for example, Kroll and Potter 1984), or it may be made difficult by utilizing nonobjects that have more subtle substitutions of parts in their correct position (for example, a cow with a donkey's head or a knife blade with scissor handles). Riddoch and Humphreys presumed that even difficult object decisions can be performed on the basis of structural knowledge alone. We do not share this view; rather we suspect that an object decision task, if appropriately designed, may test the ability to identify perceptual instances of concepts. An object decision task would similarly demand higher-level processing beyond the level of a structural description. We will provide evidence from dementia patients cosistent with this idea.

We have argued that some patients with dementia of the Alzheimer type might demonstrate possible deterioration of core concept knowledge with preservation of their identification procedures for objects. Such patients might still be able to classify visual objects or pictures and would thus correctly respond to those exemplars in an object decision task. The patients might even be able to name the object, if access from the identification procedure to pronunciation remained intact. When shown a picture, they would be able to answer probe questions about perceptual and functional characteristics that form part of the identification procedure.

Given the verbal label of the object, however, we might expect a different pattern of results from the patients. Because the conceptual attributes that form part of an identification procedure are specifically designed for the classification of *visual* instances, there is no reason to assume complete overlap between them and the attributes that are activated by words. If adequate comprehension of words depends on the integrity of semantic properties that exist outside the set delimited for identifying visual objects (that is, in the core concept), and if these are more vulnerable to brain damage, then the patient would be more severely impaired in his ability to answer probe questions on words than pictures, providing the latter retain their identification procedures. For pictures that are not identified, however, no difference is expected on probe questions relative to words.

Our evaluation of the Alzheimer's disease patients provided converging evidence that all 10 demonstrated degradation within their semantic memory store, using several different neuropsychological tests. We now examine the possibility that some of these patients retain identification procedures for a percentage of objects, relying on a version of the object decision task to provide us with a measure of identification.

Line drawing of 18 animals were obtained, all of which were used previously as test stimuli. We generated structurally plausible nonanimals by substituting other animal heads on the drawing (figure 7.2). Animals and nonanimals were then presented in random order. Patients were required to answer yes or no to the question, Is this a real animal? The test was repeated on two separate occasions over a month to ascertain that answers were consistent.

Figure 7.2
Examples of animal decision test stimuli: nonanimals on the left and animals on the
right

234 Chertkow and Bub

Table 7.7
Performance on Animal Decision Task: Mean over 3 Trials

Patient	Score (out of 32 max.)	Group
CR	31	A
AC	30	A
JM	25	C
ES	20	C
KF	24	C
DC	26	C
HR	22	C
AT	17	B
SB	17	B
TA	18	B

Results

Three Patterns of Performance   The 10 patients completed the test and displayed three different patterns of results. We have grouped these together for analysis as A, B, and C:

Group A: Two patients (CR and AC) were able to identify real and nonreal animals correctly, with little difficulty (table 7.7). They were consistently correct over three trials, scoring 31 and 30 out of 32 respectively.

Group B: Three patients (TA, SB, AT) performed essentially at chance on the test. Their mean scores over three trials were 18, 17.3, and 16.7 respectively. They each assumed different strategies: One rejected all pictures as being unfamiliar (AT), one accepted all pictures as representing real animals (SB), and the third (TA) appeared to guess in a pattern that was not consistent over trials.

Group C: Five patients (JM, ES, KF, DC, HR) were able to correctly identify a subset of the animals. For these, true animals were accepted, and false animals (wrong body to fit the head) were rejected. On the remaining animals the patients were unable to accurately identify true or false pictures. Responses were consistent over repeated sessions. For 5 animals (out of 90 responses) the pattern was unclear, and there were therefore discarded from analysis.

Probe Knowledge in the Groups
Performance of the patients on the probe questions presented in this chapter was reanalyzed in terms of group membership. The 2 pa-

Table 7.8
Group A—Probe Errors for Animal Pictures and Words (excluding superordinate questions)

Patient	No. Items	Picture Errors	Word Errors
CR	18	17/108	40/108
AC	18	32/108	55/108
Total	36	49/216 (22.7% errors)	95/216 (44.0% errors)

tients in group A has no difficulty performing the animal decision task. Examination of the errors made on attribute probe questions to the 18 animals (table 7.8) shows that they made a total of 49 errors out of 216 tries on probes on picture presentation and 95 errors out of 216 tries on probes on word presentation. It appears that their performance for pictures was considerably better than for the corresponding words. Analysis of these error data via a t-test confirms the impression that there were significantly more errors for words than for pictures ($t = 3.11$, $p < .05$).

Considering only the items that these two patients were unable to name, the same pattern persists. CR was unable to name 18 items. For these items 17 errors were made on picture probes, and 40 errors were made on word probes. AC was unable to name 33 items. For these items 65 errors were made on the picture probe questions, and 111 errors were made for words. The pictorial advantage therefore exists both for named and unnamed items.

The 3 patients in group B were essentially performing at chance on the animal decision test, suggesting that they failed to identify the majority of animals. Examination of the errors made on detailed probe questions of the 18 animals (table 7.9) shows that they made a total of 126 errors out of 324 tries on probes with picture presentation, and 116 errors out of 324 tries on probes on word presentation. It appears that their performance for pictures was no better (and in fact marginally worse) than their performance on words. Results of a t-test

Table 7.9
Group B—Probe Errors for Animal Pictures and Words (excluding superordinate questions)

Patient	No. Items	Picture Errors	Word Errors
TA	18	45/108	47/108
SB	18	45/108	37/108
AT	18	36/108	32/108
Total	54	126/324 (38.9% errors)	116/324 (35.8% errors)

Table 7.10
Group C—Probe Errors for Animal Pictures and Words (excluding superordinate questions)

| Patient | Items Not Correct on Animal Decisions | | | Items Correct on Animal Decisions | | |
	No. Items	Picture Errors	Words Errors	No. Items	Picture Errors	Words Errors
DC	5	15	18	11	16	28
KF	8	31	29	10	17	31
ES	7	25	21	8	15	22
JM	5	11	13	13	15	19
HR	10	35	35	8	14	28
Total	35	117/210	116/210	50	77/300	128/300
Percent	—	55.7%	55.2%	—	25.7%	42.7%

confirms that the performance on pictures was not significantly different from performance on words in this group ($t = 1.14$, $p = .37$).

The 5 patients in group C shows a *consistent* inability to identify certain animals only on the animal decision test. It was hypothesized that they might have lost identification procedures for these animals only, while retaining the procedures for the other exemplars. The probe errors were therefore divided in two groups: item on which the patient consistently failed on the animal decision task and items that the patient consistently identified correctly on the animal decision task. Note that the exact items in each group varied from patient to patient. Examination of the data (table 7.10) reveals that for the 35 items total on which the patients consistently failed on the animal decision task, there were 117 errors out of 210 tries on probe questions on pictures, and 116 errors out of 210 tries on words. It appears that the performance on this group of items is equally impaired for pictures and words. This is confirmed by a t-test, which failed to show a significant difference between error scores on words and pictures ($t = .155$, $p = .854$).

For the 50 items that the patients consistently identified correctly on the animal decision task, there were 77 errors out of 300 tries on picture probes and 128 errors out of 300 tries on word probes. The subjects therefore appear to be much more impaired on probe questions for words than for pictures. A t-test confirms this impression; there were significantly more errors on words than on pictures in this group ($t = 5.07$, $p < .01$).

Discussion

We have made several assumptions about the possible nature of identification procedures in an effort to construct a preliminary framework. It was argued that a dementia patient with deterioration in semantic memory may nevertheless retain the knowledge mediating the visual identification of an object concept. We assumed that if identification procedures were retained, the semantic knowledge dedicated to their function might be retrievable on probe questions to nonverbal material (pictures). Furthermore a decision test between real and nonsense animals would be a legitimate means of determining the status of an identification procedure. We therefore predicted an *item-specific* association between preserved identification procedures (measured in terms of correct answers on the animal decision test) and a pictorial advantage in answering probe questions of semantic attributes.

This hypothesis was confirmed; all 10 patients demonstrate that they have significant loss of conceptual knowledge.The 2 patients in group A showed evidence of intact ability to identify animals in the animal decision test. Both patients showed the expected pictorial advantage on probe questions. The 3 patients in group B showed evidence of degraded identification procedures on the animal decision test. Their answers to probe questions all showed equivalent impairment on pictures and words.

The 5 patients in group C displayed the most interesting pattern of results. Their performance on the animal decision test suggested that they had lost identification procedures for some animals only, retaining identification procedures for others. Their responses to probe questions display the appropriate dissociation: For items that were not perceptually identified, they are equally bad on pictures and words, whereas for items that were correctly classified as legitimate instances, they are better on pictures than on words.

Structural Description and Core Concept Knowledge
The three of patients demonstrated different patterns of impaired semantic memory. Further examination of their deficit can provide us with relevant evidence regarding two related questions, discussed in the introduction to this section.

Question 1: What Sort of Knowledge Can be Derived from the Structural Description Level Alone?
As we have seen, the claim has been made by Riddoch and Humphreys (1987) and Riddoch, Humphreys, Coltheart, and Funnell

Table 7.11
Performance of "No Semantic Memory" Group on Picture Probe Questions for *Dog*,
Cat, and *Cow* Only

Probe Question	Correct Answer	Incorrect Answer
Does it have long fur or no fur?	15	1
Does it have claws or hooves?	16	0
Is it a domesticated or a wild animal?	11	1
Does it live in our country or is it foreign?	11	1
Does it live on farm or in a house?	10	0
Does it bark or moo?	10	0
Is it safe or dangerous?	10	0
Is it for riding or for milking?	4	0

(1988) that the structural features of an object may be used by the patient to answer questions regarding perceptual and even abstract properties that are inferred from visual cues, even though the object has not made contact with its semantic description.

This proposal can be directly tested in the DAT patients. As we argue here, the 3 patients in group B have a functional deficit that appears to involve both core conceptual knowledge and identification procedures. Because they failed to identify most of the animals, any residual ability to derive attribute information must be guided by structural elements in their physical description. The same holds true for a percentage of the animal items in the group C patients, namely, those items that were not positively identified in the object decision task. If these patients still manage to correctly answer a significant number of probe questions on items they reject as unfamiliar, it would be reasonable to conclude that structural properties allowed them to infer certain attributes of the objects.

Before checking on this possibility, we should mention that even the most severely impaired of our patients retained a small number of animal concepts — the exemplars *dog*, *cat*, and *cow* were almost invariably responded to correctly on probe questions. This corpus of intact items allowed us to ascertain that the patients were attending to probe questions correctly because many of the attributes tested (for example, *dangerous* or *safe*) were sampled over a wide range of items (table 7.11).

The remaining animals, falsely rejected in the object decision task, were then examined to ascertain what attributes could be derived sufficiently from the retained representations to yield accurate responses on probe questions. The results are displayed in table 7.12.

Table 7.12
Performance of "No Semantic Memory" Group on Picture Probe Questions for
Degraded Animals

Probe Question	Correct Answer	Incorrect Answer
At chance		
Is it safe or dangerous?	12	12
Does it have claws or hooves?	16	15
Does it have long fur or hide only?	21	21
Poor performance		
[Bear]—Is it bigger or smaller than a person?	2	4
[Rhinocerous]—(same question)	4	2
[Monkey]—(same question)	2	2
[Snake]—Does it crawl or hop?	2	2
Good performance		
[Camel]—Does it have a hump or horns?	6	1
[Zebra]—Does it have stripes of spots?	5	0
[Snake]—Does it have legs or no legs?	4	0
[Mouse]—Is it bigger or smaller than a person?	4	0
[Elephant]—(same question)	4	0
[Elephant]—Does it have tusks or horns?	4	0

Clearly certain questions led to chance levels of accuracy. In particular
the patients were unable to determine whether the animal was safe or
dangerous, had fur or skin, or had claws rather than hooves. The
patients were able to make fairly accurate size estimates, however,
when the differences were extreme (that is, size of elephant and
mouse compared with a person), but were at chance when size judgments were more demanding (for example, size of a bear, rhinoceros,
or monkey, in comparison with a person).

The patients in this group were apparently capable of answering
very few probe questions, limited to basic physical properties occuring in the picture (that is, whether zebras have stripes or spots,
whether a snake has legs, whether a camel has a hump or a horn,
whether an elephant has tusks or horns). The data suggest that
knowledge derived from structure provides Alzheimer patients with
mininal information regarding the attributes of a depicted animal.

Question 2: Is the Core Concept Amodal?
Although pictures or visual objects initially access a stage of identification procedures dedicated to perceptual classification, we favor

the view that conceptual knowledge is not globally differentiated into verbal and nonverbal stores. Pictures may activate a specific set of attributes for their identification, but such activation would occur within a representational system common to all sensory forms of a concept.

We have argued that the two patients (CR and AC) in group A had no difficulty in performing the animal decision task and therefore correctly identified the targets as conceptual instances. For group C patients there existed a subset of animal items that were similarly classified.

If we consider the animals that were positively categorized, we find that many probe questions to them are answered correctly. The knowledge needed for a response may be derived from the intact identification procedure or the undegraded portion of the core concept. If a particular question remains *unanswerable*, though, the probed attribute must be lost from stored knowledge that does *not* form part of the identification procedure. Assuming this knowledge to be amodal (that is, held in common for verbal and nonverbal material), we should observe the same conceptual impairment whether the probe question was directed to the picture of an item or its written label. Thus the notion of amodal conceptual representations would predict that for items with demonstrably intact identification procedures, questions answered erroneously on picture probes should also be answered erroneously on word probes. If there exist multiple conceptual stores, however, no such correlation would be expected.

When the relevant set of pictorial items were examined, it was found that 84 probe questions had been answered erroneously. When the same questions were administered as word probes, 73 of them (87 percent) were responded to incorrectly. This represents a very strong association and provides no support for material-specific semantic stores.

Conclusion: A Two-Component Model of Semantic Memory
Investigating patients with brain damage producing visual agnosia, Warrington and Taylor (1978) and Warrington (1982) concluded that there must be two postsensory categorical components of visual object recognition. The first component consisted of perceptual categorization on the basis of an object's structure, and Warrington identified it with the *structural description*, a postsensory, presemantic level of representation. The second component, functionally independent from the first, involved semantic categorization of visual objects.

In studies of brain-damaged patients as well as normal subjects (Guenther and Klatzky 1978, Guenther, Klatzky, and Putnam 1980), there has often been the suggestion that a stage of processing exists for visual representations that occurs subsequent to the structural description and yet is not identical to the semantic memory store for words. This semantic component is more closely tied to visual representations and can produce effects in semantic tasks separate from the amodal semantic store. Such models of semantic memory might be classified as hybrid, in that they do not support a view of semantic memory as consisting of multiple stores, yet at the same time they propose the existence of different processing patterns for pictures and words. We suggest that these models are consistent with the theoretical standpoint that we have argued for in this chapter.

References

Appell, J., Kertesz, A., and Fisman, M. (1982). A study of language functioning in Alzheimer patients. *Brain and Language* 17: 73–91.

Balota, D. A., and Chumbley, J. I. (1984). Are lexical decisions a good measure of lexical access? The role of word frequency in the neglected decision stage. *Journal of Experimental Psychology: Human Perception and Performance* 10: 340–357.

Battig, W. F., and Montague, W. E. (1969). Category norms for verbal items in 56 categories: A replication and extension of the Connecticut category norms. *Journal of Experimental Psychology Monographs* 80: 1–46.

Bayles, K. A. (1982). Language function in senile dementia. *Brain and Language* 16: 265–280.

Bayles, K. A., and Kaszniak, A. W. (1987). *Communication and Cognition in Normal Aging and Dementia*. Boston: Little, Brown.

Beauvois, M. F. (1982). Optic aphasia: A process of interaction between vision and language. *Philosophical Transactions of the Royal Society of London, B* 298: 35–47.

Benton, A. (1977). Interactive effects of age and brain disease on reaction times. *Archives of Neurology* 34: 369–370.

Burke, D., White, H., Diaz, D. (1987). Semantic priming in young and older adults: Evidence for age constancy in automatic and attentional processes. *Journal of Experimental Psychology: Human Perception and Performance* 13: 79–88.

Butterworth, B., Howard, D., and McLoughlin, P. (1984). The semantic deficit in aphasia: The relationship between semantic errors in auditory comprehension and picture naming. *Neuropsychologia* 22: 409–426.

Carr, T. H., McCauley, C., Sperber, R. D., and Parmelee, C. M. (1982). Words, pictures, and priming: On semantic activation, conscious identification, and the automaticity of information processing. *Journal of Experimental Psychology: Human Perception and Performance* 8: 757–777.

Chertkow, H., Bub, D., Caplan, D. (submitted). Two stages of semantic memory: Evidence from dementia.

Chertkow, H., Bub, D., Seidenberg, M. (1989). Priming and semantic memory in Alzheimer's disease. *Brain and Language* 36: 420–446.

Chertkow, H., and Bub, D. (1990). Semantic memory loss in dementia of the Alzheimer type: What do various measures measure? *Brain*, 113: 397–417.

Collins, A. M., and Loftus, E. F. (1975). A spreading-activation theory of semantic processing. *Psychological Review* 82: 407–428.

Collins, A. M. and Quillian, M. R. (1969). Retrieval time from semantic memory. *Journal of Verbal Learning and Verbal Behavior* 8: 240–248.

Coslett, H. B., and Saffran, E. (1987). Preserved object recognition and reading comprehension in optic aphasia. *Neurology* 37(Suppl. 1): 312–313.

Coughlan, A. K., Warrington, E. K. (1978). Word-comprehension and word-retrieval in patients with localized cerebral lesions. *Brain* 101: 163–185.

Denes, G., and Semenza, C. (1975). Auditory modality-specific anomia: Evidence from a case of pure word deafness. *Cortex* 11: 401–411.

Fischler, I. (1977a). Associative facilitation without expectancy in a lexical decision task. *Journal of Experimental Psychology: Human Perception and Performance* 3: 18–26.

Fischler, I. (1977b). Semantic facilitation without association in a lexical decision task. *Memory and Cognition* 5: 335–339.

Fischler, I., and Goodman, G. (1978). Latency of associative activation in memory. *Journal of Experimental Psychology: Human Perception and Performance* 4: 455–470.

Fleiss, J. L. (1981). *Statistical Methods for Rates and Proportions*. New York: John Wiley and Sons.

Gewirth, L., Shindler, A., and Hier, D. (1984). Altered patterns of word association in dementia and aphasia. *Brain and Language* 21: 307–317.

Guenther, R. K., and Klatzky, R. (1977). Semantic classification of pictures and words. *Journal of Experimental Psychology: Human Learning and Memory* 3: 498–514.

Guenther, R. K., Klatzky, R. L., and Putnam, W. (1980). Commonalities and differences in semantic decisions about pictures and words. *Journal of Verbal Learning and Verbal Behavior* 19: 54–74.

Hachinski, V., Illif, L. D., Zilhka, E., Du Boulay, G. H., McAllister, V. L., Marshall, J., Russel, R. W. R., and Symon, L. (1975). Cerebral blood flow in dementia. *Archives of Neurology* 32: 632–637.

Howard, D. V., McAndrews, M. P., and Lasaga, M. I. (1981). Semantic priming of lexical decisions in young and old adults. *Journal of Gerontology* 36: 707–714.

Huff, F. J., Corkin, S., and Growdon, J. H. (1986). Semantic impairment and anomia in Alzheimer's disease. *Brain and Language* 28: 235–249.

Kertesz, A., and Poole, E. (1974). The aphasia quotient: The taxonomic approach to measurement of aphasic disability. *Canadian Journal of Neurological Sciences* 1: 7–16.

Kroll, J. F., and Potter, M. C. (1984). Recognizing words, pictures, and concepts: A comparison of lexical, object, and reality decisions. *Journal of Verbal Learning and Verbal Behavior* 23: 39–66.

Kucera, H., and Francis, N. (1967). *Computational Analysis of Present Day American English*. Providence, RI: Brown University Press.

Lhermitte, F., and Beauvois, M. F. (1973). A visual-speech disconnexion syndrome: Report of a case with optic aphasia, agnosic alexia and colour agnosia. *Brain* 96: 695–714.

Marcel, A. (1980). Explaining selective effects of prior context on perception: The need to distinguish conscious and preconscious processes in word recognition. In R. Nickerson (Ed.) *Attention and Performance VIII*. Hillsdale, NJ: Erlbaum.

Martin, A., and Fedio, P. (1983). Word production and comprehension in Alzheimer's disease: The breakdown of semantic knowledge. *Brain and Language* 19: 124–141.

McKhann, G., Drachman, D., Folstein, M., Katzman, R., Price, D., and Stadlan, E. M. (1984). Clinical diagnosis of Alzheimer's disease: Report of the NINCDS-ADRDA work group under the auspices of Health and Human Services Task Force on Alzheimer's Disease. *Neurology* (Cleveland) 34: 939–944.

Meyer, D. M., and Schvaneveldt, R. W. (1971). Facilitation in recognizing pairs of words: Evidence of a dependence between retrieval operations. *Journal of Experimental Psychology* 90: 227–234.

Milberg, W., and Blumstein, S. E. (1981). Lexical decision and aphasia: Evidence for semantic processing. *Brain and Language* 14: 371–385.

Miller, G. A., and Johnson-Laird, P. N. (1976). *Language and Perception.* Cambridge, MA: Harvard University Press.

Nebes, R., Boller, F., and Holland, A. (1986). Use of semantic context by patients with Alzheimer's disease. *Psychology and Aging* 1: 261–269.

Nebes, R. D., Martin, D. C., Horn, L. C. (1984). Sparing of semantic memory in Alzheimer's disease. *Journal of Abnormal Psychology* 93: 321–330.

Nebes, R. D., Brady, C. B., and Huff, F. J. (1989). Automatic and attentional mechanisms of semantic priming in Alzheimer's Disease. *Journal of Clinical and Experimental Neuropsychology* 11: 219–230.

Neely, J. H. (1977). Semantic priming and retrieval from lexical memory: Roles of inhibitionless spreading activation and limited-capacity attention. *Journal of Experimental Psychology, General* 106: 226–254.

Posner, M. I., and Snyder, C. R. (1975). Attention and cognitive control. In R. L. Solso (Ed.) *Information Processing and Cognition: The Loyola Symposium.* Hillsdale, NJ: Erlbaum.

Postman, L., and Keppel, B. (1970). *Norms of Word Association.* New York: Academic Press.

Riddoch, M. J., and Humphreys, G. W. (1987). Visual object processing in optic aphasia: A case of semantic access agnosia. *Cognitive Neuropsychology* 4(2): 131–185.

Rosch, E. (1975). Cognitive representations of semantic categories. *Journal of Experimental Psychology, General* 104: 192–233.

Rosen, W. G. (1980). Verbal fluency in aging and dementia. *Journal of Clinical Neuropsychology* 2: 135–146.

Schwartz, M., Marin, O., and Saffran, E. (1979). Dissociation of language function in dementia: A case study. *Brain and Language* 7: 277–306.

Seidenberg, M. S., Waters, G. S., Sanders, M., and Langer, P. (1984). Pre- and postlexical loci of contextual effects on word recognition. *Memory and Cognition* 12: 315–328.

Shallice, T. (1987). Impairments of semantic processing: Multiple dissociations. In M., Coltheart, G. Sartori, R. Job (Eds.) *The Cognitive Neuropsychology of Language.* London: Erlbaum.

Shallice, T. (1988). *From Neuropsychology to Mental Structure.* New York: Cambridge University Press.

Smith, E. E., and Medin, D. L. (1981). *Categories and Concepts.* Cambridge, MA: Harvard University Press.

Snodgrass, J. G., and Vanderwart, M. (1980). A standarized set of 260 pictures: Norms for name agreement, image agreement, familiarity, and visual complexity. *Journal of Experimental Psychology: Human Learning and Memory* 6: 174–215.

Sutherland, N. S. (1973). Object recognition. In V. Carterette and M. P. Friedman (Eds.) *Handbook of Perception* 3: 157–185.

Tulving, E. (1983). *Elements of Episodic Memory.* New York: Oxford University Press.

Vanderwart, M. (1984). Priming by pictures in lexical decision. *Journal of Verbal Learning and Verbal Behavior* 23: 67–83.

Warrington, E. K. (1975). The selective impairment of semantic memory. *Quarterly Journal of Experimental Psychology* 27: 635–657.

Warrington, E. K. (1981). Concrete word dyslexia. *British Journal of Psychology* 72: 175–196.

Warrington, E. K. (1982). Neuropsychological studies of object recognition. *Phil. Trans. R. Soc. Lond. B* 298: 15–33.

Warrington, E. K., and Shallice, T. (1979). Semantic access dyslexia. *Brain* 102: 43–63.

Warrington, E. K., and Shallice, T. (1984). Category specific semantic impairments. *Brain* 107: 829–854.

Warrington, E. K., and Taylor, A. M. (1978). Two categorical stages of object recognition. *Perception* 7: 695–705.

Chapter 8

Deterioration of Language in Progressive Aphasia: A Case Study

Myrna F. Schwartz and John B. Chawluk

The central thesis of this book is that the primary degenerative diseases, because of their predilections for particular sites and substrates in the brain, often succeed in picking out or isolating functionally relevant subsystems. This chapter's case study dramatically illustrates the progressive dissolution of language functions associated with degenerative changes within circumscribed regions of the left hemisphere. The patient, Susan G., over time lost the ability to express herself in speech and writing and in parallel lost knowledge of word meaning. Her ability to recognize the words of her language, whether presented orally or in writing, remained well preserved, however, as did her ability to detect violations of grammatical category in simple phrases. Chawluk and I interpret this as evidence for the sparing of the "input systems" to language even in the face of profound phonologic and semantic impairments.

Investigations of Susan's visual processing revealed parallel findings: intact visual processing up to perceptual classification of objects, with impaired semantic/conceptual elaboration beyond that stage. This set of findings is broadly consistent with Chertkow and Bub's distinction between identification procedures and core semantics, although the detailed predictions are not confirmed. Overall the data strongly support the thesis that perceptual systems, including those that operate on linguistic material, yield outputs that are shallow, which is to say, only partially elaborated as semantic or conceptual objects.

Susan G.'s case is special in many ways: Quite aside from the slow rate of symptom progression and its relatively circumscribed nature, the combination of her indomitable will to persevere and her premorbid artistic talents made it possible to explore potential dissociations more extensively, and over a longer period of time, than is generally the case. The flip side of the coin is that one cannot know for sure how much that unique history accounted for the particular pattern of results that was obtained. It is in the nature of the single casestudy method that the ultimate interpretation rests on the accumulation of evidence from related cases. We hope that this study will serve as a stimulus for future neurolinguistic case studies involving patients with progressive aphasia and other dementia presentations that feature language loss.

M.F.S.

In 1982 Marsel Mesulam described six patients who suffered from aphasia of insidious onset and progressive course, with few if any cognitive or behavioral disorders outside the domain of language. In four of the six patients, aphasia remained the only deficit 5 to 11 years after onset. In the remaining two patients generalized dementia did gradually emerge, but only 7 years postonset, at a point when the aphasic disorder was already quite severe. In all six patients neurodiagnostic evaluation showed left peri-Sylvian involvement. In the one patient in whom a biopsy was performed, the biopsied tissue, taken from the left superior temporal gyrus, showed nonspecific changes only: mild neuronal loss and lipofuscin accumulation and none of the histopathological changes diagnostic of Alzheimer's or Pick's disease. Based on these findings, Mesulam (1982) hypothesized a distinct type of degenerative disorder with predilection for the peri-Sylvian area, particularly on the left.

The existence of progressive aphasia as a clinical syndrome is now well documented (for example, by Assal, Favre, and Regli 1985, Heath, Kennedy, and Kapur 1983, Kirshner et al. 1984, Mehler, Horoupian, and Dickson 1987, Poeck and Luzzatti 1988), and the focal distribution of the underlying pathology has been confirmed in regional metabolic studies using positron emission tomography (PET) (Chawluk et al. 1986). The notion that this entity is nosologically distinct from Alzheimer's or Pick's disease was received with some skepticism (Foster and Chase 1983, Gordon and Selnes 1984), and the question remains unsettled today. On the one hand it is known that both Pick's and Alzheimer's disease can, in rare cases, present with isolated progressive aphasia preceding for a year or more the onset of global dementia (Holland et al. 1985, Pogacar and Williams 1984, Wechsler 1977). Progressive aphasia is also a significant feature of a familial dementia described by Morris and colleagues (1984; see especially cases 6 and 7), in which the neuropathological picture combines features of Pick's disease (asymmetrical focal atrophy), Alzheimer's disease (profuse neuritic plaques) and Parkinson's disease (degeneration of substantia nigra), in addition to a nonspecific spongiform degeneration of the superficial cortical layers.

On the other hand progressive aphasia does, in some patients, present distinct pathological findings. In the one of two patients reported by Mehler, Horoupian, and Dickson (1987) who underwent autopsy, there was asymmetric cerebral atrophy with nonspecific histopathologic changes. Neurochemical studies revealed that choline acetyltransferase (CAT) activity, virtually always reduced in Alzheimer's disease, was normal, whereas somatostatin levels were reduced in frontal, temporal, parietal, and hippocampal cortex. Whereas reduced somatostatin levels are also frequently seen in Alzheimer's disease (Beal et al. 1986), the dissociation between CAT and somatostatin reported by Mehler and colleagues is more characteristic of Pick's disease. However, because the histopathological studies revealed neither Pick cells nor Pick bodies, Mehler and colleagues refer to the condition as *non-Pick lobar atrophy*[1] and suggest that the underlying pathological process is degeneration of intrinsic cortical neurons with sparing of the basal forebrain.

Evidence provided by Kirshner and colleagues (1987) speaks to the remarkable focality of the pathological changes underlying progressive aphasia. In postmortem examination of two typical patients, brain sections were found to exhibit focal spongiform changes with neuronal loss and gliosis, occuring primarily in layer 2 of the involved neocortex. In one patient these findings were restricted to the left inferior frontal gyrus and superior temporal gyrus, and in the other only the left inferior frontal gyrus was affected (the superior temporal gyrus not having been examined). Kirshner and colleagues conclude that although vacuolation and gliosis of the superficial cortical layers are not unique findings, their very focal distribution here, in conjunction with the clinically focal syndrome of isolated progressive aphasia, is at least suggestive of a specific disease entity.

In an editorial accompanying the report of Kirshner and associates, Mesulam reviews the current understanding of "primary progressive aphasia" based on the evidence from seven published cases (Mesulam 1987). Two of the seven patients turned out postmortem to have Pick's disease; the other five (including the patients of Mehler and Kirshner) showed nonspecific focal changes. None of the patients showed pathological changes diagnostic of "pure" Alzheimer's disease (but see Pogacar and Williams 1984). Mesulam concludes his editorial by emphasizing the current trend to overdiagnose Alzheimer's disease, which may lead unwary clinicians to overlook the strikingly different features of atypical cases.

The patient we report on here is one of these atypical cases. Susan G. evinced an isolated progressive aphasia for approximately four years, after which she began to show a variety of frontal signs suggestive of Pick's disease. Before the onset of symptoms, Susan G. was a gifted artist and musician. The combination of her premorbid talents, the gradual course of the language deterioration, and certain unique features of her personality provided an unusual opportunity to explore the nature of the language dissolution in progressive aphasia and its selectivity or nonselectivity with respect to other cognitive domains.

From February 1984 to August 1986, Susan was studied on a regular basis as part of a larger dementia study conducted by Schwartz. During this period she was tested extensively, first on a monthly basis in the laboratory and later, weekly, in her home. This 30-month period, which began approximately four years after the onset of symptoms, marked the period in which her language functions underwent global dissolution. The nature of this dissolution is one of the major concerns of this chapter; the second is the extent to which the degenerative disorder compromised visual, and especially visual semantic, processing of pictures and objects.

Clinical History

Susan G., a right-handed white woman, was 51 years old in 1979 when family and friends began noticing disturbing changes: problems recalling names of people and things, a tendency to ramble in conversation and to reiterate events from the past, and difficulty understanding and remembering the content of conversations and written texts. Over the next few years, as the condition worsened and a serious language disorder was revealed, Susan underwent a number of medical and neurological examinations, among them an evaluation in the cerebrovascular research center of the University of Pennsylvania in May 1983, as part of its PET-dementia project. These evaluations ruled out cerebrovascular disease, tumor, or global dementia as the basis for the progressive language disorder. In the University of Pennsylvania study, CT (computed tomography) and PET scans documented left temporal lobe pathology (See Chawluk et al. 1986, where Susan appears as patient 1). Further discussion of these findings are presented in the final section of this chapter, along with results from a follow-up PET study conducted in January 1986.

A wife and mother of five, with a B.A. in music theory, Susan continued to function effectively as an animal portraitist and a piano instructor for approximately three years after the onset of symptoms. She also continued to manage the affairs of her household, including routine finances, and to participate in numerous church and community events. She drove a car and experienced no difficulty finding her way to new destinations. Sometime in year 4, however, personality alterations began to be noticed. She became garrulous and physically demonstrative, even toward strangers. Her judgment grew less reliable.

In subsequent years, as her language and social behavior deteriorated, Susan was forced to curtail her outside activities. Inside the home, however, she maintained an active, organized schedule. She arose at the same time each day, saw to the care of her horses and dogs, engaged in daily prayer, praticed piano, prepared meals, and took long walks—all in adherence to a strict, self-imposed schedule.

For most of her adult life, Susan had kept a notebook diary, in which she planned upcoming events and recorded significant experiences of the day. She continued to maintain it long after the language deterioration had compromised word retrieval and spelling so severely as to make spontaneous writing impossible. Her husband provided some help, but mostly she proceeded on her own, crafting each entry with reference to prior entries, address books, TV magazines, and the like. The determination and self-discipline she displayed in doing this was to persist long into the course of the disease. In November 1985, when her spoken and written language had become severely limited, she was observed painstakingly copying addresses from a long-ago assembled mailing list onto Christmas card envelopes, several cards each day for more than a week. She had planned for this in her notebook, and she made it part of her daily schedule.

For as long as Susan was able to communicate, she was able to recount the events and episodes of the distant and recent past accurately and precisely. What undoubtedly helped her maintain this orientation to person, place, and time was her habit of regularly rehearsing the diary entries of the past, along with the note cards, letters, and photo albums that she kept on hand to review with family and guests.

Susan taught piano up through 1984 and even after that continued to perform for her church congregation. In the course of our study, we saw her repertoire become narrowed and fixed to just those pieces that she practiced daily, in morning and afternoon rehearsals. This repertoire comprised some popular and Christian tunes and three classical pieces: a Bach prelude, Mozart's Sonata in C Major, and Debussy's "Claire de Lune." For the latter pieces she referred to sheet music, and we were able to confirm that she was indeed reading the music by having her play new, albeit simple, pieces. On these occasions she succeeded in playing the right notes, but her rhythm and timing were aberrant.[2]

Although Susan was aware from the outset of the difficulties she was having with her language, her consistently cheerful attitude belied the gravity of the situation. Episodes of incontinence, sporadic at first, then increasingly frequent, were met with indifference. So too was the insatiable craving for sweet food and drink that she began to experience in early 1986 and the marked weight gain that attended it. In the latter months of 1986, Susan became apathetic toward her family and her surroundings and less inclined to act without prodding. Mute and withdrawn, she descended into a condition of global dementia.

The Dissolution of Expressive and Receptive Language

Spontaneous Speech and Writing

In February 1984, the start of our study, Susan G. was a lively, affable 56-year-old woman, well dressed and well groomed. She was fully oriented to time, place, and person, and indicated an awareness of her problem. She provided a full autobiographical narrative and answered questions posed to her about her work and recreational schedule.

In contrast to this fluent and voluble recounting of her personal history, Susan was hesitant and evasive in response to probes for factual memories and familiar tales. Particularly surprising in this life-long, observant Christian was her inability to recall once familiar prayers and Bible stories, even with substantial verbal and pictorial prompting.

On the Boston Diagnostic Aphasia Examination (Goodglass and Kaplan 1972) Susan obtained a profile consistent with anomic aphasia of moderate severity. Scores fell at or below the aphasic means on several subtests: body part naming, recitation, written confrontation naming, spelling to dictation.

Confrontation naming was assessed by means of the Boston Naming Test (Kaplan, Goodglass, and Weintraub 1983) in an abridged (42-item) version.[3] Without prompts Susan succeeded in naming only six items. Semantic prompting had no effect, but providing her with the target's initial sound resulted in an additional nine items being named correctly.

Over the ensuing months Susan's expressive language became less fluent. In the latter months of 1984 her attempts to describe pictures were marked by word searches and by agrammatism of the constructional type (that is, minimal phrase structure but preserved syntactic morphology; Saffran, Schwartz, and Marin 1980, Tissot, Mounin, and Lhermitte 1973). Here are some examples:

Cookie theft picture (Goodglass and Kaplan 1972)
That's the guy, the kid, is in the, uh, thing and it's, it's a . . . it's . . . getting off, getting off [demonstrates tilting motion with body]. And then, uh, um, the kid is, uh, getting cookie jar [points to lettering on jar]. And then he's getting this [points] to the girl and then the mom is, uh, you know, doing the, thing. And then,

that's, ah, your water, water, lying down there. [*Interviewer: Any-thing else?*] Well, that's in the kitchen. And then that's the, you know, outside, you know, that's, uh, that's uh, a walk, you know, and that's . . . trees . . . and that's, uh, the grass [*points to bush*]. Well, uh, the, uh, you know, uh [*long pause*]. That's the grass, here [*points to grass*].

Picture of a girl watching a mother bird feed baby birds in a nest
The girl, uh, is getting the, uh, birds, and the birds, Mom bird, is getting the three birds. . . . Well, that's on the uh, tree, and she's getting on the, uh, window.

Picture of a hand placing a key into a door lock
Lock, the door. Lock the door. He, or she's locking the door. Key, key, lock the door.

A number of investigators have attributed constructional agram-matism to the impoverishment of verb representations in the mental lexicon (for example, McCarthy and Warrington 1987, Saffran, Schwartz, and Marin 1980, Byng 1987). In Susan's case the verb loss was prominent, but not selective, that is, the lexical impoverishment was not restricted to any one grammatical category.

The deterioration of Susan's expressive language was equally evi-dent at home, where over time she initiated less conversation and became less responsive to conversational probes, preferring to answer with nods or gestures and often not answering at all. When she did speak, it was most often to recount the events of the past day or week as these were recorded in her diary notebook. Table 8.1 pre-sents transcripts of some diary-driven conversations. The deteriora-tion is evident; by late 1985 she had no spontaneous speech apart from the phrases "Pat's day care; Tuesday, Thursday; here, here, here," which she mumbled repetitively in a whispered voice.

A review of the diary entries in this same time period reveals paral-lel dissolution in the domain of written language (see table 8.2). One interesting feature of her later entries is the frequent substitution of words of high subjective frequency: family names, church-related vocabulary (for example, *Tina fish* for *tuna fish*, *pray to piano* for *play the piano*). This same substitution pattern was also prominent in her oral reading performance.

The picture of progressive language deterioration that has been sketched so far omits one distinctive and quite remarkable feature: Recall that when first evaluated for aphasia in February 1984, Susan generated a fluent and highly detailed autobiographical narrative, be-lying the word-finding difficulties that surfaced on formal testing.

Table 8.1
Excerpts from Conversations

June 1985

Susan: Maryland, Maryland. And, um, Dan and I, then, um, I got here at eight-forty-five, here, eight-forty-five. And, um, there, uh, uh, yeah, here. Ann and Paul, and inn. And Dan and I, boat, eleven-forty-five, our boat, and, um, Bible and Upper Word and Saint Steven's Church, prayer list, and then I did, uh, prayer list for forty-five minutes and then, uh, um, restaurant, breakfast, restaurant, and then, uh, Acme Market.

September 1985

Susan: I did uh apples, horses . . .
M.S.: You picked the apples?
Susan: Yes.
M.S.: Or did you feed the horses?
Susan: Uh . . . apples.
M.S.: Did you pick the apples?
Susan: Horses, uh . . . hair.

June 1986

M.S.: Is that a new dress you're wearing?
Susan: Here, good, here, good, good.
M.S.: How was the wedding?
Susan: Good, here, good, good, here [*goes to calendar to point to entry for wedding*]. Here, here.
M.S.: I see, St. Joseph's Church.
Susan: Here, church, church, here, Pat's day care, Tuesday and Thursday, here.
Susan: [*Continues to mumble repetitively while materials are being arranged*] Pat's day care, Tuesday, Thursday, Pat's day care . . .

According to her family, Susan had been retelling this narrative for several years. Indeed she had been overheard many times rehearsing parts of it to herself.

In time this narrative became stylized and stereotyped around several episodes, and these came to occupy an increasingly prominent role in her conversations. The phenomenon was reminiscent of the *gramophone syndrome* described by Mayer-Gross (1937-38) in a patient with Pick's disease. In Susan's case the most notable feature of these narratives was that they remained relatively immune to the linguistic breakdown that characterized her spoken and written discourse. Consider, for example, this narrative recorded in September 1985:

And, um, I graduated magna cum laude in music in '73 in Westchester State College, and I did art all my life and I did art in '74 in Westchester State College. Dan wanted me to get a Brittany spaniel for his Christmas present. And I got him for a Christmas

Table 8.2
Excerpted Entries from the Notebook Diary

___

August 1984

—Pick up Loretta 8:30—go to Bill's Pharmacy
—go to SE Natl Bank—deposit 15–
—Ask Ron when we pick the potatoes up in our vegetable garden
—go to Hobbys and Craft and get 3 Portraits
  20″ × 16″ Artists Canvas
—go to Acme mkt
—Mary Jo was in the postoffice
—go to Charlotte 2:30 and swim. I got back at 5:30
—Did 3 Trash
—Did water plants
—Play the piano 8:30–10:30

January 1985

—feed horses
—clean stalls
—call Ted got my portrait to Mary? And she just love it!
—I did sweep the garade
—Prayer List 45 min.
—I did wood at 10:
—I did vacuum to dining room and living room
—I did vacuum 9:30 to 11:30 family room, kitchen, Den, Bathroom.
—Do portrait for Charlotte 4: to 5:30
7:– Tic Tac Doug
7:30 Wheel of Fortune

August 1985

—feed horses
—clean stalls
—I did trash in our garden
—washing in the clothes
—did trash in the road
—did trash in garage
—did the birds feeder
—8: Vinnie—Happy Birthday to you

December 1985

—feed horses
—clean stalls
8: Terry and Bear and Bingo and food
—pray the piano
9:30–10:30 Trash
Tina fish—apple
Prayer list for 45 min.
1-2-3-4 Christmas cards
1:30 Myrna Schwartz
4: Wheel of Fortune
5: Little house of Praisin

___

present. "Professor, for the final," I said, "Dan and I and four daughters and one son go to church Christmas Eve and when we get back to our farm we dig out our Christmas tree. Can I do the Brittany spaniel for his Christmas present?" And he said, "Sure." And then, when I did it for the final, he said, "Susan, you have to do animal portraits and sell notepaper." And I've been selling notepaper for six card shops for 11 years, and I've been doing animal portraits for 11 years. Good, good.

The diary-driven exchange recorded on that same day went as follows:

> M. S.: Have you been going to that day care center you've been telling me about? Pat's?
>
> Susan: Pat's day care
>
> M. S.: Have you been doing that?
>
> Susan: Day care, um, Pat's day care, um, um, Pat's day care, Pat's day care . . . um . . . Thursday and Friday and then . . .
>
> M. S.: Every week?
>
> Susan: Um, Tuesday, and then the piano, piano

The corresponding diary entry reads as follows:

> —Pat's Day Care
> 7:30 vacuum 1-2-3-4-5-6
> 10:30 play to piano

The episodic narrative recorded above was spoken rapidly, at a rate of 194 words per minute, and with an exaggerated, almost sing-song intonation. The impression was of a soliloquy being delivered, a speech learned by rote. It is therefore tempting to deny these narratives the status of propositional language in favor of an alternative, "automatic" mode that bypasses the normal speech planning mechanism (Hughlings Jackson 1874, 1878). Close inspection of the structure of these narratives suggests that this is not the case and that they do indeed have the status of propositional language: First of all, the narratives were not completely stereotyped; although the lexical content and basic ideas were preserved in successive retellings, there was substantial variety in the particular details included and as well in the grammatical forms in which they were expressed (see table 8.3). Second, when interrupted by questions in the course of a narrative, Susan was generally responsive to the question and, in continuing, was not bound to start again from the beginning. Third, these narratives did eventually deteriorate along with the rest of her

Table 8.3
Longitudinal Record of an Episodic Narrative: Variation in Form and Content

---

February 1984

Well, I play two and a half hours, every Wednesday afternoon. And uh, so then . . .
[*Interviewer: Do you bring students with you?*]
No, no. I play the piano. And we sing old-fashioned popular pieces and Christian
songs . . . and uh, I play, for a half an hour, when they're eating, lunch. And I play
classic pieces and old-fashioned popular pieces and . . . Christian songs.
Yeah . . . yeah.
[*Interviewer: So they must enjoy that a lot.*]
Well they, yes they do. Well, did I tell ya? I made an arrangement when I was walking
home from high school when I was sixteen years old. I was . . . making the,
uh . . . chords.
[*Interviewer: Chords?*]
Chords.
[*Interviewer: I'm not sure I understand.*]
And um . . . and then when I got back I walked home, two miles, and I got back to our,
my house, and I played the piano . . . and [*momentary interruption*]. So then I made
forty-eight arrangements of popular pieces, and I didn't write it down! And I do it now,
you know?

June 1985

[*pausing after piano piece*]
I walked, when I was a teenager, I was walking and I did the melody and the chords of
popular pieces, and I made forty-eight arrangements of popular pieces when I was a
teenager.

September 1985

I was a teenager and I was picturin' the melody and the chords of popular pieces. And I
made *forterange* arrangements popular pieces and, teenager. And, Step-by-Step I
Follow Jesus, What a Friend We Have in Jesus, How Great Thou Art, Do-a-Deer, His
Name is Wonderful, Dream, Night and Day, Sound of Music, Sentimental Journey,
and Begin the Beguine.

September 1985

Ah, I *tseh*, ah, twenty-eight piano pupils five afternoons each week and two nights each
week and I teach nursery school Wednesday and *Thurday* morning and, Wednesday
and Friday morning at . . . , um, here, here [*showing piano books*].
[*Interviewer: Where do you play these songs, Susan?*]
Uh, um, *Estwestcher*, uh, Sunday afternoon Westchester s-s-, yeah, here, and um.
[*Interviewer: Is that that senior citizens place?*]
Yeah, se-senior *cihzens* place, and um, pictured the melody and chords of popular
pieces . . . [*begins to play*].

language. Over time they were subject to distortion in the form of phonemic paraphasias, internarrative intrusions, and uncompleted starts (some of this can be seen in table 8.3). By early 1986, when Susan's productive vocabulary was limited to a few stereotyped words and phrases, the narratives were no longer in evidence.

Rather than viewing these episodic narratives as frozen forms that bypass the damaged speech production system, we associate them with the maximal functioning of that system. We assume that the effect of the regular rehearsal was to create the condition where form and content were overdetermined and the role of semantically driven access was minimized. Under these conditions she displayed a residual capacity for retrieving and combining lexical and grammatical forms, at least those forms that had the benefit of regular rehearsal.

Viewed in this way, the preservation of the episodic narratives suggests two accounts of the output disorder that so restricted her communication outside of this rehearsed context: (1) a failure of semantically driven lexical access and (2) a failure of phonological retrieval, subject to long-term facilitation through rehearsal.

It is our contention that both of these accounts are correct, that is, that the output disorder in this case reflected the progressive involvement of both the semantic and the phonological components of the language system. The evidence for semantic involvement comes from studies of her comprehension of words, phrases, and pictures. The evidence for the phonological disorder comes primarily from studies of her oral reading. We turn now to this evidence.

Oral Word Reading
In patients who evince word retrieval problems in the context of degenerative dementias, oral reading at the level of single words is often well retained (Nelson and O'Connell 1978, Schwartz, Saffran, and Marin 1980). The significance of this is that it points to preserved access to output phonology and locates the word-retrieval deficit more centrally, that is, in semantics or semantic access to the lexicon. Quite early in our study of Susan G., it became clear that she did not show that expected preservation of written word pronunciation.

In March 1985 we administered Coltheart and colleagues' (1979) lists of words with regular and irregular spellings. Susan succeeded in reading just 44 of the 78 items—24 regular words (62 percent) and 20 irregular words (51 percent). This small difference in favor of regular words is not statistically reliable ($\chi^2 = .83$, $p = .36$). On the other hand post hoc analysis revealed a much more robust effect of word frequency, with twice as many high-frequency words pronounced correctly as mid- or low-frequency words. Subsequently a new list of

Table 8.4
Written Word Pronunciation Test: Number of Words Pronounced Correctly (max.
20 per cell)

	Frequency		
	High	Intermediate	Low
April 1985			
Regular spellings	17	12	5	[34]
Irregular spellings	15	9	2	[26]
	[32]	[21]	[7]
October 1985			
Regular spellings	10	3	2	[15]
Irregular spellings	11	5	2	[18]
	[21]	[8]	[4]

120 words was assembled to allow a more thorough investigation of the effects on her reading of word frequency and sound-spelling regularity.

Forty words were selected from each of three frequency levels of Francis and Kucera's (1982) norms. The high-frequency words were drawn from the range 100 to 500 per million, the medium-frequency words from range 20 to 50, and the low-frequency words from range 1 to 3. At each frequency level half the words had pronunciations derivable from spelling rules (regular orthography); the other half did not (irregular orthography). Word length in syllables was balanced across the frequency levels; within each level there were 10 monosyllabic words (4 to 5 letters) and 30 bisyllabic words (4 to 8 letters).

The entire 120-word reading test was administered to Susan on two occasions: once in April 1985 and again in October 1985. Results are shown in table 8.4.

Results   Sixty of the 120 words were pronounced correctly on the first administration, and 33 of 120 on the second. Application of the log-linear model showed that the likelihood of correct pronunciation was significantly affected by administration (April versus October; likelihood ratio (L.R.) $\chi^2 = 9.8$, degrees of freedom (df) 1, $p < .01$) and by frequency (L. R. $\chi^2 = 37.1$, df 2, $p < .001$). The effect of orthography was not significant, neither were any of the interaction terms significant ($p > .20$ in all cases).

The character of Susan's errors changed markedly from the first to the second administration. In April her errors bore an obvious phonologic relation to the target: More than half of the errors (36 of 60) were nonword approximations (for examples, *tyrant/tranit*, *vessel/vezzel*);

Table 8.5
A Sample of Targets that Elicited Pronunciation Errors on Both the April 1985 and
October 1985 Tests: A Comparison of the Errors

Freq.	Orthog.	Target	April Response	October Response
high	reg	treat	steet	sprit
high	reg	county	country	country
high	irreg	union	yunun	untin
high	irreg	design	desnine	don
med	reg	textile	texter	tin
med	reg	jungle	jungler	june
med	reg	modest	moedest	mount stay
med	irreg	subtle	supley	sib come
med	irreg	ocean	aukine	august
med	irreg	ballet	balt	ball game
med	irreg	mortgage	mort gage	man kray
med	irreg	sweat	sweet	scare
med	irreg	circuit	circus	koon ken
med	irreg	cafe	calf	cattle
low	reg	veneer	verrin	virgin
low	reg	zebra	dee brite	zee bird
low	reg	rampage	rambakes	ron
low	reg	splice	prouse	sherry
low	reg	tether	tetter	tedder
low	reg	tyrant	tranit	loretta
low	reg	ozone	ozin	august
low	reg	sequin	sookin	sue here
low	reg	tycoon	lichen	ten con
low	reg	walrus	walter	water
low	reg	portend	porten	portrait
low	irreg	pristine	pristen	pristen
low	irreg	lapel	lapping	lan pop
low	irreg	scourge	sorgks	shore
low	irreg	anise	adnye	anter
low	irreg	chassis	chaquis	christian
low	irreg	womb	worm	boon
low	irreg	respite	rest	rey plant
low	irreg	lotus	locust	lit all
low	irreg	zealot	seelot	zee lote
low	irreg	gist	guist	give
low	irreg	penal	pendle	penn state
low	irreg	scion	stun	soon
low	irreg	suave	saved	shave

the remaining errors were phonologically related real words (*sweat/ sweet, suave/saved*). These errors did not have the character of "regularizations"; only 16 of the 60 errors conformed to the very liberal criteria we used to identify those that might conceivably have arisen from overgeneralization or misapplication of spelling rules (Marcel 1980, Shallice, Warrington, and McCarthy 1983). The errors had more in common with complex phonemic paraphasias in that they featured substitutions, additions, omissions, and/or transposition of constituent phonemes.

The errors in the October corpus were much less tightly constrained by the phonology of the target (see table 8.5). On the average only 45 percent of target phonemes were present in the response, as compared with 68 percent in April.

A most striking aspect of the October data was the tendency to omit the stress pattern on bisyllabic responses. With each syllable receiving equal stress, the effect was to transform bisyllabic targets into two-syllable compounds. Furthermore the syllables of these compounds tended strongly to be real words; for 26 of the 30 two-syllable compounds (87 percent), at least one of the two syllables was a real word; for 18 of the 30 (60 percent), both syllables comprised words.

This strong real-word bias in the October data was not restricted to two-syllable compounds. Of the remaining 55 errors (that is, monosyllabic responses and bisyllabic responses with recognizable stress pattern), 44 (80 percent) were words. The comparable figure for the April error corpus is 34 percent (18 of 53).

A survey of the word substitutions from the October corpus shows a marked influence of frequency, both structural and subjective. A total of 74 of her errors comprised or contained (within a two-syllable compound) an actual word of English. Thirty-one of these (42 percent) were terms and proper names well known to us from her diary entries and conversation. In the remaining cases very high-frequency items were overrepresented, relative to targets (see figure 8.1).

Thus by October 1985 the pronunciations Susan derived from written input were essentially limited to a small inventory of well-rehearsed words and words of high subjective familiarity. Although this reading vocabulary was certainly larger than her speaking vocabulary at that same time, it appears to have been subject to the same limitation. What was the nature of this limitation? We know that the correct pronunciation of written words is not necessarily precluded by even severe lexical-semantic disorders (Bub, Cancelliere, and Kertesz 1985, Schwartz, Saffran, and Marin 1980, Shallice, Warrington, and McCarthy 1983). Thus if that were the only factor limiting her speech production, we would probably not have seen parallel find-

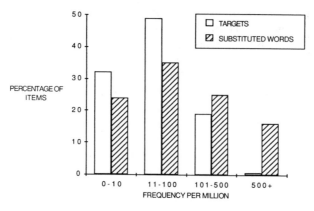

Figure 8.1
The influence of frequency on Susan's word substitution errors in the October 1985 test of written word pronunciation. *Targets* are those test words that yielded real-word substitutions other than proper names and words from her stereotyped corpus (see text) (n = 43). *Substituted words* are those words not excluded by the aforementioned criteria, which comprised the error or contributed to it as part of a two-syllable compound (n = 51). Frequency values are taken from Francis and Kucera 1982.

ings with written word pronunciation. This parallel points to the involvement of the *final common path* for reading and speaking, that is, the phonological output system.

Evidence from Repetition   Studies involving repetition confirmed the presence of a phonological output disorder. Susan's ability to repeat sentences deteriorated markedly over the first year of this study. By April 1985 she was producing errors of omission, substitution, and phonemic paraphasia in repeating even short (4- to 5-word) simple sentences. Repetition of unrelated strings yielded marked lexical effects. With digits she achieved a normal span (6 forward), but with monosyllabic words she broke down with a string length of two. Her error rate was twice as high on low-frequency strings as on high-frequency strings and featured phonemic paraphasias. Thus the evidence points to a serious disorder in lexically mediated phonological retrieval.

A question that arises at this point is why there was not evidence in Susan's reading performance of phonological retrieval that was not lexically mediated, that is, evidence for rule-based, grapheme-to-phoneme conversion. Recall that she was not more successful in reading regular words than irregular ones and showed no tendency to regularize irregular pronunciations. Informal investigations of her reading of nonwords indicated that she showed the same tendency there to substitute real words and words of high subjective familiarity. There are several possible explanations for this: One is that Susan's phonological problem was peripheral to the phonological lexicon, involving the mechanisms for assembling or holding phonological segments. The evidence that contradicts this comes from single word repetition, which should have been similarly affected on this account but was not. Throughout 1985 Susan's repetition of single words was errorless, even for long words (3 or more syllables) and pseudowords. A second possibility is that the nonlexical route to reading was specifically and perhaps independently compromised by the pathology. A third, more parsimonious alternative is that nonlexical reading makes use of the same inventory of phonological forms as lexical reading (Shallice and McCarthy 1985, Shallice, Warrington, and McCarthy 1983) and that her inability to retrieve the elements of that inventory precluded normal reading via either the lexical or nonlexical routes. This is the alternative that we believe best accounts for the overall pattern of the evidence from both reading and speaking, including the facilitating effects of her self-taught rehearsal strategy and the ultimate descent into mutism.

Comprehension of Word Meaning
As alluded to previously, lexical-semantic functions were also implicated in Susan's language dissolution. Receptive vocabulary, as measured by the Peabody Picture Vocabulary Test (PPVT), was dramatically compromised. Between February 1984 and April 1985, Susan's raw score declined from 82 (mental age 11.0) to 49 (mental age 5.0).

Lexical Comprehension Test   That semantic factors played a role in this receptive vocabulary loss was shown by her performance on our laboratory's lexical comprehension test, which, like the PPVT, requires the selection of a named object from a set of four photographs. This test assesses 32 object names, 4 from each of 8 categories (for example, from the furniture category: *desk, bureau, sofa, cabinet*; from the musical instruments category: *clarinet, trombone, banjo, tuba*). Each name is assessed twice: once with picture distractors drawn from the same category as the target and a second time with distractors drawn from other categories. The latter, across-category condition requires less in the way of semantic processing. As long as subjects understand the type of object the word refers to, they will choose correctly. Over the years we have administered this test to many patients with language disorders. The within-category condition is sensitive to even mild lexical-semantic impairments; errors on the across-category condition are indicative of a very severe impairment.

We gave Susan the 32-item lexical comprehension test on four occasions: in February 1984, March 1985, October 1985, and March 1986. Her within-category score declined with each successive administration: 28, 23, 17, 6. On the across-category condition she obtained a perfect score on the first two administrations; however, in October 1985 her score dropped to 29 and in March 1986 to 20. The results suggest a serious deterioration in ability to attach meaning to object names.

Vocabulary Test For a more comprehensive assessment of word comprehension, our laboratory uses a vocabulary test that alternates concrete with abstract terms matched for frequency on the Thorndike-Lorge count. The test is administered in two sessions. Each session begins with high-frequency items, which the subject is asked to define or otherwise indicate the meaning of, and progresses through words of decreasing familiarity. This vocabulary test was administered to Susan in February 1985. Despite her output limitation, she did succeed in conveying some understanding of the early list items. As frequency declined, however, she became increasingly vague, inappropriate, and unresponsive in her replies. In contrast to frequency the concreteness of the target did not have a detectable influence on her performance. Examples of her responses are provided in table 8.6. In several instances Susan was asked to elaborate on her responses through drawings. A sample of these is reproduced in figure 8.2.

Superordinate Matching Test The vocabulary test results, in combination with the longitudinal findings from lexical comprehension, attest to a growing imprecision in the meaning representations recoverable from the spoken name, with words of lesser familiarity more affected than familiar terms. Subsequently we confirmed and extended these findings in a procedure in which Susan would match a spoken or written name to its written category label. The stimuli for this study were taken from Battig and Montague's (1969) category norms: 20 exemplars from each of 6 categories. Within each category half the exemplars were strong, and the other half weak. Strong exemplars from the vehicles category included *car, airplane,* and *bicycle;* weak exemplars included *van, sled,* and *tank.* In general weak exemplars tended also to be less familiar, both as objects and as names, but the correspondence between strength and frequency was not perfect.

Table 8.6
Sample of Responses to the Vocabulary Test (February–March 1985)

Target (category, frequency[a])	Response
choice (abstract, A)	One or two
desk (concrete, A)	[*Outlines a large rectangular shape with her hands*] Dan is gonna do desk, and here [*mimes writing*].
prize (concrete, A)	Devon horse show, prize.
pride (abstract, A)	That's great! [*makes facial gesture suggesting smugness or self-satisfaction*].
dread (abstract, 45)	That's lousy! [*hand gesture as though wiping something away, facial gesture suggesting disgust or horror*].
drum (concrete, 40)	I, uh, here [*pointing to piano; gestures with hands around face, vaguely suggestive of having, though not fingering, an instrument (e.g., clarinet or flute) at the mouth*].
mood (abstract, 27)	The people moods off and on; moods off and on [*exemplifies with blabbering noises*].
stain (concrete, 28)	Lousy things; lousy stain.
phase (abstract, 15)	Thinking here, phase.
jaw (concrete, 11)	I sing, the jaw.
fraud (abstract, 10)	Fraud [*gestures happy face; points to smile*].
moose (concrete, 8)	That's animal [*indicates something close to ground, puppy-sized (see figure 8.2)*].
myth (abstract, 8)	No response.
crag (concrete, 8)	No response.
pleat (concrete, 2)	Pleat? [*shakes head uncomprehendingly; then rocks hands back and forth*].

[a] Thorndike-Lorge (1944) frequency count

For presentation the materials were divided into two sets: Set 1 tested recognition of the categories *animal, furniture, vehicle* and set 2 the categories *body part, clothing, musical instrument*. In session 1 we tested set 1 exemplars in spoken form and set 2 exemplars in writing. In session 2 these conditions were reversed. Within each session trials were blocked by presentation modality, but randomized as to category and strength of exemplar.

On each trial Susan indicated her response by pointing to one of three cards labeled with the superordinate name. To ensure that she understood at least the extensions of these written labels, we incorporated a training procedure in which each superordinate label was paired with a picture (taken from children's vocabulary books) depicting multiple exemplars. For example, the card labeled ''musical in-

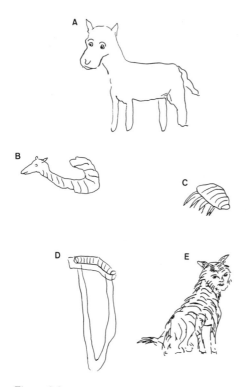

Figure 8.2
Susan's attempts to draw items named as part of the vocabulary test conducted in February 1985. (A) moose, (B) frog, (C) guitar, (D) telephone, (E) cat.

struments" was paired with a picture of an orchestra, the card labeled "body parts" with a picture of an unclad body, and so on. After a single pairing Susan succeeded in matching superordinate label to picture with perfect reliability. At this point the pictures were removed and the experiment initiated.

The results of this superordinate matching test, conducted in October 1985, are summarized in table 8.7. Susan produced correct matches on 86 of 120 spoken word trials (72 percent) and 80 of 120 written word trials (67 percent). Strength of the exemplar exerted a significant effect with both spoken ($\chi^2 = 5.9$) and written ($\chi^2 = 5.4$) presentations (in both modalities, df 1, $p < .05$). There was a marked category effect, which patterned similarly in spoken and written versions: Performance was best on animals and musical instruments, worst on furniture and clothing. Overall there was high agreement between words answered correctly in the two modalities ($\kappa = 0.26$, $z = 2.84$, $p < .01$).

Table 8.7
The Superordinate Matching Test (October 1985)

	No. Correct (max. 10)			
	Spoken		Written	
	Strong	Weak	Strong	Weak
4-legged animals	9	8	10	7
Furniture	6	2	5	5
Vehicles	10	9	8	7
Body parts	7	5	10	5
Clothing	8	4	3	1
Musical instruments	9	9	10	9

	Total Correct (max. 60/cell)	
	Spoken	Written
Strong exemplars	49	46
Weak exemplars	37	34

These results confirm that by late 1985 Susan's understanding of object terms was so imperfect as to preclude reliable matching to superordinate labels. Furthermore the fact that her performance was influenced by semantic variables (strength of exemplar and category membership) and not at all by modality (that is, the same words tended to be missed in spoken and written presentations) together located the problem in the meaning representation shared by these two input modalities, rather than in the mechanisms of access (see Shallice 1987 and Warrington 1975 for further discussion of storage versus access accounts of semantic disorders).

Syntactic Competence
One of the strongest and most significant generalizations to come out of the literature on the language disturbance in dementia is the preservation of syntactic competence in the face of impaired semantic processing (for example, Irigaray 1973, Kempler, Curtiss, and Jackson 1987, Schwartz, Marin, and Saffran 1979, Whitaker 1976). That generalization was only weakly upheld in Susan's case. For example, in mid-1985, when the severity of the semantic processing disorder had become evident, Susan was given a battery of grammaticality judgment tasks previously constructed for the evaluation of syntactic knowledge and syntactic processing in aphasic patients (Linebarger, Schwartz, and Saffran 1983, Pate and Saffran 1988). She reliably detected only those violations that grossly deformed the basic phrase structure of a sentence, for example, 1b and 2b. Violations of agree-

ment, including the agreement between the fronted auxiliary of yes-no questions and the form of the inflection on the main verb (3b), were not reliably detected.

1a. They baked a chocolate cake.
  b. *They baked a cake chocolate.
2a. They have been reading magazines.
  b. *They reading have been magazines.
3a. Is the boy sleeping today?
  b. *Has the boy sleeping today?

Moreover numerous sentence repetition tasks were run that provided her the opportunity to correct syntactically ill-formed sentences (compare Whitaker 1976), but she evinced no such tendency. Nor was it the case that syntactically ill-formed sentences generally resulted in more repetition errors or different types of errors. The only exception occurred with complete scrambling of sentences; in repeating such "sentence anagrams," Susan did make frequent omission of major lexical items, a type of error that did not occur on other conditions of repetition. In summary the body of evidence that relates to syntactic processing in this case provides evidence only for preserved sensitivity to the basic phrasal organization of the sentence as manifested in word order. In the next section we present additional evidence bearing on the syntactic-semantic dissociation.

Spared Input Systems to Language

In the previous sections we have documented the devastating disorder that compromised all aspects of language function: expressive and receptive; spoken and written; semantic, syntactic, and phonologic. Apparently the disease process had compromised the neural circuitry for language in a manner that did not allow for differential sparing within that system. The issues we address in this section and the next concern the functional boundaries of the language system as it was affected in this case.

The jumping-off point for these inquiries was the investigation of Susan's oral reading described previously and the attempt to further pinpoint the locus of the reading problem. Recall that the data from written word pronunciation showed a decrease in the likelihood of correct pronunciations over time, coupled with an increase in the phonological distance between target and response. By October 1985 Susan's correct pronunciations were almost entirely limited to high-frequency words, and her errors revealed a strong tendency to substitute for the actual targets other words with high subjective frequency.

In discussing these results, we suggested that the parallels between the reading and speaking pattern implicated the final common path for the two expressive functions—the phonological .output system. But there is another possibility, namely, that the reading system was compromised at the level of visual-orthographic analysis. Impairment at that level would certainly stand in the way of normal written word pronunciation, by any of the routes that reading theorists have proposed (for example, chapters in Patterson, Marshall, and Coltheart 1985). As for the high rate of word substitutions in the October corpus and the bias toward highly familiar vocabulary, these could have arisen as a consequence of a guessing strategy applied to highly degraded orthographic forms (Saffran 1985).

As part of the investigation of Susan's reading disorder, then, we investigated her ability to perform written lexical decision under conditions where the nonwords bear a close orthographic resemblance to the real word targets. If Susan's reading deficit were due to progressive breakdown at the level of visual orthographic analysis, her performance on this written lexical decision test should have been problematic at the start and subject to increasing errors over time.

In this lexical decision test, which required a yes/no judgment, the 120 words of the oral reading test were interspersed with 120 pronounceable pseudowords differing in one- or two-letter segments from the corresponding words (for example, *prestige/prostige, ballet/ fallet, anxious/tonxious*). The test was administered on two occasions: the first in May 1985 (four weeks after the first oral reading test), and the second in February 1986 (four months after the second reading test).

The results, summarized in table 8.8, revealed a high degree of sensitivity to the word/pseudoword distinction, especially for highly and moderately frequent word forms $d' = 2.97$ and 2.32, respectively) and no evidence of deterioration in the interval between administrations (that is, the largest d' difference, occurring to high-frequency words, is not statistically significant; $z = .58$, $p = .28$, one-tailed). These results rule out any serious involvement of visual decoding processes up through recognition of visual word forms.

Moreover results from auditory lexical decision showed that the same was true for auditory word processing. The auditory lexical decision test utilized the same 120 words, but with some modification of the distractor set aimed at ensuring that target and distractor deviated by not more than two phonemes. It was conducted within the same time frame as the written version, but not within the same session.

The results, summarized in table 8.9, provide evidence for preservation of auditory phonological processing and the integrity of

Table 8.8
Written Lexical Decision Test

	Frequency		
	High	Medium	Low
May 1985			
Prop. hits[a]	.98	.95	.58
Prop. false alarms[b]	.18	.25	.28
D-prime (*d'*)	2.97*	2.32*	0.79*
(SE²)	(.26)	(.16)	(.08)
February 1986			
Prop. hits[a]	.98	.93	.53
Prop. false alarms[b]	.30	.18	.28
D-prime (*d'*)	2.57*	2.39*	0.66*
(SE²)	(.25)	(.14)	(.08)

[a] Number of "word" responses to actual words ÷ 40
[b] Number of "word" responses to pseudowords ÷ 40
*reject H_0 ($d' = 0$), $z > 1.96$, $p < .05$

auditory word forms over the time span of the study. All d' values are significant (that is, $z > 1.96$, $p < .05$), and there is no significant change between the first and second administrations (that is, for the largest d' difference, occurring to high-frequency words, $z = 1.04$, $p = .15$, one-tailed).

The results from auditory and lexical decision indicated that Susan recognized most of the words she was unable to pronounce and offered a methodology for studying what additional information might be available to her about these words. To this end a phrase decision test was constructed, based on a 40-item subset of the words of the oral reading test. For each word we constructed two phrasal contexts, one appropriate to the grammatical category of the target, the other inappropriate. Here are some examples:

4a.   it's a treat
  b.   *it's not treat
5a.   the first person
  b.   *to person it
5a.   not too subtle
  b.   *where's the subtle?

For presentation the phrases were scrambled and pseudorandomized with respect to well-formedness. Each phrase was read aloud twice, and Susan indicated by pointing to a response card whether the phrase was "good" or "lousy." She had no difficulty understand-

Table 8.9
Auditory Lexical Decision Test

	Frequency		
	High	Medium	Low
May 1985			
Prop. hits[a]	1.00	.95	.55
Prop. false alarms[b]	.20	.33	.23
D-prime (d')	3.16*	2.09*	0.87*
(SE²)	(.40)	(.15)	(.09)
February 1986			
Prop. hits[a]	.95	.95	.75
Prop. flase alarms[b]	.23	.33	.35
D-prime (d')	2.38*	2.09*	1.06*
(SE²)	(.16)	(.15)	(.11)

[a] Number of "word" responses to actual words ÷ 40
[b] Number of "word" responses to pseudowords ÷ 40
*reject H_0 ($d' = 0$), $z > 1.96$, $p < .05$

ing the requirements of the task, which were conveyed through demonstration trials and modeling. The actual test was conducted in four parts within a single session.

The phrase decision test was administered on three different occasions between May 1985 and February 1986. The results are shown in table 8.10. It can be seen that Susan retained the ability to discriminate well-formed from ill-formed phrases, with no evidence of decline over the three administrations (the largest drop in d', occurring between October 1985 and February 1986, did not approach significance; $z = .84$, $p = .20$, one-tailed). Thus it appears that Susan continued to be sensitive to the match between the grammatical category of the target word and the category assignment dictated by the phrase context. The implication of this result is that as late as February 1986 her language system was capable of parsing these simple phrases to the point of assigning grammatical roles based on information in the mental lexicon. This is consistent with the evidence from sentence grammaticality judgments and sentence repetition described previously.

Susan's success with this phrase decision test stands in marked contrast to her inability to extract meaning from simple phrases. This was shown clearly in a second phrase decision study, conducted as an extension of the superordinate matching test previously described.

The 20 terms from the animals and furniture categories of the matching test were embedded in phrase contexts for well-formedness

Table 8.10
The Phrase Decision Test

	May '85	Oct. '85	Feb. '86
Prop. hits[a]	.75	.78	.78
Prop. false alarms[b]	.23	.25	.38
D-prime (d')	1.42*	1.44*	1.08*
(SE²)	(.10)	(.10)	(.09)

[a] Number of "good" responses to grammatical phrases ÷ 40
[b] Number of "good" responses to ungrammatical phrases ÷ 40
*reject H_0 ($d' = 0$), $z > 1.96$, $p < .05$

judgments. Two types of contexts were created: *Bare grammatical contexts* were as previously described for the phrase decision test—in well-formed versions the context was appropriate to the term's grammatical category; in the ill-formed versions it was not. In addition to the 20 animal and furniture terms, 20 adjectives and 20 verbs were assessed in these bare grammatical contexts.

The second type of context combined these same animal and furniture terms with predicates appropriate or inappropriate to the semantics of the terms. In addition to the 20 animal and furniture terms, 20 event terms were studied. Corresponding to each type of term, there were three types of predicates: animal predicates like *is sleeping, is dead, is hungry*; artifact predicates like *is broken, needs repair, is made of wood*; and event predicates like *lasted an hour, occurred yesterday, was accidental*. Each term occurred once with its corresponding predicate type, to make a semantically well-formed phrase, and once with one of the other two predicate types to make a semantically ill-formed phrase. Examples of these semantically rich contexts are

7a. the mule is sleeping
  b. #the mule occurred yesterday
8a. the desk is broken
  b. #the desk is sleeping
9a. the fire occurred yesterday
  b. #the fire is broken

The two context conditions were run in separate sessions throughout November 1985. The 60 semantically rich contexts were run first, 30 trials in each of two consecutive sessions. The phrases were presented auditorily, but we made use of combined visual and verbal instructions and demonstration with modeling to convey to Susan the idea that she should listen for whether the sentence said something silly or not. Susan indicated her decision by pointing to one or

Table 8.11
Judgments on Bare Grammatical Contexts (November 1985)

	Animal Terms	Furniture Terms	Adjectives	Verbs
Prop. hits[a]	.85	.85	.80	.90
Prop. false alarms[b]	.20	.30	.35	.05
D-prime (d')	.88*	1.56*	1.22*	2.93*
(SE^2)	(.22)	(.21)	(.19)	(.37)

[a] Number of "good" responses to grammatical phrases $\div$ 20
[b] Number of "good" responses to ungrammatical phrases $\div$ 20
* reject H_0 ($d' = 0$), $z > 1.96$, $p < .05$

another side of a response sheet showing a figure in a clown outfit labeled "silly" and an unadorned version labeled "OK." This was followed by two sessions of bare grammatical contexts, 30 trials per session, with Susan indicating by pointing whether the phrase spoken aloud to her sounded "lousy" or "good."

Results The results for the bare grammatical contexts are presented in table 8.11. Overall Susan responded correctly to 130 of the 160 sentences (81 percent correct). Significant d's were obtained for all four conditions ($z > 1.96$, $p < .05$ for each of the four). Pairwise comparisons between d's for the four conditions yielded significance only for adjectives versus verbs ($z = 2.31$, $p < .05$, two-tailed). Susan's success with phrases containing furniture terms ($d' = 1.56$) is particularly interesting in view of her poor performance with these same terms in the superordinate matching test (see table 8.7).

In contrast to the bare grammatical contexts, semantically rich contexts produced minimal evidence of discrimination (table 8.12). Overall Susan responded correctly to only 69 of the 120 sentences of this condition (57.5 percent correct). d's for the animal-term and furniture-term conditions did not approach significance ($z = 1.07$ and 0.00, respectively). On the other hand judgments in the event-term condition were accomplished with reasonable accuracy, the d' of 0.78 falling just short of significance ($z = 1.90$, $p = 0.57$). The latter result affords some confidence that Susan was on-task, so that her overall poor performance on these semantic judgments can reasonably be attributed to the severity of the semantic processing disorder, rather than to some problem with the task demands.

The studies described in this section reveal some sparing within the language system, particularly in those input systems that operate on auditory and visual stimuli to assign them linguistic descriptions, including lexical status and grammatical category (Fodor 1983).

Table 8.12
Judgments on Semantically Rich Contexts (November 1985)

	Animal Terms	Furniture Terms	Event Terms
Prop. hits[a]	.80	.50	.60
Prop. false alarms[b]	.65	.50	.30
D-prime (d')	0.46^{ns}	0.00^{ns}	0.78^{ns}
(SE^2)	(.19)	(−)	(.17)

[a] Number of "OK" responses to well-formed phrases ÷ 20
[b] Number of "OK" responses to ill-formed phrases ÷ 20
ns accept H_0 ($d' = 0$), $z \leq 1.96$, $p \geq .05$

Although Susan made errors on lexical and grammatical-phrase judgment tasks, probably more than she would have premorbidly, we are impressed by the fact that her performance here remained stable and at reasonably high levels of accuracy. This of course stands in marked contrast to the various results bearing on output phonology and semantics, which showed dramatic decline to nonfunctional levels over this same time period.

Visual Processing and Visual Object Identification

As an artist Susan had achieved commercial success selling her animal portraits and notepaper reproductions. However, her family and friends had noticed a decline in the subtlety and quality of her paintings beginning around the same time as the language problems. Figure 8.3 reproduces samples from her portfolio at different time periods.

Although she no longer displayed the same artistic talent, Susan continued throughout the course of this study to perform competently on tasks requiring visual analysis and visual reproduction (see figure 8.4). Results from various standardized tests confirm the integrity of basic visual perceptual processing throughout this time period; those results are summarized in table 8.13. Note especially that the scores on the Benton Face Recognition and Line Orientation tests remained in the normal range even late in the study, when language functions were severely deteriorated.

From the cognitive neuropsychological standpoint, a crucial question concerns the status of object recognition and the semantic interpretation of visual arrays. Previously we asserted that the results of the superordinate matching test pointed to the dissolution of meaning representations contacted by written and spoken words. If those same meaning representations are used to interpret nonlinguistic

Figure 8.3
A sampling of Susan's oil paintings from the pre- and postmorbid period. (A) from 1972, (B, C) from 1976, (D, E) from 1984, (F) from 1985.

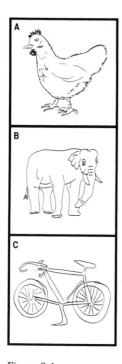

Figure 8.4
(A) Drawn by Susan to copy, July 1984; (B) drawn to copy, January 1986; (C) drawn from real-life model, November 1985.

symbols as well, we should expect to see similar problems in Susan's understanding of objects and events, both real and pictured. And indeed, as early as 1984, there were indications to this effect: her occasional failure to discriminate vegetable plants from weeds while gardening, a tendency to select the wrong implements for grooming the horses, mishandling food preparations (for example, substituting popping corn for uncooked rice in a casserole preparation). Later, when she was taking daily walks and gathering "trash" on the road, she would frequently have to be prevented from picking up with bare hands the rotted carcasses of dead animals, spoiled foods, or even fecal matter. It can be presumed that these sorts of errors would have been still more prominent but for the strict routinization of her daily schedule.

Observers of these recognition failures would often comment on the paradoxical sharpness of acuity and attention to visual detail. She was forever picking up tiny specks of dust from floor and furniture

Table 8.13
Scores on Standardized Perceptual Tests

Date	Test	Score	Interpretation
11/84	Ravens Standard Progressive Matrices	41	86th %ile
5/85	Ravens Standard Progressive Matrices	35	71th %ile
7/85	Benton's Visual Retention Test		
	Copy	0 (error score)	normal
	5-min. delay (adm. A)	8 (error score)	borderline IQ
9/85	Facial Recognition Test (long form)[a]	42 (corrected)	normal
9/85	Judgment of Line Orientation[b]	27 (corrected)	high normal
6/86	Judgment of Line Orientation	23 (corrected)	normal
12/85	Rey-Osterrieth Complex Figure Test[c]		
	Copy	31	25th %ile
	Immed. memory	2	defective

[a] Benton, Van Allen, Hamsher, and Levin 1978
[b] Benton, Varney, and Hamsher 1975
[c] Lezak 1983, p. 400

and uncovering half-hidden objects—coins, rings, pencils—that had gone unnoticed by others.

Neuropsychologists are well acquainted with this paradox. Indeed it has become standard in neuropsychological writings to differentiate between the early stages of visual object recognition, up through the identification of the object, and the more "semantic" or interpretative operations that yield an appreciation of the object's function and its relation to other objects (for example, DeRenzi, Scotti, and Spinnler 1969, Ratcliff and Newcombe 1982, Warrington 1982, Warrington and Taylor 1978). There is general agreement that the minimal evidence for intact presemantic perceptual processing is success in matching nonidentical presentations of a given object, that which Warrington termed *perceptual classification*. We assessed Susan's perceptual classification, along with other aspects of her recognition and interpretation of pictures, in a series of matching and sorting tasks.

Recognition and Interpretation of Pictured Objects

Perceptual Classification   The test we use to assess perceptual classification requires the subject to match a black and white photograph of an object (the probe) to the one of three choices that depicts that same object from an alternative viewpoint. Thirty-three different items are examined twice, once in a familiar orientation, the second time in an unfamiliar (odd) orientation (Warrington and Taylor 1978, Humphreys and Riddoch 1984). This test was administered to Susan twice, the first time in March 1985 and the second in June 1986, very late in the study. On both occasions Susan performed without errors. Even more impressive was her ability to redraw objects in their canonical orientations when given the odd-view probes (see figure 8.5).

Object Categorization   The results just presented indicate that Susan was capable of perceptually classifying photographed objects, which implies that she apprehended at least their token identity. The next question was whether she was capable of classifying depicted objects by type (that is, as an instance of a basic-level category; see Rosch et al. 1976). We assessed type-identification (object categorization) by means of a second matching test with photographs. Here again the task is to match a probe to one of three choices, but in this case the choice is made on the basis of shared category membership rather than identity. Nine categories of objects are evaluated, three from each of three superordinate categories (animals: *cats, dogs,* and *fish*; vehicles: *trucks, cars,* and *airplanes*; furniture items: *sofas, chairs,* and *lamps*). The choices on each trial are exemplars from the three categories that share a superordinate (for example, a car, a truck, and an airplane), and the probe is a different exemplar from one of the three. The photographs that constitute the choice set all represent prototypical exemplars of the various categories, as judged by raters, whereas the exemplars used as probes vary from typical to highly atypical. It is worth noting that although the categories tested are all highly familiar, the task is demanding because of the wide typicality range sampled and also because on each trial the subject chooses between two categories with perceptual features that overlap considerably (*dog-cat, chair-sofa, truck-car*). A group of 28 patients with suspected Alzheimer's disease made an average of 7 errors on this 54-item test (SD 4.4, range 0–17) significantly more than a matched control group (mean 1.5 errors, SD 1.4, range 0–5) ($t = 4.60, p < .01$). Susan was given this test on three occasions. Each time her performance was within the normal range: two errors in February 1984, three in October 1985, five in March 1986.

Function Matching Test   This test requires the subject to pair two of three photographed objects on the basis of shared function, where the third object bears a strong visual similarity to one of the other two. For example, a button must be paired with a zipper rather than a coin of the same size and shape.[4] A group of 10 normal adult control subjects scored a mean 34.2 of 36 correct on this test (SD 2.15, range 29–36). Susan's score of 17 of 36 correct was well outside the normal range.

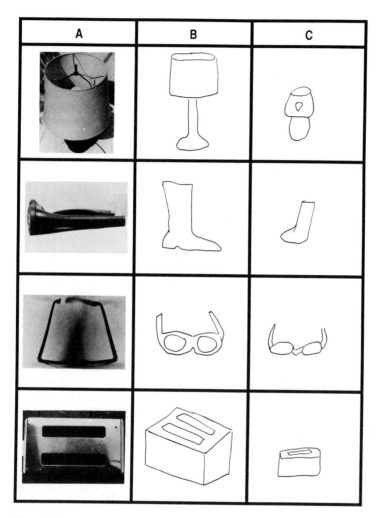

Figure 8.5
Susan's redrawing of objects presented in unusual views photographs (A). From March 1985 (B); from June 1986 (C).

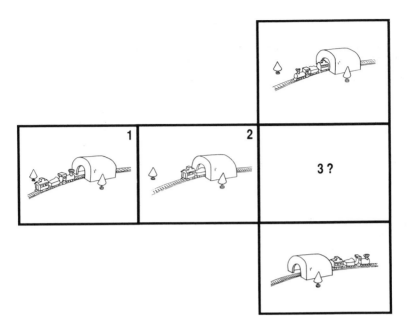

Figure 8.6
Sample item from spatial sequences

According to Warrington (1982), failure on function matching tests of this type, in the face of preserved perceptual classification, reflects a failure of object recognition at the level of semantic categorization. We therefore sought additional evidence bearing on the semantic categorization of pictures.

Interpreting Picture Sequences   In April 1985 Susan was tested on the Picture Arrangement subtest of the WAIS and achieved an age-equivalent scaled score of 3. The comparable scores for Block Design and Object Assembly, assessed in the same session as Picture Arrangement, was in both cases 15. Although all three are perform-ance subtests, only the first requires semantic interpretation of visual arrays. We subsequently clarified the nature of Susan's semantic in-terpretation deficit by means of a procedure based on Veroff's (1978) work. Like Picture Arrangement this test examines the subject's understanding of the logic of pictured sequences. Here, however, a distinction is drawn between the logic of perspective and directional movement (in *spatial sequences*) versus the logic of conceptual relations (in *semantic sequences*). The latter but not the former call upon informa-

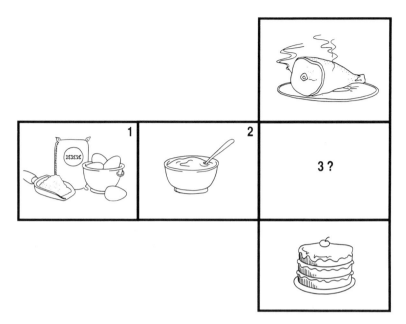

Figure 8.7
Sample item from semantic sequences

tion having to do with the nature and meaning of objects (see figures 8.6 and 8.7 for examples).

As it turned out, Susan made no errors on the spatial sequences, but missed 6 of the 18 semantic sequences. This pattern of results— better performance on spatial than semantic sequences—is opposite to that obtained by a group of 16 normal adults, who scored a mean 16.3 correct on spatial sequences (SD 1.6, range 12–18) and 17.7 on semantic sequences (SD 0.6, range 16–18). Indeed, of the 15 control subjects who made errors, not one showed Susan's pattern. Susan's results therefore suggest a problem in picture interpretation that is specific to the semantic sequences, a problem, that is, in appreciating the logic of conceptual relations among the depicted objects.

The problems in visual semantic processing revealed in these tests are nowhere near as severe as those involving language. Still, they pose an interesting parallel. It appears that in visual processing, as in language, input systems continue to operate normally up to the point of delivering a *categorized percept*, in this case a percept of the object, place, or event depicted. The problem comes with the requirement of interpreting the percept or, as some would have it, associating that percept with other representations in memory (Geschwind 1965).

This summary explains much of the data from tests of Susan's perceptual processing and object recognition. However, there are some discrepant findings that suggest that the story may be more complicated. To explore these complications, it will be helpful to turn to a more detailed account of visual object recognition recently put forth by Chertkow, Bub, and Caplan (in press; Chertkow and Bub, chapter 7).

In a synthesis of the now substantial literature dealing with both normal and brain-injured subjects, Chertkow, Bub, and Caplan attempt to differentiate several processing stages involved in the recognition of objects and pictures. The first stage yields a *structural description* of the visually presented object: a 3D, object-centered representation that encodes information pertaining to contour, major axis of orientation, and the spatial organization of parts (Marr 1980, Ratcliff and Newcombe 1982, Riddoch et al. 1988). Structural descriptions serve as input to the second stage, in which *identification procedures* bring to bear information in long-term semantic memory concerning what various object-types look like, are used for, and so on (see also Miller and Johnson-Laird 1976). This processing stage can be thought of as a classification judgment in which the object is evaluated for membership in one or more categories, hence "identified." The evidence we have presented thus far suggests that Susan's visual processing is intact up through the stage of identification procedures.

Further information about the identified object, for example, information bearing on the contexts in which it typically appears and the relations it bears to other objects, is stored in long-term memory structures, which Chertkow and colleagues call *semantic core concepts*. Retrieval processes operate on these core concepts, and the information they recover is amodal—providing meaning to both linguistic and nonlinguistic symbols (words and pictures). Susan's performance on our various tests of verbal semantics pointed to a dissolution in the core concept; her difficulty with the semantic sequences, which draws upon this same amodal core, is thus predicted by Chertkow and colleagues' model. So too, it would seem, is the dissociation between the two picture matching tasks: the object categorization test, which taps identification procedures and which was performed so well by Susan, versus the function matching test, which presumably draws upon core concepts and which was performed poorly. But here we encounter the first wrinkle in the story: For according to Chertkow and colleagues the function matching test does not tap core concepts, rather it calls upon information that should be available through identification procedures—information pertaining to the habitual uses of objects. Nor is this an arbitrary assumption of the theory; Chertkow and colleagues require this to be true to explain why the optic aphasic patient reported by Coslett and Saffran (1987), who was otherwise incapable of accessing semantic information from pictures, could nevertheless perform this same function matching test at a normal level (29 of 32 correct). Does this mean that Susan did in fact have some problems at the level of identification procedures? Some additional findings suggested this was so.

Nonobject Decision Task   One of the indexes that Chertkow and colleagues use to assess the integrity of identification procedures in brain-damaged patients is the nonobject decision task (Kroll and Potter 1984), in particular the most demanding version of that task (see Riddoch and Humphreys 1987) in which the nonmeaningful objects (that is, nonobjects) are depictions that combine parts of objects from the same superordinate category (for example, a dog with a cow's head, a knife blade with a scissor handle), thus forming a probable or familiar contour. According to Chertkow and colleagues, failure to discriminate meaningful objects from nonmeaningful objects of this type, in the face of otherwise adequate perceptual processing, suggests problems at the level of identification procedures.

We used the stimuli of the Riddoch and Humphreys's (1987) nonobject decision tasks[5] to assess identification procedures in Susan and in 10 normal control subjects. The 60-item task consists of 30 meaningful and 30 nonmeaningful object depictions randomized and presented one at a time for a yes/no judgment. Nonmeaningful objects were all of the probable or familiar type described above. Susan performed the task in June 1985. She made a total of 16 errors: 7 misses (no to a meaningful object) and 9 false acceptances (yes to a nonobject composite). This is better-than-chance discrimination ($d' = 1.26$, $z = 3.60$, $p < .05$), but outside the normal range (0–9 errors, mean 3.4, SD 2.7).

Object Color   According to Chertkow and colleagues for those items whose colors are an integral part of their identification, information pertaining to color should be stored as part of their identification procedure. Assuming intact identification procedures in Susan, the prediction is for good success in discriminating correctly colored from incorrectly colored depictions of objects. But this prediction was not borne out. In April 1986 we presented her with line drawings of 22 objects, all with highly predictable color (for example, butter, elephant, corn), and asked her to color the drawing after selecting the appropriate crayon from a choice set of three, which varied from trial to trial.[6] On this task Susan erred on 7 of the 22 trials; for example, she colored the butter blue, the peas orange.

This task was followed two weeks later by a multiple-choice version, which required Susan to select the correctly colored drawing from a set of three. With the same set of 22 items, Susan erred on 8. Of the 8, 4 were items that she had missed on the prior version as well, but there was no correspondence between the erroneous color selection in the two versions.

Susan's difficulty with these tasks, especially the multiple-choice version, suggests deficient knowledge about the color of objects. Does this mean that her identification procedures do not bring color information to bear in the identification of real and depicted objects? And does the nonobject decision result imply the same about parts and features? If so, it is quite mysterious how she managed to perform the matching views test and picture classification test with such high accuracy.

But consider this: the matching views and picture classification tests require judgments on the *outputs* of input systems, that is, the identity of the object represented in different views or the identity of the category instantiated by an object. In contrast the nonobject decision and color matching tests require judgments about some aspect of the information stored in, or accessed by, these input systems. The same can be said of the function matching test; the basis for the match, whether two objects have a common function, is presumably information that is *available* to identification procedures, but it is not the information that the identification procedures *deliver*. Conceivably Susan's problem lies in accessing for purposes other than identification those details of form, color, function, and the like that continue to be available to identification procedures.

To demonstrate that this is the case, it would be necessary to show that Susan failed to recall crucial identifying features associated with objects that she clearly recognized. In a series of studies dealing with picture codes in visual short-term memory, we obtained evidence to this effect.

Picture Codes in Short-Term Memory
Early in our study we sought to exploit Susan's drawing talent to study how she processed pictures. The idea was to impose delays of varying lengths between the inspection of the target and the opportunity to reproduce it to elucidate the characteristics of the encoded representations (presumably iconic at short delays, categorical at longer delays). To our surprise we discovered that Susan's success in reproducing line drawings broke down with the introduction of even

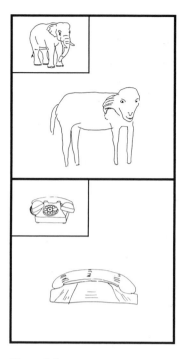

Figure 8.8
Drawings from memory attempted immediately following a 10-second inspection of the model (shown in the insert) (July 1984)

momentary delay. Figure 8.8 shows two of her drawings from immediate memory, following a 10-second inspection period. These attempts are typical in that they are devoid of critical identifying features (for example, the trunk of the elephant, the dial of the telephone). In her drawings all four-legged animals had a single, generic look.

It was clear to us as we watched Susan perform this task that her problem was not in recognizing the model: invariably she took it in casually, with just a glance before reaching out for the drawing material. (Still we required that she inspect it carefully for the full 10 seconds, and she complied with this). Once the model was removed from view, she worked quickly for the first few strokes, then more slowly and with evident puzzlement. The impression conveyed was that she was guided in those first few strokes by an iconic image (Neisser 1967) and that with the fading of that image she was left with insufficient information about the model to reproduce it in detail. Did she encode the stimulus beyond the raw image? The answer was clear when we substituted printed letters for object drawings: Her reproductions of these were uniformly accurate not only from immediate memory, but also after a 10-second delay filled by counting. Because Susan was no more successful at naming letters than familiar objects, it is not possible to attribute her differential success with letters to verbal mediation. Nevertheless it was clear that she was encoding more than the veridical appearance of the letter stimuli from the fact that her reproductions tended to preserve the *category* of the letters, but not the style or script. Evidence obtained later from picture matching with delay confirmed that she was also encoding object depictions categorically, despite her inability to reproduce them.

The Delayed Match-to-Sample Task   The general procedure was to show Susan two pictures on cards for an inspection period of 5 seconds, then turn the cards face down for a filled interval in which the experimenter and Susan counted together from one to ten. Following this, a probe card was produced and Susan was required to turn face up the one of the two samples that matched the probe. Two types of stimuli were used—letters of the alphabet and animal drawings—and each was examined under two matching conditions: identity match (A-A, $monkey_1$-$monkey_1$) and category match (A-a, $monkey_1$-$monkey_2$). Within each condition, which consisted of 48 trials, the role of visual similarity was examined as follows: In the identity match conditions half the trials consisted of sample pairs with the same overall shape or a common set of features (for example, O and Q, duck and chicken), and the other half consisted of pairs that were visually dissimilar (O and R, duck and cow). If Susan were matching on the basis of the physical similarity, she should be expected to make more errors on the visually similar trials. The manipulation of visual similarity in the category match conditions centered on the visual similarity between the category probe and the sample to be matched with it; an example of a visually similar probe-sample pair is C-c, of a visually dissimilar pair, R-r. In these conditions visual similarity would be expected to *aid* performance if the match were being performed on the basis of physical similarity, hence there should be more errors to the visually dissimilar probe-sample pairs.

The results of this study, which was conducted between April and June of 1986, are presented in table 8.14. On the identity-match conditions Susan responded correctly to 85 percent of the trials with letters and 79 percent of the animal trials. In both cases performance is above chance and well below ceiling. The visual similarity of the sample pairs did not affect her performance with either stimulus set ($\chi^2 \leq 1.5$, $p > .20$ for both). On the category-match conditions Susan responded

Table 8.14
The Delayed Match-to-Sample Task (April–June 1986)

	Number Correct	
	Letters	Animals
Identity Match		
Visually similar distractors (n = 24)	22	19
Visually dissimilar distractors (n = 24)	19	19
Category Match		
Visually similar category probes (n = 24)	18	21
Visually dissimilar category probes (n = 24)	18	19

correctly to 75 percent of the letter trials and 83 percent of trials with animals, neither result differing significantly from the respective identity-match conditions ($\chi^2 \leq 2.0$, $p > .20$ for both). The degree of visual similarity between sample and category probe did not affect performance with either letters or animals ($\chi^2 \leq 1.5$, $p > .20$ for both).

The comparability of her performance on identity- and category-match conditions, together with the absence of any similarity effects, suggest that in both conditions Susan was basing her matches on an encoding of the type-identity of the stimuli. Moreover the fact that she made as many errors on the identity-match condition as on category-match also implies that the source of the errors was not categorization failures. More likely the errors arose from the memory and/or attentional requirement of the task (see table 8.13 for additional evidence of a visual short-term memory problem).

We used these results to examine the question posed earlier: Does Susan sometimes fail to recover for purposes other than identification the perceptual details on which successful identification is based? Periodically, during the category-match blocks with animals, we followed up a correct match by immediately having Susan reproduce the probe with pencil and paper. The results replicated that which we had found earlier: With the letter probes her reproductions from memory were uniformly accurate, whereas with animals she reproduced few distinctive features, even despite our vigorous prompting for more detail (see figure 8.9). The combined results from delayed matching and drawing support the idea that Susan had access to the output of identification procedures, but not to the information that entered into these procedures.

There are several possible explanations for why this dissociation might obtain: The first is that Chertkow and colleagues are wrong in suggesting that identification procedures access information in the

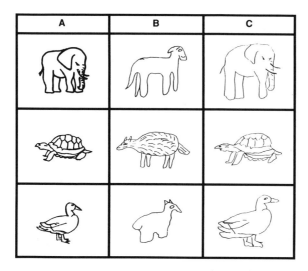

Figure 8.9
(A) Probes from successful category-match trials in the delayed match-to-sample test; (B) Susan's attempted reproductions of these probes from immediate memory; (C) copy renditions performed in a later session. The delayed match-to-sample test was carried out between April and June 1986.

semantic core. The alternative is that the information relevant to identification is duplicated in memory structures dedicated to that function and that in Susan's case these memory structures were spared the dissolution that affected core concepts. The problem with this account is that it ignores the very evidence that suggested identification procedures in the first place, evidence pointing to the breadth and multidimensionality of information bearing on identification (Chertkow, Bub, and Caplan, in press, Miller and Johnson-Laird 1976, Jackendoff 1983). If there is no limit in principle to what can enter into the identification procedure, then this first account reduces to the unlikely notion that all of semantic memory is duplicated in memory stores serving identification.

The second possibility relates to the distinction between effortful and automatic processing. It is now well recognized that brain damage sometimes compromises the availability of information to conscious deliberation, but not to more automatic modes of access such as are brought into play by various priming procedures (for example, Chertkow, Bub, and Seidenberg 1989, Milberg and Blumstein 1981, Nebes, Martin, and Horn 1984). An argument could be made that whereas identification procedures operate automatically and without conscious effort (Warren and Morton 1982), the various matching and drawing tasks on which Susan performed poorly all require conscious, directed retrieval of information from semantic memory. For example, in the nonobject decision task the demands are to decide whether a line-drawing depiction contains all and only the features appropriate to the object in question, and the color- and function-match tests require that particular features or attributes be evaluated. Thus it is possible that Susan's failure on these tasks did not reflect the dissolution of the relevant information in semantic memory as much as the inability to recover that information via effortful, conscious retrieval mechanisms.

The final possibility is that the information relevant to identification procedures had indeed undergone dissolution in Susan's semantic memory, but that the dissolution was not so advanced as to preclude successful identification from taking place under most conditions. Semantic information that is too weakly represented to be recalled or correctly assessed in a feature-by-feature match might nevertheless enter into identification procedures based on global pattern match. For example, on the logic of connectionist, spreading-activation models, a weakening of the strength of the association between concept nodes and corresponding features would certainly decrease the likelihood of particular features becoming activated as a consequence of activation of the concept node. Still insofar as the identification procedures provide bottom-up input to concept nodes, they might act to reinforce the weakened associations sufficient to accommodate a successful pattern match.

Assuming this is correct, can we continue to maintain that identification procedures were spared? Certainly further erosion of the semantic core would be expected to negatively affect identification. Indeed it is tempting to reinterpret the examples of her agnosic errors in real life—for example, the failure to distinguish weeds from cultivated plants in the garden—as true identification failures that arose out of the need to examine and evaluate particular perceptual features. But this suggests a blurring of the theoretical distinction between identification procedures and postidentification semantic elaboration. If identification procedures operating on the basis of global pattern match require, under certain circumstances, to be supplemented by a more deliberate and extensive examination of information in the semantic core, then the retrieval operations that Chertkow and colleagues designate as postidentification are in fact playing a role in the identification process.

Where does all this leave us with respect to the previously stated generalization regarding the sparing of input systems? We believe that it is defensible, but with qualification. The data from Susan's picture processing unambiguously support the integrity of visual perceptual processes, at least through the level of perceptual classification (Warrington 1982) or structural descriptions (in the sense of Chertkow, Bub, and Caplan, in press, but not necessarily that of Riddoch and Humphreys 1987 or Riddoch et al. 1988). Beyond that the evidence supports a further distinction, which may be graded rather than categorical, between identification and the retrieval of information from semantic memory for purposes other than identification.

Neuroimaging Studies

Susan was a participant in the PET-dementia study conducted at the Hospital of the University of Pennsylvania's Cerebrovascular Research Center, where she underwent full neurodiagnostic evaluation on two occasions. The first of these was in May 1983, more than three years after the onset of the progressive aphasia and before the emergence of other signs or symptoms of dementia. To summarize the findings on that occasion: Neuropsychological testing revealed a marked discrepancy between verbal IQ (71) and performance IQ (122) and severely deficient scores on verbal memory and confrontation naming. The neurological examination was unremarkable, EEG was normal, but CT scan showed mild widening of the left Sylvian fissure. The PET scan demonstrated significant reductions in local glucose metabolism (LCMRglc) in the middle and superior temporal gyri on the left, as well as the left lenticular nucleus, using absolute LCMRglc (mg/100 g brain/min) normalized to the global LCMRglc.

The second study was performed in January 1986, when the clinical deterioration had become marked. Table 8.15 summarizes the changes in metabolic rates from the first to the second study. The rates presented in the table are normalized (individual LCMRglc divided by mean LCMRglc for all regions: a so-called metabolic profile) to facilitate a meaningful comparison of the patterns of abnormality seen in the two scans. This was necessary because of various technical changes in the PET methodology (instrument calibration factors, procedure for synthesizing the tracer for measuring LCMRglc), which precludes direct comparison of LCMRglc at the two time periods. Both normalized and absolute metabolic rates for the two time periods were evaluated against two separate age- and sex-matched control groups whose PET studies were performed contemporaneously under the same technical conditions.

The first PET scan (May 1983) exhibited a metabolic profile with significant decrements in the following left hemisphere structures:

Table 8.15
Results of PET Studies, 1983 versus 1986

	Scan #1 (5/83)		Scan #2 (1/86)		Controls (SD)	
Affected Regions	L	R	L	R	L	R
1. Frontal eye fields	112	137	68[c]	106	107(6)	108(7)
2. Frontal pole	102	101	73[c]	92	96(6)	96(5)
3. Inf. frontal gyrus	113	136	75[c]	118	115(8)	117(8)
4. Middle frontal gyrus	106	113	61[a]	94	90(12)	93(7)
5. Insular cortex	95[a]	115	84[b]	112	116(8)	117(4)
6. Mid. temporal gyrus	50[c]	89	76	117	95(11)	102(7)
7. Sup. temporal gyrus	42[a]	80	36[a]	68	73(15)	83(14)
8. Amygdala	41[c]	67	63[b]	88	100(11)	96(15)
9. Hippocampus	27[c]	77	93	102	98(13)	97(13)
10. Caudate nucleus	90[a]	101	52[c]	81	106(7)	103(8)
11. Lenticular nucleus	93[b]	124	92[b]	116	117(8)	120(3)
12. Thalamus	108	118	96[a]	123	112(7)	116(7)

[a] > 2 SD below controls
[b] > 3 SD below controls
[c] > 4 SD below controls
Values are normalized metabolic rates for affected (hypometabolic) PET regions (see text for details).

amygdala, hippocampus, middle temporal gyrus, superior temporal gyrus, insular cortex, lenticular nucleus, and caudate. No right hemisphere abnormalities were seen (see table 8.15). Overall absolute hemispheric values were 3.40 mg/100 g brain/min for the left hemisphere (controls = 4.67 ± 0.82) and 3.83 for the right hemisphere (controls = 4.60 ± 0.81). The ratio of left hemisphere to right hemisphere metabolism was 0.89, compared with a value of 1.015 ± 0.026 for control subjects. Regionally all significant lateral asymmetries favored the right hemisphere. Thus in May 1983 the PET scan demonstrated abnormalities of brain function involving and limited to the left hemisphere, specifically the left temporal lobe, insular cortex, and basal ganglia.

On the follow-up scan (January 1986) the comparison of Susan's metabolic profile with that of the control group revealed significant decrements in the left frontal eye fields, frontal pole, middle frontal gyrus, inferior frontal gyrus, insular cortex, superior temporal gyrus, amygdala, lenticular and caudate nuclei, and thalamus. Again no right-sided abnormalities were seen. Regional metabolic decreases in left hemispheric structures averaged 35 percent to 40 percent compared with control values. Absolute hemispheric values were 4.97 mg/100 g brain/min on the left (5.81 ± 0.67 for controls) and 5.63 on the right (5.70 ± 0.53 for controls). The left/right ratio was 0.88 (control value of 1.02 ± 0.02). Significant lateral asymmetries again all favored the right hemisphere. Thus the follow-up PET scan showed a definite spread of metabolic abnormality to the left frontal lobe, with continued sparing of the right hemisphere.

In summary the two PET scans, separated by almost three years, both showed abnormalities overwhelmingly lateralized to the left hemisphere, the first predominantly demonstrating a left temporal metabolic disturbance, the second showing additional involvement of the left frontal lobe. Absolute metabolic rates for the two scans are not directly comparable due to the technical factors cited. It would appear, however, that even at a time when the clinical picture had deteriorated markedly (January 1986), *global* brain glucose metabolism was not much diminished. The crucial metabolic change was the *focal* left hemisphere decrease in relative glucose utilization.

Conclusion

Susan's most prominent pathological feature is of course the erosion of language functions, both expressive and receptive. Word-finding difficulty was the presenting sign, the expression of an amnestic aphasia that subsequently compromised fluency and grammatical form and that in the end degenerated to complete wordlessness. Studies of written word pronunciation revealed that a major factor in this erosion of expressive language was an inability to retrieve the output phonology of any but the most frequently uttered word forms. Other studies demonstrated the presence of a lexical-semantic disorder that limited her understanding of words and phrases and presumably also her ability to access the lexicon via semantics. This semantic disorder was not restricted to linguistic material but affected too her understanding of objects and depicted events.

The results of the PET studies strongly suggest that the pathological events originated in the left hemisphere temporal lobe and related limbic structures and later extended to frontal and subcortical areas, also on the left. We presume that this spread to frontal and subcortical structures was responsible for the social-affective changes that emerged some three or so years into the progressive aphasia, as well as for the later incontinence and bulimia. Together these changes suggest Pick's disease. Such a diagnosis is not contraindicated by the asymmetry of the metabolic changes; it is not uncommon to find asymmetric lobar atrophy in Pick's disease, and it is the left hemisphere that is most often disproportionately affected (Neumann 1949). Moreover we know from the patients who have come to autopsy that

Pick's disease is not ruled out by an initial presentation of isolated progressive aphasia, even of many years' duration (Mesulam 1987).

Whether this turns out to be a case of Pick's disease is not material to our central point, which is this: Progressive aphasia arises from degenerative processes that operate with remarkable. selectivity on the neural substrate for a major system of cognition. Cases like Susan's therefore provide a rare opportunity to examine the modular organization of the brain with respect to cognition. The clear distinction that emerged in Susan's case between input systems that deliver categorized percepts, versus the semantic and phonological systems that act on them, exemplifies the potential that these cases have for teasing apart functional subsystems.

In the domain of visual processing, similar distinctions have been drawn before, also based on the findings from atypical dementia presentations (Marin, Glenn, and Rafal 1983, Taylor and Warrington 1971). Marin and colleagues' report of a patient provides an especially clear demonstration of preserved visual analysis, perceptual grouping, and visual problem solving in the absence of semantic processing of visual (and linguistic) symbols. Their patient resembles Susan in many ways, except that there the visuorecognition disorder kept closer pace with the dissolution of language. Thus five years into the disease their patient was without any expressive or receptive language and incapable of recognizing or categorizing pictured objects. CT findings in the Marin and colleagues' patient showed bilateral atrophy of frontal and anterior temporal lobes, typical of Pick's disease. It is thus tempting to suggest that in Susan's case it was the sparing of the right hemisphere anterior structures that modulated the severity of the semantic disorder.

On the other hand it is of substantial interest that unilateral left hemisphere damage with neocortical foci limited to the temporal and frontal lobes had even this great an effect on the semantic processing of linguistic, and especially visual, symbols. Although there is some evidence from visual agnosia studies to suggest that the left hemisphere plays a privileged role in the semantic elaboration of visual concepts, the evidence there suggests a more posterior focus (Warrington and Taylor 1978, Farah 1984).

Clearly there is a good deal to be learned about the neocortical substrate for linguistic and semantic processing by careful study of these atypical dementia cases, and so too for other neurocognitive systems outside of language. There is now an accumulation of reports in the literature of patients with dementia characterized by insidious onset and progressive deterioration within a circumscribed cognitive domain (for example, Hagberg 1978, Moscovitch 1982, DeRenzi 1986,

Saffran and colleagues, chapter 9). Such patients provide important opportunities for studying the brain systems serving cognition. At the very least they call attention to the mosaic of specialized abilities that comprise human intelligence and to the multifocal character of the degenerative diseases of the brain that devastate the expression of that intelligence.

Acknowledgments

Myrna Schwartz's work on this project was supported by NIH grants #AG02231 and #NS18429, and John Chawluk's work was supported by USPHS Program Project Grant NS 14867, NIA Teaching Nursing Home Award PO1-AG03934, and NIH Clinical Research Center Grant MO1-R00040. We wish to acknowledge others who provided support on this project: Abass Alavi, Martin Reivich, Howard Hurtig, and the PET Center Staff of the University of Pennsylvania. Eleanor Saffran and Morris Moscovitch made helpful suggestions on early drafts of the manuscript. Finally, we acknowledge with gratitude the kindness and cooperation shown to us by Susan G. and the members of her family, all of whom have been given pseudonyms in this report.

Notes

1. There is an ironic historical twist in this. When Onari and Spatz first used the term *Pick's disease* in 1926, they explicitly rejected basing the diagnosis on the presence of those histological features, which Alzheimer had identified in 1911. Observing that the ballooned cells and cytoplasmic inclusion bodies were in noncomplementary distribution with the characteristic and highly specific atrophic changes first identified by Pick, they took the latter condition to be defining of Pick's disease. Over the years as investigators have sought to further differentiate Pick's disease from other dementing conditions, they have placed more emphasis on the histopathological features and less on the circumscribed atrophy. In fact, however, Mehler's *non-Pick lobar atrophy* corresponds to the majority of patients previously reported as having *Pick's lobar atrophy*, or simply *circumscribed lobar atrophy*. (For more on the tortuous history of ideas and terms relating to the degenerative dementias, see Schwartz and Stark, chapter 2.)
2. These investigations of Susan's musical competence were conducted by Louisa Saffioti in April and May 1985 in partial fulfillment of her Ph.D. in psychology at the University of Pennsylvania. Saffioti also helped conduct the studies of list and sentence repetition described in this chapter.
3. We are grateful to Jacob Huff for providing us with these abridged, equivalent forms of the Boston Naming Test.
4. We wish to thank H. Branch Coslett, who constructed this function matching test, for making it available to us.
5. We are grateful to Riddoch and Humphreys for making their stimuli available to us.
6. Before carrying out this procedure, we determined that Susan was capable of selecting crayons to match targeted colors. In a pretest we presented patches of color one at a time and asked her to duplicate the patch with the appropriate crayon, which she was required to select from a set of eight. The crayons of this choice set were graded along the spectrum yellow-green-blue-magenta-red-orange. Ten trials were run, and she performed correctly on all of them.

References

Assal, G., Favre, C., and Regli, F. (1985). Aphasie degenerative. *Revue Neurologique* 141: 245–247.

Battig, W. F., and Montague, W. E. (1969). Category norms for verbal items in 56 categories: A replication and extension of the Connecticut Category Norms. *Journal of Experimental Psychology Monographs* 80 (3, part 2).

Beal, M. F., Mazurek, M. F., Svendsen, C. N., Bird, E. D., and Martin, J. B. (1986). Widespread reduction of somatostatin-like immunoreactivity in the cerebral cortex in Alzheimer's disease. *Annals of Neurology* 20: 489–495.

Benton, A. L., Van Allen, M. W., Hamsher, K. deS., and Levin, H. S. (1978). *Test of Facial Recognition, Form SL*. Department of Neurology, University of Iowa Hospitals and Clinics, Iowa City.

Benton, A. L., Varney, N. R., and Hamsher, K deS. (1975). *Judgment of Line Orientation*. Department of Neurology, University of Iowa Hospitals and Clinics, Iowa City.

Bub, D., Cancelliere, A., and Kertesz, A. (1985). Whole-word and analytic translation of spelling to sound in a non-semantic reader. In K. E. Patterson, J. C. Marshall, and M. Coltheart (Eds.) *Surface Dyslexia*. London: Erlbaum.

Byng, S. (1987). Sentence comprehension deficit: Theoretical analysis and remediation. In M. Coltheart, G. Sartori, and R. Job (Eds.) *The Cognitive Neuropsychology of Language*. London: Academic Press.

Chawluk, J. B., Mesulam, M. -M., Hurtig, H., Kushner, M., Weintraub, S., Saykin, A., Rubin, N., Alavi, A., and Reivich, M. (1986). Slowly progressive aphasia without generalized dementia: Studies with positron emission tomography. *Annals of Neurology* 19: 68–74.

Chertkow, H., Bub, D., and Caplan, D. (1988). Two stages in semantic memory processing: Evidence from dementia. *Cognitive Neuropsychology*, in press.

Chertkow, H., Bub, D., and Seidenberg, M. (1989). Priming and semantic memory loss in Alzheimer's disease. *Brain and Language* 36: 420–446.

Coltheart, M., Besner, D., Jonasson, J. T., and Davelaar, E. (1979). Phonological recoding in the lexical decision task. *Quarterly Journal of Experimental Psychology* 31: 489–508.

Coslett, H. B., and Saffran, E. (1987). Preserved object recognition and reading comprehension in optic aphasia. *Neurology* 37 (suppl. 1): 312–313.

DeRenzi, E., Scotti, G., and Spinnler, H. (1969). Perceptual and associative disorders of visual recognition. *Neurology* 19: 634–642.

DeRenzi, E. (1986). Slowly progressive visual agnosia or apraxia without dementia. *Cortex* 22: 171–180.

Farah, M. J. (1984). The neurological basis of mental imagery: A componential analysis. *Cognition* 18: 245–272.

Fodor, J. A. (1983). *The Modularity of Mind*. Cambridge, MA: MIT Press.

Foster, N. L., and Chase, T. N. (1983). Diffuse involvement in progressive aphasia. *Annals of Neurology* 13: 224–225.

Francis, W. N., and Kucera, H. (1982). *Frequency Analysis of English Usage: Lexicon and Grammar*. Boston: Houghton Mifflin.

Geschwind, N. (1965). Disconnexion syndromes in animals and man. *Brain* 88: 237–294.

Goodglass, H., and Kaplan, E. (1972). *The Assessment of Aphasia and Related Disorders*. Philadelphia: Lea and Febiger.

Gordon, B., and Selnes, O. (1984). Progressive aphasia "without dementia": Evidence of more widespread involvement. *Neurology* 34 (suppl. 1): 102.

Hagberg, B. (1978). Defects of immediate memory related to the cerebral blood flow distribution. *Brain and Language* 5: 336–377

Heath, P. D., Kennedy, P., and Kapur, N. (1983). Slowly progressive aphasia without generalized dementia. *Neurology* 13: 687–688.

Holland, A. L., McBurney, D. H., Moossy, J., and Reinmuth, O. M. (1985). The dissolution of language in Pick's disease with neurofibrillary tangles: A case study. *Brain and Language* 24: 36–58.

Hughlings-Jackson, J. (1874). On the nature of the duality of the brain. *Medical Press and Circular* 1: 19, 41, 63. Reprinted in J. Taylor (Ed.) (1931) *Selected Writings of John Hughlings-Jackson*. Vol. 2. London: Staples, pp. 129–145.

Hughlings-Jackson, J. (1878). On affectations of speech from disease of the brain. *Brain* 1: 304–330. Reprinted in J. Taylor (Ed.)(1931) *Selected Writings of John Hughlings-Jackson*. Vol. 2. London: Staples, pp. 155–170.

Humphreys, G. W., and Riddoch, M. J. (1984). Routes to object constancy: Implications from neurological impairments of object constancy. *Quarterly Journal of Experimental Psychology* 36: 385–415.

Irigaray, L. (1973). *Le Langage des Dements*. The Hague: Mouton.

Jackendoff, R. (1983). *Semantics and Cognition*. Cambridge, MA: MIT Press.

Kaplan, E., Goodglass, H., and Weintraub, S. (1983). *Boston Naming Test*. Philadelphia: Lea and Febiger.

Kempler, D., Curtiss, S., and Jackson, C. (1987). Syntactic preservation in Alzheimer's disease. *Journal of Speech and Hearing Research* 30: 343–350.

Kirshner, H. S., Webb, W. G., Kelly, M. P., and Wells, C. E. (1984). Language disturbance—an initial symptom of cortical degenerations and dementia. *Archives of Neurology* 41: 491–496.

Kirshner, H. S., Tanridag, O., Thurman, L., and Whetsell, W. O., Jr. (1987). Progressive aphasia without dementia: Two cases with focal spongiform degeneration. *Annals of Neurology* 22: 527–532.

Kroll, J. F., and Potter, M. C. (1984). Recognizing words, pictures, and concepts: A comparison of lexical, object, and reality decisions. *Journal of Verbal Learning and Verbal Behavior* 23: 39–66.

Lezak, M. D. (1983). *Neuropsychological Assessment*. 2nd ed. New York: Oxford.

Linebarger, M., Schwartz, M. F., and Saffran, E. M. (1983). Sensitivity to grammatical structure in so-called agrammatic aphasics. *Cognition* 13: 361–392.

Marcel, A. J. (1980). Surface dyslexia and beginning reading: A revised version of the pronunciation of print and its impairments. In M. Coltheart, K. E. Patterson, and J. C. Marshall (Eds.) *Deep Dyslexia*. London: Routledge & Kegan Paul.

Marin, O. S. M., Glenn, C. G., and Rafal, R. D. (1983). Visual problem solving in the absence of lexical semantics: Evidence from dementia. *Brain and Cognition* 2: 285–311.

Marr, D. (1980). Visual information processing: The structure and creation of visual representations. *Philosophical Transactions of the Royal Society of London (B)* 290: 199–218.

Mayer-Gross, W. (1937–38). Discussion of the presenile dementias: Symptomatology, pathology, and differential diagnosis.*Proceedings of the Royal Society of Medicine* 31: 93–104.

McCarthy, R., and Warrington, E. K. (1987). Category specificity in an agrammatic patient: The relative impairment of verb retrieval and comprehension. *Neuropsychologia* 23: 709–727.

Mehler, M. F., Horoupian, D. S., and Dickson, D. W. (1987). Reduced somatostatin-like immunoreactivity in cerebral cortex in nonfamilial dysphasic dementia. *Neurology* 37: 1448–1453.

Mesulam, M. -M. (1982). Slowly progressive aphasia without generalized dementia. *Annals of Neurology* 11: 592–598.

Mesulam, M. -M. (1987). Primary progressive aphasia—Differentiation from Alzheimer's disease. *Annals of Neurology* 22: 533–534.

Milberg, W., and Blumstein, S. E. (1981). Lexical decision and aphasia: Evidence for semantic processing. *Brain and Language* 14: 371–385.

Miller, G. A., and Johnson-Laird, P. N. (1976). *Language and Perception*. Cambridge, MA: Harvard University Press.

Morris, C., Cole, M., Banker, B. G., and Wright, D. (1984). Hereditary dysphasic dementia and the Pick-Alzheimer spectrum. *Annals of Neurology* 16: 455–466.

Moscovitch, M. (1982). Multiple dissociations of function in amnesia. In L. S. Cermak (Ed.) *Human Memory and Amnesia*. Hillsdale, NJ: Erlbaum.

Nebes, R. D., Martin, D. C., Horn, L. C. (1984). Sparing of semantic memory in Alzheimer's disease. *Journal of Abnormal Psychology* 93: 321–330.

Neisser, U. (1967). *Cognitive Psychology*. New York: Appleton-Century-Crofts.

Nelson, H. E., and O'Connell, A. (1978). Dementia: The estimation of premorbid intelligence levels using the new adult reading test. *Cortex* 14: 234–244.

Neumann, M. A. (1949). Pick's disease. *Journal of Neuropathology and Experimental Neurology* 8: 255–282.

Onari, K., and Spatz, H. (1926). Anatomische Beitrage zur Lehre von der Pickschen umscriebenen Grossrindenatrophie. *Zeitschrift fur die gesamte Neurologie und Psychiatrie* 101: 470–511.

Pate, D. S., and Saffran, E. M. (1988). Sensitivity to syntactic structure in a Wernicke's aphasic: A case study. Unpublished manuscript.

Patterson, K. E., Marshall, J. C., and Coltheart, M. (Eds.) (1985). *Surface Dyslexia*. London: Erlbaum.

Poeck, K., and Luzzatti, C. (1988). Slowly progressive aphasia in three patients. *Brain* 111: 151–168.

Pogacar, S., and Williams, R. S. (1984). Alzheimer's disease presenting as slowly progressive aphasia. *Rhode Island Medical Journal* 67: 181–185.

Ratcliff, G. and Newcombe, F. (1982). Object recognition: Some deductions from the clinical evidence. In A. W. Ellis (Ed.) *Normality and Pathology in Cognitive Functions*. London: Academic Press.

Riddoch, M. J., and Humphreys, G. W. (1987). Visual object processing in optic aphasia: A case of semantic access agnosia. *Cognitive Neuropsychology* 4: 131–185.

Riddoch, M. J., Humphreys, G. W., Coltheart, M., and Funnell, E. (1988). Semantic systems or system? Neuropsychological evidence re-examined. *Cognitive Neuropsychology* 5: 3–25.

Rosch, E., Mervis, C. B., Gay, W. D., Johnson, D. M., and Boyes-Braem, P. (1976). Basic objects in natural categories. *Cognitive Psychology* 8: 382–439.

Saffran, E. M., Schwartz, M. F., and Marin, O. S. M. (1980). Evidence from aphasia: Isolating the components of a production model. In B. Butterworth (Ed.) *Language Production*. London: Academic Press.

Saffran, E. M. (1985). Lexicalisation and reading performance in surface dyslexia. In K. E. Patterson, J. C. Marshall, and M. Coltheart (Eds.) *Surface Dyslexia*. London: Erlbaum.

Schwartz, M. F., Marin, O. S. M., and Saffran, E. M. (1979). Dissociations of language function in dementia: A case study. *Brain and Language* 7: 277–306.

Schwartz, M. F., Saffran, E. M., and Marin, O. S. M. (1980). Fractionating the reading process in dementia: Evidence for word-specific print-to-sound associations. In M. Coltheart, K. E. Patterson, and J. C. Marshall, (Eds.) *Deep Dyslexia*. London: Routledge & Kegan Paul.

Shallice, T. (1987). Impairments of semantic processing: Multiple dissociations. In. M. Coltheart, R. Job, and G. Sartori (Eds.) *The Cognitive Neuropsychology of Language*. London: Erlbaum.

Shallice, T., and McCarthy, R. (1985). Phonological reading: From patterns of impairment to possible procedures. In K. E. Patterson, J. C. Marshall, and M. Coltheart (Eds.) *Surface Dyslexia*. London: Erlbaum.

Shallice, T., Warrington, E. K., and McCarthy, R. (1983). Reading without semantics. *Quarterly Journal of Experimental Psychology* 35: 111–138.

Taylor, A., and Warrington, E. K. (1971). Visual agnosia: A single case report. *Cortex* 7: 152–161.

Thorndike, E. L., and Lorge, I. (1944). *The Teacher's Word Book of 30,000 Words*. New York: Teacher's College.

Tissot, R. J., Mounin, G., and Lhermitte, F. (1973). *L'Agrammatisme*. Brussels: Dessart.

Veroff, A. (1978). A structural determinant of hemispheric processing of pictorial material. *Brain and Language* 5: 139–148.

Warren, C., and Morton, J. (1982). The effects of priming on picture recognition. *British Journal of Psychology* 73: 117–129.

Warrington, E. K. (1975). The selective impairment of semantic memory. *Quarterly Journal of Experimental Psychology* 27: 635–657.

Warrington, E. K. (1982). Neuropsychological studies of object recognition. *Philosophical Transactions of the Royal Society of London (B)* 298: 15–33.

Warrington, E. K., and Taylor, A. M. (1978). Two categorical stages of object recognition. *Perception* 7: 695–705.

Wechsler, A. F. (1977). Presenile dementia presenting as aphasia. *Journal of Neurology, Neurosurgery and Psychiatry* 40: 303–305.

Whitaker, H. (1976). A case of isolation of the language function. In H. Whitaker and H. A. Whitaker (Ed.) *Studies in Neurolinguistics*. vol. 2. New York: Academic Press.

Chapter 9

Visual Disturbances in Dementia

Eleanor M. Saffran, Eileen J. Fitzpatrick-DeSalme, and H. Branch Coslett

---

The pioneering studies of Mishkin and colleagues established that the primate brain has two cortical visual systems: one concerned with locating arrays in space, and the second concerned with semantically interpreting these arrays. The previous two chapters have dealt with the "What" system. Here Saffran, Fitzpatrick-DeSalme, and Coslett take up issues surrounding the "Where."

Carl, the first of the two patients presented, would presumably fall within Alex Martin's visuoperceptual subgroup (chapter 5). His most prominent symptoms have to do with orienting in space and reconstructing spatial arrays of objects. Under controlled experimental conditions Saffran and coauthors demonstrate the presence of a simultanagnosia in this patient, that is, a restriction in the number of objects that can be simultaneously perceived. The authors go on to show that this restriction is not present at the level of preattentive feature extraction and that indeed a good deal of high-level processing is being carried out on the "nonperceived" target. Thus the restriction appears to be "at the articulation between perceptual processes and conscious awareness."

According to the framework set out by Moscovitch and Umilta (chapter 1), this articulation between visual perception and conscious awareness is achieved by the mechanism of selective attention, which makes the output of the dedicated central processor (that is, the type II module that carries out feature integration) available to working memory. On that formulation there are three types of deficit capable of bringing about such a restriction in the number of items consciously apprehended: (1) a problem in the allocation of attention, (2) a reduction in capacity of working memory, or (3) a problem with the feature integration process that mimics a reduced working memory capacity.

The modality specificity of Carl's deficit rules out the first and second of these accounts and hence by exclusion implicates the feature integration process. But Saffran and coauthors provide evidence that the impairment arises subsequent to feature integration (in Carl, but not in Marie, their second patient), leading them to argue for a specialized visual attentional resource and/or a visual short-term memory system (see also Coslett and Saffran, in press).

However this issue comes to be resolved, the existence of selective visuoper-ceptual deficits involving attentional factors will have been established. There is little doubt that future investigators will chart their course from Saffran and coauthors' meticulous observations and the theoretical framework in which they are cast.

M.F.S.

Disturbances of visual perception and visually guided motor behavior are well-recognized features of intellectual decline in dementia. Although these deficits are not usually among the early signs of cognitive dysfunction, except perhaps as they are manifested in con-structional tasks such as copying (for example, Cummings 1982), there are exceptional cases in which visual disturbances dominate the clinical picture from the outset. As early as 1908 Pick described a pa-tient who presented with severe visuoperceptual deficits at a point where other intellectual functions were only moderately impaired.[1] More recently, Bender and Feldman (1972) reported four cases marked by early and severe visual impairment. All of these patients demonstrated failures of visual object recognition (visual agnosia) in association with other visual disturbances that were less consistent across subjects; prominent among them were visual field defects, mislocalization of objects in space, and the ability to recognize small letters but not large ones. Two patients distinguished by the severity of their visual symptomatology in contrast to their relatively pre-served verbal functions have been described by De Renzi (1986), and additional cases have been reported by Cogan (1985), by Nissen and colleagues (1985), and most recently by Benson and coworkers (1988). In addition to these case reports, evidence for a subgroup of patients particularly impaired in visuoconstructional tasks has emerged from a factor analytic study of Alzheimer's patients conducted by Martin and colleagues (1986). The selective behavioral deficits of these patients were associated with asymmetries in cerebral hypometabolism as re-vealed by positron emission tomography (PET). In contrast to the bilaterally symmetrical patterns of cerebral hypometabolism found in most AD patients, the visuoconstructive subgroup showed a rela-tive decrease in metabolic activity in the right parietal and temporal regions.

But although the clinical manifestations of progressive visuoper-ceptual impairment have repeatedly been described, little effort has been made to define the nature of the cognitive disturbance in these patients. Pick's early study is an exception in this regard. Among his most striking observations was that the patient had greater difficulty recognizing large objects than small ones and often identified a part of an object rather than the whole (for example, fingers but not the hand). The perceptual limitation could not be accounted for by low-level sensory deficits, such as visual field cuts, or by loss of knowledge of objects. Pick suggested that the deficit reflected impairment of an attentional process that serves to integrate information across the retinal array.

In this chapter we report case studies of two patients with progressive dementias characterized by disproportionate visual impairment. As Pick did, we center our analysis of these disturbances on attentional requirements for visual perception. Our approach to studying these patients has been influenced, in particular, by distinctions that have been drawn between early visual operations, involving the activity of separate processors that extract feature information (color, line orientation, movement, and so on) in parallel across the retinal array and subsequent operations in which this information is integrated (for example, Treisman and Gelade 1980). Later operations are characterized as capacity limited and therefore serial in nature, requiring focused attention to a limited region of the display. (A metaphor often used for selective attention in the visual modality is that of a spotlight beam that illuminates an area of the visual field.) The notion that early visual processes are carried out in parallel by separate subsystems is consistent with recent studies of the anatomy and physiology of the primate visual system (for example, Livingstone and Hubel 1988) as well as with perceptual evidence that indicates that elementary visual features can be detected automatically and in parallel (for example, Treisman and Gelade 1980). These demonstrations are associated with a set of experimental paradigms that we have adapted for the study of patients with visuoperceptual disorders, which include manifestations of focal brain disease (Coslett and Saffran 1987, Fitzpatrick, Coslett, and Saffran 1988) as well as progressive visual disturbances.

The two patients we report on here were not ideal subjects for experimental investigation. We examined their visual deficits in the context of progressive decline in other cognitive capacities, which limited the manner and extent of perceptual testing, and in one patient the severity of the visual deficit itself proved an obstacle to testing. However, the phenomena are fascinating in their own right, and the data provide at least a preliminary characterization of perceptual deficits that figure prominently in some cases of degenerative brain disease.

Case 1: Carl

Clinical History and Neurodiagnostic Information
Carl is a 67-year-old, right-handed man who had worked as a morti-
cian and funeral director until his illness. His wife dates the onset
of symptoms to approximately 1980–1981, when Carl was 60. The
family began noticing episodes of disorientation such as Carl's los-
ing his way to a cemetery that was well known to him. Characterized
as always a bit impractical and absent-minded, the family found
nothing otherwise remarkable about Carl's behavior. His son was
being groomed to take over the family business and was increasingly
responsible for the day-to-day operations. In retrospect it is unclear whether this was a response to Carl's difficulties or a normal
progression.

By 1984 Carl had declined sufficiently to warrant a neurological
evaluation. The physical and neurological examinations were nonfocal
and unremarkable. He had adequate visual acuity and full visual
fields. Laboratory results as well as the Hamilton Depression Scale
were within normal limits. The CT scan revealed cerebral atrophy. A
diagnosis of presumed Alzheimer's disease was made. A SPECT
scan, performed in 1986, demonstrated decreased activity in the
posterior parietal and parietooccipital regions bilaterally. A recent
ophthalmological examination (April 1988) confirmed the earlier report of normal visual acuity and full visual fields to confrontation,
though Carl was at that point unable to perform formal computerized
fields.

We first met Carl in late 1984, when he entered an experimental
drug trial, and have followed him since. (The trial was terminated
when the drug was deemed ineffective.) From early on the distinctive
flavor of Carl's illness was apparent to us. Thus as Carl sat before a
visuoperceptual task, completely unable to perform even the simplest
sample item, he exclaimed that the task was "diabolical"!

In the period from 1984 through 1986, Carl's rate of decline was
gradual. He was generally oriented to all but the specific day and
date. Although his attention and initiation were markedly below his
premorbid level, he remained able to withstand several hours of testing at a time. He was always socially appropriate and retained his
interest in and concern for others.

His language skills were remarkably well retained with only occasional signs of word-finding problems. Conversation was fluent,
directed, and meaningful. In fact Carl was quite glib and commonly
made puns and various plays on words. There was never a problem
with recognition of familiar faces, and he often initiated conversations

with people in the lab that followed up on earlier discussions. Oral reading was preserved, though comprehension of extended text was compromised. He could write sentences to dictation, but the letters were at times awkwardly formed. In contrast his figure copying was poor except for the simplest of forms.

Until 1986 Carl continued to slalom waterski, but he would not take a boat out alone. He had ceased driving a car in 1984. He could ride his bike alone in the environs of his second home at the seashore, but would occasionally get lost. At times he confused the layouts of his two houses. His favorite relaxation, playing the guitar, continues to this day to give him pleasure. He remains able to play familiar songs and to jam, but for several years now he has been unable to tune the guitar himself. He has a moderate ideomotor apraxia, dramatically demonstrated by his complete inability to simulate playing a guitar just after having skillfully played one.

Over the past year Carl's decline has become more apparent and has encroached on areas of function that were previously relatively preserved. His attention span has markedly decreased. At times his conversation is rambling and difficult to follow. He comes confused and disoriented in his home, particularly at night. His recall of recent events and conversations has deteriorated. He often remembers some aspect of an event, but confuses or misinterprets the specific details. He is unable to dress or bathe himself and when feeding himself occasionally uses the wrong utensil.

Carl's world has markedly narrowed. He no longer skis or rides a bike. He never goes out without his wife, and in fact he clings to her now, to the point of waiting outside the bathroom door for her. There is increasing tearfulness as he witnesses and remarks on his own decline. He continues to want to be of help, yet even has to be told where to place his hands when he carries something. Nevertheless, in the face of this obvious deterioration, Carl is still able to make pithy and appropriate remarks in context, often drawing on a fund of knowledge that remains considerable.

Pattern of Cognitive Impairments
Carl's performance on a range of neuropsychological and cognitive tests is summarized in table 9.1. As tracked by repeated administration of the Mattis Dementia Rating Scale (Coblentz et al. 1973), his mental status clearly declined over the three-year period of this study. Also evident from the data in table 9.1 is the significant discrepancy between verbal and perceptual functions.

This discrepancy was evident in the pattern of WAIS-R scores. Though the WAIS verbal IQ obtained in 1984 no doubt represents

Table 9.1
Results of Neuropsychological Testing: Carl

Test	1984	1985	1986	1987
Dementia Rating Scale	112/144	115/144	93/144	72/144
WAIS verbal IQ	98	103	93	
performance IQ	70	68	62	
Vocabulary (S.S.)	15	14	14	
Comprehension (S.S.)	12	14	11	
Similarities (S.S.)	11	10	14	
Digit span (S.S.)	8	8	7	
Arithmetic (S.S.)	4	5	4	
Picture completion (S.S.)	7	6	3	
Block design (S.S.)	3	2	2	
Boston Naming Test	78/85	68/85	66/85	37/60
Lexical Comprehension Test[a]				
Within category	32/32	32/32	32/32	28/32
Across category	32/32	32/32	32/32	32/32
Peabody Picture Vocabulary	163/175		138/175	
Word Fluency (Mean of 3)				
Letters	12	16	16	12
Semantic categories	3	4	1	1
NART-Revised[b]	47/50	45/50	44/50	41/50
Benton Tests				
Visual form discrimination	can't do at all			
Line orientation	12/30			
Facial recognition	13/27			
Dot Localization	18/20		11/20	
Wechsler Memory Scale	66	62		
Logical memory	6	5		
Visual reproduction	no scorable renditions			

[a] Word-picture matching test with 4 picture choices. See Schwartz and Chawluk, chapter 8, for further description of this task.
[b] This is a version of the New Adult Reading Test (Nelson and O'Connell 1977), adapted for use with American subjects.

a significant decline from premorbid levels, it is still in the normal range; in contrast performance IQ is well below normal. There is scatter within the verbal scales as well; scores on vocabulary, comprehension, and similarities are at average or superior levels, and digit span and arithmetic scores are below the normal range.

Language functions per se were very well preserved at the outset. The verbal facility evident in Carl's conversational speech was borne out in formal testing. Thus naming and word comprehension performance, which were in the normal range in 1984–1985, only began to show significant decline in 1987. The lack of impairment on naming and comprehension tasks indicates that semantic processes were relatively intact in the early phases of this study. Reading at the single-word level, as measured by a 50-item list of orthographically irregular words (the NART-Rev, a modified version of Nelson and O-Connell 1977), remained relatively intact over the course of the study period; however, reading of text, which was initially well preserved, rapidly deteriorated. The difficulty here appeared to be in scanning across a line of text and moving to the next line, suggesting a perceptual rather than linguistic limitation.

Indeed many visuoperceptual tasks proved extremely difficult for Carl from the outset. He was completely unable to perform the Benton Visual Form Discrimination Test, which requires matching of an array of three geometric forms to an identical array in a set of four choices. His performance on the Benton line orientation and face perception tests was severely impaired; on the latter he failed to match identical photos (2 of 6 correct) as well as different poses of the same individual (11 of 21 correct). Constructional tasks, such as copying figures, were performed very poorly. Periodic attempts to test him on the Tower of London task (Shallice 1982), a test of nonverbal planning, always resulted in complete failure. The task involves rearranging three colored balls, arrayed on pegs, to match a pattern illustrated on a card; Carl was unable to perform even the simplest training trials, which require movement of a single ball to an adjacent peg.

Carl's most striking failures occurred on tasks that required him to make comparisons across two sets of stimuli, as in the Benton and Tower of London tests, for example. This suggested that the source of his difficulty might lie in performing comparison operations. Results of two studies argued against this hypothesis, however. He performed well on a task, adapted from Warrington (1975), in which he had to decide which of two objects would in real life be the larger (for example, *squirrel* versus *butterfly*). The objects were represented in the form of line drawings in one version of the task and as word pairs in another. In the pictorial version the two objects were approximately the same size. In 1984 Carl was 20 out of 20 correct on the pictorial version and 19 out of 20 on the verbal version. (As in most tasks there are indications of a recent decline in performance: Carl scored 14 out of 20 on the pictorial version and 18 out of 20 on the verbal version in 1987.) His ability to perform this task indicates that he is not impaired in making comparative judgments per se; rather the difficulty appears to be specific to certain kinds of materials. The specificity of the deficit was most clearly demonstrated by Carl's performance on the spatial semantic test. This test, which is modeled on a task described by Veroff (1978), contrasts spatial versus semantic abilities using the event-sequencing format of the picture arrangement subtest of the WAIS. Rather than requiring subjects to rearrange individual cards as in the WAIS, we simplified the task by presenting a fixed 3-item sequence in which there is a choice of two pictures at one of the three event slots. (See figures 8.6 and 8.7.) In the spatial subtest the choice is governed by spatial constraints (for example, the trajectory followed by an arrow in its path from bow to target); in the semantic subtest the choice is governed by conceptual information (for example, the stages in the life cycle of a butterfly). In 1984 Carl's performance was virtually normal on the semantic sequences (17 of 18 correct; the mean for age-matched controls was 17.7, SD = 0.6), but poor on the spatial sequences (12 of 18; the normal mean was 16.3, SD = 1.6). These results indicate that Carl is particularly impaired in dealing with visuospatial information.[2]

The claim is not, however, that other cognitive capacities remained entirely intact. Thus though Carl did not appear grossly amnesic in daily life or in our informal contacts with him, he performed poorly on formal memory tests from the outset. When initially tested in 1984, he obtained a Wechsler memory quotient of 66, which is comparable to his WAIS performance score. He was impaired on verbal memory subtests of the WMS as well as on the visual reproduction subtest (on which he scored 0); only his digits forward score (7) was in the normal range. But even in the context of more general intellectual decline, the severity of his visual deficits was striking, the more so in contrast to his verbal facility.

Studies of Carl's Visual Impairment
Although Carl found some visual tasks extremely difficult, he performed quite well on others. In particular his ability to identify objects remained intact until the latter stages of our three-year study. Thus he performed well on picture naming tests (table 9.1) and also on the various comprehension and judgment tasks involving pictures that

were described previously. Not surprisingly he had little difficulty on an "object decision" task in which the distractors were composites of two real objects (for example, scissor handles with a screw replacing the cutting blades)[3]; his score as recently as February 1987 was 90 percent correct. When first tested (see table 9.1), he performed as well as age-matched controls on our laboratory's version of Warrington and Taylor's (1973) "unusual views" task, which involves naming objects photographed at unconventional angles (for example, a toaster seen from the top).

The critical factor in Carl's ability to perform visual tasks appeared to be the number of discrete elements in the array. Thus he had little difficulty with stimulus configurations that constituted unitary and familiar patterns; he identified single objects and words, for example, with relative ease. He was also able to locate specific targets in multi-item arrays, as in picture-word matching tasks involving multiple distractors. The tasks that proved difficult for him required him to respond to novel configurations of a number of discrete elements. Tasks that impose such demands, like the Benton Visual Form Discrimination and Tower of London tests, were beyond him from the first. Later he began to have difficulty with tasks that involve simpler arrays, such as dot localization (table 9.1). The stimuli for this task consist of two squares, each containing a single dot; the subject's task is to determine which of the two dots is off-center (Warrington and Rabin 1970). Carl's poor performance on these tasks suggested the possibility of a *simultanagnosic* disorder.

Although there is some disagreement about the nature of simultanagnosia (Bay 1953, Bender and Feldman 1972), and even with respect to the set of clinical phenomena over which this label should be applied (Balint 1909, Wolpert 1924, Luria 1959, Kinsbourne and Warrington 1962), for our present purposes it is a useful one. We use it here to indicate a perceptual disturbance that emerges with arrays consisting of more than a single familiar element. To determine whether Carl's visual deficit could properly be characterized as a simultanagnosia, a number of experimental investigations were carried out.

Tachistoscopic Recognition of Shapes and Objects   One of the hallmarks of simultanagnosia is an inability to perceive two distinct objects at once. One measure of such a disorder is a significant increase in the time required to recognize a pair of items versus a single item under tachistoscopic conditions.

Carl's ability to identify single objects remained well preserved until 1987. As early as 1985, however, he was markedly slow in identifying two geometric shapes. Shape recognition was examined using a Gerbrands four-field tachistoscope with a central fixation marker presented for 500 ms before stimulus presentation. Carl indicated his response by pointing to the correct item in an array of five choices. At a 150-ms exposure he was able to recognize a single form such as a circle subtending 1.8° of visual angle at 85-percent accuracy (n = 20). In contrast, when presented with two shapes arrayed vertically, 1 cm apart, at a 1500-ms exposure, Carl was able to identify both items on only 60 percent of the trials (n = 20). Increasing the exposure time to 2000 ms did not improve performance. More recently (1987) he was asked to identify drawings of common objects (for example, airplane, heart) presented either singly or in sets of two. The stimuli, presented tachistoscopically, were each approximately 2 to 3 cm in diameter, subtending an average of 2.3° of visual angle. The two presentation conditions were blocked, using an ABBA design, with 20 trials per condition. In the two-item condition the drawings were again arrayed vertically, 1.5 cm apart. Carl was familiarized with the set of objects (n = 10) before testing. Each trial was preceded by a 500-ms central fixation marker. At a 200-ms exposure he was able to identify 90 percent of the single pictures correctly, whereas at 2000 ms he could identify both items on only 30 percent of the trials. Carl always reported at least one of the two targets, but there was no consistent pattern to its location.

Carl therefore demonstrates simultanagnosia in the recognition of objects. Before inquiring further into the nature of this impairment, we sought to determine whether it was specific to objects or would occur with printed words as well.

Word Reading under Brief Exposures   In this study we examined Carl's ability to read single words and pairs of words under controlled presentation conditions. We asked, in addition, whether his ability to read word pairs might be influenced by relations between the items.

Carl was able to identify three- to five-letter words presented singly for 150 ms on an Apple IIe green-screen monitor at 94-percent accuracy (n = 110). When pairs comprised of these same words were presented, his performance was markedly worse. The stimuli consisted of 90 pairs of words arrayed side by side in the center of the screen, with two spaces between them. A central fixation marker (an asterisk) remained on the screen until the trial was initiated. Thirty of the paired items were semantically unrelated (for example, *pie ache*), 30 were semantically related (for example, *lemon lime*), and 30 were potential compounds (for example, *honey moon*). Word frequency was equivalent for the three conditions. The task was administered four

Table 9.2
Reading of Words and Word Pairs: Carl

Single-Word Presentation

Exposure	Number of words read correctly
150 ms	100/110
	94%

Two-Word Presentation

	Number of trials on which both words read correctly			
Exposure	Unrelated	Related	Compounds	Total
300 ms	28/60	32/60	41/60	101/180
	47%	53%	68%	56%
800 ms[a]	20/30	21/30	27/30	68/90
	67%	70%	90%	76%
	Number of trials on which one word read correctly			
300 ms	28/60	23/60	12/60	63/180
	47%	38%	20%	35%
800 ms[a]	10/30	8/30	3/30	21/90
	33%	27%	10%	23%

[a] Due to a coding error, only one of the 800-ms data sets could be used.

times over two sessions—twice at a 300-ms exposure and twice at 800-ms—using an ABBA design.

Comparing first his performance on single words versus two-word arrays, we see a clear effect of stimulus number. Although Carl read 94 percent of single words presented at 150 ms, his performance dropped to 70 percent of total words when two unrelated words were presented at 300 ms. Two normal subjects of the same age showed essentially no effect of array size. Tested with single words at 50 ms, one subject was 96 percent correct, and the other 92 percent correct; tested with word pairs at 100 ms, their performance levels were 95 percent and 89 percent, respectively.

Carl's performance as a function of the relatedness of the word pairs is summarized in table 9.2. At a 300-ms exposure there was a significant difference in the proportion of trials on which both words were reported correctly ($\chi^2(2) = 8.65$, $p < .01$). There was no difference between semantically related and unrelated pairs ($\chi^2(1) = 1.20$, $p < .3$), but the compounds yielded better performance than did the unrelated condition ($\chi^2(1) = 7.58$, $p < .01$). At 800-ms exposure his overall performance improved, but the pattern was similar; the effect of stimulus type did not reach significance, however ($\chi^2(2) = 5.17$, $p < .08$). On trials on which a single word was reported correctly, items were reported equally often from both positions.

Although the effect is not quite as dramatic for verbal stimuli as it is for objects, we again see that the presence of the second item exacts a significant toll. However, this effect is tempered somewhat by relations between the items. Performance improves significantly if the two words form a potential compound—if they constitute, in effect, a single item. We have demonstrated a similiar effect in a patient with simultanagnosia due to bilateral focal lesions (Coslett and Saffran 1987).

For the compound word effect to occur, both items have to be processed to a level at which the relation between the words is represented. Carl's simultanagnosia could not, therefore, reflect a low-level restriction of visual input, such as would result from a visual field defect. It seems unlikely, as well, that the difficulty reflects a general slowing in the rate of visual processing; slowing could limit the number of stimuli identified in a brief exposure and has in fact been demonstrated in some patients who have difficulty identifying objects presented simultaneously (for example, Kinsbourne and Warrington 1962). The more than tenfold increase in the exposure time that Carl required to identify a second object argues against an explanation solely in terms of decreased processing rate per item, as does a trend toward better performance when two words were presented sequentially at 150 ms per word, as compared with simultaneous presentation for 300 ms (60 percent versus 49 percent of pairs read correctly; McNemar Test, $\chi^2(1) = 3.27$, $.10 > p > .05$).

We next considered the possibility that the deficit was the result of a limitation on selective attention.

Attentive versus Preattentive Processing   Current theories distinguish between two different modes of processing visual information: a *preattentive* mode, characterized by parallel processing, and an *attentive* mode, in which processing is capacity limited and sequential. As defined in the work of Treisman and her colleagues (for example, Treisman and Gelade 1980, Treisman and Souther 1985), the preattentive level involves the parallel processing of elementary visual features, such as color, line orientation, and movement. Preattentive processing is illustrated by the seemingly effortless detection of a stimulus that differs from distractors by a single parameter, such as a green letter in a field of red letters, that pops out of the field independent of the number of distractors in the array. Normal seeing requires the integration of information across the several feature maps. According to Treisman, this process is mediated by a limited-capacity, effort-requiring mechanism, often called *selective attention*, which links corresponding regions (in the sense of shared spatial

PREATTENTIVE -12

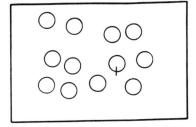

ATTENTIVE-12

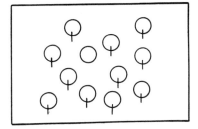

Figure 9.1
Examples of stimulus cards for the preattentive and attentive conditions

coordinates) of the maps to achieve integration. An attentive task commonly involves the conjunction of features, takes significantly longer than featural detection, and is highly sensitive to the number of elements in the array. Could Carl's impairment reflect a limitation at one of these processing levels?

Adapting a paradigm from Treisman and Souther (1985), we presented 6- and 12-circle arrays under preattentive and attentive conditions, as well as a simple detection task in which the target was a single circle appearing anywhere on the card. The preattentive target, which appeared on half of the trials, consisted of a circle subtending .5° of visual angle and intersected by a vertical line at the 6 o'clock position to form a figure similar to a Q. The subject's task was to respond by pressing a key when the target was present. In the attentive condition the target was a plain circle in a field of Q's; the task was to respond when a circle was present. Sample stimuli from the preattentive and attentive conditions are presented in figure 9.1. As demonstrated by Treisman and Souther (1985), these conditions satisfy the criteria for the preattentive/attentive distinction; their subjects showed no significant effect of array size in the Q-detection task, but did show a clear effect of number of distractors in detecting a circle in a field of Q's. The Q-detection task is simpler, one presumes, because activation anywhere in a line feature map is sufficient to signal the presence of a single Q; to detect a circle in an array of Q's, however, it is necessary to integrate across circle and line feature maps and search for a location at which only the circle is present.

A Gerbrands four-field tachistoscope, controlled by an Apple computer, was used to present the stimulus cards, which were preceded by a 1000-ms fixation stimulus. The stimulus array remained in view for 4000 ms or until the trial was terminated by a key press signalling detection of the target. Half of the targets were to the left and half to the right of fixation, but their location, as well as that of distractors, was otherwise random. Targets were present on half the trials. Normal age-matched control subjects (n = 8) performed the full complement of 480 trials: 160 in the simple detection condition and 80 in each of the other conditions; the experiment was administered in four sessions, each of which began and ended with a block of 20 simple detection trials. Each of the other conditions was split into two blocks of 40 trials and presented in a counterbalanced design across the four sessions. Each block of trials was preceded by training items. As Carl proved unable to perform the attentive task, these conditions were deleted after the first session.

The results are summarized in table 9.3. Though Carl is notably slower than age-matched controls, he shows an essentially normal pattern—that is, no effect of array size—on the preattentive condition. However, in contrast to control subjects, who show no visual field differences, he tends to respond more slowly to targets in the left visual field. The visual field difference is significant on the preattentive-12 condition ($t = 2.67$, $p < .02$) and approaches significance on the preattentive-6 condition ($t = 1.70$, $.10 > p > .05$). Where he differs most dramatically from control subjects is on the attentive condition: Carl was completely unable to perform the attentive task at either array size under tachistoscopic presentation. Given that he was

Table 9.3
Target Detection under Preattentive and Attentive Conditions: Carl

| | Reaction Time (ms) | | | | | |
| | Carl | | | Normal Subjects (n = 8) | | |
	RVF	LVF	Mean	RVF	LVF	Mean
Simple Detection	857	764	810	490	488	489
Preattentive-6	1026	1166	1076	591	599	595
Preattentive-12	951	1190	1070	651	672	662
Attentive-6	Unable to do			1042	963	1002
Attentive-12	Unable to do			1990	1529	1762

able to explain the task verbally and could occasionally identify a target in free field with unlimited exposure, his poor performance could not be attributed to failure to comprehend the task requirements. The pattern Carl demonstrated—a right visual field advantage on the preattentive task and complete failure on the attentive condition—has been seen in some patients with neglect due to focal hemispheric lesions (Fitzpatrick, Coslett, and Saffran 1988; see also Riddoch and Humphreys 1987).[4] Using a somewhat different experimental paradigm, adapted from Sagi and Julesz (1985), we have demonstrated a similar pattern in a patient with simultanagnosia due to bilateral focal lesions (Coslett and Saffran 1987).

Carl's performance pattern on the detection task is indicative of an attentional limitation. In light of his performance on the word reading task, however, it does not appear that the attentional problem impinges on feature integration per se. The fact that his ability to read a second word is influenced by the relation between the two words indicates that the normally unseen item must be processed to a fairly high level. Exclusion of a second stimulus item must occur not early in visual processing but at the level of conscious perception of the array. The question of whether attentional capacity is required early or late in visual processing is in fact controversial (for example, Duncan 1980, Kahneman and Treisman 1984, Pashler and Badgio 1985). As we suggest elsewhere in discussing similar results in another simultanagnosic patient (Coslett and Saffran 1987), it may be that attentional resources are required at more than one stage in the processing of visual information.

Summary: Carl

Carl's condition represents a form of progressive dementia in which visuoperceptual impairment is the most prominent feature. The perceptual deficits appear to reflect a limitation on the number of discrete elements that can be explicitly identified in the visual display, the ability to recognize single objects and words remaining relatively intact, that is, simultanagnosia. We have characterized this limitation as an attentional problem that arises at a late stage in visual processing, subsequent to feature integration and to the matching of integrated features to a stored pattern. The restriction appears to lie in the articulation between perceptual processes and conscious awareness.

Case 2: Marie

The severity of the deficits manifested by our second patient, Marie, greatly restricted the manner and scope of our investigation. The phenomena are striking, however, and appear quite similar to deficits described in other patients with progressive visual disorders (for example, Pick 1908, Bender and Feldman 1972, Cogan 1985). Though incomplete, these observations allow at least a provisional characterization of a profound and disabling form of visual impairment that may be specific to degenerative brain disease.

Clinical History and Neurodiagnostic Information
Marie was born in rural France, where she attended school until the seventh grade. Marie met her husband during World War II and returned with him to the United States, where they settled in rural Pennsylvania. Marie worked for a number of years in a clothing factory and in her late forties became involved in purchasing and selling antiques. The first signs of her illness occurred in 1982, when she seemed to have great difficulty coming out of mourning after the death of her brother. Marie began misplacing things; pepperoni was found in the silverware drawer, the keys often couldn't be located. She was referred to a neurologist and then a psychologist who largely ascribed the symptoms to normal grief and mourning. Marie was 57 then. She was still involved in the antique business and still drove herself around the eastern part of the state. In the summer of 1983 she was able to travel alone to see her family in France. Sometime that following year, though, Marie had to be helped home from an antique show. She began to have difficulty driving and would get confused on right/left directions. She was increasingly fearful around the house, afraid to use an iron, afraid to use the stove, but was unable to explain her fearfulness. Previously a gracious and competent hostess, she began withdrawing from people. Her husband, who had retired, gradually took over the household chores.

When Marie was again examined by a neurologist in 1984, difficulty in eye-hand coordination was noted. Her visual exam was normal. The neurologic exam was otherwise normal except for some frontal release signs and impaired recent memory after a brief delay. The CT scan was interpreted as normal with what was characterized as age-appropriate atrophy. A diagnosis of progressive dementia, presumably of the Alzheimer type, was made. This same diagnosis was made when Marie came to Temple University Hospital in late 1985. The dementia evaluation performed at that time revealed no neurological evidence of focal pathology. What was striking, however, was the profound degree of visual and visual-motor involvement in the face of normal acuity, normal eye movements, and normal visual fields on confrontation testing. (She was unable to perform formal computerized visual fields.) Marked deficits were noted in visually guided behavior during visits to our laboratory. She was unable, for example, to find the handle of the door to the ladies' room or to locate the starting point on the trail making test even after her finger was placed on it by the examiner.

Over the next year anecdotes related by her husband were very revealing. Although Marie was often unable to read material placed in front of her, there were instances when she quickly and accurately read a sign at some distance from the car in which they were riding. If she dropped an object, she was generally unable to find it, even when he pointed to the floor at her feet. In contrast other areas of function remained relatively preserved. Thus her memory impairment remained mild, and although she needed help in selecting her clothes, she was otherwise able to dress herself and needed no assistance with her personal hygiene. Socially Marie could well hold her own, and she has an elegance and grace that remains to this day.

In the past year and a half, there has been continued decline. Marie has become disoriented at home and confuses the upstairs and downstairs. She cannot leave the yard and reliably find her way home. She can no longer dress without assistance, but continues to bathe herself and to eat with the proper utensil. Her husband reports that Marie now often picks up his fork, which is to her right, rather than her own. He also describes incidents in which she denies seeing an object (for example, an antique lamp) placed in front of her and then, after shifting her position, suddenly notices the object and describes the importance of the piece. Marie herself reports often seeing only part of things and guessing from there. When she takes an object in her hand, she will generally use it correctly, but there have been times, when asked to identify an object or picture that she is holding, that she has turned it on end or backward. Marie is having much more difficulty maneuvering around without bumping into things and on occasion has sat down on the trash can instead of a chair. She is also beginning to have difficulty recognizing familiar faces. Nevertheless, despite increasing difficulty in word retrieval, she still carries on a coherent conversation and can relate events accurately that occurred days before. She knows the general time of day and usually the season and the place. She is also very much aware of her difficulties and maintains her interest in and concern for others.[5] Although Marie's abilities have declined, the severity of her visual deficits remains disproportionate to her general level of functioning.

Pattern of Cognitive Impairments
By the time this study began early in 1986, most standard neuropsychological tests were beyond Marie's capabilities. In addition to the

visual impairment, which ruled out the use of materials containing complex visual arrays, difficulty with word finding further limited the scope of formal testing.

From the outset Marie exhibited word-finding difficulty in conversational speech, as well as in formal testing. Word retrieval appeared to be less impaired in her native French than in English, though she groped for words in French as well. (In formal testing credit was given for correct responses in French.) When initially tested early in 1986, Marie was only able to identify 5 of the first 15 line drawings of objects on the Boston Naming Test without cuing; an additional 7 were named after a semantic (n = 5) or phonemic cue (n = 2) was provided. In some instances she appeared to be responding to a part of the picture rather than the whole (for example, she identified a picture of a car as "a wheel" and a tree as "leaves"). Naming of a set of real objects was somewhat better (9 of 22 correct in English; 15 of 22 correct in French), as was naming to verbal description of another set of objects (11 of 14 correct). She also responded correctly to all 10 items on the responsive naming subtest of the Boston Diagnostic Aphasia Examination.

The effect of presentation mode on naming was systematically explored in a subsequent study (administered in June 1987), in which the same items were presented under three conditions: visually as line drawings and as objects and in the form of verbal descriptions. The task was administered in three sessions. The order of conditions was counterbalanced across sessions, and each object was tested only once per session. Marie named 2 of 27 items correctly in the picture condition, 14 of 27 in the object condition, and 10 of 27 to description. (Normal subjects made no more than one error on any condition.)

Although naming is impaired irrespective of the manner in which it is probed, the disproportionate difficulty in identifying line drawings of objects suggests that there is an agnosic disturbance in addition to a language deficit. The impairment in visual object identification is further demonstrated by Marie's performance on a categorization task, in which she was asked to determine whether an object, represented either in a line drawing or named auditorily, belonged to a particular category (*animal* or *food*). The animal set contained 30 items and the food set 36; half of the items in each set were distractors from other categories. Overall Marie was 62 out of 66 correct on the words and performed at chance (32 of 66 correct) on pictures.

Marie's performance on object decision tasks provides additional evidence of difficulty in visual object recognition. In a task in which she had to determine which of two line drawings represented a real object, she performed poorly (14 of 20 correct), though the distractors had little resemblance to known objects. In a more difficult task administered in August 1986, the nonobjects were comprised of parts of two real objects[3]; half of the 40 nonobjects were composites of two objects from the same category, and half of objects from different categories. Marie was presented with a single object per trial, and she indicated her judgment verbally. Performance was essentially at chance; she responded correctly to 22 of 40 real objects and classified 11 of 20 of the across-category composites and 9 of 20 of the within-category composites as real.

Because Marie often had difficulty locating a single visual stimulus on a page, let alone in scanning multiple items for comparison, testing was necessarily restricted to single items. Working within these limitations, it was possible to determine that perception of colors was reasonably intact; Marie named 8 of 10 color patches correctly. She was also able to read single words fairly adequately; thus she was correct on 65 out of 78 words on the Coltheart list (Coltheart et al. 1979), which consists of orthographically regular and irregular words matched for frequency. Letter naming was also well preserved; she named 23 of 26 upper-case letters correctly. Her relatively good performance with graphemic stimuli provided a baseline from which effects of various perceptual factors could be evaluated.

Nature of Marie's Visual Impairment

Effect of Size on Word and Letter Identification   In view of Marie's visual impairment, reading was initially tested using large print. She failed completely on these tasks, only to succeed later when tested using standard typewritten stimuli. The effect of size on word and letter identification was investigated systematically.

Marie was asked to read high-frequency, three- to five-letter words printed in $\frac{1}{4}$- or 1-inch letters at a distance of 18 inches. She read 24 of 30 words correctly in the smaller print but only 7 of 30 of the same words in the larger print. The effect of print size was highly significant (McNemar Test: $\chi^2(1) = 14.7$, $p < .001$). Word length appeared to be a limiting factor in reading the larger print. Thus Marie correctly read 5 of 10 of the three-letter words, 2 of 10 of the four-letter words, and none of the five-letter words. There was no comparable effect with the smaller letters; in fact 4 of a total of 6 errors on the $\frac{1}{4}$-inch print occurred on the three-letter words. Of the total of 29 errors across both print sizes, 6 involved report of a single letter, in most instances (4 of 6) from the end of the word; most of the remainder were substitution errors (for example, *earth* $\longrightarrow$ "artery," *queen* $\longrightarrow$

"quit"), which incorporated some of the letters in the target word, but not consistently from any particular location.

The size factor was also investigated using single letters. Marie was 23 out of 25 (the letter I was omitted from this task) correct on $\frac{1}{2}$-inch letters, 16 out of 25 of 1-inch letters, and 7 out of 25 on $2\frac{1}{2}$-inch letters, all displayed at a distance of 15 inches. The effect of size as highly significant (Cochran's Q = 22.7, $p < .001$).

The size effect indicated that the deficit was due, at least in part, to a spatial restriction on perceptual processing. Restriction of the effective visual field could also account for other observations, such as Marie's failure to recognize objects directly in front of her while at the same time being able to read signs at a distance and her tendency to identify part of an object rather than the object as a whole. Reducing line drawings to a diameter of 2 to 3 cm did not, however, produce any consistent improvement in object naming or categorization tasks.

Other Effects on Letter Identification   In addition to size we examined the effects of altering the letter stimuli in various ways: complicating the letter form by using block letters, rendering the letter form discontinuous, and adding extraneous elements (straight and wavy lines) to the display. These manipulations are illustrated in figure 9.2. Two sets of letters with extraneous lines were prepared: one with the lines drawn in red ink and the other with black lines that were somewhat less saturated than the black letters. Examples from the latter set are provided in figure 9.2E.

The results are summarized in table 9.4. All departures from standard letter forms (conditions A and E.1 in table 9.4) resulted in per-

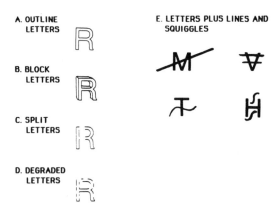

Figure 9.2
Examples of stimuli from letter identification tasks

Table 9.4
Factors Affecting Letter Identification: Marie

Factor	% Correct
A. Outline letters (n = 25)	76
B. Block letters (n = 25)	44
C. Split letters (n = 25)	24
D. Degraded letters (n = 25)	20
E. Letters + Extraneous elements	
1. Letters alone (n = 25)	80
2. Letter + red (n = 40)	48
3. Letter + black (n = 40)	30

formance decrements. Even block letters, which are in fairly common use and do not involve degradation of the letter form, proved difficult for her, perhaps because of their additional complexity. In many instances she appeared to be responding on the basis of part of the stimulus pattern. For example, the V in figure 9.2E was identified as an F, and the H as an S; the split R in figure 9.1C was called a 3. Normal subjects had no difficulty rapidly identifying letters under any of these conditions.

Thus although Marie was quite good at identifying canonical letter forms, her ability to recognize letters was markedly disrupted by increasing the size of the letter or the complexity of the letter form, by making the letter form discontinuous, and by adding extraneous elements to the display. Often she appeared to be responding on the basis of a restricted portion of the stimulus.

Could visual field defects account for her performance pattern? Marie's inability to fixate reliably precluded formal assessment of her visual fields. When first examined in 1986, however, her fields did appear full on confrontation testing. Upon reexamination in March 1988 her performance on confrontation testing was inconsistent, and the status of her visual fields equivocal. Further information relevant to early visual processing was obtained using the attentive/preattentive paradigm discussed previously.

Attentive versus Preattentive Processing   The Treisman and Souther (1985) task that was administered to Carl was also given to Marie. She had various difficulties, from positioning her head in the viewer of the tachistoscope (one of us had to manipulate her head into place and hold it there), to complying with the instruction to focus on the fixation stimulus (we were unable to monitor fixation and cannot be

Table 9.5
Target Detection under Preattentive and Attentive Conditions: Marie

	No. Correct	No. of Errors		
		Left	Right	False +
Simple detection	35/40	1/10	4/10	0/20
	38/40[a]	1/10	0/10	1/10
Preattentive-6	72/80	8/20	0/20	0/40
Preattentive-12	59/80	15/20	3/20	3/40
	27/40[a]	8/10	2/10	3/20
Attentive-6	Unable to do			
Attentive-12	Unable to do			

[a] Yes/no verbal response without manual response

sure that she did fixate reliably, even though a verbal check was carried out), to reliably pressing the response key (frequently she would acknowledge the presence of the target verbally, but neglect to press the key). Though reaction time data were unreliable, the error data yielded consistent patterns.

The data for this task are summarized in table 9.5. Marie's overall performance on the simple detection condition with a manual response was fairly good, though she missed some targets on the right; her performance was better when this task was repeated using a seemingly more reliable verbal (yes/no) response. On the preattentive conditions detection of targets was significantly better on the 6-item than 12-item arrays ($\chi^2(1) = 4.62$, $p < .05$). Combining across both preattentive conditions, targets were more likely to be detected in the right visual field than in the left ($\chi^2(1) = 20.6$, $p < .001$). This same right-sided superiority emerged when a half set of the preattentive-12 condition was run using a verbal response. In fact Marie performed fairly well in detecting targets on the right in the preattentive condition, showing little effect of the size of the array. She was, however, completely unable to perform the attentive task at either array size, even with unlimited presentation under free field conditions.

Marie's reasonably good performance on the simple detection task indicates that she is able to detect the presence of a stimulus at all locations in the approximately 8° tachistoscopic field. However, because fixation was not monitored and the pattern remained in view until she responded, it is not possible to rule out visual field defects on the basis of these data. On a later occasion the simple detection task was administered using brief presentation (220 ms) to eliminate the possibility of eye movements. Marie had become virtually untestable by the time this study was performed late in 1988, and it was only possible to run a small number of trials on this task. Nevertheless she performed correctly on 16 of 18 trials, missing 1 target (out of 8) and producing 1 false alarm. Although it is not possible to draw firm conclusions on the basis of these limited data, the fact that she was able to detect stimuli subtending .5° of visual angle appearing in random locations in an 8° field does weigh against an account of her deficit in terms of severe constriction of the visual fields.

Moreover, though visual field constriction might explain the effect of size on letter and word recognition, it does not account for other observations obtained with letter stimuli, such as the effects of complexity and of extraneous elements in the display. An alternative to the field cut hypothesis is a spatial restriction of attentional capacity—in effect a narrowing of the spotlight of visual attention. Whereas the visual field restriction hypothesis implies that fixed portions of the retinal array are excluded from higher levels of visual processing,[6] the attentional hypothesis allows the region that receives limited, or suboptimal, processing to vary. The attentional hypothesis also predicts that detection of targets will vary as function of the number of elements in the array.

One further attempt was made to examine Marie's ability to detect stimuli over the visual field, this time in a more natural context.

Detecting Visual Stimuli: The Tablecloth Experiment   Marie generally had difficulty locating and reaching for objects in space, in real-life settings as well as in tasks performed in the laboratory. Informal observations suggested, however, that the difficulty was more acute in complex or "busy" environments. In this study we examined Marie's ability to retrieve objects as a function of background complexity. We reasoned that if Marie's visual impairment were attributable solely to a static restriction in the size of her visual field, her performance would not be greatly influenced by the background against which the object was placed; the field would have to be scanned irrespective of background complexity. On an attentional hypothesis, in contrast, serial search would be necessary only when the background was busy.

To test this hypothesis, Marie was seated at the end of a large (4 × 10 ft) table covered by a tablecloth. An object was placed on the table while she sat quietly with her eyes closed. Marie was instructed to open her eyes and pick up "the thing that's on the table." Six different tablecloths, representing three distinct levels of visual complexity, were used as background. Solid cloths, one white and one mauve, were judge to be the least busy; tablecloths containing pastel checks (approximately 3-inch squares) and blue and white checks (approximately $\frac{1}{2}$-inch squares) provided an intermediate level of complexity; and two tablecloths with elaborate large scale prints (one floral, one batik) provided the greatest degree of background complexity. Target objects included a plastic flower, a red wooden ball approximately one inch in diameter, a metal spoon, and a small ($1.5 \times 2 \times 1$ inch) cardboard box. A single object was placed at one of four positions located 12 inches to the right and to left of Marie's midline, and 9 and 24 inches from the table's edge. No attempt was made to constrain movement of Marie's head or eyes.[7] After a series of practice trials, 16 blocks of 6 trials each were performed. Each tablecloth was used once in each block. The location of object presentation was randomized.

The procedure was recorded on videotape. Two judges who were naive with respect to the nature of the experiment independently recorded (to the nearest 0.1 s, using a handheld stopwatch) the time elapsed from initiation of visual search to grasping the object.

There was, in general, excellent agreement between the two judges; they differed by more than 2 s on only 3 of 96 trials. For the purposes of the analysis, data from both judges were used to generate a mean response time for each trial. Marie was unable to locate the object on 11 of the 96 trials. Because successful trials seldom took more than a minute, an elapsed time of 60 seconds was recorded for trials on which she failed to locate the object.

A two-factor ANOVA was performed in which the independent variables included the visual complexity of the background (plain, checked, print) and side of presentation (right, left), and the dependent variable was the time required to locate the object. The analysis revealed a significant effect of visual complexity ($F = 29.98$, df $= 2$, $p < .0001$). Marie required 5.1 s to locate objects presented on the plain backgrounds, 3.9 s on the checked backgrounds, and 28.3 s on the print backgrounds. Post hoc assessment (Tukey) demonstrated that performance with the print backgrounds differed significantly from the other two conditions ($p < .01$).

A significant effect of side of presentation was also noted ($F = 5.79$, df $= 1$, $p < .02$); Marie required 8.9 s to locate objects presented on the right side, but 15.9 s on the left. Analysis of the 11 trials on which she failed to locate the object was consistent with the results described here. All failures occurred with the print backgrounds; 8 of the 11 occurred on trials on which the stimulus was presented on the left.

Marie's ability to locate an object in space is therefore greatly affected by the complexity of the background against which objects are presented. The apparent difficulty in discriminating figure from ground is not surprising; more significant, for our present purposes, is that she was able to locate objects fairly easily in the absence of distractors in the visual field. Although these data do not exclude the possibility of visual field defects, her performance on this task suggests that the primary source of her difficulty is not constriction of the visual fields, which would be expected to impede stimulus detection irrespective of background complexity.[8]

An alternative explanation of Marie's impairment is, as suggested previously, a narrowing of the *attentional* field. On this hypothesis the difficulty is not in processing feature information across the retinal array, but in the capacity to integrate that information. There are a number of forms that an attentional deficit hypothesis could take. One is that the amount of attentional capacity—to use the spotlight analogy, the intensity of the "beam"—required to achieve an integrated representation is abnormally high in this patient. The narrowing of the beam follows from the fact that the efficacy of the attentional spotlight is inversely related to its diameter (for example, Eriksen and St. James 1986); hence where a powerful beam is required to achieve integrated representation, visual percepts will be spatially restricted. Although speculative, this account of Marie's deficit provides a parsimonious explanation of her impairment pattern. Consider, for example, the fact that Marie continued to be able to identify letters and words at a point when object drawings of comparable dimensions were completely unrecognizable. Though the size of the stimulus class may be a factor here, it seems likely that the perception of object forms, which are generally more complex than letters, entails a greater requirement for integrative capacity. It is noteworthy that Marie's performance on letters declined when more complex letter shapes (block letters) were used (table 9.4).

An account of the deficit in terms of decreased integrative capacity is also compatible with the characterization of Alzheimer's disease that is emerging from recent anatomical studies. Not only does the regional distribution of the pathological changes indicate a predilection for association cortex, but the laminar distribution indicates that the cells that sustain internal cortical connections are the primary targets of the degenerative process. On the basis of these data, AD has been characterized as a *cortico-cortical disconnection syndrome* (Morrison et al. 1986). Because early visual processing appears to involve parallel extraction of feature information (color, line orientation, movement, and so on) by processors that are anatomically discrete as well as functionally differentiated (for example, Zeki 1981), a decrease in cortical connectivity is likely to result in serious disruption of basic perceptual functions. The deficit pattern that we see in Marie, which closely resembles the behavioral description of other reported cases of progressive visual dysfunction, is a plausible manifestation of visual system disintegration. Pathological diagnoses are generally not available for these patients, but at least one patient has been histologically verified as having AD (Cogan 1985).

Summary: Marie

Marie's severity of visual disturbance again appears disproportionate to her general level of cognitive impairment. The difficulty in Marie's case extends to object recognition and includes apparent restriction of the effective visual field. Though our data are not conclusive, we suggest that the difficulty is best explained in terms of an impairment involving the integration of information in the visual system.

General Discussion

We have examined two patients with progressive cognitive dysfunction in whom visual impairment was a predominant feature from the outset. In the first patient, Carl, the most salient characteristic of the visual deficit is its simultanagnosic quality. Carl does fairly well in processing single visual stimuli, but his performance breaks down when the array contains multiple, discrete targets. We have characterized this as a deficit involving visual attention. The fact that Carl was found to have normal acuity and full visual fields gives support to the attentional hypothesis. The deficit in the second patient, Marie, is more profound. Marked for some period of time by failures in object recognition, the deficit is manifested, within the domain of stimuli that can still be identified, as a size limitation. We have suggested that this pattern can also be accounted for in terms of processes involving selective attention.

Though not studied in as much detail, phenomena similar to those we have described here have been reported in other patients with progressive dementia. For example, the two patients studied by De Renzi (1986) had difficulty recognizing pictures of objects and performed poorly on a range of perceptual tests, including discrimination of line length and visual angle; both had full visual fields and verbal IQ's in the normal range. Cogan (1985) reported on three patients with progressive dementia in whom visual disturbances were prominent. All experienced severe agnosic deficits and difficulty in reading, though other visual functions, such as acuity and color perception, were well preserved; one demonstrated a progressive left hemianopia. Pick's (1908) patient showed size constraints in visual perception and a tendency to recognize parts of objects rather than wholes. The four patients described by Bender and Feldman (1972) all demonstrated visual agnosia along with mislocalization of objects in space and generally worse performance on the left. There were indications of visual field deficits, particularly on the left, in all of their patients, but formal perimetric examinations could not be carried out and the defects were not consistently present. Patient 4 of their series appeared most similar to our patient Marie; this patient could read only small print, and this primarily in her right visual field. Bender and Feldman account for their observations in terms of the combined effects of low-level visual deficits and general intellectual impairment.

As dementia patients are subjected to increasingly extensive and rigorous examination, evidence of impairments at early levels of visual processing is indeed emerging. Hinton and colleagues (1986) have described degeneration in the optic nerves of Alzheimer's patients, and Sadun and Bassi (1987) have reported evidence for degeneration at all levels of the visual pathway, including retinal ganglion cells. Nissen and coworkers (1985) found that contrast sensitivity thresholds were elevated at all spatial frequencies in a group of 14 Alzheimer patients studied (but see Schlotterer et al. 1983 for negative findings). However, though cognitive deficits were present in this group, as indicated by WAIS scores and tests of memory function, none of these patients demonstrated difficulties in object or face recognition; evidently the decrease in contrast sensitivity did not have significant consequences for high-level perceptual functions. Data for one additional patient, who did manifest perceptual impairment, are reported separately. This patient, who had a right inferior homonymous quadrantopia, but an otherwise normal ocular examination, named colors well, but recognized only 1 of 20 line drawings of familiar objects. This patient also

> extinguished to double simultaneous stimulation on the right (in the superior as well as the inferior quadrant), and misreached with both hands in both visual fields. She was unable to discriminate faces . . . and reported that she recognized people by their voices or by remembering the color of clothing worn on a particular day. She and her husband reported that although she often failed to notice large objects and sometimes bumped into them, she nevertheless could detect a small spot or identify a small object on the floor. (p. 668)

Visual impairment, manifested as difficulty in "recognizing friends, identifying common objects, and reading," was the first sign of cognitive disturbance in this patient; signs of memory loss were not evident until four years later. This patient appears strikingly similar to our patient Marie. It is also significant that this patient showed a contrast sensitivity function that was very different from those of the other patients tested by Nissen and coworkers. Whereas her performance resembled theirs at high spatial frequencies (4 to 8 cycles per degree (cpd)), at lower frequencies (0.5 to 2 cpd) her sensitivity was markedly reduced. Because perception of the lower-frequency pattern presumably requires integration of information over a larger area of the visual field, this patient's performance on the contrast sensitivity test is consistent with the account of the deficit that we postulated for Marie. The findings on MRI are also of interest; in addition to moderately severe cerebral atrophy, the patient demonstrated asymmetrical lateral ventricular enlargement, greater in the left posterior portions of the left lateral ventricle, particularly in the left later occipital horn. The right visual field deficit is consistent with this asymmetry.

Most of the reported patients have in contrast exhibited greater impairment in processing stimuli presented in the left visual field (for example, Bender and Feldman 1972, Cogan 1985). Our patients demonstrated a greater deficit on the left even in the absence of demonstrable hemispheric asymmetries in structure and function as demonstrated by CT or SPECT scan. Although it is possible that this pattern of performance reflects an asymmetry in the distribution of the underlying pathology, an alternative possibility is that it reflects hemispheric asymmetry in the mechanisms mediating selective attention. Evidence consistent with this hypothesis comes from work by Posner and colleagues (1984) and Coslett, Saffran, and Fitzpatrick (1988) demonstrating more difficulty in shifting visual attention into the contralateral visual field after right as compared with left hemisphere CVA. In light of these data one might expect the bilateral hemispheric involvement commonly found in AD (for example, Martin et al 1986) to result in greater impairment in the deployment of attentional capacity in the left as compared with the right visual field.

Further understanding of the visual deficits in such patients will clearly require wide-ranging longitudinal studies of visual function, encompassing basic capacities as well as high-level perceptual functions. It seems unlikely, however, that the symptomatology that we have described in our patients can be explained on the basis of low-level visual deficits alone. Thus field cuts do not, in and of themselves, result in agnosias. We are also skeptical of Bender and Feldman's (1972) claim that the agnosic phenomena reflect an interaction between low-level visual disturbances and a nonspecific decline in intellectual function. Whereas cognitive deficits no doubt limit patients' ability to compensate for defective sensory input, it seems difficult to account, in these terms, for the severe and often quite selective perceptual deficits that we see in these patients. Explanations of this sort are also of little utility as heuristics for further research. We suggest that in many patients the deficits are more likely to be the manifestation of impairments involving higher—perhaps as well as lower—levels of visual processing, in which attentional processes figure either primarily or secondarily.

Acknowledgments

This research was supported by grants AG 06791 and K07 NS 00876 from the National Institutes of Health. We thank Myrna Schwartz for helpful comments on an early version of the manuscript.

Notes

1. We thank Jacqueline Stark for making a translation of Pick's paper available to us.
2. Note that Susan G., the progressive aphasic patient reported on by Schwartz and Chawluk (chapter 8), showed precisely the reverse performance pattern on this task. In general these patients present sharply contrasting test profiles, which appear to reflect the differential involvement of linguistic and visuoperceptual systems in the two.
3. Subsequent to this study Carl was assessed for neglect using tasks such as line bisection and line cancellation. He did indeed demonstrate neglect of stimuli on the left in these tasks.
4. See chapter 8 by Schwartz and Chawluk for further discussion of this task.
5. Interestingly Benson and colleagues (1988) comment on the preservation of personality characteristics in several of their patients with progressive visual disorders.
6. Or at least from conscious perception. The phenomenon of blindsight—the ability to respond to the presence of visual stimuli in the "blind" field without consciously perceiving them—has been reported in patients with dense hemianopias (for example, Weiskrantz et al. 1974).
7. Because fixation was not controlled, we make no claims with respect to the lateralization of stimuli within Marie's visual fields.
8. If the patient does indeed have an attentional disorder that results in narrowing of the effective field, the standard visual field examination, which requires fixation on a central stimulus, is like to yield spurious results. Attending to the fixation stimulus will limit the patient's ability to detect a target at another location. Several authors have in fact commented on the difficulty of obtaining consistent visual field data on patients with deficits similar to Marie's (for example, Bender and Feldman 1972, Cogan 1985).

References

Balint, R. (1909). Seelenlahmung des "Schauens," optische ataxie, raumlichestorung der aufmerksamkeit. *Mschr. Psychiat. Neurol.* 25: 57–71.
Bay, E. (1953). Disturbances of visual perception and their examination. *Brain* 76: 515–550.

Bender, M. B., and Feldman, M. (1972). The so-called "visual agnosias." *Brain* 95: 173–186.

Benson, D. F., Davis, J., and Snyder, B. D. (1988). Posterior cortical atrophy. *Archives of Neurology* 45: 789–793.

Coblentz, J. M., Mattis, S., Zingesser, L. H., Kasoff, S. S., Wisniewski, H. M., and Katzman, R. (1973). Presenile dementia: Clinical aspects and evaluation of cerebrospinal fluid dynamics. *Archives of Neurology* 29: 299–308.

Cogan, D. G. (1985). Visual disturbances with focal progressive dementing disease. *American Journal of Ophthalmology* 100: 68–72.

Coltheart, M., Besner, D., Jonasson, J. T., and Davalaar, E. (1979). Phonological recoding in the lexical decision task. *Quarterly Journal of Experimental Psychology* 31: 489–508.

Coslett, H. B., and Saffran, E. M. (1987). Simultanagnosia: Semantic factors and performance. (Abstract) *Neurology* 36: 134.

Coslett, H. B., Saffran, E. M., and Fitzpatrick, E. J. (1988). Impaired movement of selective attention in neglect. (Abstract) *Journal of Clinical and Experimental Neuropsychology* 10: 21.

Cummings, J. (1982). Cortical dementias. In D. F. Benson and D. Blumer (Ed.) *Psychiatric Aspects of Neurological Disease,* Vol. II. New York: Grune and Stratton.

De Renzi, E. (1986). Slowly progressive visual agnosia or apraxia without dementia. *Cortex* 22: 171–180.

Duncan, J. (1980). The locus of interference in the perception of simultaneous stimuli. *Psychological Review* 87: 272–300.

Eriksen, C. W., and St. James, J. D. (1986). Visual attention within and around the field of focal attention: A zoom lens model. *Perception and Psychophysics* 40: 225–240.

Fitzpatrick, E. J., Coslett, H. B., and Saffran, E. M. (1988). Preattentive and attentive processes in brain-damaged patients. (Abstract) *Journal of Clinical and Experimental Neuropsychology* 10: 29.

Hinton, D. R., Sadun, A. A., Blanks, J. C., and Miller, C. A. (1986). Optic-nerve degeneration in Alzheimer's disease. *New England Journal of Medicine* 315: 485–487.

Kahneman, D., and Treisman, A. (1984). Changing views of attention and automaticity, In R. Parasuraman and D. R. Davies (Eds.) *Varieties of Attention.* New York: Academic Press.

Kinsbourne, M., and Warrington, E. K. (1962). A disorder of simultaneous form perception. *Brain* 85: 461–486.

Livingstone, M., and Hubel, D. (1988). Segregation of form, color, movement and depth: Anatomy, physiology and perception. *Science* 240: 740–749.

Luria, A. R. (1959). Disorders of "simultaneous perception" in a case of bilateral occipitoparietal brain injury. *Brain* 83: 437–449.

Martin, A., Brouwers, P., Lalonde, F., Cox, C., Teleska, P., Fedio, P., Foster, N. L., and Chase, T. N. (1986). Towards a behavioral typology of Alzheimer's patients. *Journal of Clinical and Experimental Neuropsychology* 8: 594–610.

Morrison, J. H., Scherr, S., Lewis, D. A., Campbell, M. J., and Bloom, F. E. (1986). The laminar and regional distribution of neocorticfal somatostatin and neuritic plaques: Implication for Alzheimer's disease as a global neocortical disconnection syndrome. In A. B. Scheibel, A. F. Wechsler, and M. A. B. Brazier (Eds.) *The Biological Substrates of Alzheimer's Disease.* Orlando: Academic Press.

Nelson, H. E., and O'Connell, A. (1977). Dementia: The estimation of premorbid intelligence levels using the New Adult Reading Test. *Cortex* 14: 234–244.

Nissen, M. J., Corkin, S., Buonanno, F. S., Growdon, J. H., Wray, S. H., and Bauer, J. (1985). Spatial vision in Alzheimer's disease. *Archives of Neurology* 42: 667–671.

Pashler, H., and Badgio, P. (1985). Visual attention and stimulus identification. *Journal of Experimental Psychology: Human Perception and Performance* 11: 105–121.

Pick, A. (1908). Zur Symptomatologie des atrophischen Hinterhauptslappens. Studien zur Hirnpathologie und Psychologie. Sonderabdruck aus der deutschen psychiatrischen Universitatsklinik in Prag.

Posner, M. I., Walker, J. A., and Rafal, R. D. (1984). Effects of parietal lobe injury on covert orienting of visual attention. *Journal of Neuroscience* 4: 1863–1874.

Riddoch, M. J., and Humphreys, G. (1987). Perceptual and action systems in unilateral visual neglect. In M. Jeannerod (Ed.) *Neurophysiological and Neuropsychological Aspects of Spatial Neglect*. Amsterdam: Elsevier.

Sadun, A. A., and Bassi, C. J. (1987). The visual system in Alzheimer's disease. *Archives of Neurology* 44: 1209.

Sagi, D., and Julesz, B. (1985). "Where" and "What" in vision. *Science* 228: 1217–1219.

Schlotterer, G., Moscovitch, M., and Crapper-McLachlan, D. (1983). Visual processing deficits as assessed by spatial sensitivity and backward masking in normal aging and Alzheimer's Disease. *Brain* 107: 309–325.

Shallice, T. (1982). Specific impairments of planning. *Philosophical Transactions of the Royal Society of London B.* 298: 199–209.

Shiffrin, R. M., and Schneider, W. (1977). Controlled and automatic human information processing: II. Perceptual learning, automatic attending, and a general theory. *Psychological Review* 84: 127–190.

Treisman, A. M., and Gelade, G. (1980). A feature-integration theory of attention. *Cognitive Psychology* 12: 97–136.

Treisman, A. M., and Gormican, S. (1988). Feature analysis in early vision: Evidence from search asymmetries. *Psychological Review* 95: 15–48.

Treisman, A. M., and Souther, J. (1985). Search asymmetry: A diagnostic for preattentive processing of separable features. *Journal of Experimental Psychology: General* 114: 285–310.

Veroff, A. (1978). A structural determinant of hemispheric processing of pictorial material. *Brain and Language* 5: 139–148.

Warrington, E. K. (1975). The selective impairment of semantic memory. *Quarterly Journal of Experimental Psychology* 27: 635–657.

Warrington, E. K., and Rabin, P. (1970). Perceptual matching in patients with cerebral lesions. *Neuropsychologia* 8: 475–487.

Warrington, E. K., and Taylor, A. M. (1973). The contribution of the right parietal lobe to object recognition. *Cortex* 9: 152–164.

Weiskrantz, L., Warrington, E. K., Sanders, M. D., and Marshall, J. (1974). Visual capacity of the hemianopic field following a restricted occipital ablation. *Brain* 97: 709–728.

Wolpert, I. (1924). Die simultanagnosia: Storung der gesamtauffassung. *Z. gesamte Neurologie und Psychiatrie* 93: 397–413.

Zeki, S. M. (1981). The mapping of visual function in the cerebral cortex. In Y. Katsuki, R. Norgren; and M. Sato (Eds.) *Brain Mechanisms of Sensation*. New York: Wiley.

Author Index

Subject Index

Acetylcholine, xx, 88. *See also* Alzheimer's disease, cholinergic hypothesis of
Acquired dyslexia. *See* Reading disorders
Actions, skilled. *See* Motor processes
Agnosia, xi, 16, 17, 25, 45, 67, 68, 76, 77, 95, 240, 287, 291, 298, 314, 323, 324. *See also* Object recognition; Visuoperceptual deficits
  for objects, 6, 12, 18, 23
  progressive visual disorders, xiv, 156, 312, 322, 325n5
Agrammatism. *See* Aphasia
Alexia. *See* Reading disorders
Alz-50, 90–91
Alzheimer's disease (AD), xx–xxiii, 10
  cerebral blood flow in. (*See* Cerebral blood flow)
  cholinergic hypothesis of, xx–xxi
  diagnostic criteria, xix–xx, 91–92, 210
  diverse clinical presentations, xxii, 143, 144–146, 164–170, 209. (*See also* Subgroups)
  early accounts, 70–73, 75–78
  early (presenile) vs. late (senile) onset, xxii, 73, 104, 181, 184
  familial form, 105, 184
  modern accounts, xix–xxiii
  multicomponent account, 177, 199. (*See also* Subgroups)
  neurochemical alterations in, xxi–xxii, 149, 164–165
  neuropathology of, xix–xxi, 84–92
  regional cerebral glucose metabolism in. (*See* PET)
  relation to senile dementia, xix, 61–79
  a single disease entity, xxii
  stages of, 78–79, 166–167, 177–178
  subtypes of. (*See* Subgroups)

Amnesic syndrome, xi, 6, 43, 93, 97
  invariably present in Alzheimer's disease, 93, 107, 304
  isolated, progressive amnesia, 161–162, 199
  and medial temporal damage, 166
Amygdala, 87, 148, 166
Amyloid, xxi, 71
  amyloid plaques. (*See* Neuritic plaques)
Anomia. *See* Naming defect; Word finding impairment
Aphasia, xi, 17, 45, 68, 76, 77
  agrammatic, 14, 16–17, 116, 158, 250–251. (*See also* Syntactic processing)
  amnestic. (*See* Naming defect; Word finding impairment)
  Broca's aphasia, 158
  conduction aphasia, 31
  and domain specificity, 6
  optic. (*See* Optic aphasia)
  progressive. (*See* Progressive aphasia)
  receptive aphasia, 17
  transcortical sensory aphasia, 69–70
  Wernicke's aphasia, 10
Apraxia, xi, xiv, 67, 74, 76, 77, 301
  constructional apraxia. (*See* Visuoperceptual deficits)
  ideational, 18, 23
  praxis and findings from PET, 116
Association cortices, 95, 148
  histopathological changes in, 88, 160
  regional metabolic changes in. (*See* Cerebral blood flow; PET)
  temporal vs. parietal involvement in DAT, 132, 150–159, 168
Associative processes. *See* Strategic processes
Atrophy. *See* Cerebral atrophy